Pitt Series in Policy and Institutional Studies

Organizing Governance

&

Governing Organizations

Colin Campbell, S.J., and B. Guy Peters

Editors

University of Pittsburgh Press

Published by the University of Pittsburgh Press, Pittsburgh, Pa., 15260
Copyright © 1988, University of Pittsburgh Press
All rights reserved
Feffer and Simons, Inc., London
Manufactured in the United States of America

Library of Congress Cataloging-in-Publication Data

Organizing governance, governing organizations.

(Pitt series in policy and institutional studies)
1. Public administration. 2. Civil service.
3. Organization. I. Campbell, Colin, 1943–
II. Peters, B. Guy. III. Series.
JF1351.075 1988   350   87-19160
ISBN 0-8229-3570-8

Chapter 11 was originally published in the *Canadian Journal of Political Science* 19, no. 1 (March 1986), 3–27.

Contents

Acknowledgments

A<small>LTHOUGH THIS</small> book bears our names on the title page, it is the product of the labors of a number of individuals. We would like to acknowledge their many contributions to the success of this project.

This book is the product of the first conference of the International Political Science Association Research Committee (then Study Group) on the Structure and Organization of Government, known lovingly around the world as SOG. The participants at that conference, who became contributors to this volume, were central to the enterprise. They accepted the advice and criticism of the editors with good grace, and made the completion of the project a pleasure.

Just as the conference could not have been successful without able participants, it could not have been successful without funding. We gratefully acknowledge the funding provided by the University Center for International Studies of the University of Pittsburgh and the International Programs Office of Georgetown University.

Broomcroft Hall of the University of Manchester provided an excellent site for our first conference. Brian Putt, the Senior Resident, and the members of the staff made us welcome and most comfortable, and helped to dispel some rumors about British cuisine. Professor Geraint Parry and Professor Roger Williams, both of the Department of Government of the University of Manchester, also made us feel most welcome.

Once the conference itself was complete, Jenefer Ellingston of Georgetown and Sandra Mathews of Pittsburgh very capably prepared the final manuscript. Jane Flanders, the rest of the staff at the University of Pittsburgh Press, and our series editor Bert Rockman have been both highly professional and pleasant to work with as we have pushed toward the publication of this project.

To all the people mentioned above, as well as to two anonymous reviewers, we express our gratitude.

Organizing Governance, Governing Organizations

Introduction

B. Guy Peters

ARE THE structural features of government systems and the characteristics of the organizations that compose government important? This book is dedicated to investigating that deceptively simple question. Governments have existed for centuries, have experimented with a huge variety of structural mechanisms for attempting to accomplish their tasks, and yet there is still no clear answer to the question of the importance of structure. The scholars whose work is assembled within these covers have devoted considerable time and energy to investigating the impact of those structural features of government, and thus consider those features to be paramount when trying to understand governmental performance. Also, given the number of attempts made by practical persons involved with government to alter performance by altering structure, it appears that many working within the system itself regard structure as crucial to performance.[1] However, there remains a great need for more extensive conceptualization, empirical investigation, and informed analysis before these intuitive notions about government can receive anything more than the Scottish verdict of "Not proven."

Our concern with the importance of government structure and the relationship of structural elements to performance is closely related to the emergence of the "new institutionalism" in political science and (perhaps to a lesser extent) in the other social sciences.[2] Traditional approaches to political phenomena have stressed the importance of institutions and in a somewhat formalistic manner have related the characteristics of government institutions to what government does.[3] The traditional conception was that formal structures—the products of constitutions, laws, and other legal documents—determined how government performed. While traditional work was largely descriptive and did not pretend to develop the nomothetic statements to which the "new institutionalism" appears to aspire, there was a strong implicit statement that structures and institutions do matter and are indeed central to the understanding of government activity. While much of this work involved the unrealistic assumption that human beings in organizations would necessarily follow formal lines of authority and legal directions, it certainly regarded government institutions as central to political inquiry. What appears to be needed, therefore, is a regeneration of the concern with institutions, while retaining some better understanding of the behavior of individuals within organizations and institutions.

Much of the behavioral revolution in political science, beginning in the early 1950s, rejected these institutional models in favor of explaining government performance by either environmental factors—such as political culture, characteristics of the social system—or by the attitudes and behavior of those in government.[4] Government institutions were essentially empty bottles into which different types of individuals could pour different ideas and beliefs and in turn produce different types of policies. Formal structures and organizations did not matter nearly so much as the informal patterns of organizational behavior created by individuals to make the formal structure work in certain desired ways. In this view, rather than being independent variables determining behavior and performance, government structures became at best dependent variables, merely the product of individual behavior. At worst, they were meaningless.

To the extent that behavioral social scientists analyzed institutions at all, it was as systems of shared values rather than as important entities in their own right. So, for example, much of the literature about socialization concentrated on the acquisition of political attitudes and information by children, and tended to ignore the socialization of adults that occurs within political institutions.[5] We have since come to realize that political institutions are very powerful socializing elements even for quite mature and sophisticated individuals—for example, the ability of the U.S. Senate to indoctrinate new members with its values. Therefore, it is important to understand the generation of those collective values in institutions and how individuals become acculturated to those values.

By rejecting some of the formalistic presuppositions of the traditional school of scholarship on government institutions, many involved in the behavioral approach to political science appear to have thrown out the proverbial baby with the bath water. Many factors associated with political life may be more difficult to explain *without* the formal structuring principles that guide behavior in organizations than with them. This is true even if the individuals involved in government are "free actors" with their own decision-making capabilities. Further, such an approach to government tends to ignore the historical nature of much of political life. Decisions simply do not happen; they happen in the context of institutions that embody a historical evolution of thinking about policy issues and a set of rules, understandings, and values. Decision makers are not totally free but are free only within the parameters of values and ideas made manifest in government institutions.

What may be required for more substantial progress in the study of government performance is some blending of the two alternative (although not necessarily clearly dichotomous) approaches to the study of politics. From the behavioral approach can come a concern for the development of "lawlike" statements about how governments perform their tasks and the correlates of observed differences in performance. Such correlates are not, by any means, determinants but they are patterns of association that help us to understand. From the more structuralist approach to political phenomena can be derived a better understanding of institutions as organizing principles for the behavior of individuals, as well as some concern for how those institutions function as collectivities of individuals with both collective and individual values and rules.

While it is possible to reify institutions excessively, it is important to see them as political actors in their own right. Like the state in the burgeoning literature on state theory, lesser government institutions may also have interests of their own, and therefore may be analyzed as though engaging in purposive collective behavior.[6] Many of the questions that have been raised about the behavior of the state, such as its autonomy of action, may also be raised about the behavior of institutions such as the civil service or individual organizations functioning within the context of the state.[7]

Fundamental Questions

Our concern with the importance of government structures and organizations raises a number of quite fundamental questions about the study of government that will be investigated in the following chapters and by the International Political Science Association Study Group on the Structure and Organization of Government (SOG). The essays in this volume were presented at the first research meeting of this study group at the University of Manchester in November 1984. The questions they raise must be answered before any adequate progress can be made in reconceptualizing the impact of government structure and organization on government decision making and performance.

What Is Structure? What Is Organization?

Before we are capable of arguing whether a characteristic of government is important, we must identify and classify it. In other words, what are the basic building blocks of government structures with which we should be concerned? Thus far we have argued for the importance of government structures in explaining differences in performance without a working definition of essential concepts.

The next essay will discuss these questions in great detail; here I will only point to the importance of some types of formal organizational structures and definitions of patterns of interactions among them. For example, we can find in the *U.S. Government Manual* an enumeration of formal organizations and their organizational charts.[8] However, if we begin to discuss government structures and organizations, we have a difficult time identifying them. There are difficulties in defining *public* organizations, and in defining public *organizations*. We have discussed these problems elsewhere; the fundamental point here is that a great deal of conceptual and empirical work needs to be done before we can make detailed statements about government organizations.

Of course, even if we can isolate government organizations, this does not tell us exactly how those organizations will function, although we can derive some suppositions about behavior simply by examining carefully their formal structures. For example, the Department of Housing and Urban Development is organized with relatively few independent agencies under its umbrella, while the Departments of Agriculture and of Commerce have a large number of independent agencies. Therefore, we would expect the latter departments to be more decentralized less successful in producing policies which redistribute resources within the whole policy area than would more centralized departments such as HUD. In addition, if we compare the decentralized structures in American public administration with the more centralized ministries in most European countries we can see the difficulty of maintaining tight control in a U.S. Cabinet department.[9]

Principles such as federalism, which define the relationships among the portions of government systems, are also important components of this definition of government organization and structure.[10] Such overarching structural features are rarely embodied with organizations themselves (except perhaps for organizations such as the Federal Provincial Office in Canada or the Advisory Commission on Intergovernmental Relations in the United States) but rather are defined by patterns of interactions, often determined by both formal constitutional statements and the historical evolution of the relative powers among the several levels of government. So, for example, federalism in the United States has evolved by legislation and by custom, although the written constitutional principles that established it have changed almost not at all.

As the example of federalism would imply, many of the important structural features of contemporary governments are interorganizational rather than simply organizational. Significant theoretical development has already occurred with respect to systems of organizations loosely linked by the implementation process; the concept of the "implementation structure" as a closely linked set of organizations involved in the execution of a particular policy is an important advance here.[11] However, that thinking has rarely been extended to more general concerns regarding government structure. Therefore, one important task for those of us studying the structural features of government is the development of terminology and theory about *populations* of organizations as well as about single organizations.[12] We must be able to identify and conceptualize the patterns of interaction that occur among government organizations, as well as simply identifying those organizations.

In addition to patterns of interaction among public-sector organizations, an increasing number of structural relationships exist between public and private organizations. One of the fundamental features of government in the late twentieth century is "third-party government" and the increasing mixture of public and private activities.[13] Therefore, any understanding of government structures must include those patterns of interaction as well as the many formal and informal relationships that exist across the public-private divide. Some organizations themselves bridge that gap. Organizations at "the margins of the state" have been discussed in some scholarly and even more political writings, but still require better conceptualization in light of their important structural relationships to government activity and authority.[14]

Another aspect of the links between the public and private sectors is the linking of private organizations to public organizations through a variety of mechanisms described under the term of "corporatism."[15] While the literature on third-party government discusses the devolution of government functions onto nongovernment actors, the literature on corporatism discusses that phenomenon, as well as the "capture" of government organizations by private-sector interests. What may differentiate this type of relationship from other forms of capture, however, is the formalization of the relationships between public- and private-sector organizations. These have become sufficiently institutionalized in many political systems to be considered structural features of government, and therefore require some consideration as we begin to examine the structure of modern governments. Particularly for economic policy, it is virtually impossible to understand policymaking in many European countries without understanding these state-society linkages.

So, what is structure? What is organization? We do not yet know.

Perhaps the most important element of the structure of modern governing systems is their complexity and the difficulty of describing and categorizing them. Relatively few efforts have been made to apply the technology and concepts skills of modern political science to the enduring questions regarding the nature of government organizations. Those that have been made, such as the work of Hood and Dunsire and various contingency theory studies, have been largely unsatisfying.[16] While they address some of the relevant questions, the independent variables used (especially in the contingency analyses) fail to capture the richness and complexity of modern political life. The chapters in this volume begin to identify and to employ relevant explanatory variables and concepts, but much basic conceptual and theoretical work remains to be done.

Does Reorganization Matter?

Many people in government appear to believe that government organization and reorganization does matter; they spend so much time doing it. Although if we look at governmental structures over time at a high level of generality we see relatively few changes, when we examine these structures at a more disaggregated level we see huge number of changes. New organizations are born, others die, but most are simply changes in existing organizations.[17] The question, then, is what does all this organizational activity add up to, and does it really matter?

Most important, we have no good guidance for what a "good" organizational structure in government is. If a strong theoretical position had gained empirical support and could be used to guide presidents, prime ministers, and other tinkerers with the machinery of government, then organizational changes might produce desired results. However, there is no such agreed-upon body of knowledge. Any number of government commissions have met and propounded their own views on what good organization and management are (the Brownlow Commission, the Hoover Commissions, the Grace Commission, the Haldane Commission, the Fulton Commission, the Nora Commission). Unfortunately, however, the results of these investigations are often locked in time and into a particular set of problems facing government at that time. They rarely develop generic principles to guide decision makers or to adequately justify their own recommendations. Therefore, a great deal of reorganization activity appears to replace one set of problems with another, which in turn may produce a return to those first problems at the next reorganization.

The absence of any strong principles of organization may not reflect the weaknesses of the commissions or the academics who advised them. Rather they may suggest the rather disheartening proposition that all forms of government organization are equally bad. That statement is not intended to denigrate government or its employees; much the same could be said about the organization of firms or other private-sector entities. Further, the statement merely points out that the selection of any organizational arrangement involves a range of costs and benefits, and that achieving one goal may mean losing ground on several others.

This skepticism about the efficacy of any particular organizational arrangement is to some degree expressed in Herbert Simon's critique of the "proverbs of administration" developed by scholars such as Gulick and Urwick in the United States, and contained in another form in the Haldane report in the United Kingdom.[18] Those "proverbs" are soundly criticized by Simon as inconsistent and ultimately useless because they are internally contradictory.[19] For example, on the one hand, the proverbs stress the importance of a limited number of hierarchical levels between the top and the bottom of an organization. One the other hand, they stress the importance of a limited span of control for any one supervisor. The problem is, of course, that both of these adages are correct—each has its advantages and disadvantages—but they cannot be achieved at the same time. The trick, therefore, for the analyst and the proponent of government reorganization is to understand the particular problems besetting any organization at any time and to fashion proposals that address those problems. The organizational analyst in government must understand, however, that the successful implementation of any proposal is likely to engender new problems that are likely to be exactly the opposite of those that spawned the original reorganization. The new problems may well, before long, become the reason for a new round of reorganization. Problems with government organization are virtually without end.

In addition to the goal of improving organizational performance, reorganization is definitely a political activity. When all else fails, or even before trying anything else, a political leader may find it advantageous to use reorganization as a response to problems in government. While any particular reorganization may be of a very meager nature—merely moving around the boxes within the context of a larger, more immutable structure—it may well be a response to a real problem. In addition, reorganization can be used to express the political power of groups in society, and may alter the relative political success of interest groups. Some reorganizations, such as the formation of the U.S. Department of Education, give interest groups a new and ready target for their activities. That reorganization also provided a powerful advocate for the interests of education, when previously those interests had tended to be swallowed within the larger Department of Health, Education, and Welfare. As with everything else in government, organizational change can never be simply a technical exercise but inevitably is an exercise in political power—either its use or its acquisition. Reorganizations may express the political power of interests that favor them, and they can at times create powerful interests themselves.

In the United States there is a tendency to think of government reorganization as a dramatic activity involving the president, Congress, and all the principal institutions of political power. However, frequently in the United States and even more frequently in other political systems, reorganization is not a manifestation of *haute politique* but merely the day-to-day politics of jiggling and poking with organizations. The United States tends to provide a public law basis for most government organizations, while in many other countries those organizations can be created and destroyed with considerably less formal activity. Therefore, when we look at the reorganization of government cross-nationally, we should be expecting many small changes rather than a few dramatic events. The analysis of these changes will, therefore, require a nuanced and detailed understanding of those other governments.

With all these caveats about the practical effectiveness of reorganization, we should remember that reorganization to a great degree reflects what those in government think about the structures within which they work, as well as the prevailing theoretical wisdom about organizations and management in the public sector. Thus, reorganizations may be more indicative of the prevailing climate of ideas than of any revealed wisdom about how to govern. Therefore, studying reorganization can reveal a great deal about what the relevant actors are *thinking* about government, even if it tells us next to nothing about the real efficiency or effectiveness of government.

This discussion implies that a great deal of reorganization activity is cosmetic; it is a wonderful exercise which in the end may produce next to nothing. A great deal of effort may be expended to produce very little real enhancement of performance, and at times there may even be reductions in effectiveness. Despite good intentions, it may be undertaken without the type of information about organizational design that would be needed to make any accurate predictions of performance.[20] Again, it may simply be a political mechanism for reducing pressures for action; although far from costless, it may be much cheaper than trying to change an organization's policies.

Organizations and Government Growth

One topic of continuing interest in the comparative study of politics, and especially the politics of advanced industrialized societies, is the

expansion of government activity.[21] While this is to some degree an ideological issue, and opposition to such expansion has vaulted several very
conservative governments into office in the late 1970s and 1980s, it is
also an issue that should be analyzed objectively. The public sector is, in
most countries, substantially larger relative to the total resource base in
the country than it was in the 1950s, 1960s or even early 1970s. For our
inquiry into the organization and structures of government, this growth
may be considered both an independent and a dependent variable.

First, the expansion of the public sector and the various "crises"
associated with it may be expected to have affected organizations in several ways. First, as there is more to do, there should be more organizations, and existing organizations should be expected to have ramified their
internal structures considerably. This is a major component of the organizational change we have measured within the U.S. federal bureaucracy
and to a lesser extent in other bureaucracies. Examined at a high level of
abstraction, the number of cabinet departments has increased slightly, but
for the most part the structure is quite similar to that found decades ago.
However, underneath that top level, there have been literally thousands of
changes.[22]

The crises associated with government growth also tend to place different
types of organizations in more powerful positions than they might otherwise
have been in. When it is believed that government is spending too much more
or taxing too much, the central agencies, the "superbureaucracies," come to
the fore if control is perceived to be the most important function in government.[23] On the other hand, when resources for government seem at least
adequate, then program analysts who can plan and advocate "better" programs may have the more relevant skills. In extreme cases, however, no form
of analysis may be desired: very blunt instruments such as Gramm-Rudman
may be used simply to turn off the flow of money without any real thought
about the impact of such a program.

The growth of the public sector may also be seen as a dependent
variable. One school of analysts regard the public bureaucracy itself as a
major source of pressure for the expansion of the public sector. This
argument is based upon the premise that public bureaucrats have much
the same motives as private businessmen—to maximize their "profits."[24]
As few public-sector organizations actually make a profit in the usual
sense of the term, they attempt to maximize the size of their budget and
work force. They might do this for at least three reasons. Niskanen and
others suggest that the larger the organization, the greater the personal
benefits for the leader of that organization.[25] Therefore, the "bureaucratic
entrepreneur" will have a very personal and remunerative incentive to
attempt to expand the size of an organization.

A second reason is that even if it is impossible to receive any personal benefits for running an expanded organization, it will still be a source of prestige and self-satisfaction to "bureaucratic-entrepreneurs." They can cut a larger figure on the cocktail party circuit if they are successful in their budget appeals or if they run a very large budget. This may also make them more successful in their internal management of the organization; if employees believe that managers are successful on the outside, they will have more clout on the inside.

Finally, expansion of a bureau's budget, if possible, (because of a short-term budgetary surplus, the popularity of the agency's programs, or just blind luck) may shield the agency from future difficulties. It allows the organization to build "fat" into its budget so that future cuts can be imposed without affecting the central core of agency programs.[26] It may be rational for managers to poach on a budgetary commons in the short run to provide for essential needs at some time of stringency in the future.

Despite the logic and plausibility of these arguments about the role of the public bureaucracy in the expansion of the public sector, they require, as we have said throughout this introductory essay, a great deal of additional research. Although many of us believe that organizations and structures do have a central role to play in the understanding of political phenomena, we must pay very costly dues to substantiate that belief.

The Remainder of the Book

Each of following sections concerns an important set of issues in the study of government structure and organization. The first section opens with my attempt to present an initial framework for the systematic analysis of government structure. As with most such efforts, however, it raises may more questions than it can possibly answer but perhaps will serve as a starting point for our discussions. Colin Campbell's essay is narrower but far more definitive. He builds on his long experience in the study of central agencies in a number of political systems to assess their effectiveness in producing coordination and control in government. In so doing, he also touches on a number of important themes in the study of government reorganization, while my own essay is more concerned with static characteristics of governing systems.

The second section contains explicit attempts at comparison, and the development of theoretical issues in the study of government organization. First, Joel Aberbach and Bert Rockman examine one of the enduring, but still significant, questions for those interested in the structure of government, particularly the executive branch: the comparative powers of politi-

cal and career officials in the construction of public policy. They undertake this task within a somewhat novel context, however, with a particular
concern for the role of policy analysis in contemporary political systems.
Richard Rose discusses another enduring question mentioned above—the
expansion of the public sector in most contemporary political systems and
the role of government organizations in that expansion. Finally, Norman
Thomas examines the effects of continuing economic strains in Western
democracies on the organization of government, and patterns of organizational responses to those economic problems. While short-term crises
come and go, Western democracies are unlikely to return to the affluence
they enjoyed for the twenty-five or thirty years following World War II,
and we need to understand how governments have responded to their new
situations. Thomas certainly improves our understanding of these very
important issues.

The third section focuses on the United Kingdom as a particular case
of a government attempting to cope with massive changes in its economic,
and to some degree political and social, environment. Richard Chapman
provides a useful background for understanding changes in the British
civil service in the postwar era by describing the changing culture of
public administration in Britain. This is followed by Peter Hennessy's
discussion of the contemporary debate about the nature of the British civil
service and its role in policymaking. This debate has become especially
important because the Thatcher government has questioned the traditional
role of the civil service and has sought to return policymaking powers from
the mandarins to political executives. As such, this is a discussion, within
the context of the single nation, of some of the issues raised by Aberbach
and Rockman. Finally, Brian Hogwood looks at organizational changes
within a single ministry to attempt to understand more general issues
about government reorganization and policy change in Britain. This type
of research is especially difficult to do in the United Kingdom, since
government structures tend to be quite fluid and the changes which occur
are not well documented. Thus, a single study makes a major contribution
to the more theoretical discussion of organizational change in the public
sector.

The final section is composed of single-nation studies of organizational
change in government. Although these studies cover countries as different
from one another as the United States and Bangladesh, they are united by
a common concern with change and "reform." What is perhaps most
interesting in these studies is the recurrence of common themes about
government reorganization in a variety of political and cultural settings.
One is the utilization of "rational" management and managerial tech-

niques, as discussed by Peter Aucoin, regarding Canada, and Ulrich Klöti, about Switzerland. Another theme is the struggle between political leaders and the career civil service. This conflict arises in a number of different contexts, as John Warhurst's examination of recent administrative reforms in Australia and Mohammad M. Khan's analysis of Bangladesh point out. Finally, Michael G. Hansen, Charles Levine, and Johan P. Olsen touch on some general issues of organization theory—some of them classic concerns such as centralization and decentralization—when they discuss administrative reform in the United States and Norway.

Again, what is perhaps most interesting in this collection of individual case studies (including those from the United Kingdom discussed earlier) is the commonality of the themes across nations. Although we are an international group of scholars, we find that the language and theoretical terms of discourse (when translated) are really quite similar. This gives us hope that while we have discovered problems that are perhaps insuperable, they are at least real problems facing real governments and can perhaps be better addressed in light of the experience of other nations.

Notes

1. Peter L. Szanton, *Federal Reorganization: What Have We Learned?* (Chatham, N.J.: Chatham House, 1981).

2. James G. March and Johan P. Olsen, "The New Institutionalism: *American Political Science Review* 78 (1984), 734–49.

3. Any textbook in comparative government published prior to the 1950s will quickly demonstrate the important role ascribed to institutions.

4. See Jorgen Rasmussen, " 'Once You've Made a Revolution Everything's the Same': Comparative Politics," in *The Post-Behavioral Era,* ed. George J. Graham, Jr., and George W. Carey (New York: David McKay, 1972).

5. See, for example, Kenneth P. Langton, *Political Socialization* (New York: Oxford University Press, 1969).

6. Such purposive behavior has been ascribed to public bureaucracies in the public choice literature, as will be discussed below.

7. Eric Nordlinger, *On the Autonomy of the Democratic State* (Cambridge, Mass.: Harvard University Press, 1980); Roger Benjamin and Stephen L. Elkin, *The Democratic State* (Lawrence: University Press of Kansas, 1988).

8. B. Guy Peters, *Through A Glass Darkly: American Public Bureaucracy in Comparative Perspective* (University, Ala.: University of Alabama Press, 1988).

9. Harold D. Seidman, *Politics, Position and Power,* 3d ed. (New York: Oxford University Press, 1980).

10. See the discussion of federalism in chapter 1.

11. Benny Hjern and David O. Porter, "Implementation Structures: A New Unit of Organizational Analysis," *Organization Studies* 2 (1980), 211–24.

12. H. E. Aldrich, *Organizations and Environments* (Englewood Cliffs, N.J.: Prentice-Hall, 1979).

13. Lester B. Salamon, "Rethinking Public Management: Third-Party Government and the Changing Forms of Government Action," *Public Policy* 19 (1981), 255–75.

14. Ira Sharkansky, *Wither the State?* (Chatham, N.J.: Chatham House, 1979).

15. Phillipe Schmitter, "Still the Century of Corporatism?" *Review of Politics* 23 (1979).

16. Christopher Hood and Andrew Dunshire, *Bureaumetrics* (Farnborough, Hants.: Gower, 1981).

17. Brian W. Hogwood and B. Guy Peters, *Policy Dynamics* (New York: St. Martin's, 1983).

18. Luther Gulick and L. Urwick, eds., *Papers on the Science of Administration* (New York: Institute of Public Administration, 1937).

19. Herbert A. Simon, *Administrative Behavior* (New York: Free Press, 1945).

20. Paul C. Nystrom and Williamc C. Starbuck, *Handbook of Organizational Design* (New York: Oxford University Press, 1981).

21. See, for example, Patrick D. Larkey, Chandler Stolp, and Mark Winer, "Theorizing about the Growth of Government: A Research Assessment," *Journal of Public Policy* 1 (1981), 147–220.

22. Peters, *Through A Glass Darkly.*

23. Colin Campbell and George Szablowski, *The Superbureaucrats* (Toronto: Macmillan of Canada, 1979).

24. William Niskanen, *Bureaucracy and Representative Government* (Chicago: Aldine/Atherton, 1971).

25. Ibid.

26. Anthony Downs, *Inside Bureaucracy* (Boston: Little, Brown, 1966).

PART I

Major Organizational Issues

CHAPTER 1

The Machinery of Government:

Concepts and Issues

ॐ

B. Guy Peters

THIS CHAPTER discusses a number of issues arising in the study of the structure and organization of government.[1] It is hoped that the identification and arrangement of the issues and the literature on this complex subject will contribute to our understanding.

Why Be Concerned About the Structure of Government?

The most basic question about the structure and organization of government is why we should be concerned about this question at all. Many scholars trained in political science programs during the "behavioral revolution" were taught to believe that government structures were insignificant as a focus for research. The structures of government were encapsulated in an opaque black box; they were merely that part of the political system where decisions were made. Fortunately, this view no longer prevails. There is increasing interest in structural questions, generated in part by the increasing interest in the state as a focus for political inquiry, as well as by the recognition of the need for improved institutional analyses of politics.[2] Much of the work on the state, however, still leaves that concept largely undifferentiated and has not dealt systematically with the structure of the state apparatus. In addition, there is as yet little well-developed institutional theory, or theory linking government institutions to public policy. Thus, concern for the development of state theory, as well as public policy, has returned structural questions to a more central position in political science.

Government structure can first be seen as a dependent variable in the political process. For example, as Christopher Pollitt points out, one aspect of what he terms the "political science" approach to the machinery of government has been to hypothesize that economic scarcity will influence organizational developments within government.[3] Bert Rockman has made a more specific point, arguing that scarcity tends to accelerate the development of units for policy analysis within government organizations, particularly line agencies, so that they can attempt to counter macroeconomic priorities being imposed upon them by central financial agencies.[4] Manfred Kochen and Karl Deutsch have developed a number of hypotheses relating characteristics of the the tasks of public organizations to the structural forms that are most suitable, especially regarding centralization and decentralization.[5] The size of government may also influence organizational patterns.[6] In particular, one might hypothesize that the magnitude of government operations would be exponentially related to growth in the number of organizational units within a single government, if not across political systems. That is, there are limits to any one large organization's ability to manage large volumes of work or multiple policy areas, and therefore as government grows organizations may proliferate. Insofar as the structure of government can be analyzed as a dependent variable according to the usual canons of social science, that structure can be examined, with no loss of "scientific" rigor, as more closely approximating the political realities being studied.

Structures of government can also be used as independent variables to explain policy outcomes, or political behavior. As Gerald Caiden points out: "The implied rationale [of many efforts at administrative reform] is that administration really does matter, that it is not something that can be ignored or cast aside, and that an improvement in administration will pay handsomely in the attainment of other objectives."[7] For one obvious example, a federal system would be expected to have less uniformity in the implementation of policy than unitary systems. Likewise, more highly differentiated and decentralized bureaucracies such as those of the United States will likely be more susceptible to pressure-group influence than more unified bureaucracies such as those of the United Kingdom. The important tasks, therefore, are to develop appropriate concepts, and appropriate operational indicators of those concepts for describing structures of government and to develop theoretical linkages between structures and policy outcomes.

The importance of the structure of government, as both independent and dependent variable, is made even clearer by James March and Johan Olsen in their discussion of the new institutionalism.[8] They point out that much contemporary political theory assumes that government is influenced by social factors such as interest groups or ethnicity, but that the reverse is not true.[9] They argue, however, that government institutions are important for structuring patterns of interaction in society: "An institutional theory would specify how historical processes are affected by specific characteristics of political institutions, and it would provide greater theoretical understanding of the inefficiences of history."[10] Such an institutional theory would be crucial for understanding how the machinery of government influences the development of public policy, and could be an important complement to existing theories of politics based on societal factors.

What Is the Structure of Government?

The next question is just what are we talking about? The words *structure* and *organization of government* have been used in various ways. The most restrictive is to talk just of the government, that is, the organization of cabinets and the division of portfolios and power among cabinet members. For example, Jean Blondel ranks the top executive structures in the modern world into categories ranging from hierarchical governments generally dominated by a single ruler, through collective governments such as the British cabinet system, to divided governments—including both the United States and the Communist countries.[11] This is an interesting approach to the structure of government, but seems excessively restrictive and misses important structural changes occurring in contemporary political systems.

Other rather restrictive studies of the machinery of government are typified by Christopher Hood's and Andrew Dunsire's study of internal structures of departments in British central government.[12] Again, internal structure is an important component of the question, but takes for granted larger structural questions within government, such as the number and type of organizations. Other works deal with very similar issues in the context of the United States federal government.[13] However, the concentration on internal structure does not link these types of concerns to broader organizational issues.

At the other extreme are comprehensive studies such as Arend Lijphart's analysis of twenty-one democratic systems, which includes some of the same factors about the structure of the political executive that Blondel discusses, but also includes factors related to party structure, legislative behavior, and the heterogeneity of the population.[14] Building on Lijphart's earlier work, this study explores the existence of two alternative models of democracy: the majoritarian (Westminster) model and the consensual (or consociational).[15] The classificatory system developed by Lijphart has been shown to have some utility for explaining patterns of public policy in democratic countries, but this whole-system approach may be too broad and too much related to the structure of political inputs to help us understand the organization of government itself.[16] The structures of government seem again to be reduced to a black box for transmitting the demands of the mass public into policies with little understanding of how that box itself functions. Despite the importance of the linkages between government and mass politics and mass society, there is a need to develop a better understanding of politics *within* government, and of the impact of structural variables on those politics.

A third approach is represented by the "machinery of government" literature.[17] It comes closer to the mark because of its concern with macrolevel organization of systems of governing. However, perhaps it gives excessive attention to the departments of central government and too little to both nondepartmental bodies and their importance to the formulation and execution of public policies, and to the central government's relationship to other levels of government.

Peter Hall takes a very broad approach to the machinery of government in his discussion of the capacity of governments to innovate effectively.[18] He enumerates three structural factors important in explaining that capacity. First is the structure of the state itself, including such attributes as the relationship between political and career executives and internal decision-making structures of government departments. Second is the relationship between state and society, or the leverage government can exert over society. Of course, many others working from the perspective of corporatism, or from that of state autonomy might be more interested in society's power over the state.[19] Finally, Hall is interested in the social structure itself that enables the state to intervene effectively. For example, government may be more effective in implementing an incomes policy in a society with industrial unions rather than craft-based unions. Hall's first two dimensions are essential for an understanding of the structural aspects of governing systems, but the third may go beyond our immediate concerns. However, such social factors may well have to be brought back into the analysis if, as they are for Hall, government performance and/or state autonomy are important features of any research on government structures.

James Sundquist asks the same type of question as Hall did—what factors explain the relative success of government in making policy interventions?[20] Comparing the United States to Western Europe, he argues that four factors explain the relatively greater success of European countries in planning for, and controlling, population movements. These are: (1) different levels of bureaucratic capabilities, (2) different degrees of bureaucratic discipline, (3) differences in the institutional environment of planning, and (4) differences in the stability and authority of party programs. He concludes by arguing, "It may well be that institutional differences that have evolved quite accidentally are more important than differences in geography or resources or ideology in making the United States stand out among the industrial democracies as the one with by far the most conservative domestic policies."[21] While one may question whether European countries are as homogenous as they appear in this description, and institutional factors may well explain differences among the policies of different countries, this analysis does provide an interesting starting point for further analysis.

Clearly, a rather broad conception of the "structure and organization of government" is the most beneficial approach for research. Such a conception should include the two topics mentioned above—the division of ministerial offices and the internal structuring of government departments—but should also contain additional information about the structure of the governing system, including the relationships, division of power, and responsibilities of central government and subnational governments. We should also be concerned with how government organizes its own work and the extent to which nondepartmental bodies, public corporations, and quasi-public corporations are used to implement public policy. There is evidence that such government structures do make a difference both in the performance of functions and how government is regarded by citizens.[22] We would like to be able to test those assumptions as well as the correlation of those characteristics of government with other structural characteristics of governing systems. In addition, we should look at those structures as mechanisms by which the state influences society; mechanisms that are picked for administrative convenience or to mask the true size of the public sector may be less effective as well as less responsible. Even public corporations organized on a corporate format to gain the presumed advantages of a businesslike structure may be less effective in implementing a government program than an executive department performing the same function.[23] Finally, it appears that some *structural* aspects of organized participation in government should be included in a conceptualization of government organization. This need not be a complete replay of the corporatist and corporate-pluaralist themes.[24] We should, however, be concerned with the existence of structural elements in government that either facilitate such participation, or produce variations in the representation of groups in government.[25]

Approaches to the Structure and Organization of Government

Now that we have a better idea of the basic issues to be addressed, we can turn to alternative approaches for understanding the machinery of government. This chapter will deal more with the analysis of existing structures of government and less with questions of reorganization and pressuress for change, which would require another chapter to discuss. Many assumptions about the existing machinery of government are implicit in attempts at reorganization, so that the two questions are by no means unrelated. A number of approaches to understanding and explaining existing government structures have been advanced.

Traditional Explanations

Pollitt labeled one approach to the structure of government *traditional*.[26] In the context in which the term is employed, it refers to scholars of the British "machine" whose work tended to be highly descriptive and to some extent oriented toward government practitioners rather than scholars—especially those attempting to develop theoretical explanations of government structure.[27]

Much of the descriptive literature on the machinery of government in other countries could be called traditional.[28] Like traditional political science, much of this work is descriptive, formal, and legalistic. This approach can be very useful in simply gaining an idea of the structures one is either trying to conceptualize, or in the case of the practitioner, to manipulate.

Growth of Government

A second group of explanations relate the "overload" phenomenon to changes in government structures.[29] Several hypotheses—for example, that increasing demands would be related to greater internal specialization—could be developed from this approach. However, concentrating on merely the growth of government as a source of change in political structures is a quite limited approach to the impact of political change on government organization.[30]

Overload—to the extent that it can be adequately conceptualized and measured—is but one of many changes in society that are mediated through the political system and may influence the machinery of government. To the extent that it is different from overload, financial scarcity for governments can also be expected to have significant structural effects.[31] Likewise, technological change has been found to be important for explaining the existence of certain types of organizations.[32] In addition, societies with ethnic or regional differences, or other forms of fragmentation, may require different structural arrangements than are needed in more homogenous societies.[33] In other words, a number of political and/or social variables influence the nature of government that are not captured by the overload concept, and it may be as important to identify the *types* of demands placed upon government as their quantity. In a longitudinal analysis of a single government which has experienced variations in "load," the use of quantity alone may be quite appropriate, but to develop a theory for the comparative analysis of government structures, it is an inadequate measure of the impact of politics on structure.

Organization Theory

Organization theory has been applied more frequently to private-sector organizations than to the public sector.[34] In addition, most of the relatively few applications of organization theory to the structure of government have merely applied contingency theory to explain the structure of government departments or local governments.[35] These empirical studies have met with limited success; the factors usually related to organizational structures do not correlate strongly with characteristics of public organizations. It is unclear how such an approach could explain the macrolevel structural concerns we have already outlined. Further, as Christopher Hood points out, these contingency approaches have even less ability to prescribe the right type of organization for a particular environment than they do to *describe* patterns of organizations.[36] Similarly, Herbert Kaufman and David Seidman find no connection between environment and organizational form in a number of agencies in the U.S. federal government and argue that variations in form are a function of micropolitical forces rather than the task environment, as is assumed in the contingency approach.[37]

One aspect of organizational environments that may explain a great deal about the structure of public organizations is the need to deliver different public services in different ways.[38] Kochen and Deutsch develop a number of hypotheses relating the characteristics of services to structures, especially the possibilities of plualizing service delivery with large numbers of similar organizations.[39] Scholars have noted that social service organizations rely on their street-level personnel much more than would be expected in a hierarchical organization and hence have developed different structures for accountability and control.[40]

Of course, organization theory has been used in any number of ways to explain organizational behavior *within* public organizations, but used much less to explain the structure of those organizations, or sets of organizations.[41] Such approaches are more concerned with internal management than with the structures of organizations or sets of organizations; for John Kimberly, these are research *in* organizations rather than *on* organizations.[42]

Contingency theory need not be the only formal organization theory applied to the structure of government. At a high level of abstraction, population ecology models may be useful in explaining the survival or death of public organizations.[43] The assumptions behind this approach may be somewhat more deterministic than those usually found in analyzing public-sector organization; most approaches stress making choices about organizations rather than pressures arising in a group of organizations. However, the approach may have some utility, at least for the study of departmental and subdepartmental bodies.[44] For example, using these models we could predict a drop in the number of organizations following a rapid increase in their number. We might expect this politically, as new organizations are more vulnerable to political pressures and mistakes are inevitable in the establishment of new organizations. However, population ecology models yield interesting predictions which, if validated, may provide greater insight into the dynamics of public-sector organizations.[45]

Another organizational theory that may have some relevance stresses the implementation of programs.[46] The principal virtue of the work of this group, centered at the International Institute of Management in Berlin, for the analysis of the machinery of government is that they direct our attention away from readily identifiable organizations toward underlying government structures—as identified by their approach. Their basic concept is the *implementation structure,* defined as an "administrative entity which programme implementors use for accomplishing objectives within a programme."[47] Such an implementation structure typically involves components of several public and private organizations. This metaunit forces us to think about how public services are rendered and the implications of certain organizational formats for implementation structures. It has a certain similarity to the economic theory of teams, to be discussed, in that it posits the existence of quasi-organizations within and across other organizations. The members of these implementation structures may have more in common with other members of their unit than with the members of the organization of which they are nominally members. For empirical research, however, this approach requires careful attention to the margins of identifiable government organizations. It also does little to help us understand the upper echelons of public organizations that have come to be regarded as a central focus for the analysis of government structure.

Social Action Theory

Social action theory argues that governmental structures, or indeed any other aspects of the social world, cannot be understood without a firm understanding of their premises.[48] Thus, it is similar to *verstehen* approaches to the social sciences, as it requires the observer to understand the "act" meaning (the meaning to the participants) as well as the "action" meaning of social behavior. Government actors designing public organizations bring with them a range of ideas, beliefs, opinions, and traditions that affect their designs. These ideas may be in part the mythology and proverbs of public administration, and in part a function of the society and culture in which the organization functions. Thus many things that appear quite unexpected to the outside observer—such as the dependence of the executive branch in the United States on a large number of political appointees rather than civil servants—must be understood within the U.S. social and political milieu.

It is difficult to deny that political structures should be understood within their own context; the difficulty arises, however, in making comparisons. An action-theory approach to the machinery of government may make meaningful comparisons difficult, since any government structure or any attempts to change the structures would have to be understood almost as sui generis. The approach may be quite useful within a single country within a relatively short period, as Pollitt argues, but its utility diminishes as comparative analysis becomes more important.[49]

Political Economy and Policy Analysis

Political economy and/or policy analysis have been given less attention as approaches for analyzing the structures of government. That is understandable, since the majority of analyses in these closely related fields are concerned with *processes* of decision making rather than the role of structure in influencing those processes. For example, authors such as William Niskanen and Gordon Tullock have been concerned primarily with the behavior of individual bureaucratic decision makers working within the public bureaucracy rather than the structures of those organizations.[50]

Those concerned with decision making do not, however, exhaust the concerns of political economists discussing organizations and more especially public organizations.[51] Williamson, for example, considers that a firm's internal form has much to do with its decision making.[52] He distinguished two basic organizational forms, the unitary (U) form and the multidivisional (M) form. In the U-form, specialized units such as sales, finance, and personnel, perform their specialized functions for all product lines of the firm. In the other, operating divisions are responsible for those functions concerning their own product lines. The analogy between the models of business and organization in the public sector is clear. The U-form can be seen as a government with a number of relatively strong central agencies capable of imposing standards on operating divisions, while an M-form organization would be more decentralized, with each component making potentially different decisions about matters such as personnel and budgeting.

Williamson also developed hypotheses about the effects of these two organizational forms on a firm's behavior. In the first place, he was concerned with a possible loss of control caused by the expansion of a U-form organization.[53] Not only would there be a loss as each organization expanded its number of hierachical levels, but also there as horizontal communication deteriorated; for example, the Office of Personnel Management would find it more difficult to coordinate effectively with the Office of Management and Budget because of its own internal layering. The U-form is also hypothesized to make strategic planning difficult, as operational goals of individual units are incommensurate and power struggles over different goals develop. Williamson argues that a strong executive is required to manage such an organization. In the business world, the M-form organization is considered a superior form of organization, as each portion of the firm is in itself a quasi-firm and has the same types of incentives for profit and efficiency as the firm as a whole.

It is by no means clear that the same logic applies to the public sector. In fact, central agencies have been developed to try to prevent the operating agencies of government from becoming quasi-firms and to impose some coordination on what might otherwise be an even more chaotic pattern of governance.[54] The fundamental difference would seem to be that the firm can use a measurable profit to serve as a guide for action, whereas government agencies must use other, less directly measurable, criteria to extract resources from the center. Thus, there will almost certainly be some goal conflicts between operating line agencies and the central agencies.

The economic theory of teams is also related to Williamson's models of firm structure. Like implementation structures, teams are theoretical constructs, although unlike implementation structures they exist *within* rather than *between* organizations.[55] The team is a subset of the entire organization that derives its utility primarily from the success of the team rather than from that of the entire organization; as such it presents problems similar to those of displacement of goals in sociological theories of organization.[56] Also, the theory of teams touches at important points the new agency theories of organizations.[57] One of the basic questions of the theory of teams is how to structure organizations to allow for the optimal use of information, and particularly the impact of centralization or decentralization on the use of information. As with most economic models, the purpose of this approach is normative rather than descriptive, but it does demonstrate a point of contact between formal economic theory and administrative theory that is often overlooked.

Theories of the State

Another possible approach to the structure of government is the theory of the state, especially the state in capitalist society.[58] The importance of this theory for our undertaking may appear limited, since little has been done on the internal structure of the state. Rather, the dominant concern has been relationships between the state and its international environment, and between the state and its society.[59] State theorists have been concerned with the internal structure of government, insofar as structures in dependent capitalism differ from those of advanced industrial capitalism.[60] In particular, much of the theoretical work on the state and society has concentrated on the question of the relative autonomy of the state vis-à-vis either the capitalist classes, for those working from a Marxist perspective, or organized interests in the society, for those working from other perspectives.[61] The argument on behalf of giving the state a higher degree of autonomy than usually assumed constitutes an interesting contradiction of much of the corporatist literature on state-society linkages.

The concept of state autonomy also may be useful for our analysis of government structure. It is another way of looking at the policymaking capacity of contemporary governments.[62] There may well be structural features of the political system that contribute to the relative decisional autonomy of state actors, and thereby make government more effective. Hall, for example, argues that the power of government to make innovative policy would be higher if: (1) power is concentrated in a relatively few hands; (2) the power lies in the hands of actors who are free of vested interest in the policy area; (3) organizational structures enhance access to information and expertise in the policy area; and (4) government organization facilitates informal alliances between political executives and career civil servants.[63] To some degree then, Hall's analysis of decisional autonomy uses some of the same factors Richard Rose found useful in explaining the effectiveness—or lack of effectiveness—of party government.[64]

Management

A final means of approaching the machinery of government is from the perspective of a political executive, or some other government manager, attempting to put a program into effect; this is the perspective of "government against subgovernment."[65] Whereas the implementation literature uses a bottom-up perspective, this is to some degree implementation from the top down.[66] Rose cites structural factors to explain why party government is difficult to sustain, as well as many of the features cited by those who analyze the barriers to implementation, or the "nothing works" interpretation of government.[67] The management approach appears particularly useful because it is directly concerned with the impact of structure on government performance, and more exactly its implementation of the wishes of political leaders.[68] Such an approach is, however, of little use in explaining the development of government structures, especially since many, such as those designed by the U.S. Constitution, seem more suitable to preventing anything from happening rather than to assist in policymaking. It may be, as Sundquist argues, that government structures develop almost accidentally, although there does appear to be at least the nub of theory guiding the reorganization of governments, and perhaps their formation.[69]

Even if this approach may have some weaknesses as a means of explaining the development of structures, it does appear the most useful means of examining structures as an independent variable. Such a perspective allows us to integrate a concern with structural features, such as central agencies, that may affect the effectiveness of political executives, procedures, and techniques, with a characteristics of individual executives themselves.[70] This helps to explain the relative success of political leaders in achieving their policy goals, and the contribution of structural considerations to successful policymaking.

Dimensions of Government Structure

The structures of modern governments are complex and varied. In this section we will discuss several broad dimensions of government structure, as well as several subdimensions of each. For each of these subdimensions I will propose (when possible) some possible empirical indicators. Finally, I will propose some hypotheses concerning the relationships between each subdimension and government policymaking.

Extensiveness

The first dimension of government is its extensiveness. Government in the late twentieth century is far more extensive than government in the eighteenth century, or even the early twentieth century. This increase in government activity influences both other structural aspects of government and policymaking. For example, as government increases in size, very likely the number of organizations increases, as does the demand for their more effective coordination. Hugh Heclo describes the growth of programs and the need for coordination as the "implosion" of programs into the organizational structure of government.[71]

Thus, as government becomes more extensive, presumably central agencies are used more and new procedures are developed as mechanisms for coordination.[72] In addition, it is no longer possible to go boldly into new policy areas, and the mode of policymaking becomes one more of policy succession rather than policy initiation—a hypothesis supported by some empirical evidence.[73] Of course, technological and social change may present new demands and opportunities for policy initiations, but the dominant mode of policymaking in an already extensive government should be policy succession.

Size.   There are several dimensions of extensiveness. The one most often discussed is the "size" of government. This is usually measured by a relatively simple indicator such as the ratio of public expenditure or public revenue to gross national product, or the ratio of public employment to the total labor force.[74] We have already pointed out, as have others, that public expenditures and public revenues do not exhaust the activities of government that influence their economies and society and therefore should be counted into some measure of size; however, unlike the GNP for the economy, there is no comprehensive measure for the size of government.[75] We will return to the questions posed by governments operating with nonconventional mechanisms when discussing hierarchical control.

While acknowledging the measurement problem, and using a commonsense definition of size in government, we can agree that size may have a significant influence on a government's structure and organization. If we are thinking of size solely in terms of levels of revenue and expenditure, size need not increase complexity and cause the proliferation of central agencies. If government chooses to deliver a small range of services through relatively simple transfer and grant programs, it may be able to accomplish its ends without the need for many organizations and large numbers of people.[76] There will still be problems, as the difficulties in coordinating social service transfer programs in most countries well illustrate, but not as severe as those in labor-intensive, highly organized systems. On the other hand, a government might choose to do fewer things but to provide service directly rather than through transfer or grants. This would tend to create a good deal more organizational complexity in government and produce greater problems of coordination.

Range. Another aspect of the extensiveness of government is the range of its activities. Virtually all industrialized societies are extensively involved with their economy and society, to varying degrees. One of the most important areas of variation is in the role of government in the economy and especially public ownership of industries. Table 1.1 shows in very rough terms the proportion of various major industrial groups or enterprises owned by government. As expected, the United States appears quite uninvolved with the economy as compared to its major trading partners, and might appear even less interventionist if the role of state and local governments was excluded.

We must, however, be careful not to assume that just because a country does not nationalize an industry that it is uninvolved in that industry. Banking is a particularly good example. Other than the involvement of the federal government with the Continental Illinois Bank and a few state-owned banks in the upper Midwest, there has been little direct involvement of the U.S. government in bank ownership. On the other hand, the Government National Mortgage Association (GNMA, or "Ginnie Mae"), Federal National Mortgage Association (FNMA, or "Fannie Mae"), Student Loan Marketing Association (SLMA, or "Sallie Mae"), and the several intermediate credit institutions in the Department of Agriculture and the Department of Housing and Urban Development constitute a very important set of banking institutions. None of these offers ordinary checking accounts, as might be true for nationalized banks in other countries such as France or Sweden, but they are certainly elements of the banking and credit system that are nationally owned and operated.

Portfolios. Size in government can also be measured by the number of ministries and agencies. Both Rose and Blondel have discussed the growth of the number of ministerial portfolios as an evolution of government indicating greater involvement in the economy and society.[77] There need not be any necessary correlation, as they point out, as a larger number of functions can be performed within the same number of ministries by giving each more work, but empirically there does appear to be a relationship.

TABLE 1.1
Public and Private Ownership of Industries in Five Countries, 1986

	Italy	*France*	*Sweden*	*Britain*	*United States*
Transportation					
Railroads	G	G	M/G	G	M/P
Airlines	G	G	M/G	E	P
Auto manufacturing	M/P	M/P	P	M/G	P
Communications					
Radio and television	G	G	M/P	M/G	M/P
Telephone service	G	G	G	M/P	P
Postal service	G	G	G	G	M/G
Power					
Gas	M/G	G	E	G	M/P
Electricity	M/G	G	M/G	G	M/P
Coal	M/G	M/G	M/P	G	P
Oil	M/G	E	M/P	M/P	P
Banking	M/G	M/G	M/P	M/P	M/P

Source: Adapted from Charles F. Andrain, *Politics and Economic Policy in Western Democracies* (North Scituate, Mass.: Duxbury, 1980).
Key: P   = private ownership
     G   = government ownership
     M/P = mixed ownership, private dominant
     M/G = mixed ownership, government dominant
     E   = approximately equal ownership

As well as being important for workload management and having symbolic and political value indicating governmental interest in a certain function or set of clients, the development of more ministerial portfolios may also be important for policy outcomes. One might say that extensiveness in government escalates as more agencies or ministries are developed. Creating an agency gives those interested in its particular function a clearer target for exerting pressure; this has been seen, for example, in the relationships between the National Education Association and the U.S. Department of Education after it was removed from the Department of Health, Education, and Welfare. In addition, the development of new agencies means the appointment of a minister and, more importantly, a group of civil servants to monitor developments in that policy area. This will likely lead to an elaboration of the laws and regulations in the policy area and an increase in the extensiveness of government. Such elaboration may have occurred eventually, but is likely to develop more rapidly once there is an independent agency.

The number of portfolios may also influence the extensiveness of government through coalition building. If policymaking in cabinet governments is carried on through coalitions rather than under the direction of a prime minister or perhaps a minister of finance, then more interests have to be assuaged in order to secure a winning coalition and the larger government expenditures and employment are likely to become. Cabinet governments vary considerably in their use of voting and coalitions in policymaking, both across time within countries as well as between countries, but in general larger cabinets are assumed to be associated with larger expenditures.[78]

Centralization

A second important dimension of government is the centralization of power and authority. Centralization has been discussed many times in studies of constitutional forms, such as discussions of unitary versus federal government. However, although it seem obvious, it is not as simple a concept as is sometimes assumed, and several subdimensions should be mentioned. Further, centralization is closely connected with the next dimension—hierarchy—and both are very important for the ability of central decision makers in national government to make and implement decisions effectively. Everything else being equal, we can hypothesize that the more decentralized and the less hierarchical a governing system is, the less capable it will be of producing desired results. There may be, of course, some virtues to a lack of uniformity across subnational areas and federalism has been praised as providing a natural laboratory for trying out different policy innovations.[79] However, from the top-down perspective employed here, federal structures present significant managerial problems.

Numbers of Governments.   Political systems differ in the number of governments within their borders. For some small Caribbean and Pacific nations there may be but one government that performs all the functions that are performed by national, intermediate, and local governments in other countries. Even for larger countries, there is a great deal of variation in the numbers of subnational governments, as shown in table 1.2. In this highly selective listing of countries, France and Czechoslovakia have the most governments per capita, while the United Kingdom has by far the fewest.

Leaving aside the formal structuring of relationships among levels of

TABLE 1.2
Local Governments in Fourteen
Countries, 1982

	Number	Population per Unit
Ireland	111	31,000
Denmark	277	18,400
Bulgaria	356	24,500
Sweden	279	29,800
Norway	454	9,000
Finland	461	10,400
United Kingdom	548	102,500
Belgium	596	16,700
Netherlands	820	17,000
Italy	8,053	7,100
Czechoslovakia	8,099	1,900
West Germany	8,510	7,200
France	36,391	1,500
United States	38,732	6,700

Source: Statesman's Yearbook.

government, we can assume that a large number of governments may present difficulties. One is simply that there are many more organizations to coordinate, especially if subnational governments implement some central government policies, so that central government may have to expend more of its resources and energy on maintaining control. In addition, large numbers of subnational governments may constitute a more effective political base for intergovernmental lobbying. Finally, citizens appear to be more satisfied with smaller governments, feeling that they have greater influence and that government is less remote, but the ability to satisfy local needs may limit the effectiveness of central direction.[80]

However, there are efficiency considerations in the choice of the number and size of subnational governments. Of course, different types of public services are best provided by different sizes and types of governments.[81] Vincent Ostrom and others have advocated using different types and sizes of government depending upon the services to be delivered.[82] Although rarely chosen strictly for efficiency reasons, special district governments in the United States and other countries such as Australia illustrate the use of different types and sizes of governments to provide services. If one is willing to accept variations in how services are provided and in the taxes and user fees associated with their delivery, this may be an efficient structural mechanism. The Tiebout analysis would, of course, argue that this type of decentralization would be the most efficient means of providing local public services as it would allow citizens to pick a bundle of services and prices.[83] Regardless of the impracticalities of the approach, decentralization of many functions to small local units may produce greater efficiency but at the loss of central control. Thus, those designing systems of governance, if indeed they are consciously designed, must be cognizant of such a tradeoff.[84]

Formal Federalism.   An important determinant of centralization and decentralization is a government's formal structure as a unitary or federal state. Of the over 150 countries in the world, 18 are federal in one form or another; of the 51 democratic governments identified by Lijphart, 10 are federations of one sort or another.[85] The phrase, "of one sort or another" is important because federalism is by no means a simple concept and there are a number of variations in federal constitutions and politics. In all, some power is shared between the central government and subnational governments, and the latter may have dominant policymaking authority over some policy areas. Some, such as education, tend to be controlled by subnational governments in almost all federal arrangments, while others such as defense and monetary policy are central functions, and many policy areas may be controlled by either.

If we think of federalism and decentralization from a theoretical rather than legal perspective, then the loss of control usually associated with federalism may not be as great as sometimes thought. Given the difficulty of governing large social systems, decentralization may be a rational strategy of governance.[86] It allows for adjustment without the grave errors that might occur in more centralized systems; it encourages strategic rather than synoptic decision making.[87] Although there may be some rationality in the redundancy built into federal systems, that still makes central control, which we are using as our "handle" to assess governmental structure, more tenuous.[88]

Fiscal Federalism.   As well as sharing formal powers over decision making, federal systems share revenue and expenditure powers. This form of sharing is not confined to federal systems; virtually all countries allow subnational governments some independent powers to raise revenues and make discretionary expenditures. Table 1.3 demonstrates the variations in the revenue-collecting and spending powers exercised by subnational governments in a number of political systems. As expected, unitary governments tend to have more centralized collection of revenue, although in only one country does the central government collect less than 50 percent

TABLE 1.3
Local Government Taxation and Expenditure
in Twenty-one Countries, 1982
(percent of total not under the central government)

	Taxation	Expenditure
Switzerland	59	63
Canada	50	57
Germany	49	51
United States	43	45
Sweden	38	40
Japan	35	36
Norway	30	35
Austria	30	31
Finland	30	36
Denmark	29	46
Australia	20	40
Luxemburg	18	18
Iceland	17	18
United Kingdom	13	26
France	12	15
Ireland	8	15
New Zealand	7	10
Belgium	7	14
Spain	6	8
Israel	4	11
Netherlands	2	24

Sources: Arend Lijphart, *Democracies: Paterns of Majoritarian and Consensus Government in Twenty-One Countries* (New Haven, Conn.: Yale University Press, 1984), table 10.2; International Monetary Fund, *Government Finance Statistics Yearbook, 1982* (Washington, D.C.: IMF, 1983).

of the taxes. Expenditures are somewhat less centralized, with subnational governments in three countries accounting for more than 50 percent of total public expenditure.

The centralization or decentralization of public finance is obviously important for our "top-down" view of the machinery of government. If a subnational government has considerable revenues of its own, as in Switzerland or Canada, it can perform functions following its own priorities to an extent that subnational governments in more centralized countries such as the Netherlands or Israel would not. This effect is compounded when local governments have relatively large expenditures but few revenue sources; their dependence upon central government revenues makes them equally dependent upon central government directions. In this regard, local government in the Netherlands, with only 2 percent of the revenues but one-quarter of expenditures, may be expected to be much more dependent (everything else being equal) than local government in countries such as Spain, France, or Iceland where revenues and expenditures are approximately equal.

Administrative Federalism.   Personnel is another resource that may be shared among levels of government.[89] Even in unitary states, many central programs are administered by personnel employed by subnational units.[90] This pattern is particularly common in education and health. The Federal Republic of Germany has the most extreme administrative decentralization of any of the industrialized countries (see table 1.4). The federal government has few civilian employees other than those in the post office and the state railway and those it does have are in planning and "policymaking" positions rather than in service delivery positions. The *Land* governments are largely charged with the actual delivery of services.[91] Quite obviously, the more subnational units of government are used to administer central government programs, the more likely the administration of programs will vary, although this may be desirable if there are marked regional differences in ethnicity, language, and religion. Further, administrative decentralization allows central governments to appear smaller to their citizens; despite all the rhetoric, employment in the federal government in the United States has been declining as a percentage of the labor force.[92] This has been true even when the federal government was perceived by students of intergovernmental politics as an increasingly dominant actor in the federal system.[93]

Hierarchy

While centralization as a concept is primarily concerned with the distribution of power and authority among levels of government, the concept of hierarchy as used here will be concerned with the ability of decision makers in the central government to govern effectively within government itself. We have several analyses of the difficulties faced by even nominally powerful actors in producing the elusive quality of "governance."[94] What factors are significant in affecting the ability to provide governance?

Quangoism.   One factor that clearly affects the ability of those in political office to govern is the extent to which their government is "on-line," meaning the extent to which government operations are directly under the control of ministers or other responsible political officials.[95] The extent to

TABLE 1.4
Distribution of Public Service Employment in Six Countries, Early 1980s
(percent of total public employment)

	Employer			
	Central Ministry	*Trading Enterprises*	*Local and Regional Governments*	*Other*[a]
France	45	17	23	15.0
Italy	37	30	13	20.0
United States	20	7	72	0.4
Sweden	19	23	54	4.0
Britain	14	25	39	22.0
West Germany	13	36	41	10.0

Source: Richard Rose et al., *Public Employment in Western Nations* (Cambridge: Cambridge University Press, 1985).

a. "Other" includes quasi-governmental organizations, health services, in some instances higher education, and a variety of public services organized to be outside the direct control of either central or local government.

which government has come to be operated "off-line" had particular relevance in the United Kingdom with the discussion of the number of "quangos" (quasi-nongovernmental organizations) found in British government.[96] Similar types of bodies operating at the "margins of the state" are found in virtually all governments, and governments in the 1970s and 1980s appeared to have a particular interest in moving their operations out of ministerial organizations into quasi-governmental or quasi-private bodies.[97] This was in part a means of hiding the real costs of the public sector, as budgets for these entities often are not included in the national budget. These organizations also allow government to distance itself from some activities that may be politically embarassing or unsuccessful; as William "Mate" Cobblers said, "It's nothing to do with me, mate." In addition, some activities performed by quangos, such as the Marriage Guidance Council in Great Britain, might be considered "inappropriate" for government itself to do.

As we have been adopting a top-down approach to the study of the machinery of government, quangos and other parastate bodies present a major problem of control for any political leader. Even if funding for the organization comes from government sources, these organizations tend to be insulated from political control and capable of ignoring changes in governments while they continue with their own activities. From a more bottom-up perspective, they also present a great problem in holding government accountable for the actions of the public sector. This may be intentional, as government in the United States, for example, would not like to be held accountable for the performance of Amtrak trains nor salaries paid to officials of the Synthetic Fuels Corporation.

Nationalized Industries. Nationalized industries, in that they tend to have rather loose connections with political leaders in government, may also be no more than fringe bodies. This relationship is rarely unintended, as governments may not want to be responsible for actions of such industries, and it may appear more appropriate to society as a whole to have a nationalized industry removed from direct political control so that it can operate like a business. The 1984 coal strike in the United Kingdom is a very good example of a government distancing itself from a nationalized industry and trying to say that the strike was the business of the National Coal Board and not the government. Further, there is little evidence to suggest that nationalized industries necessarily conform more to government policies than do private industries.[98]

Nationalized industries are different from most fringe bodies in that they can be to some degree self-financing. Given that most nationalized industries tend to be losers rather than winners, they have some continuing financial relationship with government.[99] Even then, however, their ability to generate revenues and to engage in other economic activities gives them substantial independence. This independence is increased when the nationalization process is conducted at one remove from government through mechanisms such as state holding companies. For example, in Italy, the Ministry for State Participation indirectly controls the activities of the major state holding companies IRI and ENI; the National Enterprise Board has played a similar role in the United Kingdom, although with greater political supervision, as has Stats Företag AB in Sweden. The latter company has investments in firms producing, among other things, textiles, pharmaceuticals, shale oil, steel, and tobacco. In some cases the ownership is complete; in others it is only partial. A similar problem of control arises when nationalized industries develop subsidiaries that may or may not be operating in the same general industry as the nationalized industry itself. This is not intended to be a discussion of the means through which the public sector may become involved in the economy, but perhaps it does point out that nationalized industries with access to revenues and credit markets may make the job of a minister trying to control them very difficult, and may present the same or even greater problem of accountability encountered in other forms of off-line organization in the public sector.[100]

Contracting.   Contracting out public services has become an increasingly popular means of attempting to control government costs. [101] Although it is not a structure per se (as we shall see regarding procedures), contracting does seem relevant to the structuring of the public sector, and certainly has relevance for hierarchical control of government by public officials. For example, contracting for defense purchases in the United States produces over 2 million jobs in the private sector; contracting for building highways produces 260,000 jobs. Those same jobs could be in the public sector if government chose to produce all its own weapons and build all its own roads. [102]

It is generally assumed that contracting will produce lower costs for government for the same services; one of the contentions of the Grace Commission in the United States was that contracting a variety of federal programs would save $12.75 billion over four years. [103] Whether these cost savings could be realized or not, there appear to be the same control problems in contracting as are found in off-line government organizations. Some are related directly to cost, as the numerous cost-overrun scandals in the Department of Defense have demonstrated. Other problems are more the product of the quality of the services being rendered and the nature of government as a service provider. Protections for clients and citizens, such as freedom of information, may be available in public programs that are not available in contracted services.

Subdepartmental Structure.   Even within government itself there are numerous problems of control of subordinate organizations, and the characteristics of organizational structures below the cabinet or executive department level may exacerbate those problems. In the United States we are accustomed to well-defined and politically powerful organizations existing below executive departments; the "agency" is an important building block of official Washington and is a major actor in the politics of "iron triangles."[104] The Canadian government has a rather similar subdepartmental structure, and *styrelsen* in the Swedish government constitute semiautonomous boards administering public programs. In most European countries, however, subdepartmental structure is not so clearly elaborated; contrast the *Civil Service Yearbook* from the United Kingdom to the *United States Government Manual.* The latter publication provides detailed organization charts and descriptions for several tiers of subdepartments; there is little evidence of any formalized subdepartmental structure in the *Civil Service Yearbook,* although devolution of authority can be followed by watching the grade level of civil servants responsible for the tasks mentioned. Further, changes in subdepartment organization in the United

States will almost certainly be noted by some official piece of paper such as an executive order, while subdepartmental structure in the United Kingdom appears to be changed almost at will.

Everything else being equal, a more elaborated and formalized subdepartmental structure will make the exercise of central control more difficult. This has been the traditional analysis of policymaking in the United States were agencies' permanence and contacts with both client groups and Congress give them substantial power in relation to political actors who are brought in by a president to supervise them.[105] In such a structure, the cabinet-level department, having little ability to speak as a whole on issues or to control the activities of its components, is reduced to a holding company for the operating agencies. The absence of a cabinet form of government in the United States makes even the cabinet-level departments themselves somewhat independent of the president and perhaps more tied to their clients and to their congressional committees than to the program of the president.[106] As we shall see, such decentralization of the executive branch requires either a very strong president or a set of well-developed procedures to maintain—or gain—control.

Political Executive/Bureaucratic Relationships. Related to the various powers of cabinet-level departments and their components is the question of the relationship between political executives and career civil servants. As is not true of most other industrialized countries, hierarchies within departments in the United States are truncated; civil servants can rise only so far before they reach positions reserved for political appointees. These appointees are typically in Washington for a rather short time, have limited experience and even limited knowledge about the policy area they are intended to manage. As any number of authors have pointed out, this limits their ability to impose effective leadership on the Washington bureaucracy and to implement presidential priorities successfully.[107] This is somewhat paradoxical, since the usual justification for political appointees is that they give the president more control over government.

The United States is at one extreme of a continuum describing relationships between career and political officials. At the other is the blending of the two into virtually a single career. So, for example, in 1977 the president of France, the prime minister and thirty out of thirty-six ministers were former civil servants; as members of the *grands corps* they could return to the civil service at the end of their political career if they wished.[108] Also, French civil servants are in the ministers' *cabinets* and thereby serve as their personal advisers with substantial political influence.[109] A similar blending of political and administrative careers can be found in other European countries. Between these poles (represented by the United States and France) are policymaking systems such as the United Kingdom where civil servants go to the top of the administrative and policy hierarchies, but where political and civil service careers are distinct.

Central Agencies.   One resource for those in the center of government attempting to impose control over the rest of government are the central agencies.[110] These agencies, such as the Office of Management and Budget and the Office of Personnel Management in the United States, the Treasury in the United Kingdom, and the Treasury Board Secretariat in Canada, are designed to coordinate interdepartmental aspects of policy, develop policies that departments must follow (for example, budgeting and personnel procedures), and monitor performance by the operating departments. These are the staff agencies in traditional public administration, but they are also something more. Staff agencies implies rather bloodless bureaucrats making arcane rules about public personnel procedures. Those in central agencies are increasingly vital political actors rather than mere technocrats. Colin Campbell stresses the importance of the central agencies in imposing executive control (to the extent possible) in the United States, Canada, and the United Kingdom, and the growing importance of these agencies as stress on governments increases.[111]

Countries vary substantially in the need for such organizations and in their development. Countries such as the United States and Canada, with both a federal system of government and relatively strong subdepartmental structures, would appear to require stronger central agencies than a unitary system such as the United Kingdom with relatively weak subdepartmental structures. Quantitative data presented by Campbell shows the responses of these countries to demands for central control, with the United States and Canada devoting substantially more resources to these efforts than the United Kingdom.[112] Staffing and expenditures in the United Kingdom are in fact higher than might have been expected, given other structural characteristics, indicating perhaps a greater need for control than in the other two countries.

Not all organizations and agencies performing coordinative roles assigned to central agencies need be identifiable as budgeting, personnel, or financial organizations such as the central agencies mentioned above. Another option may be the use of "superministries" to coordinate such functions within a large policy area. This was tried in the United Kingdom during the Heath government, and was proposed for the United States by President Nixon, among others.[113] The expenditure envelope system in Canada is the functional equivalent of a system of superministries.[114] Similarly, little discussed parts of government such as cabinet committees can perform this coordinate role in conjunction with central agencies.[115] Hall, for example, notes the importance of the Elysée staff and interministerial committees as coordinating mechanisms within French government, and the extent to which they have been able to overcome the formalism of the administrative system for greater effectiveness.[116]

Procedures. It may appear inappropriate to consider procedures as a structural element of government, but they demonstrate many features associated with political institutions. In addition, they are associated with central agencies and may be essential to the functioning of the central agency. In addition, procedures may be important for either the central agencies or political executives exercising their political control over the business of government. For example, the development of the machinery for controlling public expenditure in the United Kingdom, going from PESC through cash limits to "funny money" represents changes in procedures that have been very important for Treasury control.[117]

Participation

The final major dimension of the structure of government is participation. While not usually considered a structural variable, the manner in which participation is channeled into the political system can be argued to have a significant impact on policy outcomes.[118] These effects have most commonly been noted in the corporatist literature, but appear to be more general.

Interest-Group Participation. As noted, the most common form of structured participation in government is the role assigned to interest groups in corporatist political systems. Although it is difficult to define corporatism, or to determine whether it really exists in any meaningful sense, how interest groups are permitted access to policymaking can be hypothesized to influence policy. In particular, giving certain groups rights of participation and requiring the consultation of affected parties when new legislation or regulations are being considered reduces a political official's power to grant access, and hence lessens the possibility of closed, symbiotic relationships between political actors and a limited set of interest groups. The openness of "legitimate" interest-group arrangements then can be hypothesized to produce more direct bargaining among interest groups and perhaps more redistributive policies.[119] On the other hand, from the perspective of theories of the state, legitimate ties between interest groups and government may lessen the state's autonomy in making decisions that would potentially harm the societal interests represented by those groups. However, such arrangements have the virtue for governments seeking autonomy that, once the decision has been made, all affected parties have had a part in making decision. They are to some degree bound by the decision that may enhance the autonomy of the state in implementing decisions that might be unpopular with some groups.[120] Thus, the relationships of interest groups to government decision making, and the role of structured access for interest groups, is more complex than is sometimes assumed, and any discussion of the structure and organization of government must include some attention to that topic. From the top-down perspective we have been using, structured access of interest groups at once decreases control by sharing decision-making power and increases control by gaining acquiescence through the policymaking process.

Political Parties.   Political parties are more conventionally assumed to be related to policymaking than interest groups, and James Sundquist makes the point that the stability and authority of political parties are important for explaining the relative success of European planning efforts in population policy.[121] This is a part of the continuing saga of the search for responsible political parties in the United States. The argument is that if parties are responsible and decisions about policies are made collectively, then the type of individual policy entrepreneurship that sometimes characterizes Cabinet and subcabinet officials in the United States can be reduced or eliminated.

As well as responsibility, simple factors such as the number of parties and their need to form coalitions in order to govern may also affect policymaking and the ability of political leaders to make authoritative decisions. For example, with coalition governments, especially those involving large numbers of parties, one would expect more side payments to be necessary, and, as a result, policies to be less coherent than in single-party governments. Similarly, one might expect coalition governments, everything else being equal, to expand the scope of government since again, side payments in policy terms would have to be made to more interests in the society. Everything may not be equal, and a coalition of conservative parties may be quite effective in restraining the expansion of government, but the general tendency would be for expansion.

Summary

As we said at the outset, this chapter was not intended to break a great amount of new ground, but perhaps it has plowed some old ground in useful ways. It has argued that one fruitful manner in which to approach the machinery of government is from a managerial perspective, that is, from the perspective of someone in government who is trying to make effective policy and have it implemented. The numerous aspects of the machinery of government we have discussed should be seen, however, as more than simply barriers to implementation but rather as a set of choices and options. Governments designed with only implementation in mind may well fail to meet other criteria for good government, especially good democratic government. The "top-down" perspective, however, does provide a handle with which to think about the design of government, and the design of governing institutions has important implications for academic analysts, practitioners, and citizens.

Notes

1. In this chapter the words "structure" and "organization" of government are used synonymously. Both terms are used because they both appear frequently in the literature. The phrase "machinery of government" was not used because of its somewhat mechanistic connotations and because its use is largely confined to the Anglo-Saxon parts of the world.

2. Kenneth H. F. Dyson, *The State Tradition in Western Europe* (Oxford: Martin Robertson, 1980); Roger Benjamin and Steven L. Elkin, *The Democratic State* (Lawrence: University of Kansas Press, 1985); Douglas E. Ashford, "Welfare States as Institutional Choices," prepared for the Fifth International Conference, Council for European Studies, October 1985.

3. Christopher Pollitt, *Manipulating the Machine: Changing the Pattern of Ministerial Departments, 1960–83* (London: George Allen and Unwin, 1984).

4. Bert A. Rockman, "Scarcity and the Analytic Capacity of Government," manuscript, Department of Political Science, University of Pittsburgh, 1984.

5. Manfred Kochen and Karl W. Deutsch, *Decentralization* (Cambridge, Mass.: Oelgeschlager, Gunn and Hain, 1980).

6. B. Guy Peters and Martin O. Heisler, "Thinking About Public Sector Growth," in *Why Governments Grow*, ed. Charles L. Taylor (London: Sage, 1984); Richard Rose, *Understanding Big Government* (London: Sage, 1984).

7. Gerald E. Caiden, *Administrative Reorganization* (Chicago: Aldine, 1970), p. 200.

8. James G. March and Johan P. Olsen, "The New Institutionalism: Organi-

zational Factors in Political Life," *American Political Science Review* 78 (1984), 734–49.

9. Ibid., p. 735.

10. Ibid., p. 743.

11. Jean Blondel, *The Organization Of Governments: A Comparative Analysis of Government Structures* (Beverly Hills, Calif.: Sage, 1982).

12. Christopher Hood and Andrew Dunsire, *Bureaumetrics* (Farnsborough, Hants.: Gower, 1981).

13. B. Guy Peters and Brian W. Hogwood, *The Changing Face of Washington Bureaucracy*, forthcoming.

14. Arend Lijphart, *Democracies: Patterns of Majoritarian and Consensus Government in Twenty-One Countries* (New Haven, Conn.: Yale University Press, 1984).

15. Ibid.; Arend Lijphart, "Typologies of Democratic Systems," *Comparative Political Studies* 1 (1968), 3–44; *Democracy in Plural Societies: A Comparative Exploration* (New Haven, Conn.: Yale University Press, 1977).

16. B. Guy Peters, John C. Doughtie, and M. Kathleen McCulloch, "Types of Democratic Systems and Types of Public Policy," *Comparative Politics* 9 (1977), 327–55.

17. Pollitt, *Manipulating the Machine*; D. W. Chester and F.M.G. Willson, *The Organisation of British Central Government, 1914–1964*, 2d ed. (London: George Allen and Unwin, 1968); Christopher Hood, "The Machinery of Government Problem," *Studies in Public Policy*, no. 28 (Glasgow: Centre for the Study of Public Policy, University of Strathclyde, 1979); Audrey D. Doerr, *The Machinery of Government in Canada* (Toronto: Methuen, 1981).

18. Peter A. Hall, "Policy Innovation and the Structure of the State: The Politics-Administration Nexus in France and Britain," *Annals* 466 (1983), 43–60.

19. Eric A. Nordlinger, *On the Autonomy of the Democratic State* (Cambridge, Mass.: Harvard University Press, 1981).

20. James L. Sundquist, "A Comparison of Policy-Making Capacity in the United States and Five European Countries: The Case of Population Distribution," in *Population Policy Analysis*, ed. Michael E. Kraft and Mark Schneider (Lexington, Mass.: D.C. Heath, 1978).

21. Ibid., p. 79.

22. Anthony Barker, *Quangos in Britain* (London: Macmillan, 1982); D. C. Hague, W.J.M. MacKenzie, and A. Barker, *Public Policy and Private Interests* (London: Macmillan, 1975); Ira Sharkansky, *Wither the State?* (Chatham, N.J.: Chatham House, 1979).

23. Raymond Vernon, "Linking Managers with Ministers: Dilemas of State-Owned Enterprises," *Journal of Policy Analysis and Management* 4 (1984), 39–55; Harvey B. Feigenbaum, *The Politics of Public Enterprise* (Princeton, N.J.: Princeton University Press, 1985).

24. Phillipe C. Schmitter, "Still the Century of Corporatism?" *Review of*

Politics 36 (1974), 85–131; Martin O. Heisler, "Corporate Pluralism Revisited: Where Is the Theory?" *Scandinavian Political Studies* 2 (1979), 277–97.

25. B. Guy Peters, *The Politics of Bureaucracy*, 2d ed. (New York: Longman, 1984).

26. Pollitt, *Manipulating the Machine*, p. 168.

27. Chester and Willson, *The Organisation of British Central Government.*

28. L. M. Short, *The Development of National Administrative Organization in the United States* (Baltimore: Johns Hopkins Press, 1923); William Andersen, *Units of Government in the United States* (Chicago: Public Administration Service, 1945).

29. Richard Rose, "Overloaded Government: The Problem Outlined," *European Studies Newsletter* 5 (1975), 13–18; Anthony King, "Overload: Problems of Governing in the 1970s," *Political Studies* 23 (1975), 284–96.

30. Patrick Dunleavy, "Demand Pressure and Structural Change in the Political System," manuscript, Nuffield College, Oxford University, 1976.

31. Charles H. Levine, "Organizational Decline and Cutback Management," *Public Administration Review* 38 (1978), 316–25; Daniel Tarschys, "Rational Decremental Budgeting," *Policy Sciences* 14 (1981), 49–58; Rockman, "Scarcity and Analytic Capacity of Government."

32. C. Grafton, "Response to Change: The Creation and Reorganization of Federal Agencies," in *Problems in Administrative Reform*, ed. R. Miewald and M. Steinman (Chicago: Nelson-Hall, 1984).

33. Lijphart, *Democracies.*

34. Hal G. Rainey, "Public Organization Theory: Current Contribution and Research Directions," presented at the annual meeting of the American Political Science Association, Washington, D.C., 1984.

35. Douglas C. Pitt and B. C. Smith, *Government Departments: An Organisational Perspective* (London: Routledge and Kegan Paul, 1981); Royston Greenwood and Christopher R. Hinnings, "Contingency Theory and Public Bureaucracies," *Policy and Politics* 5 (1976), 159–80; Royston Greenwood, Christopher R. Hinnings, and S. Ranson, "Contingency Theory and the Organization of Local Authorities, I and II," *Public Administration* 53 (1975), 1–23, 169–90.

36. Hood, "The Machinery of Government Problem."

37. Herbert Kaufman and David Seidman, "The Morphology of Organizations," *Adminstrative Science Quarterly* 15 (1970), 439–51.

38. Vincent Ostrom and Elinor Ostrom, "Public Goods and Public Choices," in *Alternatives for Delivering Public Services*, ed. E. E. Savas (Boulder, Colo.: Westview, 1977).

39. Kochen and Deutsch, *Decentralization.*

40. Michael Lipsky, *Street-Level Bureaucracy* (New York: Russell Sage, 1980); Douglas Yates, *The Ungovernable City* (Cambridge, Mass.: MIT Press, 1977).

41. David Braybrooke and Charles E. Lindblom, *A Strategy of Decision* (New York: Free Press, 1963); Michael D. Cohen, James G. March, and Johan P.

Olsen, "The Garbage Can Model of Organizational Choice," *Administrative Science Quarterly* 17 (1972), 1–25; William Niskanen, *Bureaucracy and Representative Government* (Chicago: Aldine/Atherton, 1971).

42. John Kimberly, "Issues in the Design of Longitudinal Organizational Research," *Sociological Methods and Research* 4 (1976), 321–47.

43. Howard E. Aldrich, *Organizations and Environments* (Englewood Cliffs, N.J.: Prentice-Hall, 1979).

44. Some preliminary work of this sort appears in B. Guy Peters and Brian W. Hogwood, "In Search of the Issue Attention Cycle," *Journal of Politics* 47 (February 1985), 238–53.

45. Peters and Hogwood, forthcoming.

46. Benny Hjern and Chris Hull, "Implementation Research as Empirical Constitutionalism," *European Journal of Political Research* 10 (1982), 105–15; Kenneth Hanf, "Regulatory Structures: Enforcement as Implementation," ibid., pp. 159–72; Benny Hjern and David O. Porter, "Implementation Structures: A New Unit of Administrative Analysis," *Organization Studies* 2 (1981), 211–27.

47. Hjern and Porter, "Implementation Structures," p. 211.

48. Michael Harmon, *Action Theory for Public Administration* (New York: Longman, 1980).

49. Pollitt, *Manipulating the Machine*, pp. 174–77.

50. Niskanen, *Bureaucracy and Representative Government*; Gordon Tullock, *The Politics of Bureaucracy* (Washington, D.C.: Public Affairs Press, 1965).

51. Terry M. Moe, "The New Economics of Organizations," *American Journal of Political Science* 28 (1984), 739–77.

52. Oliver E. Williamson, "Managerial Discretion, Organization Form and the Multi-division Hypothesis," in *The Corporate Economy*, ed. B. Marris and A. Woods (London: Macmillan, 1971); *The Evolution of Hierarchy: An Essay on the Organization of Work* (New York: Norton, 1976).

53. Peter M. Jackson, *The Political Economy of Bureaucracy* (Oxford: Philip Alan, 1982), pp. 65–67.

54. Colin E. Campbell and George Szablowski, *The Superbureaucrats: Structure and Behaviour in Central Agencies* (Toronto: Macmillan of Canada, 1979).

55. J. Marschak, "Elements of a Theory of Teams," *Management Science* 1 (1955), 127–37; R. Radner, "Team Decision Problems," *Annals of Mathematics and Statistics* 33 (1962), 857–81.

56. Robert Merton, "Bureaucratic Structure and Personality," *Social Forces* 18 (1940), 560–68.

57. Moe, "The New Economics of Organizations"; Barry Mitnick, *The Political Economy of Regulation* (New York: Columbia University Press, 1980).

58. Dyson, *The State Tradition in Western Europe*; Theda Skocpol, *States and Social Revolutions* (Cambridge: Cambridge University Press, 1979); Claus Offe, *Contradictions of the Welfare State* (London: Hutchinson, 1984); Benjamin and Elkin, *The Democratic State*.

59. Raymond D. Duvall and John R. Freeman, "The State and Dependent

Capitalism," *International Studies Quarterly* 25 (March 1981), 99–118; Stephen D. Krasner, "Approaches to the State," *Comparative Politics* 16 (January 1984), 223–46.

60. Duvall and Freeman, "The State and Dependent Capitalism"; John R. Freeman and Raymond D. Duvall, "The Technobureaucratic State and the Entrepreneurial State in Dependent Industrialization," *American Political Science Review* 77 (September 1983), 569–87.

61. Goran Therborn, *What Does the Ruling Class Do When It Rules?* (London: New Left Books, 1978); Nordlinger, *On the Autonomy.*

62. Sundquist, "A Comparison of Policymaking Capacity"; Hall, "Policy Innovation."

63. Hall, "Policy Innovation."

64. Richard Rose, *The Problem of Party Government* (London: Macmillan, 1974); B. Guy Peters, "The Problem of Bureaucratic Government," *Journal of Politics* 43 (1981), 56–82.

65. Richard Rose, "Governments Against Subgovernments," in *Presidents and Prime Ministers*, ed. Richard Rose and Ezra N. Suleiman (Washington, D.C.: American Enterprise Institute, 1980).

66. For an analysis, see Stephen H. Linder and B. Guy Peters, "The Fallacy of Misplaced Prescription," manuscript, Department of Political Science, University of Pittsburgh, 1985.

67. Christopher Hood, *The Limits of Administration* (New York: John Wiley, 1976); George C. Edwards, *Implementing Public Policy* (Washington, D.C.: Congressional Quarterly Press, 1980).

68. James W. Fesler, "Politics, Policy and Bureaucracy at the Top," *Annals* 466 (1983), 23–41.

69. March and Olsen, "The New Institutionalism."

70. Campbell and Szablowski, *The Superbureaucrats.*

71. Hugh Heclo, "Frontiers of Social Policy in Europe and America," *Policy Sciences* 6 (December 1975), 403–21; "Toward a New Welfare State," in *The Development of the Welfare States in Europe and America*, ed. Peter Flora and Arnold J. Heidenheimer (New Brunswick, N.J.: Transaction Books, 1981), pp. 383–406.

72. Campbell and Szablowski, *The Superbureaucrats.*

73. Brian W. Hogwood and B. Guy Peters, *Policy Dynamics* (New York: St. Martin's, 1983).

74. Richard Rose et al., *Public Employment in Western Democracies* (Cambridge: Cambridge University Press, 1985).

75. Peters and Heisler, "Thinking About Public Sector Growth," pp. 177–97.

76. See Brian W. Hogwood and B. Guy Peters, *The Pathology of Public Policy* (Oxford: Oxford University Press, 1985), pp. 43–48.

77. Richard Rose, "On the Priorities of Government: A Department Analysis of Public Policy," *European Journal of Political Research* 4 (1976), 247–89; Blondel, *The Organization of Governments.*

78. Michael Rush, *The Cabinet and Policy Formation* (London: Longman, 1984).

79. Herbert Jacob, *German Administration Since Bismarck: Central Authority versus Local Autonomy* (New Haven: Conn.: Yale University Press, 1963).

80. S. Sonenblum, John J. Kirlin, and John C. Ries, *How Cities Provide Services: An Evaluation of Alternative Delivery Structures* (Cambridge, Mass.: Bollinger, 1977).

81. D. P. Bradford, R. A. Mott, and Wallace E. Oates, "The Rising Cost of Local Public Services," *National Tax Journal* 2 (1969), 185–202; Kenneth Newton, "Is Small So Beautiful? Is Big So Ugly?" *Studies in Public Policy*, no. 18 (Glasgow, Scotland: Centre for the Study of Public Policy, University of Strathclyde, 1977).

82. Vincent Ostrom, *The Political Theory of the Compound Republic* (Blacksburg, Va.: Public Choice Center, Virginia Polytechnic Institute and State University, 1971).

83. Wallace E. Oates, *Fiscal Federalism* (New York: Harcourt, Brace, Jovanovich, 1972); C. Tiebout, "A Pure Theory of Local Expenditure," *Journal of Political Economy* 64 (1956), 416–24.

84. See Ira Sharkansky, "Intergovernmental Relations," in *Handbook of Organizational Design*, ed. Paul C. Nystrom and William H. Starbuck (New York: Oxford University, 1981), 1:456–70.

85. Lijphart, *Democracies*.

86. Donald Schon, *Beyond the Stable State* (New York: Random House, 1971).

87. John J. Kirlin, "A Political Perspective," in *Public Sector Performance: A Conceptual Turning Point*, ed. Trudi C. Miller (Baltimore: Johns Hopkins University Press, 1984).

88. Martin Landau, "Federalism, Redundancy and System Reliability," in *The Federal Polity*, ed. Daniel Elazar (New Brunswick, N.J.: Transaction Books, 1974).

89. Richard Rose, *Understanding Big Government* (London: Sage, 1984).

90. John Greenwood and David Wilson, *Public Administration in Britain* (London: George Allen and Unwin, 1984).

91. Nevil Johnson, *State and Government in the Federal Republic of Germany* (Oxford: Pergamon); Edward C. Page, *Political Authority and Bureaucratic Power* (Brighton: Wheatsheaf, 1984).

92. Frederick C. Mosher, "The Changing Responsibilities and Tactics of the Federal Government," *Public Administration Review* 40 (1980), 541–53.

93. Advisory Commission on Intergovernmental Relations, *The Federal Role in the Federal System* (Washington, D.C.: GPO, 1981).

94. Rose, *The Problem of Party Government*; Richard Rose, *Do Parties Make a Difference?* 2d ed. (Chatham, N.J.: Chatham House, 1984); Peters, "The Problem of Bureaucratic Government"; Colin Campbell, *Governments Under Stress* (Toronto: University of Toronto Press, 1983).

95. Rose, *Understanding Big Government*, pp. 156–65.

96. Barker, *Quangos in Britain*; Brian W. Hogwood, "The Tartan Fringe: Quangos and Other Assorted Animals in Scotland," *Studies in Public Policy*, no. 34 Centre for the Study of Public Policy, University of Strathclyde, 1971).

97. Sharkansky, *Wither the State?*

98. Feigenbaum, *The Politics of Public Enterprise.*

99. Lennart Warra, *Den Statliga företagssketorns expansion* (Stockholm: Liber, 1980); J. Redwood, *Going for Broke: Gambling with Taxpayers' Money* (Oxford: Basil Blackwell, 1984).

100. Vernon, "Linking Managers with Ministers"; Feigenbaum, *The Politics of Public Enterprise.*

101. E. S. Savas, *Privatizing the Public Sector* (Chatham, N.J.: Chatham House, 1981); RIPA, *Contracting Out in the Public Sector* (London: RIPA, 1984).

102. G. Guy Peters, "Providing Public Services: The Public-Private Employment Mix," in *Providing Public Services*, ed. Dennis L. Thompson (Lexington, Mass.: D.C. Heath, 1986).

103. President's Private Sector Survey on Cost Control, *Report to the President* (Washington, D.C.: PPSSCC, 1984); see also Joan T. Claybrook, *Deceiving the Public: The Story Behind J. Peter Grace and His Campaign* (Washington, D.C.: Public Citizen, Inc., 1985).

104. A. Grant Jordon, "Iron Triangles, Woolly Corporatism, and Elastic Netwoks: Images of the Policy Process," *Journal of Public Policy* 1 (1981), 95–123.

105. Harold Seidman, *Politics, Power and Position*, 3d ed. (New York: Oxford University Press, 1980); James W. Fesler, "Politics, Policy, and Bureaucracy at the Top," *Annals* 466 (1983).

106. Thomas E. Cronin, "Everybody Believes in Democracy Until He Gets to the White House," *Law and Contemporary Problems* 35 (1970), 573–625.

107. Sundquist, "A Comparison of Policymaking Capacity"; Bert A. Rockman, *The Leadership Question* (New York: Praeger, 1984); Rose, "Government Against Subgovernment"; Fesler, "Politics, Policy, and Bureaucracy at the Top."

108. Vincent Wright, *The Government and Politics and France* (London: Hutchinson, 1978), p. 91. See also Anne Stevens, " 'L'Alternance' and the Higher Civil Service," in *Socialism, the State and Public Policy in France*, ed. Philip G. Cerny and Martin A. Schain (London: Francis Pinter, 1985), pp. 143–65.

109. Ezra N. Suleiman, *Politics, Power and Bureaucracy in France* (Princeton, N.J.: Princeton University Press, 1974), pp. 234ff.

110. Campbell and Szablowski, *The Superbureaucrats.*

111. Colin Campbell, *Governments Under Stress* (Toronto: University of Toronto Press, 1983).

112. Ibid., pp. 16ff.

113. Pollitt, *Manipulating the Machine*, pp. 96–98; Richard P. Nathan, *The Project That Failed: Nixon and the Administrative Presidency* (New York: John Wiley, 1975).

114. S. Borins, "Envelopes: Workable Rationality at Last," in *How Ottawa Spends Your Tax Dollars*, ed. G. Bruce Doern (Toronto: Lorimer, 1982).

115. Thomas T. Mackie and Brian W. Hogwood, *Unlocking the Cabinet: Cabinet Structures in Comparative Perspective* (London: Sage, 1985).

116. Hall, "Policy Innovation."

117. Douglas E. Ashford, *Policy and Politics in Britain* (Philadelphia: Temple University Press, 1981); H. Copeman, "Analyzing Public Expenditure, Parts 1 and 2," *Journal of Public Policy* 1 (1981), 189–306, 481–500; Sir Leo Pliatzky, *Getting and Spending* (Oxford: Basil Blackwell, 1982).

118. B. Guy Peters, *The Politics of Bureaucracy*, 2d ed. (New York: Longman. 1984), p. 151; Frank G. Castles, *The Impact of Parties* (London: Sage, 1982); Charles Lockhart, "Explaining Social Policy Differences Among Advanced Industrial Countries," *Comparative Politics* 16 (April 1984), 335–50.

119. Peters, *The Politics of Bureaucracy*, pp. 150–57.

120. Martin O. Heisler, with Robert Kvavik, "The European Policy Model," in *Politics in Europe*, ed. Heisler (New York: David McKay, 1974), pp. 27–89.

121. Sundquist, "A Comparison of Policymaking Capacity."

CHAPTER 2

The Search for Coordination and Control:

When and How Are Central Agencies the

Answer?

Colin Campbell, S.J.

Modern government encompasses a complex and interlocking set of institutions administering an almost bewildering array of programs. The organizations of government are so numerous and stand in so many different relationships to the central institutions of government—legislatures, individual and collective executive authority, and courts—that the question even arises as to which belong to government and which are beyond the pale.[1] When they take over, both chief executives and their secretaries or ministers find efforts to bring order to the chaos through reforms in the machinery of government almost irresistible. The sheer size and number of interorganizational linkages make it difficult for the uninitiated, or even the more knowledgeable, to understand how the bureaucratic system operates. Reorganization presents itself as a way to gain control over the machinery of government by simplification and rationalization.[2]

To be sure, reform strategies generate problems of their own. These stem from the fact that few widely accepted principles guide such efforts.[3] Ironically, the tendency to reorganize has accelerated since the beginning of the twentieth century with the development of "scientific" administrative theory.[4] However, the theory of bureaucratic organization provided few definitive answers to the specific problems that administrators and politicians face. Somewhat like modern medicine, it seldom prescribed direct treatments for specific diseases. Rather, it tended to promote

general-purpose drugs that frequently produced side effects as dangerous
as the diseases being treated.

This chapter examines reorganization efforts in the United States, the
United Kingdom, and Canada. In each country the pace has quickened in
the past two decades. Numerous changes emerged in the allocation of
functions among operational departments. The more dramatic of these
included the birth and then death of "superministries" in Britain, the
failure of Richard Nixon's attempt to establish "supersecretaries" along
with Jimmy Carter's comprehensive and largely unsuccessful Reorganization Project in the United States, and continual proliferation and rearrange-
ment of portfolios during Pierre Trudeau's regime in Canada.

Even more striking changes in central coordination and control departments and agencies have occurred in the United States, the United Kingdom, and Canada during the past twenty years. Developments surrounding
these institutions will serve as the focus of this chapter. In the process of
counteracting fragmentation within the executive, U.S. presidents and
U.K. and Canadian prime ministers have frequently resorted to central
agency reforms. The three nations share closer historical-constitutional,
political, and cultural connections than any other trio of advanced liberal
democracies. It should come as no surprise that, with the caveat that the
United States has not derived much from Canadian efforts, the three have
copied one another extensively while altering central agency structures
and functions.[5] As well, a pattern has emerged in all three countries
whereby chief executives frequently resort to central agency reforms in
efforts to solve essentially sectoral problems. Excessive use of such solutions runs a serious risk of overloading the center, making it a mirror
image of dysfunctions and cleavages in operational departments.

Normally, reorganizations of line departments and central agencies
respond to separate sets of problems. The former usually treat stress
emanating from the perceived inadequacy of existing administrative arrangements for dealing with a particular policy sector. For example, the
reorganization of energy policymaking in the United States during the
Carter administration addressed deficiencies in machinery that became
apparent during energy crises beginning in 1973. The institutional remedies did not remove the stress. In fact, some argue that they exacerbated
it. Nonetheless, the reforms enabled the administration to buttress the
public conviction that it had taken charge by even tackling the organizational dimensions of the crisis.

Similarly, reorganization of central agencies usually stems from severe
systemic stress. However, this stress normally takes the shape of broader
disorders such as fiscal strains, poor coordination between departments, and

weak bureaucratic or political accountability. Central agency reorganization, thus, most appropriately addresses relatively global problems originating from fundamental economic, political, and governance problems.

This chapter will examine three factors that may affect political leaders' decisions to attempt reorganization of central agencies. These are: the nature of the chief executive's authority, the patterns of cabinet secretaries' exercise of discretion and collective decision making, and the managerial ethos of the executive-bureaucratic culture. An assessment of the reorganization option from these perspectives should shed light on the art of the possible regarding the machinery of government. At the end of the analysis, the chapter will derive some conclusions that may prove helpful for academics and practitioners alike.

Executive Leadership

In several respects, executive leadership plays a major role in the process whereby difficulties with machinery of government lead ultimately to reorganization. Here we must first distinguish between the "principal" and "collective" executive authority. The former denotes the president and the prime ministers, whereas the latter means the Cabinet. Three factors influence the likelihood that chief executives will resort to reorganization of central agencies when facing machinery issues. These are: the parameters of their authority, their leadership styles, and events of the day.

Parameters of Authority

Neat comparisons between the authority of presidents and prime ministers have proven elusive for scholars.[6] One can find in the literature works that look longingly at the latitude of presidents while assessing the position of prime ministers,[7] and vice versa.[8]

Any effort to enumerate the various components of a president's authority over civil service organization becomes quite arduous. The visitor to Washington soon finds that U.S. officials, especially in central agencies, invoke principles derived from the Constitution and provisions from specific statutes to define their responsibilities much more often than their opposite numbers in London or Ottawa ever would. Entrenched strands of authority give an immense profile to the president while scarcely acknowledging the existence of the cabinet. Yet these sources operate as mixed blessings. Americans' ambivalence toward executive authority, with its clearest manifestation lodged in the principle of checks and balances, accompanies their penchant for institutionalizing presidential responsibilities. As well, the clarity of statutory provisions comes at the cost of congressional scrutiny, approval, and oversight. Thus, for presidents with ambitious reorganization plans, their situation can give with the right hand and take back with the left.

Apart from the vagaries of constitutional and congressional mandates, presidents must attune themselves to conventional constraints on their authority over machinery of government. Since issues in this field affect most directly the bureaucratic community, presidents must recognize that permanent civil servants and their departments will resist initiatives that appear to encroach upon their territory.[9] Nixon's hostility toward the permanent bureaucracy spawned dramatic efforts to centralize the cabinet system and increase departments' responsiveness to the president. However, even sympathetic observers viewed these measures as exceeding the authority of the presidency.[10] Carter experienced similar constraints. For instance, career civil servants in the Office of Management and Budget never accepted the appointees and secondees brought under its roof to work on Carter's reorganization projects.

British and Canadian prime ministers find that they have relatively little entrenched or elaborated authority over the civil service. However, what prime ministers lack by way of detailed responsibilities they make up for in conventionally accepted latitude. For instance, machinery of government is one sector that often falls outside the scope of collective decision making under the British and Canadian cabinet systems. In the United Kingdom, the Ministers of the Crown (Transfer of Functions) Act (1946) enables the executive, through order in council, to shift functions between and even to disband departments.[11] This instrument leaves a great deal of room for essentially prime-ministerial initiative. To be sure, Harold Wilson's and Edward Heath's efforts toward consolidation of departments into superministries ran up against immense bureaucratic inertia and stirred cabinet jealousies.[12] However, more modest schemes— such as Wilson's creation of the Civil Service Department and Heath's establishment of the Central Policy Review Staff—came off relatively smoothly. What is more, Margaret Thatcher disbanded each of these agencies, the former in 1981 and the latter in 1983, with barely a stir either from cabinet or Parliament.

Pierre Elliott Trudeau's fourteen years in office provided a plethora of reforms. These included the creation of several new operational departments and central agencies. However, we should caution against making too clear an association of Canadian developments since 1968 with Trudeau. Lester Pearson, his predecessor, had instituted similar, though by no means so many, reforms. During his nine months in office, Joe Clark adopted a number of highly significant changes. The three prime ministers faced little resistance, either in the cabinet or Parliament, to their reorganization schemes. As for the career bureaucracy, a succession of well-placed institutional engineers—especially those in the Privy Council Office—urged plans upon the three prime ministers for rationalizing cabinet coordination and redistributing portfolios with very considerable effect.[13] In Canada, the Ministries and Ministers of State Act (1971) empowers the executive, *in consultation with the prime minister*, to operate up to five "ministries of state" on the basis of order in council.[14] Such proclamations rarely receive more than perfunctory discussion in Parliament.

Leadership Styles

Presidents' and prime ministers' actual exercise of authority over the machinery of government depends to a great degree on their leadership styles. Richard E. Neustadt argues that a president who relies heavily upon a relatively large and highly differentiated central advisory system perhaps lacks the ability or the temperament (or both) adequately to fulfill the requirements of the office.[15] Stephen J. Wayne pursues this by relating the organization of the White House to presidents' styles from Franklin Delano Roosevelt to Jimmy Carter. He credits Kennedy and Ford with finding the best balance between the need for organizational structure and operational flexibility.[16]

Chief executives may develop one of four styles for the administration of government.[17] Each of these will affect their perception of how they should organize central agencies, and which operational departments should be created or disbanded and how these should relate to one another and to central agencies. First, a *priorities and planning style* usually emerges when chief executives find themselves in a strong political position and choose to pursue an ambitious, creative, and comprehensive legislative program. Assuming this style, we might expect a considerable increase in the role of central agencies in extracting proposals from the departments and assembling coherent policies and programs. Second, the *broker politics style* develops when presidents or prime ministers maintain a reasonably strong political position but choose—because of personality, external conditions, or both—to seek only a modest legislative program. Such leaders will become relatively agnostic about both central agencies and departments. That is, they will prefer the latter to work out conflicts among themselves without reference to the former. On critical issues, however, they will expect central agencies to intervene to "knock heads together." Thus, broker-politics leaders will likely resist expanding existing central agencies or creating new ones.

The *administrative politics style* occurs most often when chief executives find themselves in a tenuous political position that presents few openings for bolder political initiatives and places a premium on ad hoc firefighting. In these instances central agencies will be reduced to more conventional process- and crisis-management functions. However, administrative politics, especially over a prolonged period, might see the proliferation of line departments designed to satisfy claims from disenchanted sectors for more attention from government. A fourth mode, the *survival politics style*, arises when an administration or government clearly faces replacement if it does not improve its performance dramatically. Here presidents and prime ministers will tend to draw decisions that ordinarily would be made by line departments into the center, with central agencies becoming more important in decision making. However, the streamlining of units and reporting lines will attempt to reduce drastically countervailing influences. In survival politics, proposals for new line departments stand a relatively slim chance of success.

This look at the relationship between style and approach to institutional reform must take into account an exceedingly long tenure—such as Pierre Trudeau's—as an exception. Over time, Trudeau revealed a strong bias toward institutional innovation oriented toward compartmentalization of machinery intended for central control and coordination. Thus, if political leaders pursues a strong interest in organizational issues we might expect them to transform machinery of government over the long haul.

Events of the Day

Notwithstanding differences in the prospects for longevity, chief executives normally want to maintain or improve their chances of staying in power. Even if constitutionally prevented from seeking another term, or if simply intending to retire, they will feel bound at least to leave their party viable in the next political combat. Here events of the day can introduce political imperatives that, in turn, force changes in the machinery of government.

Most obviously, cabinet politics often operate at the heart of organizational change. Nixon's efforts to create superagencies stemmed from a desire to curtail the activities of his secretaries by placing them under the stewardship of trusted lieutenants.[18] Trudeau's minister of industry, trade, and commerce from 1980 until fall 1982 espoused a strident economic nationalism that sparked a cabinet backlash and U.S. indignation. Thus, in January 1982, the minister faced a package of reforms—imposed by Privy Council Office fiat—that transferred his most critical policy responsibilities to a cabinet secretariat and moved authority for trade issues to the

Department of External Affairs. In 1981, Margaret Thatcher itched to neutralize the Civil Service Department, which she viewed as overly protective of the career bureaucracy. She became especially miffed over its seeming inability to quash civil service strikes. However, such a move would appear as a slap in the face of one of her most highly esteemed ministers, Lord Soames. As a solution, she used a full cabinet shuffle to retire Lord Soames gracefully. After a decent interval, she then disbanded his department—sending one part to the Cabinet Office, under the title Management and Personnel Office, and the other back to Her Majesty's Treasury from whence it had come in 1968.

In a more general sense, chief executives will employ changes in government machinery in order to tackle particularly pressing problems which, if not addressed, could seriously undermine electoral support. Presidents and prime ministers must respond to elements of public aspirations and anxieties which, taken together, comprise the electorate's mood. Often, citizens' views of whether times are "good" or "bad" hinge on events in areas where government will take the praise or blame for much of what happens. The most vital of these for any chief executive include macroeconomics, national security, domestic stability, and economic and social development.

Although administrations' and governments' management of macroeconomics appears over the last decade to have become considerably more difficult, chief executives in our three countries have tampered precious little with the machinery of government operating in this field. The key economics departments in each country—the Treasury in the United States and the United Kingdom and Finance in Canada—can thank the Keynesian era for sharply delineating macroeconomics as a government function and, therefore, spotlighting the government's role. The current monetarist period further heightens the importance of macroeconomics as the central determinant of the art of the possible in other realms.

In the United States and Britain, national security has received special attention in central agencies. Power struggles between the National Security Council and the State Department have forced perennial interventions by U.S. presidents designed to restore the credibility of their leadership in this area. In Canada, prime ministers have so far eschewed the centralization of control and coordination in this field. Although domestic instability has not occasioned major changes in U.S. or U.K. central agency machinery over the last decade, such has occurred in Canada. There Trudeau faced threats to national unity stemming from disenchantment, especially in Quebec and western Canada, with federalism. Although the agency has now shrunk in size, the creation in 1975 of the Federal-Provincial Relations Office and its rapid growth in 1976 following the Parti Quebecois victory reflected the importance Trudeau placed on the national-unity crisis.

Pressures in the economic and social development fields do not usually result in the creation of "umbrella" central agencies. However, they might bring about alterations in executive-bureaucratic processes at this level. In turn, these changes might serve as a justification for distinguishing expenditure review and/or management policy more sharply from macroeconomics in the central agency community. Since Kennedy, American presidents have placed great stock in budgeting and analytic techniques designed to reduce the incremental nature of funding. In Britain, the Public Expenditure Survey, Program Analysis and Review (PAR), Rayner scrutinies and, most recently, the Financial Management Initiative have played similar roles. Canadians borrowing both from the U.S. and British experiences, have come up with innovations of their own. Since 1979, Canada has followed an "envelope" system for expenditure review. Here, cabinet committees prevailing over broad expenditure sectors enable ministers to produce savings that will remain in program sectors, rather than simply being returned to the general treasury. The cumulative success of such innovations in their respective countries escapes verification. However, they can give the public the impression that the government has taken concrete steps to increase value for money at a time when the costs of programs, particularly new initiatives, come under constant fire.

Several instances suggest themselves in which different approaches to central control of allocation and management policies have been given added importance through central agency reforms. In the United States, the Bureau of the Budget evolved through the twenties and thirties into an organ of the presidency as incumbents increasingly viewed the annual budget estimates as a means toward greater effectiveness and efficiency.[19] The change of BOB's name to the Office of Management and Budget in 1970 signaled a largely unsuccessful attempt to make the somewhat encrusted "budget" department focus as much attention on management policy as it does on control of expenditure. In Britain, a desire to give greater attention to management led to the creation of the Civil Service Department in 1968; the institution of Policy Analysis and Review under Heath provided one of the justifications for the Central Policy Review Staff—although HM Treasury ended up with the lead in the PAR system; even Thatcher's Financial Management Initiative offers a much-needed, albeit tenuous, raison d'être for the new Management and Personal Office. In Canada, the Treasury Board Secretariat owes its formal separation from the Department of Finance in 1966 to a belief that management policy required closer attention. The envelope system resulted in two free-standing central agencies—disbanded during John Turner's brief term—which served as secretariats to the cabinet committees overseeing expenditure for economic-regional and social development.

Fragmented Versus Coordinated Cabinet Systems

Richard E. Neustadt has stressed the deepening tendencies toward fragmentation in the U.S. policy arena.[20] Here voting blocks have become less visible in Congress and, therefore, the president must work much harder to deliver his legislative program. Ad hoc problems increasingly sharpen the delineation of bureaucratic organizations. Attentive publics respond to atomization inside government by organizing in new interest groups. Neither the British nor the Canadian system is exempt from fragmentation. The practice of cabinet government and party discipline in each country frequently helps conceal the process from public view. Yet U.K. governments become particularly torn between intense and incisive attacks both from business and labor. These, as often as not, place the groups' "patron" parties in serious political dilemmas. As well, observers have been slow to account for the clear growth of factionalism in U.K. parties.[21] In Canada, party discipline has held up remarkably well. However, the strains of federal-provincial diplomacy greatly intensify the difficulties departments face both in developing and implementing their policies.[22]

Students of institutionalization such as Nelson W. Polsby have pointed up the cyclical nature of such processes.[23] As applied to cabinets, increases in size and differentiation would follow changes in the political environments to which government institutions must respond. Alterations allow governments to articulate further their relations with their client groups. At various intervals, however, diminishing returns set in. That is, governments no longer reap benefits from larger and more differentiated cabinets because of the the byzantine machinery necessary to coordinate the parts.

Pressures to streamline cabinet structures lead governments to turn to three types of remedies. They can merge units so that similar activities come under unified direction. They can rely more extensively on collective decision-making bodies that force department heads and their officials to vet their proposals and policies with a view to greater coordination. They can develop further secretariats designed to assist the chief executive and/or cabinet in managing the decision load, establishing priorities, and enforcing strategic and tactical decisions.

Cabinet Size

The U.S. government, with only thirteen departments, has kept the tightest rein on the designation of "cabinet-level" units. However, this by no means qualifies it as the least differentiated executive-bureaucratic community. In fact, departments operate as conglomerates of major policy and operational units working under subcabinet heads and reporting to cabinet secretaries. The former officials, mostly assistant secretaries, often feel greater loyalty to the president than to their secretary, as they received their appointment from and serve at the president's pleasure. Under the circumstances, U.S. departments frequently fail to adequately coordinate policies under their own roof, let alone mesh them with others' mandates. Keeping issues away from the White House becomes a major task.

Cabinet-level differentiation has thrived in both Britain and Canada throughout this century. However, British prime ministers have tended more than their Canadian counterparts to merge ministries working within roughly the same areas. The cabinet proper consists of only twenty-two of the fifty-five senior ministers who comprise the U.K. government. Clearly, the situation falls far short of Edwin Montagu's 1917 proposals for an inner cabinet of seven—including the prime minister, the chancellor of the exchequer, and five secretaries of state who would preside over umbrella ministries under which departments would operate. [24] Yet, allocation of additional senior ministers to all operational departments except Education and Science allows for a division of labor that heightens attention to several policy fields without launching free-standing bureaucratic units.

Canada operates with each minister belonging to the cabinet, which totals forty members under Brian Mulroney. Pressures in the political system for the cabinet to represent regional interests make it difficult for prime ministers to reduce its size. [25] Relatedly, that six central agencies and twenty-two operational departments report to various cabinet ministers reflects the fact that ministers come across much more convincingly as regional standard-bearers when they shoulder responsibility for an entire cabinet-level sector of government activity. Currently, only seven operational departments have more than one minister.

Committees

Short of reducing the size of the cabinet, both U.K. and Canadian prime ministers make use of multiple and specialized standing commitees to ease the full cabinet's work load. Under Ronald Reagan, the same practice appears finally to have taken root in the United States. By the mid-nineteenth century, British prime ministers had resorted frequently to ad hoc committees to prepare especially sensitive legislation.[26] However, only in defense policy did a succession of panels set up to manage responses to various military crises begin to take on the trappings of standing committees.[27] By way of partial response to pressures for streamlining cabinet during the latter part of World War I, Lloyd George created standing cabinet committees on economic defense and development, home affairs, and postwar priorities in 1918.[28] However, interest in these bodies waned soon after the war. Only after World War II did the United Kingdom move on to the next phase of committee development in which standing committees have persisted over long periods within several specialized areas of cabinet activity. Some of these sectors operate with standing subcommittees. Yet, prime ministers still rely very heavily on "miscellaneous" or "general" committees working on an ad hoc basis at especially thorny policy issues or crises.

Canadians have gone through essentially the same process of gradual evolution from an ad hoc system to a network of standing committees.[29] Trudeau, however, began in 1968 a process whereby the committee system was greatly institutionalized. In his last government, standing committees covered priorities and planning, legislation and house planning, economic and regional development, social development, foreign and defense policy, government operations, communications, labor relations, public service, security and intelligence, orders in council, and western affairs. The fact that all but three of these committees claimed ten or more members reflected again the representational imperative that makes Canada's cabinet system unwieldy in comparison to Britain's. Even Priorities and Planning—essentially the cabinet's executive committee—kept on thirteen ministers. Economic and Regional Development admitted fully twenty. While the system has undergone some paring under Mulroney, the representational imperative shows no signs of weakening.[30]

A Tradition of Secretariats

Further development of secretariats provides the third way in which chief executives can attempt to reduce fragmentation in their cabinet systems. In assessing the development of these bodies in the United States, one must take special care to distinguish between provision of advisory staff for the president and assignment of resources organized so as to assist collective decision making. Until Franklin Delano Roosevelt's second term, presidents drew upon minuscule staffs.[31] The creation of the White House Office in 1939 started the accretion of offices under the

Executive Office of the President to the current level: nine units with staff totaling nearly 1,600. However, only the National Security Council Staff, with around seventy staff members, and the Office of Policy Development, with just over forty, provide resources for assisting the administration in meshing its policy stances. Here only the NSC staff has operated fairly consistently as a cabinet secretariat. Early in the Reagan administration, Richard V. Allen's, William Clark's, Robert McFarlane's, and John Poindexter's poor selection of staff and weak leadership reduced this unit to its nadir of power and respect. Without further development of these secretariats, U.S. efforts to improve collective decision making by cabinet members will meet with little success.

Lloyd George's innovations broke the ice for units serving prime ministers in pursuit of policy goals and/or coordination of cabinets. A "garden suburb" of political advisers and a career-service cabinet secretariat emerged simultaneously during the latter stages of World War I.[32] The former concept fell out of favor immediately after the war. Beginning with Churchill during the Second World War, nearly every prime minister has brought a trusted policy adviser to No. 10 (sometimes providing him a small staff) and/or appointed political secretaries whose tasks included adding party-political perspectives to policy considerations.[33] Since Harold Wilson's second term (1974), more formalized policy units in No. 10 have successfully followed the principle that prime ministers should have at their immediate disposal five to ten trusted advisers who can track efforts to fulfill the government's most vital objectives. Mrs. Thatcher has further advanced the tradition by bringing to No. 10 exceptionally senior and notable personal policy advisers. The British cabinet secretariat has, of course, developed into the highly differentiated Cabinet Office. This overwhelmingly career organization includes cabinet support units totaling around 350 staff, the Central Statistical Office, and, as of fall 1981, the Management and Personnel Office.

In Canada, central agencies reporting directly to the prime minister and/or serving cabinet and its committees took considerably longer than in Britain to develop. While the Privy Council Office (PCO) first took shape as a cabinet secretariat in 1940, the Prime Minister's Office began to become clearly delineated as the prime minister's political switchboard only in the mid-1960s. Of course, Trudeau's period as prime minister saw perhaps the most dramatic developments in cabinet secretariats available to students of central agencies. Counting those in the Treasury Board Secretariat (TBS, hived off from the Department of Finance in 1966), the Federal-Provincial Relations Office (from PCO in 1975), the Office of the Comptroller General—(from TBS in 1976), and the ministries of state for

Economic and Regional Development, and Social Development (created in 1978 and 1979, respectively), nearly 1,700 officials worked in cabinet secretariats in 1981–1982. Two factors explain Canada's dependence on such bodies. First, as we have seen, the representational imperative intensifies the management-of-business and civil-service-guidance work load connected with resolution of cabinet-level disputes. Second, Trudeau's management style strongly favored development of finely tuned machinery to assist collective decision making.

Managerial Ethos

The degree to which government and private-sector management are comparable is a topic of perennial interest in the study of public administration. As well as being the source of endless academic wrangling, this question raises practical issues. If they believe that both public and private-sector administrations function according to compatible principles, political executives and career civil servants alike will keep a weather eye for ways of applying to government management techniques developed in business. In the context of this chapter, they will attempt more often to reorganize the structures of government according to what business views as "good" management. Thus the use of central agencies will reflect this ethos.

A Rational Cast of Mind

Even in the private sector, the manifestations of managerial ideology do not occur across the board. There administration may hinge more on the exercise of personal, almost patrimonial, authority. In government, some organizations might readily adopt strictly managerial forms of control, while others might rely on highly personalistic criteria.[34] For example, organizations directly attached to the chief executive, such as the White House Office in the United States, No. 10 in Britain, or the Prime Minister's Office in Canada, operate largely as personal fiefdoms. Membership and/or influence depend disproportionately upon the personal trust of the chief executive. Meanwhile, line departments mostly function as "normal" bureaucracies. Hence participants' involvement in issues and latitude for action are based largely on enduring institutional arrangements. The modern theory of organizations makes the fundamental point that institutional form must relate to function. Career-oriented bureaucratic units adhere more or less faithfully to this principle.

The bureaucracies of the United States, the United Kingdom, and Canada are all imbued with the empirical approach to decision making presumed to be characteristic of the Anglo-Saxon mind. In these three countries, thus, those who design the machinery of government avail themselves, at least to some degree, of rational analysis. This starts with the assumption that leaders should seek ways for making government function better in managerial terms. The manipulation of the structures and interrelationships in government is a principal way of producing such improved performance. This is true of the reorganization of line departments—for example, Carter's reorganizations in the fields of energy, human services, and international communications, and the reorganization of several British ministries into "superministries" in the late 1960s and early 1970s. It is also true of the creation and reorganization of central agencies designed to impose the policy preferences of the chief executive and/or cabinet on line departments.[35]

In both types of reorganization, unless there is a cynical attempt to pacify public opinion with simple answers or to divert attention away from the "real" issues, changes stem from the underlying assumption that machinery-of-government reforms heighten bureaucratic performance. Although the principles underlying reorganization may be similar both for changes in line departments and central agencies, there should be important differences in the relationship of the managerial approach to their occurrence. Frequently, changes at the line department level reflect straightforward managerialism. That is, the various motives for such reorganizations appear to be largely operational. As well, a cycle of concentration followed by dispersion often accompanies the reorganization of line departments.[36]

Along managerial lines, new central agencies have tried to heighten the use of analytic methods for solving servicewide problems. As we have already noted, this has spawned the formation of central agencies specifically responsible for management policy and public expenditure. It has also undergirded the creation of central-policy analysis and advice bodies such as Britain's CPRS—now abolished—or the United States' NSC staff. These attempt to improve the effectiveness of career civil servants, university and think-tank boffins, and private-sector experts potentially useful at the center of government by locating them in one place. However, the reorganization of central agencies appears to depend as much upon the whims of individual chief executives as it does upon the application of managerial principles. In fact, the reorganization of central agencies may relate inversely, or not at all, to the strength of the managerial perspective in a country. As in the case of Trudeau, preoccupation with the proper organization of central agencies might reflect an attempt on the part of those at the center of government to exercise highly personalized authority over the entire public-service apparatus.

Such differences in the reorganization rationales of line and central agencies may point to a fundamental, if misunderstood, paradox in government between maintaining accountability to political superiors and pursuing efficient management. The more organizations and their managers are closely controlled from the center, the less likely they may be to effectively manage the quotidian affairs of the organization and to plan for the future. Following closely from that observation, the more central agencies attempt to ensure compatibility of the day-to-day operations of departments with the goals of a chief executive, the less efficient those departments are likely to become in reaching their operational goals. The rise and fall of many servicewide analytic techniques reflects this paradox. Although designed to improve management in government, they ultimately collapsed under their own weight when their centralizing tendencies eventually met serious backlashes at the operational level. Such observations suggest that the perceived organizational obstacles to elective officials' reaching their policy goals often prove much more formidable than they at first appear.[37]

Facing Up to the Permanent Civil Service

The greatest resistance to reorganization efforts normally arises from permanent civil servants. More specialized patterns of civil service recruitment tend to produce senior bureaucrats who will resist reorganization. In the United Kingdom, senior civil servants enter government more on the basis of their general intellectual abilities than specialized education and training. In theory, the flexibility gained from such personnel should make reorganization relatively easy. On the other hand, U.S. recruitment patterns, based largely upon possession of specific skills, might make reorganization more difficult. If they find that their positions and units are reorganized out of existence, U.S. officials will certainly have difficulty marketing their skills elsewhere in government. The mobility of Canadian officials between departments—those who switch the most actually receive the quickest promotions—greatly mitigates the fact that most started their careers by virtue of specialized education.

A discussion of civil-service career patterns relates directly to recruitment. The British civil servant, in the tradition of the "talented amateur," tends to follow a career that calls upon adaptability to diverse experiences both inside and outside one's home department. Senior Canadian civil servants do not belong to a specific department. Thus, they usually enjoy relative mobility from one organization to another. U.S. civil servants fill particular positions in specific organizations. Although there is some movement from agency to agency, many officials spend their entire careers in

one department. In addition to custom and the value placed upon expertise, the limited circulation of information on openings, outside of the
departments where they occur, makes it difficult for U.S. officials to move
to another department. Each agency tends to maintain its own insular
career structure.

Experience in and with the private sector constitutes another aspect of
the career structure of civil servants that might favorably affect attitudes
toward reorganization. In Britain, permanent civil servants occasionally go
on short secondments to the private sector. Canadian permanent civil
servants tend more than their counterparts in the United States and the
United Kingdom to have entered government from the private sector at
mid-career. The more frequent interactions of U.S. career civil servants
with outsiders and the relative abundance of job opportunities for former
bureaucrats in the private sector should ease somewhat their resistance to
changes stemming from the specialized nature of their careers.

Notwithstanding substantial differences in the permanent civil-service
cultures in our three countries, the prevailing view of administration in
each appears to wash out some of the expected effects of career routes.
The United Kingdom is the least managerially oriented of the three. It
relies more upon the conception of public administration as service to the
crown in a rather traditional, patrimonial fashion. Those in the top positions of the pyramids of power in Whitehall may define their task less as
managing large complex organizations than of providing advice and support to their ministers.[38] Both the managerial and policy functions of the
civil servant are important in any public organization. However, the
upward-looking British civil servant may not be able to produce desired
results to the degree that a more downward-regarding, managerially oriented civil servant might be able to.

The lack of concern over management in British government is in part
reflected in the report of the Fulton committee and its results. This committee has become one of the most frequently cited in the study of British
government. It does appear, however, that the clear managerialist content
of the Fulton report was dissipated significantly in various attempts to
implement the proposed reforms.[39] Even spiritual kin of Fulton-style
"manageralism"[40] which were initial successes, such as the Public Expenditure Survey and, later, Program Analysis and Review, are now either
widely criticized, or have actually been terminated.[41] And, attempts at
reforming civil service organization and personnel management through
the Civil Service Department have met a similar fate. Even with clear
enunciation of principles or considerable follow-through by way of innova-

tive processes and institutions, it appears difficult to make managerial ideas stick in British government. This even appears to be the case with Mrs. Thatcher's overtures toward managerialism.

Managerial ideas meet with relatively widespread acceptance in much of American and Canadian bureaucracy. Rather than viewing themselves primarily as the servants of their political masters, career officials in the United States regard themselves first as managers of large organizations. Their task is to formulate policies, coordinate their policymaking with the remainder of the department and the rest of government, and make their organization function so that policies may be implemented successfully.[42] All of this takes place in a highly politicized atmosphere. But much of the discourse centers on managing internal adjustments, rather than reacting to ideas for change from above.

The emphasis on management in the United States derives in part from the political environment's positive appraisal of business and private-sector management and the increasing perception that major difficulties with government are the rigidities and inefficiencies of its organization and procedures. The attack on the "imperial president" has led to skepticism about efforts to centralize administration. This shifted demands for management improvement from the presidency to line departments.[43] Thus, as is not true in the United Kingdom, pressures for reorganization may well arise from below, not from the top. In fact, the organization of American government has proven less static than is often assumed. One analysis reveals a total of 1,757 major organizational changes from 1933 to 1979.[44] Many of these originated from the interest of lower-level managers in making their organizations more efficient.

Canadian senior officials—overwhelmingly, permanent civil servants—have become much more politicized than their counterparts in the United Kingdom. For instance, Canadian deputy ministers operate much more overtly as major participants in the policymaking process than do U.K. permanent secretaries. They routinely attend cabinet committees and, in the absence of their ministers, speak for their departments. Advancement to all deputy-minister and many assistant deputy-minister posts involves political considerations that, though of the relatively invisible executive-bureaucratic variety, place a premium on candidates who have caught the prime minister's eye and have demonstrated an ability to work well in collective decision-making forums. Canada's politicized version of the managerial approach to government, unlike the United States, has produced a very pronounced emphasis on the reorganization of central agencies and the development of managerial techniques at the center of government.[45]

Conclusion

As a comparative study of reorganization as related to central agencies, this chapter has attempted to give greater perspective to machinery-of-government reform efforts in the United States, the United Kingdom, and Canada. As well, it has uncovered a number of findings that might serve as the basis of further systematic work. First, chief executives should take greater care in assessing their strengths and weaknesses before embarking on reforms. Here U.S. presidents find themselves at a disadvantage. They usually must pilot reforms through rigorous congressional review. Chief executives in each country might take strikingly different views of reorganization efforts, depending upon their leadership style. However, they should eschew wholesale efforts. If a chief executive embraces the institutional reform ethos too religiously, he will find himself under pressure to alter his reorganization plans in ad hoc responses to crises. Such a situation appears to do the most damage if it leads to using central agencies to solve sectoral problems.

The nature of a cabinet system limits the options open to chief executives in each of our countries. Generally, a high degree of differentiation of units according to client-bound sectors will lead to more intense conflicts between departments. Heightened use of specialized committees, of course, can mitigate some of the adverse effects of differentiation. Both Britain and Canada have employed this approach extensively. As well, they have gone considerably beyond the United States in developing central agency resources designed to assist collective decision making. However, even allowing for the representational pressures on Canada's cabinet system, the creation there of central agencies to address sectoral issues ran the danger of simply mirroring fragmentation in line departments.

This chapter's treatment of managerial ethos as a factor affecting reorganization distinguished between two views of administration. One tends to see management as a tool for achieving greater effectiveness. The other views it more as advising and supporting superiors and, ultimately, political masters. In the United States, officials operating in the numerous offices and agencies under the umbrella of a department demonstrate an exceptionally strong managerial ethos. However, career civil servants' links with Congress and outside interests, along with a deep-seated deference to seniority and professional expertise in their own units, make it exceptionally difficult for administrations to influence management policy centrally. In the United Kingdom, some prime ministers have imposed from the center techniques to improve expenditure budgeting, effectiveness, and efficiency. The four most notable of these, the Public Expenditure Survey, Programme Analysis and Review, Rayner scrutinies, and the Financial Management Initiative all fought uphill battles against widespread civil-service skepticism. British prime ministers thus find that introducing a new management technique soon entails a sales job of missionary proportions. In Canada, the most senior officials place exceptional trust in the view that servicewide standardization will improve management on the operational level. This view, which largely owes its pervasiveness to his longevity and style of leadership, provided Trudeau with a virtual carte blanche for indulging his highly personalistic approach toward bureaucratic organizations—especially central agencies.

Notes

This chapter is an extensively revised and updated version of a paper originally prepared by the author with B. Guy Peters.

1. B. G. Peters and M. O. Heisler, "Government: What Is Growing and How Do We Know?" *Studies in Public Policy*, no. 89 (Glasgow: University of Strathclyde Centre for the Study of Public Policy, 1981).

2. N. Johnson, "Recent Administrative Reforms in Britain," in *The Management of Change in Government*, ed. Arne F. Leemans (The Hague: Nijhoff, 1976), pp. 272–96.

3. P. Szanton, ed., *Federal Reorganization: What Have We Learned?* (Chatham, N.J.: Chatham House, 1981).

4. P. Self, *Administrative Theories and Politics: An Inquiry Into The Structure and Processes of Modern Government* (London: Allen & Unwin, 1977).

5. C. Campbell, *Governments Under Stress: Political Executives and Key Bureaucrats in Washington, London and Ottawa* (Toronto: University of Toronto Press, 1983).

6. R. Rose and E. N. Suleiman, eds., *President and Prime Ministers* (Washington, D.C.: American Enterprise Institute, 1980).

7. H. Heclo and A. Wildavsky, *The Private Government of Public Money* (Berkeley and Los Angeles: University of California Press, 1974), pp. 368–70.

8. R. Rose, "Government Against Sub-Government: A European Perspective on Washington," in *Presidents and Prime Ministers*, ed. Rose and Suleiman, pp. 284–347.

9. B. W. Hogwood and B. G. Peters, *Policy Dynamics* (Brighton: Wheatsheaf, 1982).

10. R. P. Nathan, *The Plot That Failed: Nixon and the Administrative Presidency* (New York: Wiley, 1975), pp. 60–62, 82.

11. R. A. Chapman and J. R. Greenaway, *The Dynamics of Adminisrative Reform* (London: Croom Helm, 1980), p. 133.

12. R. Crossman, *The Diaries of a Cabinet Minister*, Vol. 3: *Secretary of State for Social Services—1968–70* (London: Hamish Hamilton and Jonathan Cape, 1977); C. Pollitt, "Rationalizing the Machinery of Government: The Conservatives 1970–1974," *Political Studies* 28 (1980), 84–98; and R.G.S. Brown and D. R. Steel, *The Administrative Process in Britain* (London: Methuen, 1979), pp. 276–80.

13. C. Campbell, "Cabinet Committees in Canada: Pressures and Dysfunctions Stemming from the Representational Imperative," in *Unlocking the Cabinet*, ed. T. Mackie and B. Hogwood (London: Sage, 1985).

14. V. S. Wilson, *Canadian Public Policy and Administration* (Toronto: McGraw-Hill Ryerson, 1981), p. 338.

15. R. E. Neustadt, *Presidential Power: The Politics of Leadership From FDR to Carter* (New York: Wiley, 1978), pp. 28–33.

16. S. J. Wayne, *The Legislative Presidency* (New York: Harper and Row, 1978), pp. 1–55.

17. C. Campbell, "Political Leadership in Canada: Pierre Elliott Trudeau and the Ottawa Model," in *Presidents and Prime Ministers*, ed. Rose and Suleiman, pp. 50–93.

18. Nathan, *The Plot That Failed*, pp. 60–68.

19. L. Berman, *The Office of Management and Budget and the Presidency, 1921–1979* (Princeton, N.J.: Princeton University Press, 1979).

20. R. E. Neustadt, *Presidential Power: The Politics of Leadership with Reflections on Johnson and Nixon* (New York: Wiley, 1980), pp. 212–13.

21. L. D. Epstein, "What Happened to the British Party Model?" *American Political Science Review* 74 (1980), 9–22; and J. E. Schwarz, "Exploring a New Role in Policy Making: The British House of Commons in the 1970s," *American Political Science Review* 74 (1980), 23–37.

22. R. J. Schultz, *Federalism, Bureaucracy, and Public Policy: The Politics of Highway Transport Regulation* (Montreal: McGill–Queen's University Press, 1980).

23. N. W. Polsby, "The Institutionalization of the U.S. House of Representatives," *American Political Science Review* 62 (1968), 144–68.

24. Chapman and Greenaway, *The Dynamics of Administrative Reform*, p. 78.

25. Campbell, "Cabinet Committees in Canada."

26. J. P. Mackintosh, *The British Cabinet* (London: Stevens, 1977), p. 147.

27. Ibid., pp. 278–86.

28. Ibid., pp. 378–79.

29. W. A. Matheson, *The Prime Minister and the Cabinet* (Toronto: Methuen, 1976), pp. 83–87.

30. Campbell, "Cabinet Committees in Canada."

31. Wayne, *The Legislative Presidency*, p. 32; and S. Hess, *Organizing the Presidency* (Washington, D.C.: Brookings, 1976), pp. 28–29.

32. Mackintosh, *The British Cabinet*, 376–77; and J. Turner, *Lloyd George's Secretariat* (Cambridge: Cambridge University Press, 1980).

33. G. W. Jones, "The Prime Minister's Aides," in *Hull Papers in Politics*, 6 (1980).

34. B. G. Peters and M. P. Smith, "The Relationship of Organizational Form and Task Requirements in the Public Sector," manuscript, Dept. of Political Science, Tulane University, New Orleans.

35. C. Campbell and G. J. Szablowski, *The Superbureaucrats: Structure and Behavior in Central Agencies* (Toronto: Macmillan, 1979).

36. C. Hood and A. Dunsire, *Bureaumetrics* (Westmead, Hants.: Gower, 1981).

37. R. Rose, *The Problem of Party Government* (London: Macmillan, 1974).

38. P. Kellner and Lord Crowther-Hunt, *The Civil Servants: An Inquiry into Britain's Ruling Class* (London: Macdonald and Jane's, 1980).

39. J. Garrett, *Managing the Civil Service* (London: Heinemann, 1980).

40. D. C. Pitt and B. C. Smith, *Government Departments: An Organizational Perspective* (London: Routledge and Kegan Paul, 1981).

41. P. K. Else and G. P. Marshall, "The Unplanning of Public Expenditure: Recent Problems in Expenditure Planning and the Consequences of Cash Limits," *Public Administration* 59 (1981), 253–78.

42. T. P. Murphy, D. E. Neuchterlien, and R. J. Stupak, *Inside the Bureaucracy: The View from the Assistant Secretary's Desk* (Boulder, Colo.: Westview, 1978).

43. L. E. Lynn, *Managing the Public's Business: The Job of the Government Executive* (New York: Basic Books, 1981).

44. Hogwood and Peters, *Policy Dynamics*.

45. Campbell, *Governments Under Stress;* R. Van Loon, "Stop the Music: The Current Policy and Expenditure Management System in Ottawa," *Canadian Public Administration* 24 (1981), 175–99.

PART II

Cross-National Dimensions

CHAPTER 3

Political and Bureaucratic Roles in Public Service Reorganization

੨ઋ

Joel D. Aberbach and Bert A. Rockman

THE RHETORIC of administrative reorganization, James March and Johan Olsen point out, emphasizes two distinctive traditions.[1] One tradition stresses administrative concepts and criteria such as efficiency, cost-effectiveness, streamlining, coordination, and program effectiveness. The second tradition stresses realpolitik—the political impact of and motivation behind reorganization efforts. This latter tradition sees administrative units, programs, and administrative roles as focal points for the play of political interests. Thus, to rearrange units, programs, or roles is, by definition, to rearrange the constellation of political interests organized around them. Furthermore, lest we mistakenly think of administrative officials as mere ciphers, they are themselves an element in the network of political interests, or at least so they are often viewed by top political leaders. This view that the senior civil service has political interests has been most vociferously voiced in Washington but it is not at all confined there.

Our point of departure in this chapter is the second of the two rhetorics of reorganization of which March and Olsen speak, that of realpolitik. Therefore, our discussion is not of the technical effectiveness of reorganization efforts as such, though this does not imply that the topic of effectiveness is unimportant, simple, or even isolatable from the politics of administrative reorganization. Our chapter, however, focuses on the political relevance of reorganization, on the methods by which some politicians seek to exert control over the bureaucracy and by which some bureaucrats seek to exert influence over policymaking or, at the very least, resist having their influence weakened.

Of the many potential lines of political conflict that can emerge as a consequence of reorganization efforts, we emphasize one that is of growing importance: conflicts between the centers of governments and their parts, particularly those with interest groups and constituencies nested within them. To borrow a line from Richard Rose, we look at reorganization from the perspective of "governments against subgovernments."[2] The reason we use this perspective is that ultimately many forms of reorganization are intended to strengthen "effective executive leadership" and to generate "broader and more integrated authority *within* the executive."[3] They are, in short, designed mostly to strengthen the integrative capacities of governments over their sometimes resistant parts.

Relevant to these considerations is the structure of administrative and political roles—and change in them. How does the struggle between the government and its component parts affect the roles of politicians and bureaucrats? Of equal pertinence, how do changes fostered by reorganization affect the roles of various types of politicians and bureaucrats?

These questions, and the way they have been phrased, no doubt seem more pertinent to government in Washington than to government in Whitehall or in European capitals. In Washington, there is no center of government, but there is a center to the executive. There is no integrated government, but there are efforts to impose an integrated executive; thus, the pressures to achieve integration at the top are felt with unusual urgency more often in Washington than elsewhere because the centrifugal forces in the American capital are so much greater. The diversity of institutions and traditions of government across national systems inhibit breezy cross-national generalizations about the nature of government/subgovernment relations, methods for seeking control, and even the specification of administrative and political roles. One cannot precisely say, for example, that there is a center to British government in any sense remotely similar to that of Washington, since the theory of British government is that it is a unified entity. Ten Downing Street is not 1600 Pennsylvania Avenue in appearance or in staffing. The former lacks an extensive noncabinet apparatus analogous to the Executive Office of the President (EOP). Nor is the immense diversity of U.S. bureaucratic and political roles matched in Europe as yet, notwithstanding the internal diversities of administrative and political roles in European states. Perhaps only in Canada in recent times, with the growth of central organization, has internal diversity within the executive grown to the point where one can draw some parallels to the U.S. case.[4]

The diversity of administrative and political roles in the American system is in some substantial measure a function of the compound fracturing of the U.S. system—the constitutionally ordained disunity of the U.S. federal government. The diversity of vantage points within both the administrative and political structures in the United States means that, to some extent, our suppositions about the relationships of role change to reorganization, as well as about the modes of reorganization, is Washington-based. However, this does not necessarily mean that these suppositions, at least in functional terms, are entirely exclusive to Washington. The constraints on governments in recent times to rationalize programs and to lessen budgetary inefficiencies are likely to heighten governmental/subgovernmental tensions. One response is to introduce at the center new technical tools for achieving rationalization, and to organize new units and new roles to centralize political control.

Having defined the principal issue of reorganization, from our perspective, as the relationship of the government to its subgovernments and the impact of methods for reorganizing that relationship on administrative and political roles, in the next section we will examine briefly some of the prevailing techniques for achieving this reorganization. We then follow by specifying different administrative and political actors and their apparent interest in, and resistance to, centralizing reorganization. Finally, we speculate on common trends placing more integrative and rationalizing pressures on government, and adaptations to these pressures that we might expect across different systems.

Approaches to Central Control

A reorganization is a change, large or small, formal or informal, in the prevailing distribution of responsibilities, lines of reporting, or personnel system in an organization. Using this expansive definition, one could argue that reorganizations occur frequently in most governments. However, highly touted major and formal reorganizations occur less frequently. Quite possibly, some of the most important reorganizations occur without much visible notice, yet they create new roles, structures, and techniques that influence patterns of relationship.

In recent times, three such approaches to affecting government/subgovernment relations by executive tinkering can be identified. The first creates or transforms roles in the bureaucracy so as to politicize the administration. The second creates or further expands coordinating and monitoring units at the center (hierarchically, at the top) of government. The emergence of such units is especially identifiable in the United States and Canada and, to a more modest extent, in West Germany and Sweden.[5] The third approach utilizes analytic techniques, at least partly to legitimate the priorities of the center. The second and third approaches are somewhat related in that analytic techniques for decision making and budgetary allocations often are spearheaded by staff units at the executive center. In Canada, for example, Colin Campbell and George Szablowski found that the "superbureaucrats" in the central agencies were much more attuned to the use of quantitative techniques of analysis than their peers in the traditional line bureaucracies.[6]

Politicization of the Administration

A classic method by which to lessen the obstacles to central authority is to politicize the administration so as to enhance its responsiveness to central policy lines. The term *administration* is used here rather than *civil service* because in the United States, expecially in the Reagan administration, the recent tendency has been to avoid rather than directly to abuse the civil service by politicizing more extremely the noncareer "in-and-out" positions above the civil service and effectively using the political component of the newly formed Senior Executive Service (SES). The in-and-out positions are typically "red-and-expert." Recruitment to them is based partly on acceptable political credentials and partly on subject expertise. During the Nixon and Reagan administrations, the "red" component of this pairing has become more salient, while the "expert" component has been reduced in importance.

In *A Government of Strangers*, Hugh Heclo details the growth of new layers of politically appointed officialdom above the civil service in the departments—a tendency he had noted earlier in the newly reorganized (1970) Office of Management and Budget.[7] This process of "layering-in" appointees between the heads of departments and the senior civil service essentially prevents the civil service from playing a significant policy advisory role within the executive, though this insulation cannot by itself deter senior civil servants from offering (especially when asked) their advice before congressional hearings or more informally to congressional staff personnel scouting for issues. This layering-in does not so much politicize the civil service as it ignores it. In so doing, it helps to politicize the administration itself by making it more fully responsive to real or anticipated political directions and needs at the top.

Politicization at the top levels of the bureaucracy is not simply an American anomaly despite the overtness of, and large number of positions involved in, the practice in the United States. The advent of the Social-Liberal coalition in West Germany in 1969 brought forth charges of *Parteibuch* administration during which large transformations in the senior civil service were reputed to have taken place. According to Renate

Mayntz, however, substantial turnover was limited by selection from within the career executive via transfer and promotion. On the other hand, at least at the level of state secretary and ministerial director, the growing tendency of civil servants to be overtly identified with a party resulted in a selective process of political recruitment into the highest positions.[8] The concern that incumbents in top civil service posts within the ministries have the right political credentials extends even more so to civil servants in the Chancellery.[9]

At the top levels of the European civil service systems, the "red" conponent of the "red-and-expert" duality seems to be emerging more visibly. F. F. Ridley emphasizes, in this regard, traditional distinctions between the role of the senior civil service in Britain and its equivalents on the continent.[10] In his view, the British tradition of personnel selection and promotion to top posts is anomalous. Even more so is the expectation that in these top posts, in contrast to continental traditions, civil servants will adapt with ease to the politics and policies of the ministers they serve. As Ridley puts it: "Most other countries have long accepted that key officials should be in sympathy with government policies and the ministers should have the right to choose their closest collaborators."[11] This view is held with special fervor in the United States. Ridley concludes that Mrs. Thatcher's modus operandi with regard to the British civil service is effectively moving the British system closer to the Continent in that it has brought in as policy advisers those whose advice is pleasing, eclipsing the advisory role of career-based regulars. Guy Peters argues, however, that Mrs. Thatcher's direction is more westward than eastward, more akin to U.S. practices even than to those of the Continent.[12] Her direction implies the separation of policy advice from management, and thus the traditional American distinction (*myth?*) between politics and administration. Thus, the permanent corps of civil servants is directed to manage, whereas a changing group of political executives is to offer policy advice and to oversee management.

These altered relationships between civil servants and political leaders do not so much reflect changes induced by reorganization as changes in the elite culture governing these relations—in other words, changes in the style of leadership and governance at the top. Reorganization itself seems almost epiphenomenal to alterations in governing style. Explicit legal tools, of course, can make the interventions by the political leadership easier or at a minimum less obviously contrary to prior traditions. In this regard, the 1978 U.S. Civil Service Reform Act (CSRA) designed in part to produce greater managerial (read "political") flexibility well expressed in statutory form an aspect of the prevailing culture of executive leadership–civil servant relations. At the same time, the CSRA has permitted further opportunities for the presidential administration to manipulate the system so as to place its most loyal minions in key positions.

The CSRA, arguably, has enabled Reagan to be a successful Richard Nixon. Indeed, Nixon's travails make it clear that the provision of legal instruments by which to conduct an administrative presidency, graciously provided by Carter, has made it rather easier for Reagan to do so. Most important, it has made what is transpiring less obvious because "management flexibility" has provided the justificatory standard for conflict with the norms of an apolitical or neutral bureaucracy. The changes authorized by CSRA whereby senior officials may be moved across departmental lines and transferred from Washington to the field are instruments of significant potential for a presidential administration inspired by a mission; so too is the provision that 10 percent of the Senior Executive Service can be selected from outside the career service. If opportunities are carefully selected, those appointments can be effectively used—or abused, depending upon one's perspective.

Not all political penetration of the civil service or of ministries has a centralizing effect, to be sure. The byzantine wiring of political circuits through Italian ministries, for example, tends to reinforce the nonintegrative character of Italian governments. Personal political organizations and alliances operating through the Italian bureaucracy act as resisters to coherence.

Penetration of the civil service as a form of political intervention in the administration can frequently be done within an existing personnel system. So long as the number of positions available is expandable, as has been the case in the United States, new layers of responsibility and supervision (and now persons to fill them) are easily added. Not surprisingly, therefore, layers of political officials have been added (because it is so easy to do so) to nearly all departments and agencies in Washington as insulation between the top and the operating bureaus. The added layers of responsibility, among other things, serve to prevent civil servants from delivering their not highly desired views to the top.

Central Agencies

The complex functions of modern government and the multitude of organizational structures performing them have required some integration at the top. Usually, in cabinet systems, one or two departments (finance, economic affairs, treasury) perform the central bargaining functions affecting budgetary allocations. Appeals usually are taken to the relevant minister and then to some form of cabinet deliberations.

It seems more or less inevitable that the coordination required in economic and foreign policy means a proliferation of interdepartmental committees in virtually all governments. Diffusion and fragmentation of governmental authority, however, makes the creation of central agencies operating beyond line jurisdictions even more compelling. Not surprisingly, the buildup of these operations in the United States has been especially impressive. This has not necessarily made them effective, however. Campbell observes, for instance, that British and Canadian central agencies tend to operate in support of cabinet decisions in ways that their more frenetic American counterparts do not.[13] One reason for this is that in both the British and Canadian systems one can speak of cabinet decision making because the cabinet is the government. To speak in such terms in Washington, on the other hand, would be at odds with virtually all known facts about how government and politics operate on the Potomac.

Regardless of differences in how central agencies are deployed in various national capitals and even differences in their degree of institutionalization, they can never be insulated from the political leadership styles and priorities at the top. Campbell's investigation of central agencies in London, Washington, and Ottawa, for example, is instructive for comparing leadership styles. He developed a fourfold typology of leadership styles. The poles of one axis are central agency dominance versus delegation of authority to line departments; the other axis moves between overlapping jurisdictions (the Neustadt formula) and discrete responsibilities in accordance with formal jurisdictions.[14] From the intersection of these axes, he derives four political styles: *brokerage*, *administrative*, *planning and priorities*, and *survival*.

Some of these stylistic differences can be seen since the late 1960s in Bonn, for instance. The buildup of the Chancellery coincided with the coming to power of the Social-Liberal coalition, Chancellor Willy Brandt's ambitious political agenda, and his (and his party's) skepticism toward the traditional line bureaucracy. The Chancellery, in large measure, became Brandt's forward planning arm. Major new social and political initiatives were undertaken during the Brandt period. The predilections of Helmut Schmidt, Brandt's successor, as well as the costs of these social initiatives, led to a use of the Chancellery to some degree as an instrument of technical analysis, not otherwise manifested in the traditionally juridical West German bureaucracy. Now in the hands of Schmidt's successor, Helmut Kohl, the Chancellery, while still retaining its large size, has returned to performing the more classic role of mediating ministerial agendas under a chancellor who, far more than his two SPD predecessors, is inclined to delegate to the line departments and to act as a broker among his ministers.

Central agency functions, then, vary with the style of the political leadership. One reason they do is their relative lack of institutionalization regarding personnel. This is abundantly true in the United States, where high officials and staff personnel of White House and EOP units are turned over to an exceptional degree when a new presidential administration comes into being. The turnover is almost directly in proportion to the president's assessment of the unit's importance. Similarly, the 1982–1983 change in government in Bonn after fourteen years of SPD-Liberal rule swept out virtually all senior Chancellery officials associated with the prior government.

Nonetheless, central units have grown in importance as the coordinative and monitoring needs of governments have grown and, with these, the quest of political leaders to instill a few overriding objectives over the "many objectives of government."[15] An obvious concern is how and on what terms the functions of coordination and monitoring and that of political leadership can coexist. Effective performance of the coordination and monitoring functions probably requires considerable continuity within the central units across changes in government or presidential administration, that is, their institutionalization. But effective performance from the political leadership perspective may be stymied (or felt to be) by close collaboration between central units and line departments.

Campbell's analysis of central agencies in three Anglo democracies suggests, in this regard, that in the White House the political use of central staff tends to create more freneticism than effectiveness. The strong emphasis on political control, that is, White House assertion over policy, means that presidents often wind up as the final source of appeal and are therefore overloaded despite all of the organizational paraphernalia around them. President Reagan is less overburdened by these concerns simply because he refuses to be and, in part, because of his administration's success in placing officials with an uncommonly homogeneous outlook in the departments and on the White House staff. In Britain, however, Margaret Thatcher's vigorous style of advocacy reflects an equally vigorous style in pursuing her priorities. Her desire to use high administrative appointments to press these priorities is a new element in British government. In the end, should the style take hold beyond Mrs. Thatcher's leadership, it may produce staffing designed to serve the priorities only of particular governments. That, ironically, would be her contribution to bringing the Washington style of government to Whitehall.

Techniques

The subject of analytic techniques is one we shall return to later because, like central agencies, these too have become more important if not necessarily in determining decisions, then surely in determining the language and operations in which the process of decision making is couched. The deployment of analytic techniques is also not merely coincidental with the growing importance of central agencies. For analysis requires that programs, operations, or expenditures be justified according to systematic and quantifiable criteria. Offcials at the level of operations tend to resist these technical interventions. At that level, data gathering required by central agencies or secretarial staffs often seems like busywork detracting from the actual routines and functions of the line programs. Skepticism at the operations level is reinforced also by the fear that the evaluative criteria employed by the operative administrative unit is incompatible with the logic of the techniques employed by units above them—a matter to be further discussed. Thus, evaluation based on assumptions not held at the operative level is feared by the operating units. Highly related to this is the concern that to standardize criteria across many programs and units is simply an effort to dissolve the complexities of each program and its special conditions into a few key and highly abstracted assumptions; the fear is that vegetable soup will be made into purée.

The tension between program officials and central officials over evaluation, language, and assumptions—and, ultimately, interpretation of results—is a key one. It leads officials at the operative unit level to cultivate "opaque" strategies, while officials at the top seek to develop transparent criteria.[16] Thus, operative units usually seek to avoid focusing on a bottom line whereas central officials want singularly to achieve one. In essence, central officials and departmental staff officials tend to ask in evaluations: "Is this program worth continuing? What are the alternative uses for its funds?" For their part, operational people ask: "How can we do our job better?"

The emergence of central units charged with assessing how the pieces of governmental activity fit together and, in some measure with rationalizing them, also pits planning or budgetary technocrats against substantively focused technocrats. In discussing the crisis of social security funding in Brazil in the face of its large international debts, for example, James Malloy notes that within the Brazilian bureaucracy the "division between macro-structural technocrats and more politically-attuned, publicly-focused types quickly emerged as a more generally deep division within the government and its support groups."[17]

How do diverse actors in the administration and the political realm relate to divisions of this sort? How are they affected by them? In the next section, we shall try to identify types of key actors and their perspectives on matters revolving around the relative ability of central or "local" units to define the criteria for evaluation.

Identifying the Players and Their Perspectives

Reorganization efforts aimed at strengthening the center of government in relation to its parts necessarily affect different sets of political and administrative actors in different ways. The immense complexity of the U.S. system, as we earlier indicated, creates a wider variety of administrative and political roles than is to be found among even the more convoluted European systems. Because the American context is so complicated, we shall begin with the key roles in the U.S. system and draw parallels where appropriate to Europe.

Political Actors

In modern governments, any strict distinction between political and bureaucratic actors is bound to be infirm. Despite the fact that parliaments are more purely political bodies than are ministries, and that in most European countries the minister is a parliamentary politician, career officials are well positioned to influence the politician-ministers. Moreover, while ministers inherently play political roles, they are not always professional politicians. This is especially true on the American scene; indeed, the absence of ostensible political credentials among cabinet members has been decried by some commentators.[18] The distinction between political and bureaucratic roles especially is blurred in the U.S. executive because the many layers of noncareer officials are often composed of hybrid "red-and-expert" officials, and because career officials have complex ties to congressional politicians.[19]

In terms of our central theme—viewing reorganization in the context of governmental/subgovernmental relations—the major determinant for the behavior of political actors as well as the bureaucratic ones is apt to be their proximity to, or distance from, the executive center. Among the key U.S. political players, then, we note four groups relevant to reorganizations that serve to strengthen the center: *central-executive politicians*, *peripheral-executive politicians*, *legislative politicians* (members of Congress), and *legislative staff politicos*.

Central-executive politicians in the United States include the president but also figures not usually considered traditional party politicians such as the OMB director, the national security assistant—indeed, all directors of major EOP staff units, and typically the appointed officials in units that Campbell designates to be central agencies operating outside the EOP. These include the secretary of the treasury's office and the director of the Office of Personnel Management (OPM).

The above, with the exception of the treasury, are structural definitions. But in practice it is hard to designate precisely what is and isn't a central unit. Much depends upon the vantage point of the designator. For instance, from a general standpoint, some departments or ministries other than the treasury are also continuously involved with the president or prime minister at the cabinet level. These other ministries typically include the foreign ministry, the justice ministry, and defense.[20] The U.S. Department of State, especially, on matters engaging the attention of other departments—notably, international trade—thinks of itself as a central unit pushing the long-range big picture in international affairs. The department sees itself as protecting the long-range national interest against the protectionist entreaties of clientele-based departments. Yet, from within the White House, the State Department is seen as an embodiment of particularistic and hypercautious thinking, fixated on regional rather than global interests.

Given all of these complications, we accept Campbell's rough designations.

Reformations of the executive that strengthen the integrating capacities of the center are obviously most strongly pushed by the officials who stand at the top of the organizational cross-hatches of government. "Coordination" and "integration" are the buzz words here. Role incumbency, however, is an imperfect indicator of where one stands, in spite of the pithy dictum to the contrary. Leadership styles, for example, do differ at the top, and a leader's willingness to delegate is apt to be related to a president's (or prime minister's) temperament. Also, the ability to appoint the proper people into positions in the line departments may lessen the perceived need for stronger controls at the top. Over time, however, presidents tend to want to draw the action closer to themselves in areas where it counts, especially politically sensitive ones. Above all, the desire to avoid embarrassment and leaks grows over time and this leads to fewer and more centrally located key players. European parallels are hard to come by in this regard, since the politics of governing in European nations is more circumscribed to begin with. Cabinet members (with frequent exceptions to be made for those representing junior parties or distinct factions in a coalition) are more nearly the center of government than they are in the United States, where they are often viewed, rightly or wrongly, as mere spokespersons for their departmental interests.

U.S. cabinet members and the multitude of subcabinet officials, with the frequent exception of the inner-cabinet members and their close aides, are peripheral political executives. They have no precise parallel in European systems except, to some extent, the ministers of client-centered departments. From the perspective of the center, the peripheral executives represent parochial departmental and subgovernmental interests. Occasionally, it has been argued that effective cabinet councils and interdepartmental committees have helped adjust the distinctive perspectives of these officials to a common denominator. The argument could be made that this was the practice in national security policymaking under Eisenhower and economic policymaking under Ford.[21]

Particularly when presidents are committed to imposing their plans upon the government (or at least wish to refrain from having someone else's plans thrust upon them), they are inclined to fear that peripheral-executive politicians willl be captives of their departmental and constituency interests—that they will be the bearers of their department's message to the president rather than vice versa.

In all governments, there is no doubt tension between the president or prime minister and the "supply" agencies that claim to speak for central authority, on the one hand, and the "demand-making" departments and their heads, on the other. In the United States, this tension attains rare heights, however, because there is no central locus for dispute mediation and bargaining. Appeals are constantly possible, and the availability of nonexecutive actors to whom information may be leaked and toward whom influence may be exercised is considerable—though, to be sure, political competition between demand-making and supply agencies is almost never neatly contained in any system.

One of the reasons, however, for the continuous appeals process in the United States has to do with another set of political actors: legislative politicians. Except as members of a government, legislative politicians have far less direct political leverage in European systems. The independent authority of the U.S. Congress makes it an explicit party to all major efforts at reorganization and usually at least a tacit party to more subtle ones. Both the independence of the legislative authority (and thus the executive's dependence on it) and the committee and subcommittee-oriented nature of the U.S. Congress are the pillars of a system of subgovernments that exists at an unusually fine-grained level of disaggregation. The American parallel to the British television show "Yes, Minister" would be "Yes, Congressman," denoting which set of officials in each country the senior civil servant finds most important. This difference is exceedingly important for all of the actors involved and for their strategies of influence, control, and evasions thereof. James Q. Wilson states the matter with great acuity:

The particularistic and localistic nature of American democracy has created a particularistic and client-serving administration. If our [U.S.] bureaucracy often serves special interests and is subject to no central direction, it is because our [U.S.] legislature often serves special interests and is subject to no central direction. For Congress to complain of what it has created and it maintains is, to be charitable, misleading. Congress could change what it has devised, but there is little reason to suppose it will.[22]

Whatever modest amendments it may require from time to time, Wilson's statement is largely correct. It illustrates, above all, that the American legislative body, in its many parts, provides a strongly centrifugal force away from the executive center. The result frequently is an atomized clientelistic relationship between interest groups, bureaus, and congressional subcommittees in which groups with narrowly definable objectives have an advantage. This tends to contrast with the levels at which these connections are made between interest groups in most European systems and their bureaucracies (often at the ministerial level). Moreover, the supervisory responsibilities that the Congress in its parts has over the executive often enables it to protect favored fiefdoms by preempting the possibility of stronger action at the executive center.[23]

Understandably, then, if central political executives try to pull control toward the center, legislative politicians, for the most part, try to exert efforts in the opposite direction. Often, the peripheral-executive politicians (mainly cabinet and subcabinet officials) are caught between these forces and try to maneuver between them.

Yet a fourth group of U.S. political actors are not formally politicians at all, but act politically on behalf of politicians. These actors are the senior personnel and committee staffs in Congress. This does not exhaust the congressional staff—many of whom despite their far larger numbers, are akin to the civil servants who staff European parliaments. It does, however, suggest that these personnel are issue-sniffers and operators for their chieftains as individual members or as committee or subcommittee chairs.[24] In many respects, they serve as the chief pipeline from the career bureaucrats to Congress. Because Congress is the type of legislative institution it is—free-wheeling, entrepreneurial, and particularistic— staff personnel do the kinds of things they do, much of which is to look for things for their bosses to do that are to their political or policy advantage. Not infrequently, this means embarrassing (sometimes deservedly) the political executives, especially when the two ends of Pennsylvania Avenue are held by different parties, and, in more symbolic form, bashing the bureaucracy.

From this complex array of political actors, we can see that in contrast to the relatively simpler European governmental/political structure, the centrifugal forces in the U.S. system are very great indeed. It is as though Congress and the central executive were polar magnets. Their distinctive perspectives on reorganization are usually developed around the pole toward which they are attracted. Occasionally, Congress can be persuaded to allow more opportunities for control to move to the center when the issues seems to be entirely abstract or seems to involve only the harmless matters of process that are the passion of professors of public administration. But on the whole, Congress only reluctantly cedes power to the executive. One last but exceedingly vital point in this regard is that Congress is almost never a single entity but a multiplicity of sometimes overlapping entities.

Bureaucratic Actors

If bureaucrats are a species, they come in many varieties—again, probably more so in the United States than elsewhere. Three varieties are of particular importance to reorganizations that shuffle the governmental/subgovernmental deck. The first and largest group at the senior level are the *program bureaucrats*. They typically serve an external set of interests directly concerned and affected by what they do. In addition, their links to Congress are usually close. These are the "Yes, Congressman" bureaucrats. Their aim is to gain the resources they need to do the job inherent in their program mandate.

A second group is the growing army of *staff analysts within the line departments and agencies*. Often, they are clustered together in units that have words like "planning," "evaluation," or "analysis" in their titles. The commanding officers of this army are the officials heading these units. These officials are in a peculiar position; while they are the synthesizers of information from the program units of their departments, they are the intermediaries for their departments when dealing with central units. In essence, they are typically looking to make a clear case for bargaining on behalf of their agency. They want to develop clear criteria and data (what we earlier called criteria based on transparency) to allow them to develop the most efficient way to expand departmental resources. When bargaining upward, however, they must also make the case on behalf of their departments.

A third group are the *staff analysts within the central units*. Before analytic models came into play, these officials often were the green eyeshade wearers situated in the green eyeshade agencies, such as the old BOB and the old GAO. They are an especially interesting group because, on the one hand, their analytical techniques (when they arrive at the right answers) are heavily favored, whereas they themselves are often ignored. Analysts doing program review, cost-benefit analysis, and so forth, favor centralized decision making which also is desired by the central political actors. Staff analysts advocate central control because they see such control as essential to employing universal (analytic) criteria in order to make decisions according to a technical definition of the public interest. They want to know whether a program is worth doing it all. Central political actors, however, while desiring central control over decisions, often wish to have it exercised on behalf of particularistic policies when there are important political payoffs. Thus, Heclo's analysis of the politicization of OMB during the Nixon administration suggests that OMB was changed from an agency designed to serve the interests of the presidency into an agency serving the interests of whoever is president.[25]

In any event, this brief description of bureaucratic types hints at how they are linked to various sources of authority in the system, and also how they are apt to respond to reorganization efforts to alter the government/ subgovernment balance. The nexus between constituency bureaucrats and legislative politicians (though not foolproof) inhibits successful manipulation by the central executive leadership. At the center of the executive, political leaders and technobureaucrats have a shared interest in central control and evaluation, but are driven sometimes by distinctly different predilections. In more ambiguous roles are the peripheral-political executives and the departmental staff analysts. The latter seek to put the best departmental face forward by pressing to eliminate obviously indefensible operations, and to reallocate departmental resources to the programs they judge most effective. The former are often in an ambiguous situation, responding to multiple constituencies and sometimes, at least by association, perceived as "marrying the natives," or internal departmental constituencies. In his short-lived second administration, President Nixon sought to eliminate these tendencies and, from the outset, so has President Reagan.

Our focus here has been on executive changes that affect governmental/ subgovernmental relations and the perspectives of key political and bureaucratic actors—perspectives that might be expected from their particular vantage points within the system. Additionally, we have hinted at the role played by technical analysis in achieving the objectives of central leaders. (We also have hinted at some of the complications occasioned by analysis as well.) We now turn to the conditions that may encourage technical analysis in the executive (a tendency that varies considerably across nations) and to some links between these tendencies and national executive systems.

Trends Toward Rationalization?

In the United States, the 1960s saw widespread program expansion—an expansion not so much of functionaries but of new administrative units (the creation of new programs and administrative housings for them is, of course, a form of reorganization), and especially of expenditures. The vast increase in expenditures, however, had a delayed effect: new programs begun with modest expenditures became established programs with significantly growing expenditures for both controllable (decisional) reasons and noncontrollable (demographic and macroeconomic) reasons. As of the late 1970s, the trend was toward what Lawrence Brown calls "policy rationalization."[26]

Budget constraints have promoted the use of analytic tools to promote "efficient" allocations of public expenditure and, thus, "rational" policy. Efforts to achieve more rational (analytically arrived at) control over expenditures begun to develop as the pace of government spending quickened. The use of analytic techniques, in turn, was stimulated by a desire to gain a more holistic grasp of the problems toward which public expenditures were directed—a desire with no inherent ideological coloration, but one that always threatens to disrupt established subgovernmental interests.

Both the use of analysis and the types of analytic exercises engaged in are conditioned by the goals of political leaders and by the environment. For example, during the expansionary period of the Johnson administration, the federal government tried to achieve a holistic planning thrust over programmatic direction as evidenced by the short-lived infatuation with PPB and systems analysis. Similarly, in some European countries, analytic planning exercises have been associated with the agendas of left-oriented governments. Such governments, notably in West Germany and Sweden, encouraged the use of analysis as a mechanism for social planning.[27]

Still, the change in emphasis in the United States came when program expansion gave way to budgetary pressures (partially promoted by this expansion) and stimulated efforts to evaluate and rationalize programs associated with the period of growth. The metamorphosis of the public agenda from program expansion to pressures for budgetary constraint, despite differences in timing and in modes of adaptation, was not exclusive to the United States.

These new pressures for greater efficiency and effectiveness also produce pressures for changes in administrative style and the development of new administrative roles. Even in Britain, where the cult of the gifted amateur still dominates (in spite of Mrs. Thatcher's efforts), one of her Majesty's civil servants writes (perhaps only in hope) that the style of British administration may likely grow more devoted to efficiency and effectiveness and more able to deal with analysis and evaluation.[28] Another British official comments, "If there is a single theme which dominates current political and publc interest in the civil service it is that of efficiency . . . not a matter central . . . to discussion a generation ago."[29] Such tendencies, however, seem to be, at this stage, most profoundly developed in the United States.

As noted previously, we do not claim that analysis in use is a politically dispassionate exercise. The motives of political leaders and those of technobureaucrats at the center diverge often enough. But the former do have problems for whch the latter seem to have solutions; above all, political leaders have needs for which technobureaucrats have legitimating language.

Analysis, then, is a mechanism not primarily for centralizing programs, but for centralizing decisions. Its growth, inevitably, is a new element in the equilibrium reached between government/subgovernment interests. How important it will become cannot as yet be conclusively assessed. But clearly in an era of pressures for constraint, more and more decisions are being moved from the production line to the finance office.

The extent to which, and precisely how, analytic tools flower within the bureaucracy depends heavily upon the mixture of traditions and skills within the bureaucracy, and the extent to which policy premises are shared across the policy sectors that the administrative state creates. No doubt some clue as to an administrative system's capacity to yield a hearty supply of technical analyses and evaluation reviews is given by the proportions of social and natural scientists in administrative enclaves. The number of economists on a government's payroll is apt to be an especially good clue to the likelihood of producing analytic grist for the policymaker's mill.

Conclusion

Efforts to rearrange the organizational apparatus of governments and the personnel to staff it are a constant of modern governments. Although people often associate reorganizations with big changes following upon the report of some hallowed commission, numerous smaller and equally important changes are continuously occurring.

The complexity of government and the difficulty of making directional inpulses reverberate throughout the operational sectors of government make the tinkerer's craft an increasingly valued trade—if, to be sure, in some locales more than others. In Washington, especially, technocratic *and* political impulses are both remarkably strong. In a strange and ironic twist, the two normally disparate urges have become symbiotic, although the goals of those supporting the production of analysis can be in conflict. The drive to centralize decision making in the American system is sustained by central executive technobureaucrats (analysts) and central political executives. But resistance comes from political urges and is expressed mainly through program technocrats and in Congress. In this, Congress remains a bastion of particular interests (as viewed, of course, by the center) and is the host for the many disaggregated objectives that government has committed itself to pursue.

The political consequences of reorganization affect how and where conflicts are resolved. For the moment, austerity (or at least the climate thereof) has given central decision makers some opportunities—ones that leaders such as Reagan and Thatcher have turned to their advantage on behalf of their radical political agendas. For each, a central element of their vision encompasses their remarkably similar ideas as to the role of civil servants—more efficient (and thus fewer) managers of a shrunken public sector.

Notes

1. James G. March and Johan P. Olsen, "Organizing Political Life: What Administrative Reorganization Tells Us About Governing," *American Political Science Review* 77 (1983), 281–96.

2. Richard Rose, "Government Against Sub-Governments: A European Perspective on Washington," in *Presidents and Prime Ministers*, ed. Richard Rose and Ezra N. Suleiman (Washington, D.C.: American Enterprise Institute, 1980), pp. 284–347.

3. Peter Szanton, "What Are We Talking About and Why?" in *Federal Reorganization: What Have We Learned?* ed. Peter Szanton (Chatham, N.J.: Chatham House, 1981), p. 32.

4. See Colin Campbell and George J. Szablowski, *The Superbureaucrats: Structure and Behavior in Central Agencies* (Toronto: Macmillan of Canada, 1979).

5. See ibid.; also Colin Campbell, *Governments Under Stress; Political Executives and Key Bureaucrats in Washington, London, and Ottawa* (Toronto: University of Toronto Press, 1983). In Sweden, the distinction between the thinly staffed policy planning ministries and the implementation boards effectively means that these smaller ministries perform some roles that are similar to those of central agencies elsewhere. The German bureaucracy, on the whole, has far less planning and analysis capacity than does the Swedish system. Most analyses are contracted out to research institutes. Additionally, the ministries tend to resist much coordination. Overall, negotiating to obtain coordination is one of the principal functions of the Bundeskanzleramt. See K.H.F. Dyson, "Planning and the Federal Chancellor's Office in the West German Federal Government," *Political Studies* 21 (1974), 348–62.

6. Campbell and Szablowski, esp. chs. 4–5.

7. Hugh Heclo, *A Government of Strangers: Executive Politics in Washington* (Washington, D.C.: Brookings, 1977), esp. ch. 2; see also Hugh Heclo, "OMB and the Presidency: The Problem of 'Neutral Competence,'" *Public Interest* 38 (Winter 1975), 80–98.

8. Renate Mayntz, "The Political Role of the Higher Civil Service in the German Federal Republic," presented at the Brookings Institution Conference, Washington, D.C., June 1983.

9. Note that the political (party) component of the civil service in Germany is viewed by Derlien and also by von Mutius et al. as essentially a long-standing phenomenon dating back to the nineteenth century. See Hans-Ulrich Derlien, "Zur einstweiligen Quieszierung politischer Beamter des Bundes, 1949–1983," Universität Bamberg, Verwaltungswissenschaftliche Beiträge, no. 16, 1984; and Albert von Mutis, ed., *Handbuch für die offentliche Verwaltung*, vol. 1 (Neuwied and Damstadt: Luchterhand, 1984).

10. F. F. Ridley, "Career Service: A Comparative Perspective on Civil Service Promotion," *Public Administration* 61 (Summer 1983), 179–96.

11. Ibid., p. 195.

12. B. Guy Peters, "A Low Cost Civil Service: At What Cost?" presented at the conference on "The Unfinished Agenda of Civil Service Reform—The President's Private Sector Survey," Brookings Institution, Washington, D.C., October 1984.

13. Campbell, *Governments Under Stress*, esp. "Conclusion."

14. Ibid., p. 24.

15. See Richard Rose, *Managing Presidential Objectives* (New York: Free Press, 1976).

16. This point was emphasized by Brian Hogwood in a discussion with one of the authors.

17. James M. Malloy, "Politics, Fiscal Crisis, and Social Security Reform in Brazil," prepared for the annual meeting of the American Political Science Association, Washington, D.C., 1984, p. 31.

18. See, for instance, Nelson W. Polsby, "Presidential Cabinet Making," *Political Science Quarterly* 93 (Spring 1978), 15–26.

19. For evidence of these complexities, summarily labeled the "end-run" model, see Joel D. Aberbach, Robert D. Putnam, and Bert A. Rockman, *Bureaucrats and Politicians in Western Democracies* (Cambridge, Mass.: Harvard University Press, 1981), pp. 228–37.

20. See, especially, Thomas E. Cronin, *The State of the Presidency*, 2d ed. (Boston: Little, Brown, 1980), ch. 8; and Richard Rose, "British Government: The Job at the Top," in *Presidents and Prime Ministers*, ed. Rose and Suleiman, pp. 1–49.

21. On the NSC under Eisenhower, for example, see Frederick C. Thayer, *An End to Hierarchy and Competition: Administration in the Post-Affluent World*, 2d ed. (New York: New Viewpoints, 1981), ch. 5. For a more critical perspective, see Paul Y. Hammond, "The National Security Council as a Device for Interdepartmental Coordination: An Interpretation and Appraisal," *American Political Science Review* 54 (1960), 899–910. On the process of economic policy coordination in the Ford administration, see Roger B. Porter, *Presidential Decision Making: The Economic Policy Board* (Cambridge: Cambridge University Press, 1980), esp. ch. 7.

22. James Q. Wilson, "The Rise of the Bureaucratic State," in *The American Commonwealth—1976*, ed. Nathan Glazer and Irving Kristol (New York: Basic Books, 1976), p. 103.

23. See Joel D. Aberbach, "Changes in Congressional Oversight," *American Behavioral Scientist* 22 (1979), 493–515.

24. See Michael J. Malbin, *Unelected Representatives: Congressional Staff and the Future of Representative Government* (New York: Basic Books, 1980); Robert H. Salisbury and Kenneth A. Shepsle, "U.S. Congressman as Enterprise," *Legislative Studies Quarterly* 6 (1981), 559–76; and Joel D. Aberbach, "Congress and the Agencies: Four Themes on Congressional Oversight of Policy and Administration," in *The United States Congress*, ed. Dennis Hale (Boston: Boston College Press, 1982), pp. 285–96.

25. Heclo, "OMB and the Presidency."

26. Lawrence D. Brown, *New Policies, New Politics: Government's Response to Government's Growth* (Washington, D.C.: Brookings, 1983).

27. On Germany, see Hans-Ulrich Derlien, "Program Evaluation in the Federal Republic of Germany," European Public Administration Group, occasional paper, 1984. On Sweden, see Harold L. Wilensky, "Political Legitimacy and Consensus: Missing Variables in the Assessment of Social Policy," in *Evaluating the Welfare State: Social and Political Perspectives*, ed. S. E. Spiro and E. Yuchtman-Yaar (New York: Academic Press, 1983).

28. John Delafons, "Working in Whitehall: Changes in Public Administration, 1952–82," *Public Administration* 60 (Autumn 1982), 253–72.

29. Sir Douglas Wass, "The Public Service in Modern Society," *Public Administration* 61 (Spring 1983), 9.

CHAPTER 4

The Growth of Government Organizations:

Do We Count the Number

or Weigh the Programs?

Richard Rose

W HAT DIFFERENCE does the growth of government make for government organizations? Does government growth produce bigger organizations, whether size be measured in terms of money spent, public employees, or some other indicator? Or does growth mean more organizations, however organizations are identified? Could government growth even mean fewer organizations, insofar as growth involved the merger of preexisting organizations? Conceivably there could be no change in the number of organizations; existing organizations could grow in program resources without growing in number.

The most common measure of the aggregate size of government, public expenditure, implies "the more, the more"; that is, the more money government spends, the bigger it is. But what does it mean to speak of more organizations? Students of public administration do not normally count the number of organizations in government. Organizations are characterized by juridical attributes, institutional characteristics, or procedures applicable to hundreds of public agencies.

Comparisons between nations remind us that organization size is relative. What appears a big organization when judged within a national context may appear a small organization in cross-national perspective. By the absolute standards of the United States, countries such as Britain or France, with one-quarter the population, may appear to have small governments. If size is judged relative to a nation's population, then a government small in an absolute sense, such as Sweden, may appear relatively large.

Everyday political comment implies a primitive idea of ordinal differences in the size of organizations. Some ministries are said to be bigger than others, whether the measure is money spent, numbers of public employees, or the variety of programs. Some ministries are said to be more important politically than others—for example, the Treasury as against Agriculture. The scale of an organization may also be judged by the population it covers or the number of clients it serves. The size of nationalized industries can be judged according to criteria applied to private-sector firms.

While theories of the growth of government are numerous, surprisingly little attention has been given to the effect upon organizations of government growth.[1] The most fundamental question—Do we count organizations or do we weigh their resources?—has hardly been considered. The purpose of this chapter is to do just that. The first section considers the place of organizations in a dynamic model of government; the second reviews alternative theories of the impact of government growth upon organizations; and the third and fourth sections examine quantitative and qualitative aspects of changes in organizations resulting from government growth.

Organizations as Instruments for Producing Programs

Government is first of all a set of organizations. Organizations are central, mobilizing resources of society and converting them into program outputs. But the centrality of organizations can be interpreted in more than one way. Organizations can be simply an intervening variable, a necessary but relatively unimportant means for producing program outputs. Organizations can also be analyzed simply on their own.

A public policy model of the growth of government views organizations as intermediaries (see figure 4.1). Organizations mobilize three principal public resources—laws, money, and employees—converting them into program outputs such as health care, roads, military defense, public transport, and so forth. Each statutorily based program is the responsibility of an identifiable organization or organizations within government. Whereas social scientists may disagree about which organizations are responsible for such abstract functions as maintaining authority, there is little disagreement about the organizations providing pensions, education, or military defense. Public organizations are properly described as agen-

FIGURE 4.1
The Principal Elements of a Dynamic Model of Government

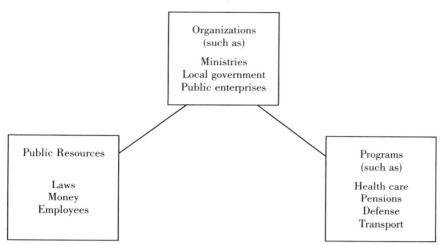

Source: Richard Rose, *Understanding Big Government: The Programme Approach* (Beverly Hills, Calif.: Sage, 1984).

cies, a term in common use in Washington, for they are indeed agents carrying out the actions laid down by laws and policies of elected officials.

Analyzing government organizations in terms of programs puts the purposes of government first.[2] From this perspective, organizations are instrumental. This is consistent with the Latin and Greek etymology of the word *organization*, which is derived from terms describing a tool or instrument. Organizations are instruments for producing program outputs; they are not just ends in themselves. It follows from this that weighing the resources that organizations mobilize is a necessary requirement.

The program approach offers clear and measurable ways of determining the growth of organizations. The size of government can be measured by the *scale* of resources required to produce programs. Insofar as government grows, then existing programs can claim more money, more personnel, and/or more laws. A bigger organization can be a government that does more of what it has been doing by claiming more resources. A second way in which an organization can grow is to increase in *scope* by adding new programs undertaking activities that had not previously been the responsibility of government or by expanding already established programs. The growth in the scale of program resources need not imply any alteration in the number of government organizations: the same organizations simply produce more of what they had been producing before. Similarly, an increase in the scope of government activities need not lead to an increase in the number of government organizations; more programs can be added to an existing organization.

The first rule for determining the dynamics of a government organization is to ask what an organization does, not what it is. We must pay more attention to the dynamics of programs than to organizational attributes. To explain why ministries of health and social security have increased their resources of money and employees, we first turn to information about the increase in the number of elderly people in the population, and changes in legislation that increase the numbers entitled to benefits or the levels of benefit per recipient.[3] To explain why defense expenditure and those in military uniforms rise or fall, we must examine perceived threats to a country's security and the political priority that the elected government gives to armed defense. Since programs differ greatly in their substantive purposes, characteristics, and clients, we would expect a variety of influences to affect the programs that are the collective responsibility of government.

The principal programs of governments in advanced industrial societies can be grouped under a small number of familiar headings. In OECD nations, six programs on average account for 38 percent of the gross domestic product, and for nine-tenths of total public expenditure. These programs are: income maintenance, chiefly old-age pensions, 14.3 percent of the national product; education, 5.8 percent; health, 5.7 percent; debt interest, 4.3 percent; economic programs, 4.8 percent; defense, 3.0 percent.[4] The organizations responsible for these programs are readily identified: social security agencies, schools, hospitals and medical practitioners' offices, the central bank, departments of industry, transportation, energy, and agriculture, and the armed services.

Much of the growth of government is not the result of present choices of governors, but reflects the inertia of past choices. Laws vesting such entitlements as education, old-age pensions, and state-assisted health care were adopted generations ago. As long as these laws remain on the statute books, government agencies are compelled to pay pensions, provide education, and fund health care. Inertia is here a force in motion, with a bias toward incremental growth.[5]

Organizations are the institutional force maintaining and expanding programs authorized by existing laws. Of itself, a law on the statute book is of no consequence: it becomes effective only when an organization is charged with producing the service it authorizes. An organization has a political base within government to make sure that a law, once enacted, is not repealed or lapses into disuse, and that program outputs are produced or expanded. Organizations are necessary but not of primary importance; they are instruments of the forces shaping public programs.

Theories of political entrepreneurship take a very different view of the growth of public organizations.[6] Theories of bureaucratic empire building postulate that the organizational power vested in the leaders of large government organizations gives them a vested interest in encouraging the growth of their organization in order to reap the extra pay, prestige, and power presumed to go with responsibility for an enlarged government agency. Micro motives of public officials are meant to have macro effects.

However, when Hood, Huby, and Dunsire employed a variety of indicators of benefits accruing to British bureaucrats, such as an increase in individual salary, staff numbers, and senior promoted posts, they found the relationship was random between growth in organizational resources and growth in their bureaucrats' advantages.[7] At lower levels of public employment, where the numbers of employees are far greater—for example, postal workers, railway workers, and ancillary staff in hosptials—there can even be an inverse relationship between numbers employed and wages, for high wages are more difficult to finance when they must be paid to tens or hundreds of thousands of workers. Similarly, a study of the political salience of the agencies headed by cabinet ministers according to four different criteria—as stepping-stones to higher office, partisan visibility in the House of Commons, press publicity, and authority in cabinet—found that the ministries with the highest political salience tend to be relatively low in their claims on public money; examples are the prime minister, and the foreign secretary. The big-spending departments, such as Health and Social Security, and Education, tend to be low in political salience.[8]

Organizations can be said to act as entrepreneurs claiming more public resources only if we include the client as part of the organization, for example, viewing the elderly as part of a social security agency, or children as part of an education department.[9] Heclo's issue network concept emphasizes that politics unites across organizational lines service providers, service beneficiaries, and officials who decide about resource allocations.[10]

Changes in the Number and Programs of Organizations: Alternative Hypotheses

Logically, an increase in the scale or scope of programs can have three different effects upon the number of government organizations: nil change;

an increase through fission; or a decrease through fusion. Plausible reasons can be given for expecting each of these alternatives.

Null Hypotheses

1.1. Pluralization: *More resources produce no change in the number of organizations, because of the multiplication of service delivery units within an organization.* In law a government organization remains a single organization, whatever the scale of resources that it mobilizes. A ministry of defense is a single ministry, whether mobilized for war or demobilized for peace. A ministry of education remains a single ministry, however many teachers and pupils it has. From this perspective, an organization does not become bigger or smaller; either it exists or it ceases to exist as a legal entity.

Organizations can adapt to demands for more output and the provision of more input through a process described as *pluralization.*[11] When the activities are the result of a well-understood technology that can readily be taught to staff and delivered by standardized organizational units, then the number of units delivering the program can be multiplied within one organization. The minister remains solely responsible at the top of a hierarchy; the organization grows at the base through the multiplication of service delivery units. The process is familiar in industry, for manufacturers expand by opening additional factories and using proven technology to train workers to produce more goods in more cities and countries. Retailers expand by opening more look-alike chain stores.

The infantry company, the primary school, a hospital, or the local post office are familiar examples of a plurality of service delivery units within a single public organization. Government relied on pluralization to expand long before the advent of Woolworths or McDonalds, made it prominent in the marketplace. When an army grows by increasing the number of its companies, brigades, and divisions, and a navy by increasing the number of its ships, the armed services remain under a single command. A ministry of health meets increased demand by building more hospitals and increasing the number of doctors trained. In order to provide more program outputs, a government does not need to establish a new organization but it does need to provide more resources to finance more standardized service delivery units.

1.2. Diversification: *An increased number of public programs requires no change in the number of organizations, because of diversification within existing organizations.* Every public organization is multifunctional. In addition to having some units responsible for internal matters (such as personnel, budget, information), the organization usually produces program outputs. For example, a defense department will be concerned with land, sea, and air services, and an education department with primary, secondary, and tertiary education. Many government organizations have a heterogeneous collection of program responsibilities for reasons of historical accident or because of taking responsibility for ancillary services—for example, a defense ministry providing health care for civilian dependents of servicemen, or an agriculture department promoting industrial development in rural areas. The process of diversification is familiar enough in private-sector firms. As conglomerates such as ITT demonstrate, the general goal of producing a profit can be achieved in diverse ways.

Fission Hypotheses

2.1. Pathologies of scale: *The more resources an organization claims, the less efficient it becomes* (diseconomy of scale) *or the less politically responsive it becomes* (remoteness of scale). Economic analysis is accustomed to making assumptions about the relationship between organizational size and efficiency.[12] Diseconomies of scale are not considered normal in the private sector, but private-sector organizations are normally much smaller than government organizations. The provision of education, for example, may account for upwards of five percent of the total labor force in a country, a magnitude very different from that of even a relatively large private employer.

Proponents of the devolution of programs to subnational, regional, or local levels of government argue that public organiztions lose political responsiveness as they grow in size.[13] The recurrence of such demands in the 1970s has sometimes been interpreted as a consequence of big government producing a degree of political alienation from remote, centralized bureaucratic organizations.

2.2. Specialization by program: *The more programs a government provides, the greater the number of organizations.* One characteristic of organizations as a set is that they are differentiated; hence, the creation of a new program not previously undertaken by government could lead to the creation of a new organization to carry it out. Insofar as there is anxiety about diseconomies of scale, this would be logical. A government that wants to undertake a hundred different programs could have ten times the number of organizations as a government that has only ten programs.

Questions may be raised about this hypothesis. The first is the assumption that new programs can be created and implemented without established organizations as sponsors. Established organizations are likely to propose new programs that they themselves want to carry out to enlarge and improve service to clients and will have the personnel with relevant experience for carrying out many new programmes.[14] Moreover, the constraints upon the number of organizations that can exist at the level of a ministry (less than twenty) are much more stringent than constraints upon the number of programs that a government can sponsor (hundreds or thousands).

The fission hypothesis—one organization is required for each program—implies that the way to alter the collective resource claims upon government is to abolish the sponsoring organization. Yet this does not follow, for money and personnel would still be required if the program was transferred to a more specialized organization. In Britain, where the prime minister has the power to change organizational forms but not to alter laws authorizing programs, organizational changes are unrelated to claims on resources.[15]

Fusion Hypotheses

3.1. Economies and equities of scale: *The more resources government mobilizes, the fewer organizations it has, because larger organizations are more efficient producers of goods and services and distribute them more equitably.* The arguments for economies of scale cannot be translated uniformly from the private sector to the public sector. Insofar as government produces collective goods, then by definition such things as military defense can only be supplied by the national government: there is no alternative to having a single organization supplying these goods. In local government, where delivery of services to individuals and households is the norm, postwar reforms reducing the number of organizations were greatly influenced by economies-of-scale arguments; it was assumed that bigger authorities would be more efficient authorities.[16]

Central government may also be considered a more equitable producer of services because it is the one level of government able to provide services to all citizens. Insofar as services are distributed by a variety of subnational units of government, then what individuals receive may vary according to the fiscal resources or competence of local or regional authorities. By drawing resources from a nationwide tax base and producing services to a common standard, central government can avoid "territorial injustice" arising from the differential provision of program outputs by local and regional governments.[17]

3.2. Coordination: *The more programs a government undertakes, the fewer organizations it has, as the need to coordinate different activities gains in priority.* The political logic is that the more a government does, the more interdependent its activities are, because of the interaction between different programs affecting the same client group, and because of competition for resources between more and more (and larger and larger) programs. In central government coordination is normally assumed to result from creating superdepartments that merge preexisting ministries into a single very large ministry—for example, health, welfare, and social security programs in a welfare ministry; or army, navy, and air force ministries in a single ministry of defense.[18] At the subnational level, coordination is often assumed to follow from merging a variety of institutions carrying out separate programs into an extensive multipurpose local authority.

Do Changes in the Scale and Scope of Government Lead to Changes in the Number of Government Organizations?

The logic of hypotheses about program change and organization change is clear, but the means of testing are not. The independent variables concerning programs are amenable to measurement, and there is much empirical evidence of the great majority of programs having increased their claims on national resources in the postwar era.[19] Most of the great expansion in public expenditure and public employment has been concentrated in familiar programs, such as pensions, education, and health care, often by the extension of coverage or improvement of benefits. The characteristic method for increasing the scope of government in an era of big government is better described as a process of policy succession than the creation of completely new programs.[20] From a historical perspective going back before the Second or the First World Wars, there has been a major increase too in the scope of public programs.[21]

However, the dependent variable—the number of organizations—is not easily reduced to a form suitable for statistical testing. It could even be suggested that elaborate multivariate statistical analyses based on data about the number of government organizations ought to carry the warning: "Excessive quantification is dangerous to understanding." While we are accustomed to quantify such measures of organizational resources as money and personnel, formal organizations are first of all defined by nominal (typically, legal) attributes.

Three different definitions of government organization must be considered: the overarching collectivity, the state, which must remain unitary in concept albeit polymorphic; a politically accountable office, such as the head of a cabinet department or a local government, each normally being responsible for a number of programs; and a service delivery unit responsible for a particular program, typically a subordinate unit within an organization.

The Overarching Collectivity—the State, the Government, the Public Sector, the Crown

The broadest and most general terms used to describe public institutions are abstract constructs not formal organizations. These terms can be made operational, although critics like to emphasize the fuzziness at the edges of any definition of the modern public sector.[22] The definition may be laid down by public law or in a constitution, by conventions of national income accounting, or as an operating definition imposed by government organization manuals, which themselves can be fuzzy. For example, the *U.S. Government Manual 1984/85* moves from a desription of the Executive Office of the President to "Executive Departments, Independent Establishments and Government Corporations, Quasi-official Agencies, Selected Multilateral Organizations, and Selected Bilateral Organizations." The boundaries of the British crown are vague in territory as well as organizational form.[23]

Organizations grouped in a single category do not thereby constitute a single organization. A country with twenty-five regions and 250 urban districts has only two categories of local government, but hundreds of separate local organizations. A public law can define and authoritatively list the bodies considered as public enterprises. But this does not make the state railway, post office, airlines, and electricity authority one organization: they remain separate, notwithstanding a common legal status. The private-sector analogue is the existence of thousands of different corporations under a single act for incorporating limited liability companies.

A few overarching collectivities are multipurpose federations of formal organizations: a cabinet is the best-known example in central government, and local government is another familiar example. A cabinet or local authority is a formal organization with identifiable members, rules of procedures, and records. But it is also a federation of politicians who head separate ministries, local councillors who chair functional committees, and specialist officers heading the various departments of the council.

Two points are particularly important about a federation of formal organizations. First, by definition a collective is a single unit: it can become bigger or smaller (that is, increase the number of federated units or resources of existing units), but it cannot multiply. Whereas ministries may increase in number, a cabinet remains a single body. Similarly, while a local authority may add or lose functions, it remains a unitary body, however many programs it administers and whatever the scale of its resources. Changes in such an abstract collectivity as the state or government are best understood as changes *within* the collectivity.

Organizations Headed by Politically Accountable Officials

Every democratic government is headed by a group of politically accountable officials who receive office due to election, appointment by an elected official, or some combination of the two. In the American system, the president is the sole elected official with authority in the executive branch; he appoints thousands of people to the leading posts in the dozens of organizations that constitute the executive branch, and they are politically accountable to him. In a parliamentary system, the cabinet is collectively accountable to a popularly elected Parliament. Most cabinet ministers have also won election to Parliament and owe their office to appointment by the prime minister or to interparty bargains between partners in a coalition government. A government in which only one person, whether king, president, or führer, was in charge of everything, would be limited in what it did by the time and resources of a single person. Big government requires a team of politically accountable officials to carry out its multiple tasks. If we wanted to take a photograph of the politicians responsible for doing most of what government does, it would be a group photograph of presidential appointees or of cabinet ministers rather than a photograph of the president or prime minister alone.

A political official is often responsible for a multiplicity of programs. A minister for defense is concerned with three different armed services, with the use of defense forces in many different contexts at home and abroad, with the retirement and recruitment of servicemen, with weapons procurement and development, and so forth. A minister for health is concerned with health programs, some of which are carried out by hospitals, some by medical doctors, and some involving collaboration with a variety of operating agencies. When health and welfare are combined in a single ministry, then one minister will be accountable for a host of different income-maintenance programs and for personal social services as well.

From an introverted perspective, a ministry is not one organization but a cluster of variously denominated bureaus, divisions, sections, and offices. Within a cluster it is an open question whether the relationship between units in a ministry is hierarchical, as in defense; unitary, with the minister being responsible for each and all as in British constitutional theory; or federative, as occurs in Washington with legal powers and responsibilities often vested in the head of a bureau whose links with legislative committees and interest groups are often stronger than with a formal superior, the secretary of the department.[24]

In much of Europe the theory of the ministry is perpendicular—the secretary of state announces, "*I* have decided," but the practice is gothic, as power is exercised in dark corners. In Germany, Renate Mayntz and Fritz Scharpf note that the basic unit of a federal ministry, a section headed by a *Referent,* is very small; two-thirds have six or fewer staff.[25] Britain's seventeen ministries are fragmented into sixty-nine or more departmental units for budget and accounting purposes.[26] For administrative direction each ministry is divided into dozens of "commands" with an undersecretary coordinating: fifty-three in Trade and Industry, thirty in Agriculture, and seventeen for the Home Office.[27] In turn, each coordinating jurisdiction is further subdivided into different units under assistant secretaries, thus generating hundreds of organizational units within less than a score of ministries.

Dividing a ministry into bureaus or sections makes it possible for one minister to be responsible for a heterogeneous range of programs. Whereas pluralization allows the reproduction of a standard type of operating unit, sectionalization permits the multiplication of diverse programs within the boundaries of a single organization. This is not the classic subdivision of interrelated tasks directed toward a common goal under a single authority. The process is more aptly labeled diversification, because it permits unrelated tasks to coexist within one ministry. The private-sector analogy is not McDonalds or Coca-Cola, but a conglomerate corporation such as ITT or Unilever. The variety of programs for which a single official is accountable can be expanded very substantially by adding new operating units to an organization, each having delegated authority for one of the programs of the ministry or the local council.

The expansion of the scope of public programs has not led to a concurrent expansion in the number of accountable organizations in central government. Since the mid-nineteenth century, governments of industrial nations have added hundreds of tasks, and since 1945 dozens of programs. But the number of ministries has not increased in proportion (see table 4.1). In the past 133 years, the cabinet of the average industrial nation has only increased its number of ministers by ten.[28] Since 1945 the number of ministries has changed very little, and in some countries the number has actually contracted. The typical minister is now responsible for more programs than a generation or two ago.

The expanded scope of public programs has led to the creation of a weighty new type of organization, the public enterprise that is state-owned but sells its goods and services—electricity, gas, coal, road, rail, and air transport, postal and telephone service, and so forth—to customers. While the motives and forms for nationalizing a firm or industry vary, in Europe the result has been to create a category of government organizations employing more than one-quarter of all public employees and responsible for basic services in the nation's economy. It has also produced

TABLE 4.1
The Number of Central
Government Ministries in 1849
and 1982

	1849[a]	1982
France	10	42
Canada	8	36
Italy	11	28
United Kingdom	12	22
Denmark	8	20
New Zealand	19	19
Sweden	7	18
Germany	12	17
Norway	7	17
Belgium	6	15
Finland	11	15
Ireland	11	15
Australia	7	14
Austria	9	14
Netherlands	9	14
United States	6	13
Switzerland	7	7
Average	9.4	19.2

Source: From Richard Rose, "On the Priorities of Government," *European Journal of Political Research* 4, no. 3 (1976), and up dated by the author. Nondepartmental ministers are included, but a ministry with an assistant or deputy minister also in cabinet is counted only once.

a. Or a date shortly after national independence, if later.

many legal problems of accountability, for nationalized enterprises are effectively hybrids, accountable to the market and to elected politicians.[29]

The important point here is that nationalization of an industry usually involves a reduction in the number of organizations active in that industry. This may come about because on taking ownership the state merges the assets of a number of private-sector firms into a single state enterprise; because the state confers monopoly status in the industry upon the firm it owns; and/or because state subsidies effectively prevent private enterprise firms from successfully competing with it in the market. Logically, state ownership of a firm need not involve monopoly; municipalization is a possible alternative to nationalization. Empirically, the expansion of public enterprises has meant a reduction in the number of organizations in industry.[30]

The creation of national health services has involved a major shift in the weight of different types of public organizations, for the health service is large, accounting for about more than one-eighth of total public expenditure, and an even larger share of public employment. Doctors are difficult to subject to bureaucratic regulation, perceiving themselves as professionals (*freie berufe*) and by virtue of their expertise claiming autonomy in making decisions about patients. Hospitals are subject to administration by many procedures common to large bureaucratic organizations, but the role of doctors in assigning, treating, and discharging patients gives experts operational authority within hospitals analogous to that of professors in a university. In many national health services the primary role of central government is that of paying for health services; doctors are normally not state employees and hospitals may be operated by subnational units of government, nonprofit philanthropic agencies, profit-making bodies, or a mixture of all three. The growing importance of health care programs has given great weight to issues of political accountability arising from a form of organization that deviates greatly from conventional political and administrative theories of bureaucratic authority and accountability.

While the scale and scope of local government has grown in the postwar era the number of local authorities has been reduced almost everywhere. The median Western nation has reduced locally elected governments by more than half since 1951; in Sweden, where program expansion has been particularly marked, the number of local authorities has been reduced from 2,500 to 279. (See table 4.2). The United States, has concurrently seen many new communities created as a function of great population growth and movements while many smaller jursidictions have merged, seeking the efficiency presumed to arise from economies of scale. In France, the persistence of a very large number of very small communes reflects the French state's preference for maintaining service delivery responsibilities in the hands of central government agencies, keeping many local authorities too small to assume major program responsibilities.

Whether central or local government is the focus, the growth in the scope of government programs has often resulted in fusion. The number of programs for which a public organization is responsible has tended to increase; multifunctional agencies add more functions. In local government, smaller units have been merged into fewer in the name of efficiency. In an industry subject to nationalization, the number of firms in the industry has been reduced.

TABLE 4.2
The Contraction in Local Government Units, 1951–1982

		No. of Units		% Change	Pop. per Unit, 1982
	Basic Unit	1951	1982	1951–1982	(in thousands)
France	commune	37,983	36,391	−4	1,500
United States	townships, municipalities	33,980	35,944	+5	6,300
Italy	commune	n.a.	8,053	n.a.	7,100
Germany[a]	*gemeinden*	24,500	8,510	−65	7,200
Norway	municipalities	746	454	−39	9,000
Finland	commune	547	461	−16	10,400
Belgium	commune	2,670	596	−78	16,700
Netherlands	municipalities	1,014	820	−19	17,000
Denmark	commune	1,388	277	−80	18,400
Sweden	commune	2,500[b]	279	−89	29,800
United Kingdom	districts	1,957	545	−72	102,500

Source: *The Statesman's Year Book, 1951, 1982–83* (London: Macmillan); Arthur B. Gunlicks, ed., *Local Government Reform and Reorganization: An International Perspective* (Port Washington, N.Y.: Kennikat Press, 1981).

a. Includes *kreisfrei gemeinden* (92), *einheitsgemeinden* (2,170), and the 6,248 villages that are the units constituting *verbandsgemeinden*. If the *verbandsgemeinden* are reckoned as the basic units, the German total is 3,353 units, with an average population of 18,400. See Gunlicks, ed., p. 175.

b. Local government reorganization in Sweden during the 1950s reduced the number of basic units to 1,032, which were further reduced by reorganizations in the 1960s and 1970s.

Service Delivery Units That Bring Programs to Recipients

The politically accountable official is rarely the individual who delivers a particular program, and this is particularly true in the modern state. Historically, government was concentrated at the center, being responsible for a minimum of programs defining the modern state, such as the courts, finance, and relations with foreign countries. Even then, in order to be effective nationwide, the king's authority had to be delegated—whether to territorial barons, *intendants*, or whatever.

The growth in the scope and scale of programs that has produced the modern mixed-economy welfare state necessarily requires the delivery of services nationwide.[31] The paradigm programs—health, education, and income maintenance—are meant to benefit individuals and families. Since most of a nation's population lives at some distance from the capital city, a nationwide network of service delivery units must be created to deliver programs where people live.[32] Public enterprises such as postal service, telephones, electricity, buses, and railways, must also be distributed in keeping with the nationwide distribution of the population. Whereas the government of George Washington or George III of England was concerned with a few matters of high politics that could be conducted over the heads of most subjects, contemporary governments are concerned with matters of "low" politics that directly affect the everyday lives of nine-tenths or more of the population.[33]

The growth of government has been a growth in services requiring delivery nationwide. Central defining concerns of the state such as defense have become relatively less important by comparison with social programs such as education, health, and income maintenance (table 4.3). While the data about total government expenditure for long periods of time can only be approximate, the pattern is clear. In every nation surveyed, social programs requiring delivery nationwide have increased their share of an enlarged public expenditure, and now account for around two-thirds of total spending; central programs have declined in relative importance.

The welfare state is consumer-oriented more than it is producer-oriented. When the delivery of services to the citizen is the principal concern, then political heads of government organizations must delegate de facto authority to act to public employees closest to program recipients.

The simplest form of formal delegation is *intraorganizational*. This is most evident in the military, where concern with central direction and control is very strong. The armed services have a recognized chain of command within the organization's hierarchy. Delegation within a ministry is important where uniform nationwide standards are meant to be maintained. For example, social security benefits may be calculated at a central headquarters, and great care taken to stipulate rules to guide officials who advise claimants in local offices. It is also evident in government activities for which a network is necessary, such as the post office, which requires links between local offices in order to deliver mail from one part of a nation to the other.

Service delivery is usually delegated on an *interorganizational* basis. Service delivery can be placed in the hands of three different types of organizations separate from ministries: local and regional authorities; public enterprises selling products in the market; and expert-dominated institutions, of which the health services are the most significant. A fourth category, advisory councils or committees, are by definition of very limited importance, since they are advisory, not executive, claim few resources, and have little tangible output.[34]

Inasmuch as services are normally delivered by public employees, the proportion of public employees working in a central government ministry

TABLE 4.3
The Shift from Central to Nationwide Programs
(% share of public expenditure)

	Centralized Programs[a]	Nationwide Programs[b]
France (central government)		
1842	91	9
1890	86	14
1935	57	43
1975	36	64
change	−55	+55
Germany (general government)		
1872	69	31
1900	55	45
1935	41	49
1975	36	64
change	−33	+33
Italy (central government)		
1872	78	22
1900	76	24
1933	66	34
1973	40	60
change	−38	+38
Netherlands (central government)		
1900	82	19
1935	58	42
1975	33	67
change	−49	+49
Sweden (general government)		
1913	51	49
1936	35	65
1974	28	72
change	−23	+23
United Kingdom (general government)		
1840	81	19
1895	58	42
1933	39	61
1975	26	74
change	−55	+55

Source: Peter Flora, *State, Economy and Society in Western Europe, 1815–1975* (Frankfurt: Campus, 1983), pp. 380–82, 387, 402f., 410f., 428, 446f.

a. Centralized programs are defense, administration, justice, and residual, primarily debt interest.

b. Nationwide headings are social services such as health, education, and income maintenance, and economic and environmental services, including transport.

is an indicator of the degree of interorganizational delegation of service delivery (see table 4.4). When public employment is examined, no central government in a major Western nation is responsible for delivering as much as half the programs of government. The proportion of public employees working for central ministries is highest in very unitary states: France (45 percent) and Italy (37 percent). It is low not only in the Federal Republic of Germany (13 percent) and the United States (22 percent), but also in unitary Britain (14 percent) and Sweden (19 percent).

Responsibility for delivering public programs is usually delegated *between* organizations. Delegation occurs even in unitary states because politically accountable heads of central government institutions only want to lay down the framework laws within which service delivery occurs and to allocate money and personnel to a given program. But the actual task of delivering particular services to particular individuals is not for them. It is beneath the dignity of politicians, and secondary to their personal and partisan ambitions. It is also a physical impossibility for a busy politician in a capital city to superintend the nationwide set of offices required to deliver major social programs. Nor is a politican likely to have any technical expertise in the content of the program. His expertise is in securing legislation to improve and expand the scope of an organization's programs, fighting for more resources for existing programs, and obtaining publicity.

When responsibility for delivering programs is handed to other organizations, the giver does not lose all interest and influence—particularly if paying a substantial portion of the cost of the program. The result of interorganizational delegation is interorganizational politics. While local authorities, public enterprises, and health service agencies may deliver programs, they remain open to influence by the officials who delegate. In unitary as in federal systems of government, interorganizational politics creates a maze or tangle of political relationships.[35]

Within an organization, delegation increases with the scale of resources committed to a program. As the volume of services to be delivered increases, so too does the process of pluralization, multiplying the number of standardized units for the delivery of standard services. All the major programs of government can alter their volume of program outputs by multiplying service-delivery units. Pluralization normally requires an increase in the resources of the organization containing the plural units. The multiplication of units requires three things: a standard technology for producing goods or services; the capacity to train staff in standard procedures; and organizational structures suitable for mass replication.

Defense is the traditional example of an organization changing scale—

TABLE 4.4
Total Public Employment by Type of Government Organization, 1980
(in percent)

	Central Ministries	Trading Enterprises[a]	Other	Local and Regional Government
Britain	14 (−17)[b]	25 (−10)	22 (+12)	39 (+15)
France	45 (−2)	17 (−14)	15 (+7)	23 (+9)
Germany	13 (+10)	36 (−14)	10 (+1)	41 (+3)
Italy	37 (−9)	30 (0)	20 (+8)	13 (+1)
Sweden	19 (−17)	23 (−11)	4 (+3)	54 (+25)
United States	22 (−35)	7 (+7)	0.5 (0)	70 (+28)

Source: Richard Rose, *Public Employment in Western Nations* (Cambridge: Cambridge University Press, 1985).

a. Central government is the principal owner of these enterprises; industries such as electricity or bus transport are sometimes owned by local or regional government.

b. % change since 1951.

whether cutting back or increasing in size—by varying the number of units producing standard program outputs. While sophisticated in conception, the military is not meant to be sophisticated in application; it is said to be "designed by geniuses to be run by idiots." The basic unit of the armed forces is small: a tank, a plane, an infantry squad, or a task-specific unit on board a ship. The methods for training the military, evolved over the centuries, make it possible for the armed services to train most new recruits in a few months. The Post Office, very important in the growth of nineteenth-century government both in employment and penetration of public service nationwide, is another example of the development of standard units (post offices) with standardized staff (postal clerks).

Education, important for a century in the growth of government, does not expand at headquarters, where politically accountable officials are located, but in the cities, towns, and villages where young people live. The basic service-delivery unit is the school or the classroom within the school, with one teacher and a few dozen pupils. Teacher training has been standardized for more than half a century. An increase of 500,000 in the number of employees in education can be achieved by producing several thousand schools with an average of twenty or twenty-five employees and fifteen or so classrooms.

Health services are delivered in two different but complementary ways: by hosptials, and by independently employed doctors. A doctor's "office" is more like a mediaeval king's office, an extension of his person, than it is a bureaucratized public office. The replication of doctors' practices occurs by training more doctors in standard medical methods. Hospitals are subject to an element of public control, requiring public approval for construction. Hospital activities may be subject to bureaucratic control of nonmedical concerns, such as budgeting or conditions of employment of nonmedical staff, but leave substantial discretion to individual doctors. This discretion is not exercised idiosyncratically; it can be pluralized because it reflects the formal training and informal socialization of doctors into a profession that can expand its numbers while keeping its standards constant.

Economic programs of government usually depend upon a standardized technology. Capital investment in such economic infrastructure as roads assumes a standard procedure for converting money into roads through engineering techniques widely diffused in the construction industry. Construction firms increase their number of crews when road building increases, and contract them with cutbacks in public investment. Nationalized industries have the engineering technology to produce electricity, gas, rail, and air transport, and so forth. The standard unit of delivery may be capital-intensive (such as an electricity generating station) or labor-intensive (such as a bus). The number of such units can be increased or decreased in keeping with political assessments of supply and demand.

Income-maintenance programs are distinctive for two reasons: their form is a transfer payment, and the output is money. The provision of old-age pensions, by far the largest single program, has expanded greatly along with the technology for computerized check writing and record keeping. In organizational terms, debt interest payment has expanded even more easily as interest rates alter daily in accord with fluctuations in supply and demand in an international market. The expansion of local offices to deal face-to-face with social security claimants occurred in conjunction with the maintenance of nationwide standards ensuring interpersonal equity, for the programs are both rule-bound and routinized; this is especially true of the biggest program, pensions.

From about 1850 to 1950 much of the growth of government involved the creation of new organizations to deliver new programs. However, since then program growth has had very different implications for government organizations. Instead of increasing the number of organizations, the change has typically involved an increase in the resources of existing organizations through pluralization. There has been nil change or even a reduction in the number of politically accountable organizations through fusion, while the basic service delivery unit has remained much the same in its size.

Commentators and politicians may exclaim with anxiety: How can we ever direct an organization that has doubled or quadrupled in the size of its total resources? The answer is: Much the same as before. As long as expansion involves the pluralization of organizations, more can readily be done because it simply means doing more of what an organization is already doing.

Do Changes in the Scale and Scope of Programs Lead to Changes in the Qualities of Organizations?

When the dependent variable is the quality of government organizations, the impact of changes in the quantity of public programs is not easily identified. Yet qualitative changes are politically as important as quantitative changes, and what is difficult to measure can only be ignored by self-fulfilling reductionism. Here, the consequences of quantitative changes can be discussed but not proven. Good grounds can be given for conclusions concerning three particularly important qualitative characteristics of organizations: effectiveness, conflicts between organizations, and popular evaluation of organization outputs.

Effectiveness

All organizations, not least government organizations, are inevitably imperfect.[36] Moreover, the program goals of public organizations vary in the extent to which there are known techniques for their achievement. Some tasks are inherently more "doable" than others, because of the existence of widely diffused means-ends technologies. For example, a department of highway engineering can be more effective in building roads than a department of social engineering can be in efforts to reduce poverty. A crucial question in the growth of government is whether the scale and scope of activities increases more among programs that service delivery units can carry out with a reasonable degree of effectiveness, or among programs with low effectiveness.

The simplest hypothesis to entertain is the null hypothesis: changes in the scale and scope of public programs make no difference to organizational effectiveness. This null hypothesis does not assume any particular level of effectiveness of organizations prior to growth. In Mediterranean countries, the state mobilizes relatively few resources, yet complaints about inefficiency are frequent. By contrast, in Scandinavia government's claims on resources are large and public organizations are assumed to be efficient. Political culture can affect the efficiency of government programs whatever their potential level of effectiveness.

Because growth in the scale of public spending and employment has occurred through pluralization, there is little reason for it to lead to a noteworthy loss (or gain) in effectiveness. The process of pluralization results in the multiplication of service delivery units; it need not lead to changes in the standard unit within an organization. A school remains a school, whether it is one of ten, one hundred, or one thousand, and a doctor's medical knowledge can be the same whether his practice is one of 5,000 or 50,000 in a country. An American president who wishes to expand the Department of Defense with more than 3 million employees and spending hundreds of billions of dollars can scarcely argue that a big organization is ineffective. In defense, as in civil programs, the typical service delivery unit is small.

Changes in the scope of government are likely to rely upon untested means-ends technologies, and thus require the creation of new service delivery units, and systems of superintendence by politically accountable officials. Jeffrey Pressman's and Aaron Wildavsky's study of implementation has argued that with the creation of new programs there is a great loss of effectiveness, not only because of shortcomings in untested technologies but also because of the obstacles to securing co-operation within and between organizations.[37] But Elinor Bowen has shown that claims about the obstacles to interorganizational cooperation are exaggerated.[38] Organizations often combine to deal with a multiplicity of interdependent problems simultaneously, and the positive-sum benefits of cooperation between interdependent organizations can overcome many problems of implementing a program for the first time.

While undoubtedly important in expressing what policymakers want to change, new programs are of very limited significance for the scale of government. The resources claimed by new programs, such as the much-analyzed American poverty programs, were small by comparison with the claims of old programs: the defense budget, interest on the national debt, and social security. By definition, new programs will have far less time to accumulate large claims on resources. Because they are untested, they will often be launched on a pilot funding basis and lack the generations of inertia that institutionalize growth in older programs.[39]

In the postwar era, increases in resources have principally been allocated to programs with known technologies. Education, health care and income-maintenance programs have expanded by a process that Hugh Heclo has described as institutional learning, and Brian Hogwood and Guy Peters as policy succession.[40] Policy succession involves adding to established programs. Heclo argues, this is usually done after existing activities produce substantial evidence of need and proposals for expansion grounded in experience. An additional program responsibility is less often "a lead in the dark" than it is the expansion of existing organizations and service units. For example, the broadening of categories of entitlement to income-maintenance grants may make it easier to administer programs and increase effectiveness (if that be judged in terms of take-up of entitlements) by simplifying the categories of eligibility. In health care, technology is often the cause of program expansion; increased expenditure on new units within a hospital or on new types of medical treatment follow from laboratory developments.

Examples can always be found of programs that are completely new in intent, completely untested, and even completely ineffective in execution. But these programs, by the very visibility of their failure, are more likely to be abandoned rather than grow, whereas the programs that are most effective are likely to have organizational and popular support for further growth.

Contradictions and coordination between organizations.

Contemporary governments are complex organizations, whether they are growing or remain constant in size. The optimist will refer to the problems presented by the multiplicity of tasks of multiple organizations as a problem of coordination; it is better referred to as a problem of conflict management.[41] This is most evident when the organizations in question are headed by separately elected officials in central, regional, and local governments, or arise between elected politicians and expert-headed public enterprises or health agencies.

The need for increased coordination is characteristically seen in demands for "improvement" in the budget process. The growth of government requires more money, and in a period of slow economic growth, this creates fiscal strains, as revenues to fund continued growth are more difficult to raise. The deficit of revenue as against expenditure claims is a perennial problem in the budget process; so too is the adjustment of competing spending claims between organizations within government, a problem that becomes more intense when the fiscal dividend of growth no longer assures prizes for all, but threatens cuts.[42] It would be wrong to label fiscal problems as an organizational problem: they are first and foremost problems of money. Organizational redesign provides less help in resolving budget problems than does the fiscal dividend generated by higher growth, or the advent to office of politicians prepared to take decisions to produce medium-term remedies for immediate budget problems. To define budget problems as organization problems is to encourage a search for treatment by that well-known placebo, the reorganization of government.

Contradictions between government organizations arise only under limiting assumptions. First of all, growth must involve an increase in the number of programs. Second, growth must involve an increase in politically accountable organizations that come into conflict because they have mutually opposing tasks. However, many government programs are unrelated or have only incidental consequences for each other. Moreover, growth in the scale of programs does not multiply the number of organizations proportionately. Coordination problems, such as they are, are more likely to occur within rather than between organizations, as a ministry becomes responsible for more and more programs.

When growth involves pluralization, coordination problems are not increased, for pluralistic organizations run in parallel (as, for example, one primary school for each neighborhood) rather than in competition or conflict. What must increase is the supervision of more service delivery units. The hierarchies generated to supervise a school system with a hundred schools will be higher than in a system with ten schools. As the distance between the politically accountable official and those delivering services increases, supervision may diminish. But the additional layering of a hierarchical organization does not cause a great problem, insofar as the primary object—the production of relatively standard goods and services for citizens—is secured through the standardization of equipment, techniques, and organizational forms, reinforced by the inculcation of common professional norms among service providers.

Popular Acceptability

Popular reactions to the growth of government are ambivalent; the benefits are welcome but the taxes needed to finance these benefits are less welcome. In a mixed-economy welfare state, political parties can compete, some stressing benefits, and others costs. The appropriate mix of the two is a matter for political judgment, not organization theory.

The growth of government has created two organizational problems for conventional theories of government by elected representatives. The first is that the increase in the scale and scope of public programs has not been matched by an increase in the number of popularly elected representatives. The ratio of voters to legislation varies widely among Western nations. The important point is that everywhere the number of voters per representative has increased since the introduction of competitive elections; the median increase is more than 600 percent.[43] Not only is the idea of direct democracy too simple in an era of big government, so too is the idea of direct links between voter and representative. The increase in associations or confederations of interest groups—often described as corporatism, but more properly described as interest intermediation—has further complicated relations between individual electors and policymakers.

To regard a dilution in the link between electors and representatives as a cause of qualitative dissatisfaction with government misconceives the role of individuals in a mixed-economy welfare state. It confuses the individual's role qua elector with his or her role qua consumer of public goods and services. Individuals vote for a party with which they identify because it stands for people like themselves, because of diffuse political principles or concerns with issues, and because of the personalities of party leaders. A ballot is a blunt instrument: it does not allow an individual to express satisfaction or dissatisfaction with particular services provided by the state.

When we turn to the major goods and services produced by government, we then see the ordinary individual as a consumer, whether the role is defined as that of a sovereign consumer or a consumer dominated by powerful producers. Here it is particularly important to consider the organizational setting in which programs are delivered. The fact that a million people may receive a benefit from an organization with 20,000 public employees does not mean that each recipient must stand in a queue with a million others, or deal with thousands of officials.

A major characteristic of the programs making government big is that they provide private benefits rather than collective goods. The use of the language of a consumer is apt, for health care, education, and income-maintenance grants are consumed by individuals. They are not like such collective goods as defense; therefore the benefits of these programs are likely to be clearly evident to the individual. If the state did not provide education, health care, and pensions, most people in an advanced industrial society could and would buy them in the market.

A particular characteristic of health and education programs is that they are provided by "human-size" delivery units. The majority of units for service delivery are small. The United States federal government is big in aggregate—but 57 percent of its 45,000 operational units have four or fewer employees.[44] A patient and a doctor have a one-to-one relationship. Education involves a pupil in a one-to-twenty relationship with a teacher, and sometimes a one-to-one relationship. A patient in a large hospital will normally be treated in a particular ward, just as a university student will be attached to a class, a department, and a faculty rather than being an atom among 20,000 students.

Social security payments to the elderly, the most important of all income-maintenance programs, are administered impersonally; the pensioner receiving a check does not see the computer that writes it. The vesting of a pension as a statutory entitlement of an elderly person, reinforced by the payment of social security taxes into trust funds, makes pensions a "self-administered" program. When an individual seeks a pension, he or she is claiming a right—and rules are written to make payment readily practicable for more than 99 percent of claimants. The problems of administration and dissatisfaction arise only where the element of discretion is substantial. Departures from clearly specified entitlement criteria or rights are relatively few, and go against the norm of public organizations as rule-bound bodies.

As for the services of trading enterprises, the individual behaves as a conventional consumer, paying a charge for the use of a service. There is little or no connection between the ballot box and the services sold by public enterprise. Public enterprises account for upwards of one-quarter of public employees, and for many basic services upon which families rely, such as electricity, gas, oil, postal and telephone services, and public transportation.

In order for an individual to register an effective choice by voting with his or her purse, the first need is money. The growth of national economies in the postwar era and the concomitant growth in household income has greatly increased personal disposable income. Nearly every family now takes it for granted that it can buy an adequate amount of electricity, heat and light, use the telephone and post, and be able to make some use of public roads and transport. While not everyone has the means to consume all that he or she would like, income limitations are not a major constraint upon the consumption of everyday necessities by a majority of people.

In order to register choice, consumers must also have a choice between suppliers. Where public enterprises are a monopoly, choice cannot be between competing suppliers. Many public enterprises are in fields where one product can be substituted for another; for example, a person may heat a house by electricity, gas, oil, or coal. Even if all four industries are public enterprises, they compete with each other for trade. Similarly, the post office competes with telephones for the communication of messages. In transport there is an even clearer choice between public buses or trains, as against automobiles. The record of public enterprises in the postwar era—some expanding, and others contracting their market share—indicates that they do respond to popular pressures, albeit through market not electoral signals.[45]

Whether the criterion is effectiveness, the generation of contradictions, or popular satisfaction, the evidence emphasizes that changes in the scale and scope of government have not caused major qualitative changes in organizations.

The problems that do exist in an era of big government are real problems, but fundamentally they are not organizational problems. First and foremost is the fiscal problem of financing a continuously growing public budget, while simultaneously avoiding a reduction in take-home pay and maintaining a reasonable level of growth in the national economy to fund future spending commitments.[46] Second is the explicitly normative question about what is the "proper" extent of government activity as against the market or the household, and how much change should occur at the margin of the public and private sectors. Since these are not organizational problems, they will not be resolved by organizational means. It is misleading for politicians or management consultants to claim that it is possible to resolve political controversies by consensual reorganization, or to produce big cash savings by introducing marginal alterations in the efficiency of public organizations based upon misleading inferences from the business world.[47]

For students of organizations, the analysis suggests two priorities, one from the top and another from the bottom. The top-down priority is to give more attention to the conditions and consequences of the pluralization of service-delivery units within a large organization. This problem is not unique to government: it is faced by every nationwide retailer, major manufacturer, and multinational firm. If private-sector organizations see no limit to the extent to which they can expand by replicating service delivery units, why—apart from the problem of finance—should there be problems in government?

From a bottom-up perspective, interactions between consumers and producers of public services are of concern. Often these involve face-to-face relationships, where personalities are important, for example, a doctor and patient or a teacher and child. If there is evidence that children learn more when they like their teacher, how can a large public bureaucracy make sure that each individual teacher is likeable or trained to be likeable? Impersonal relationships are most significant in public enterprises, where a consumer buys a service from a producer (such as an airline pilot or telephone operator) who may never be seen.

Even though growth has not created major organizational problems by claiming more resources and by producing more goods and services, government has made the qualities of public programs more important, not only to public organizations as producers but also to millions of citizens as consumers.

Notes

1. See, for example, Patrick D. Larkey, C. Stolp, and Mark Winer, "Theorizing About the Growth of Government," *Journal of Public Policy* 1, no. 2 (1981), 157–220.

2. Richard Rose, *Understanding Big Government: The Programme Approach* (Beverly Hills, Calif.: Sage, 1984).

3. See Organization for Economic Cooperation and Development, *Social Expenditure, 1960–1990: Problems of Growth and Control* (Paris: OECD, 1985).

4. Ibid.; Peter Saunders and Friedrich Klau, "The Role of the Public Sector," *Economic Studies* [OECD] 4 (1985), 5–239.

5. Richard Rose and Terence Karran, "Inertia or Incrementalism?" in *Comparative Resource Allocation*, ed. A. Groth and L. L. Wade (Beverly Hills and London: Sage Publications, 1984), pp. 43–71.

6. W. A. Niskanen, *Bureaucracy and Representative Government* (Chicago: Aldine-Atherton Press, 1971; André Breton, *The Economic Theory of Representative Government* (London: Macmillan, 1974).

7. C. C. Hood, Meg Huby, and A. Dunsire, "Bureaucrats and Budgeting Benefits," *Journal of Public Policy* 4, no. 3 (1984), 163–79.

8. Richard Rose, *Ministers and Ministries* (Oxford: Clarendon Press, 1987), tables 3.1, 4.3.

9. Chester I. Barnard, *The Functions of the Executive* (Cambridge, Mass.: Harvard University Press, 1938).

10. Hugh Heclo, "Issue Networks and the Executive Establishment," in *The New American Political System*, ed. A. S. King (Washington, D.C.: American Enterprise Institute, 1978), pp. 87–124.

11. Manfred Kochen and Karl W. Deutsch, *Decentralization* (Cambridge, Mass.: Oelgeschlager, Gunn and Hain, 1980), pp. 33ff.

12. See Wallace Oates, *Fiscal Federalism* (New York: Harcourt, Brace, Jovanovich, 1972).

13. See Sidney Tarrow, P. J. Katzenstein, and L. Graziano, eds., *Territorial Politics in Industrial Nations* (New York: Praeger, 1978); Yves Meny and Vincent Wright, eds., *Centre-Periphery Relations in Western Europe* (London: George Allen & Unwin, 1985).

14. Hugh Heclo, *Modern Social Politics in Britain and Sweden* (New Haven, Conn.: Yale University Press, 1974).

15. Phillip L. Davies and Richard Rose, "Are Program Resources Related to Organizational Change?" *European Journal of Political Research*, forthcoming.

16. Francesco Kjellberg, "Local Government Reorganization and the Redevelopment of the Welfare State," *Journal of Public Policy* 5, no. 2 (1985); Arthur B. Gunlicks, ed., *Local Government Reform and Reorganizations: An International Perspective* (Port Washington, N.Y.: Kennikat Press, 1981).

17. See Bleddyn Davies, *Social Needs and Resources in Local Government*

(London: Michael Joseph, 1968; David Heald, *Public Expenditure* (Oxford: Martin Robertson, 1983), pp. 239ff.

18. Christopher Pollitt, *Manipulating the Machine: Change in the Pattern of Ministerial Departments 1960–83* (London: George Allen & Unwin, 1984).

19. Richard Rose, "The Programme Approach to the Growth of Government," *British Journal of Political Science* 15, no. 1 (1985), 1–28; and "Accountability to Electorates and the Market," *Politiques et Management Public* 3, no. 2 (1985), 49–77.

20. Brian W. Hogwood and B. Guy Peters, *Policy Succession* (Brighton: Harvester Press, 1983).

21. Peter Flora and A. J. Heidenheimer, eds., *The Development of Welfare States in Europe and America* (New Brunswick, N.J.: Transaction Books, 1981).

22. See Murray Weidenbaum, *The Modern Public Sector* (New York: Basic Books, 1970); Anthony Barker, ed. *Quangos in Britain: Government and the Networks of Public Policy-Making* (London: Macmillan, 1982).

23. Richard Rose, *Understanding the United Kingdom: The Territorial Dimension in Government* (London: Longman, 1982).

24. Herbert Kaufman, *The Administrative Behavior of Federal Bureau Chiefs* (Washington, D.C.: Brookings, 1981).

25. Renate Mayntz and Fritz Scharpf, *Policy-Making in the German Federal Bureaucracy* (Amsterdam: Elsevier, 1975), p. 69.

26. C. C. Hood and Andrew Dunsire, *Bureaumetrics* (Farnsborough, Hants.: Gower, 1981), pp. 272–75.

27. Management and Personnel Office, *The Civil Service Year Book* (London: HMSO, 1984); Rose, *Ministers and Ministries*, ch. 8.

28. Richard Rose, "On the Priorities of Government," *European Journal of Political Research* 4, no. 3 (1976), 247–89.

29. Richard Rose, "Giving Direction to Public Officials: Signals from the Electorate, the Market, Laws and Expertise," in *Bureaucracy and Public Choice*, ed. Jan-Erik Lane (London: Sage, 1987), pp. 210–29.

30. Phillip L. Davies, "Territory and Function: The Electricity Supply Industry in Great Britain," Ph.D. diss., University of Strathclyde, 1985.

31. Richard Rose, "From Government at the Centre to Nationwide Government," in *Centre-Periphery Relations in Western Europe*, ed. Yves Meny and Vincent Wright (London: Allen & Unwin, 1985), pp. 13–32.

32. Richard Parry, "Territory and Public Employment: A General Model," *Journal of Public Policy* 1, no. 4 (1981).

33. Jim Bulpitt, *Territory and Power in the United Kingdom* (Manchester: Manchester University Press, 1983); Rose, *Understanding the United Kingdom*, pp. 157ff.

34. See A. F. P. Wassenberg and J. Kooiman, "Advice and the Reduction of Overload," in *Challenge to Governance*, ed. Richard Rose (London: Sage, 1980), pp. 127–50; Barker, ed., *Quangos in Britain*.

35. See, for example, K. W. Hanf and F. W. Scharpf, eds., *Interorganizational Policy Making: Limits to Coordination and Central Control* (London: Sage, 1978); Deil Wright, *Understanding Intergovernmental Relations*, 2d ed. (Monterey, Calif.: Brooks/Cole, 1982).

36. See C. C. Hood, *The Limits of Administration* (London: John Wiley, 1976).

37. Jeffrey Pressman and Aaron Wildavsky, *Implementation* (Berkeley and Los Angeles, University of California Press, 1973).

38. Elinor Bowen, "The Pressman-Wildavsky Paradox," *Journal of Public Policy* 2, no. 1 (1982), 1–22.

39. Harold Wilensky, *The Welfare State and Equality* (Berkeley and Los Angeles: University of California Press, 1975).

40. Heclo, *Modern Social Politics in Britain and Sweden;* Hogwood and Peters, *Policy Succession.*

41. Allen Schick, "The Coordination Option," in *Federal Reorganization: What Have We Learned*, ed. Peter Szanton (Chatham, N.J.: Chatham House, 1981).

42. Daniel Tarschys, "Curbing Public Expenditure: Current Trends," *Journal of Public Policy* 5, no. 1 (1985), 23–67; *The Public Expenditure Process: Learning by Doing*, ed. David Heald and Richard Rose (London: Public Finance Foundation, 1987).

43. Rose, *Understanding Big Government*, table 6.3.

44. Charles T. Goodsell, *The Case for Bureaucracy*, 2d ed. (Chatham, N.J.: Chatham House, 1985), table 6.1.

45. Rose, "The Programme Approach."

46. See Rose and Karran, "Inertia or Incrementalism?"

47. See Peter Grace, *War on Waste* (New York: Macmillan, 1984).

CHAPTER 5

Policy Responses to Economic Stress and Decline in Anglo-Atlantic Democracies

Norman C. Thomas

THE ECONOMIES of the three Anglo-Atlantic democracies, the United States, Great Britain, and Canada, faltered badly during the global recession that has prevailed for much of the time since 1970. Unemployment, inflation, slow growth in productivity and gross national product, and increasing vulnerability to foreign competition have imposed great stress on the three countries and their governments. The policies they adopted in response to general economic decline have had mixed results; economic performance has improved in certain respects but sustained relief from economic difficulties has not been achieved and future prospects are highly uncertain.

In this regard, the United States, Britain, and Canada do not differ markedly from other industrial democracies.[1] I have limited this study to the three Anglo-Atlantic democracies because of their common political heritage, similar patterns of economic organization, and the pluralistic basis of their sociopolitical systems. There are, of course, differences in their political and economic structures and processes, and their economic policies have manifested differences in content and timing. Each country has shown a high degree of organizational experimentation in its approach to public administration and each has modulated its use of economic policy instruments in accordance with its particular economic and political circumstances.

There are several possible explanations of the similar patterns of policy responses to economic stress and decline adopted by the United States, Britain and Canada in the 1970–1982 period and the similar outcomes of those policies. Of equal interest is the question of why those similarities have either become less striking or have been replaced by differences in policies and outcomes beginning in 1983. One of the most widely held explanations is that political institutions and processes, more than any other factors, most satisfactorily account for democratic governments' choices of macroeconomic policies. Although I do not deny the importance of governmental structures and procedures, I believe that other factors have also contributed substantially to American, British, and Canadian economic policy in the period since 1970.

Specifically, I maintain that between 1970 and 1982, when the United States, Britain, and Canada adopted similar policy responses to economic decline and experienced roughly similar results, the pluralistic pattern of democratic politics was of greater importance in determining policy than institutional factors. Since 1982, when differences in economic policies and policy outcomes in the three countries have become apparent, I maintain that pluralistic politics continues strongly to affect policy choices and outcomes; however, its influence has been modified by the strong ideological postures of President Ronald Reagan and Prime Minister Margaret Thatcher. I also contend that explanations for choosing policies to cope with economic stress and the limited success of most of those policies are primarily political rather than economic. That is to say, the explanations are not likely to be found in economic theories or in the domination in policymaking circles of one economic theory—as, for example, Keynesianism or monetarism—over another.

In this chapter I examine general and country-specific explanations of the effects of political factors on the efforts of the United States, Britain, and Canada to manage their economies since 1970. For most of that time, the economies of the three countries have been in decline. Beginning in 1983, some aspects of the economic performance of each country have improved and the United States has been, at least temporarily, more successful in restoring employment. But it is by no means clear how long the recovery can be sustained and whether the current robust American economic performance was purchased at too costly a fiscal price.

The political factors I will analyze most closely are (1) the organization of political and social forces and (2) the pattern of institutions and processes. The first focuses on how societies are organized so as to identify demands and convert them into public policy. It also concerns the effects of those organizational patterns on overall governability and the effectiveness of public policies. The United States, Britain, and Canada all manifest a highly developed pluralist pattern of social and political organization. The second factor uses as principal explanatory variables the degree of centralization in governmental and political structures and the degree of integration in decision-making processes. In the United States decision making is highly decentralized and fragmented. Britain manifests a much greater degree of centralization and decision integration. Canada is an amalgam: a highly decentralized system that has integrated decision making.

The recent emphasis on institutional factors as determinants of public policy is a healthy and appropriate corrective to approaches that rely almost exclusively on individual and aggregate measures of behavior.[2] However, I believe that structures and processes are but the products of the societies in which they function. At most, cross-national differences in governmental institutions provide different terrains and rules of the game on which social forces contend. The pluralistic pattern of politics that characterizes how social and political forces are mobilized appears to have been a more important determinant of economic policy and its effectiveness than institutional arrangements such as federalism, separation of powers, and a competitive, disciplined, responsible party system. The chapter concludes by proposing a causal model of economic decline in which a highly developed pattern of pluralistic politics is the primary determinant.

Economic Policies Under Stress: 1970–1984

This section provides a brief narrative description of major economic policy developments in the United States, Britain, and Canada during the period of economic stress that began around 1970. The purpose is not to analyze these actions in detail, but to establish a background for the subsequent attempt to explain the economic difficulties of the three countries and their apparent inability to solve them through the principal policy instruments at their disposal.

During the 1970s the United States, Britain, and Canada responded to economic decline in roughly similar ways. Monetarism replaced the Keynesian fiscal strategy of demand management as the principal instrument of macroeconomic policy. Each country experimented with an incomes policy. (The incomes policy approach proved at least moderately successful in curbing inflation without a corresponding increase in unemployment, but it was abandoned when support for it collapsed.) Elements of an industrial policy have been adopted in all three countries, but none can be said to have embraced a comprehensive industrial policy strategy. The policies that the three countries adopted in the 1970s in response to economic decline were similar, but not identical; they varied considerably in timing, and began to vary substantively in the early 1980s, especially following the advent of the Reagan administration.

The results of these policies were similar through the recession of 1981–1982. The three countries experienced unemployment figures that reached post–World War II highs, double-digit inflation rates, and little economic growth. All have shared in the recovery that began in 1983 and each has reduced the annual rate of inflation below 4 percent (4.0 percent in Britain, 2.1 percent in the United States, and 4.0 percent in Canada in 1987). However, unemployment has fallen more sharply in the United States (to 6.6 percent) than in Britain (11.0 percent) or Canada (9.6 percent).[3] Also, the American economy grew at a more rapid rate (3.7 percent in 1983 and an estimated 6.9 percent in 1984) than Britain's (2.5 percent in 1983 and an estimated 2.3 percent in 1984) or Canada's (2.0 percent in 1983 and an estimated 4.5 percent in 1984).[4] In addition, the three governments, by virtue of their function as employers, vary substantially in the leverage they exert on wages and prices. Because the British government is a very large employer, it has been able to implement a de facto incomes policy which the United States government cannot do. Canada falls somewhere between the two in this regard.

There are several possible explanations of the robustness of the American recovery, two of which have gained wide acceptance. First, it is argued that the reductions in personal and corporate income taxes legislated in 1981, as well as the massive increases in defense spending initiated at that time, combined to provide a substantial fiscal stimulus (financed by borrowing) that was not experienced in Britain or Canada. Second, real wages are said to have risen much less in the United States than elsewhere since 1981 and this has led to increased investment and consumer spending. Whether the improved performance of the U.S. economy can be sustained is not yet known. The answer will depend, at least in part, on the effect of increased federal borrowing on interest rates, investment, and savings, and on the willingness of workers to restrain their demands for increases in wages and benefits.

General Explanatory Approaches

Explanations of governments' choices of policies to combat economic stress and the limited success of those policies are not to be found in economic theories or in the domination of a particular theory in policymaking circles.[5] The two leading economic theories offer contrasting explanations and policy prescriptions.[6]

According to the Keynesians, the root of the problem lies in the decline in the aggregate demand that resulted from oil price increases in 1973 and 1979 and the failure of governments to compensate adequately for the drop in demand by expansionary fiscal and monetary policies. In contrast, monetarists view the oil price increases as temporary abnormalities that would have rapidly been disposed of by market forces but for governmental attempts to stimulate demand and prevent the decline in real wages necessary for the restoration of full employment. The monetarist prescription calls for restrictive monetary policies to control the growth of the money supply bolstered by actions to depress real wages.

Neither approach is free from serious drawbacks. If the expanded aggregate demand advocated by the Keynesians is not complemented by relatively stable wages and prices, then increased inflation rather than economic growth and full employment are the likely result. On the other hand, if controlled growth of the money supply and stimulation of investment are not complemented by falling prices and wages, then economic output and employment will decline more than inflation. The proponents of neither approach are comfortable with governmental efforts to control wages and prices, nor is it politically feasible to do so for a sustained period in any of the industrialized countries.

Explanations of the choice of policy instruments to combat economic stress and decline and the limited success of those instruments lie primarily in political rather than economic factors. Specifically, they are to be found in the limited capacity of modern industrial democracies to achieve their goals and in the interaction between economic conditions, institutional constraints, and the inertia of established policies. There are general and country-specific theoretical approaches to the subject that are based on political factors.

At least four types of general explanatory approaches can be identified: the statist approach, the social organization approach, the institutional approach, and the behavioral approach. The literature seems to fall logically into these categories, but undoubtedly other classification schemes could be devised. I will describe the principal features of each approach and examine its utility for explaining governments' policy responses to economic decline.

The Statist Approach

As an explanatory concept, the state has experienced a renaissance in recent years. The key element in the statist approach is the distinction it makes between state and society. The state is viewed as an autonomous actor that defines and pursues goals (the national interest) that are separate from those of any other social group.[7] Central decision makers in the institutions that comprise the state have a profound impact on the development and content of public policy that is "not simply reflective of the demands or interests of social groups, classes, or society."[8] The statist approach is also distinguished, then, by the importance assigned to the concept of the national interest and one identification of that interest, the collective good of society, with the goals of central decision makers.

Stephen Krasner has employed a statist approach in a study of United States policy regarding foreign raw materials investments. His approach involves: "(a) demonstrating empirically that American central decision makers have sought a consistent set of goals . . . and (b) defining the conditions under which they have been able to obtain their goals in the face of international, and more important, domestic contraints."[9] He recognizes the importance of constraints from private groups and notes that the American state has limited ability to influence private groups because of the fragmentation and dispersion of political power. His principal conclusion is that "no institution in the United States, public or private, has the power to compel others to act, but many can effectively veto initiatives that they oppose."[10]

Krasner's conclusion is hardly different from what one would expect of an analysis that employed the pluralist/interest-group liberalism approach that dominates the study of American politics. He argues that his statist approach is superior to pluralism on the ground that it explains why central decision makers, at least in the cases that he examined, often pursued goals that were at variance with those of the private interests that pluralist theory predicts would prevail.[11] The adoption of policies not directly responsive to private interests is not conclusive evidence that the state, as an autonomous actor, defines and pursues the collective good, nor does it demonstrate the inappropriateness of the pluralist perspective. There are multiple groups and interests in society and in government that pursue a wide range of interests that are ideological as well as economic and strategic.

Given that America has, as Krasner acknowledges, a "weak state" and that the British and Canadian states are marginally stronger and weaker, respectively, the statist approach is hardly better than any other for analyzing governmental policy responses to economic stress. The fundamental characteristic of the statist approach, the concept of the state as an automonous actor with objectives and resources that are qualitatively distinct from those of other social institutions and which determines and protects the common good, is lacking in empirical support. The boundary between public and private sectors is blurred in the three Anglo-Atlantic democracies. The exchange of information and personnel is continuous. Accountability for public policies is difficult to affix and the concept of a general public or national interest, although widely recognized, is only a normative standard which policymakers routinely invoke as a rationale for widely diverse policy preferences.

At most, statism directs attention to the need for policymakers and analysts to consider the welfare of society at large. The statist approach also alerts analysts to the factors that affect governments' ability to accomplish their objectives, the policy instruments at their disposal, their financial and human resources, and the domestic and international constraints that limit their actions.

The Social Organization Approach

The second category of explanatory approaches focuses on how societies are organized for the process of identifying demands and converting them into public policy, and how those organizational patterns affect overall governability and the effectiveness of public policies.

A well-known example of the social organization approach is Mancur Olson's *The Rise and Decline of Nations*. Olson's theory holds that economic growth, stagflation, and social rigidities in highly organized societies are caused by dense networks of powerful "distributional coalitions" that retard and even prevent adaptation to changing conditions. Distributional coalitions in the economy, such as cartels and national labor unions, keep real wages and prices from falling and thus prevent the use of unemployed resources. When public policies to stimulate demand are adopted, distributional coalitions react by setting higher prices and wages.

For Olson, the United States and Britain are countries with strong distributional coalitions in which unemployment and inflation rose sharply during the 1970s. In contrast, Olson points out that West Germany and Japan, countries with fewer encompassing special-interest organizations, have had lower rates of unemployment and inflation.[12] It is significant that distributional coalitions in the United States and Britain were not disrupted by World War II as were those in Germany and Japan. The longer a society goes without an upheaval, Olson argues, the more powerful its structure of interest organizations and the greater difficulty it will have in sustaining economic growth and adapting to change. The principal policy implication that Olson derives from his anlaysis is that no macroeconomic policy can work effectively without an "open and competitive environment"—hence the need for policies to restrict the market power of special interests and for government to refrain from intervening on their behalf.[13]

Olson's approach is an intellectual tour de force that holds considerable attraction because of its simplicity. He directly and plausibly explains complex phenomena that the most sophisticated economic theories have not accounted for satisfatorily. The problem, according to one critic, is that Olson attributes too much economic variance to the presence of a pluralist pattern of organization and he neglects the institutional structures in government and the economy that affect economic performance.[14] (I will argue later that with respect to the United States, Britain, and Canada, institutional factors are not as important as pluralist sociopolitical organization as determinants of economic policy and its effectiveness.)

Similar criticism can be directed at a second social organization approach—corporatism—which is best exemplified by the work of Phillipe Schmitter. The corporatist approach holds that the "relative governability" of advanced capitalist societies is a function of the "discrete processes that identify, package, promote, and implement potential interest claims and demands."[15] One of the three indicators of governability is fiscal effectiveness (the others are ruliness and stability). The key to understanding the problem of ungovernability lies in "functional interest intermediation through highly formalized and specialized organizations in direct relationship with the bureaucratic apparatus of the modern state."[16] The pursuit of self-interest by specialized organizations representing "class, sectoral, professional, regional, ethnic, sexual and generational interests" has replaced parties and elections as the primary means of placing problems and issues on the agenda of the state.

According to Schmitter, a pluralist pattern of interest intermediation (or social organization) is an obstacle to governability in advanced capitalist states.[17] In contrast, countries having a "societal corporatist" mode of interest intermediation tend to be more governable and to have greater fiscal effectiveness. Schmitter uses the term corporatism in a nonideological sense to refer to institutional behavior and structural arrangements in the political process. He defines societal corporatism as a mode of interest intermediation in which "constituent units are organized into a limited number of singular, compulsory, hierarchically ordered and functionally differentiated categories, recognized, licensed or encouraged by the state and granted a representational monopoly within their respective categories in exchange for observing certain controls on their selection of leaders and articulation of demands and supports."[18]

Schmitter uses the degree of organizational centralization and associational monopoly to measure societal corporatism in fifteen Western democracies and ranks the United States and Canada as tied for eleventh and Britain fourteenth. On a measure of fiscal ineffectiveness, based on the increase in government borrowing and the decrease in reliance on indirect taxation, the United States tied for first (with Italy), Britain ranked third, and Canada tied for sixth (with France and West Germany). The rank-order correlation between the measure of societal corporatism and fiscal ineffectiveness was −0.63.[19] However, the lack of extensive variability on the two measures by the United States, Britain, and Canada limits the utility of Schmitter's approach for this analysis. None of the three countries has a strongly corporatist pattern of social organization and all three are quite fiscally ineffective relative to other Western democracies.

The Institutional Approach

The third general approach explains the choice of economic policies and their effectiveness in terms of formal political institutions and processes. This approach uses the degree of concentration (as opposed to fragmentation) in government institutions and decision-making processes as its principal explanatory variable. The United States, with its federal system, separation of powers, weak political parties, and sprawling autonomous bureaucracy pressured by interest groups and legislative committees, provides an example of a highly fragmented polity. Britain exemplifies a more highly centralized polity with its unitary structure, a fused executive and legislative leadership that dominates Parliament through disciplined political parties, and a strong bureaucracy controlled by a cohesive elite. Canada falls between the United States and Britain: it has a federal system whose provinces are more able to influence the central government than are the American states, its central government closely resembles that of Britain, and its bureaucracy is dominated by "mandarins" who almost match their British counterparts in their ability to resist interest-group pressure and to influence public policy.

The degree of concentration versus fragmentation affects the ability to coordinate various economic policy instruments—as, for example, monetary and fiscal policies—and it influences the choice of policy instruments and the targets toward which the instruments are directed—such as whether monetary policy focuses on interest rates or the money supply.[20] James Alt and John Woolley suggest that since control of monetary policy is typically less fragmented than control of fiscal policy it is employed sooner and more often in response to economic conditions. They also suggest that corporatist arguments may be used in policy bargaining to overcome the consequences of fragmentation.

One of the most comprehensive institutional approaches is that developed by Fritz Scharpf. He argues that two sets of institutional structures, the private-sector industrial relations system and the governmental decision-making system, influence and constrain policy choices. Since all institutions generate substantial policy inertia, Scharpf continues, economic performance in the face of new problems depends on the accidental congruence between established policies and those problems. If such policies fail, he concludes, institutional structures will determine the ability of a government to adopt innovative alternatives.[21]

Scharpf's two primary structural variables are dichotomous: decision-making institutions are horizontally integrated or fragmented and vertically centralized or decentralized. The decision-making process is also characterized by two dichotomous variables: it is (1) either unilateral or multilateral among the institutional power centers involved and (2) exclusive or inclusive of the range of social, economic, and political interests involved. The United States has a decision-making structure that is fragmented and decentralized and a decision-making process that is multilateral and inclusive. Britain's structure is fragmented and centralized and its process unilateral and exclusive. Scharpf's principal expectation is that with respect to economic policy, "Concentrated and centralized institutions will be more capable of innovation than fragmented and decentralized institutions, and that countries with unilateral and inclusive patterns of decision-making are more likely to innovate (and more likely to make mistakes) than countries with a strong commitment to multilateral and inclusive decision-making."[22] It does not appear that Scharpf's structural approach can account for the modest differences in the economic policies of the United States, Britain, and Canada. Neither the decision-making institutions nor the processes in the three countries appear related to the policies adopted, the timing of the adoptions, or the limited success of the policies.

The Behavioral Approach

The fourth category of general explanations of the choice of economic policies and their limited effectiveness focuses on the behavior of political elites and masses in industrial democracies. A major variant of this approach holds that voters tend to "vote their pocketbooks" and that consequently political leaders bid for electoral support by altering economic policy according to the electoral cycle. As elections approach, expansionary fiscal and monetary policies are in vogue, while less popular, restrictive policies tend to be enforced in postelection periods. According to Edward Tufte, there is substantial political control of the economy, at least in the United States, but it often leads to "perverse outcomes in economic policy." The political business cycle results in stop-and-go economic policies in industrial democracies as politicians exhibit a bias toward policies with "immediate, higly visible benefits and deferred, hidden costs."[23] Economic policymaking tends to have a short-run focus based on the electoral cycle, and long-range planning is discouraged.

Undoubtedly democratic policymakers take electoral and other political considerations into account as they attempt to deal with economic decline. But the political-business cycle theory assumes a higher degree of predictability and control than is likely to be attainable in practice.[24] Management of the economy through public policy in response to electoral forces is somewhat beyond the capabilities of most democratic governments.

A second variant of the behavioral approach to explaining economic policymaking focuses on the politics of governmental distribution. Richard Rose and Guy Peters, in a study centered on the concept of political bankruptcy, argue that democratic politicans have failed to recognize or accept the limitations that have resulted from the slowing of economic growth in the 1970s and have overloaded their political economies. Overload occurs when the costs of public policy and take-home pay for individuals exceed the gross national product. In overloading their economies, governments risk political bankruptcy, a condition in which they lose their economic effectiveness and popular consent. Loss of effectiveness occurs when governments consistently spend more than their economies produce and loss of consent follows. A politically bankrupt government can stay in office, but it is "bereft of authority, existing in a limbo of ineffectiveness."[25]

The primary cause of the overload that brings governments to the brink of political bankruptcy is the failure to control the escalating costs of public policy that result from the establishment of new programs and the growth and maturation of existing ones. Governments facing political bankruptcy have adoped various strategies. They may have done little or nothing, waiting Micawberlike for something to turn up. Or they resort to placebos such as planning and exhortative campaigns to increase productivity. They also search seriously for means of increasing the GNP. At some point, most of them try to hide their problems through inflation. But the money illusion, which makes the GNP appear larger than it is in real terms, is of only limited duration and as people come to realize that they are increasingly worse off, "inflation itself becomes a symptom of overload."[26] Eventually, as time runs out, politicans confront two unpalatable alternatives to avoid political bankruptcy: they can either cut take-home pay by increasing taxes or reduce the cost of public policy by cutting spending. If they try to "paper over the gap between national commitment and the national product," they only encourage political bankruptcy.[27]

For Rose and Peters the choice between cutting take-home pay and curtailing the costs of public policy is a political one and they clearly favor the latter alternative. They argue that the problems resulting from cutting take-home pay—increased tax evasion and the development of an underground economy—will undermine governmental authority and thus accelerate political bankruptcy. The consequences of allowing spending for public policies to continue to expand more rapidly than productivity is a totally dependent society with ever-increasing power in public bureaucracies.

The Rose and Peters prescription is a moderate one; they advocate slowing the growth of government spending rather than reversing the direction of public policy. The task will not be easy. No set of institutional or procedural mechanisms will be sufficient to curb the escalating cost of public policy and provide assurance against political bankruptcy. The risk of political bankruptcy can be reduced only if governmental decision makers "are prepared to show the political will to limit growth."[28] Nor does the problem lie primarily with citizens and their alleged propensity to elect only politicians who will provide them with ever-expanding benefits, as the initiative for expanding spending lies with governments.

Rose and Peters place responsibility for fiscal and economic ineffectiveness squarely on public officials. They also reject the idea that patterns of social organization are primarily responsible. Indeed, they argue that corporatism is of limited effectiveness in resolving economic problems since freedom of contract means that agreements are subject to veto by each corporate party. The success of corporate agreements is contingent upon the "unlikely mutual conjunction of interest of business, labor and politicians."[29] Institutional arrangements are accorded greater weight in the Rose and Peters explanation. They maintain that the absence of an all-powerful central decision maker in democratic governments limits the ability to manage the economy in ways that economists presuppose. In addition, they argue that strengthening central banks reduces the risk of overloading the political economy. Independent central banks can pressure economically weak governments to avoid policies that cause political bankruptcy.

Although Rose and Peters give clear indications of how political decision makers must act to avoid political bankruptcy, they do not explain why some of them have the will to do so while many others do not. Nor do they indicate how a country can elect officials possessed of the requisite will to resist pressures and temptations to increase spending. In this respect their approach stops short. Is will lacking because of the excess of of pluralism, as Olson suggests, or because of responsiveness to political business cycles? Or do institutions and processes in governments impede the emergence of officials with the will to adopt politically unpopular policies that are needed to avoid political bankruptcy? Surely the presence or absence of the will to act is not merely the result of a random process.

The Rose and Peters political bankruptcy approach seems quite applicable to the United States, Britain, and Canada. Officials in each country have lacked the will to restrain the growth of spending and to take other politically unpopular measures. But the approach provides no indication of why they do not have that will.

Country-Specific Approaches

In addition to the general explanatory approaches to governments' relatively ineffective policy responses to economic decline, the literature abounds with studies of individual countries. These explanations overlap to some extent with the general approaches, so they are not necessarily idiosyncratic. In this section, I will examine several explanations of American and British economic policy and performance since 1970 (comparable Canadian literature is sparse) with a view toward identifying those elements that hold promise for comparative analysis.

The United States

Explanations of the economic difficulties of the United States since 1970 and its inability to adopt policies to cope with them range from Maxwell Newton's *The Fed* to Robert Reich's *The Next American Frontier.* I will examine these along with Lester Thurow's *Zero-Sum Society*, Alan Wolfe's *American Impasse*, and David Calleo's *Imperious Economy*.[30]

Newton combines a narrow institutional approach with an espousal of monetarist theory. He places the blame for the economic troubles of the United States and its failure to correct them squarely on the Federal Reserve and its policies. According to Newton, the Fed's independence gives it a profound influence over the economy, no matter who is president. By failing persistently to prevent excessive monetary growth, a consequence of targeting its actions on interest rates rather than the money supply, the Fed has supposedly led the economy through continuously accelerating inflationary cycles. Newton claims that the Fed's chairmen, beginning with Arthur Burns in 1971, have been activists motivated by political objectives rather than economic theory. Moreover, to compound the damage its policies have done, the Fed has seriously impaired the financial services industry through its regulatory policies. The combination of inflation caused by the Fed and increasing taxation resulting from bracket creep has, according to Newton, undermined the financial position of private corporations, forcing them deeply into short-term debt at high rates of interest. This in turn has resulted in declining growth and rising unemployment. Newton's solution is simple and direct: abolish the Fed.

In some respects one wishes that monetary policy was the omnipotent policy instrument that Newton believes it to be and that America's economic difficulties could be ended by excising the malignant institution that has misapplied it. Surely if the solution were as simple as he maintains, something along that line would have been tried by now. Even if Newton's view of monetary policy is fully accepted, he neglects to explain the alleged institutional dominance of the Fed over the political branches of government and the corporations and financial institutions it has supposedly driven to the wall. Newton's contribution is to call attention to monetary policy and the central bank as important aspects of the government's economic role.[31]

In contrast to Newton's sharply focused approach, the other four studies attribute America's difficulties to systemic features and long-term patterns of economic development and general governmental policies. All of them cite the fragmented patterns of political decision making as a primary reason for the failure of public policy to solve economic problems.

Lester Thurow argues that there is a substantial zero-sum element in economic decisions. That is, most viable policies require that some people suffer losses to balance the gains of others. Historically, American politics has been able to allocate gains but it has been unable to deal with economic losses. Until the 1970s, economic growth made it possible to avoid dealing with the question of who will bear the losses. This strategy was aptly embodied in President Kennedy's aphorism, "A rising tide floats all boats." Growth, however, has become increasingly difficult to achieve and sustain due to resource constraints, international economic interdependence, and foreign competition. Moreover, demands on government for economic security and the reduction of risks have grown more rapidly than the economy.

Policy solutions are available but the political process cannot adopt them because of its inability to allocate the necessary economic losses. Political fragmentation, weak political parties, and the lack of an effective means of holding officials accountable has resulted in political paralysis: "We each veto the other's initiatives but none of us has the ability to create successful initiatives ourselves."[32] Thurow's solution is to revamp the political system so that accountability for policy failure can be established.

Thurow's diagnosis and explanation of the problem appear to be on the mark. However, his solution, which each generation of political scientists since Woodrow Wilson's has advocated, is not in prospect. Nor does Thurow offer suggestions how it might be achieved. Furthermore, the presence of government by disciplined, responsible political parties in Britain and Canada has not spared those countries kinds of economic distress and policy failures that the United States has experienced.

Alan Wolfe and David Calleo offer somewhat similar policy-related explanations of economic decline and the inability to overcome it. Wolfe asserts that "America's impasse" is due to an unrestrained politics of growth coupled to imperial expansion. According to Celleo, the economic problems of the United States are a consequence of persistent overextension at home and abroad.

Wolfe argues that the politics of growth was conducted without "political vision" grounded in ideology. This enabled the country to avoid confronting hard redistributional choices (similar to Thurow's allocation of losses). The impasse did not result from growth itself, but from the political price paid for it: the loss of "the capacity of either major party or dominant sets of ideas to establish goals and an agenda for reaching them." Wolfe's solution calls for political revitalization based on creation of a "strong government capable of planning and intervening in the public interest" and recognition by the people of their class interest and willingness to use government to support that interest.[33]

Wolfe's ideologically oriented approach is of questionable utility. Politics in America has never had a strong class basis. Indeed, as much of the literature reviewed here points out, it is organized around powerful interests. The claim that current problems are due to the absence of class-oriented ideological politics cannot be empirically supported. Nor does it appear likely that such a politics will emerge in the foreseeable future. But Wolfe's suggestion that the unrestrained pursuit of growth has contributed to the economic difficulties of the United States is compatible with the explanations offered by Thurow and Calleo.

Calleo calls for greater discipline in defining national objectives and in economic policy itself. He would abandon the subsidies and tariffs that underwrite business failure and reduce economic adaptability and rely more on the "creative destruction" of the free market noted by Schumpeter.[34] But Calleo regards the adoption of disciplined long-range policy as unlikely because of the fragmentation of governmental authority and the institutionalization of adversarial politics in the United States. He suggests that an initial step toward political reform would be the abandonment by political scientists of the pluralist model of politics with its brokered bargaining among organized interests. Although Calleo concedes that the pluarlist model "describes a large share of reality," he warns that it risks becoming a "learned apology for a prodigiously wasteful system of government incapable of disciplining its own claims on the society's resources."[35]

The issue of whether pluralism should be abandoned as a conceptual model because of its conservative implications and the uses made of it in defense of the established regime has been extensively argued elsewhere and I will not rehash it here. Calleo is quite explicit, however, in designating it as the major obstacle to the adoption of disciplined economic policies. In this respect, Calleo reinforces Olson's argument that distributional coalitions are a major cause of economic decline.

The most comprehensive approach to explaining America's economic difficulties is that offered by Robert Reich. He argues that the critical determinant of economic progress in any society is the pattern of organization in business and government and the resulting relationship between the private and public sectors. American (and to a large extent British) prosperity in the period that ended around 1970 "was a product of the alliance between high-volume machinery and large-scale organization."[36] In the present era, organizational structures, in which the largest firms dominate each industry, have prevented adaptation to economic change. Mass-production industries in the United States have become increasingly noncompetitive as high-volume machinery has been moved into countries with low-cost, unsophisticated labor. Future prosperity for the United States, Reich argues, lies in products that are "precision-manufactured," customized, and "technology driven."[37] These products require a flexible system of production based on skilled labor that is quickly adaptable to change.

However, the United States has been slow in shifting to a flexible system of production because "its organizations are based on stability rather than flexibility."[38] Any move toward restructuring productive organization so that the relationships between business and labor and between the private and public sectors are less rigid is likely to be resisted because it threatens vested economic interests.

Reich maintains that the American political system has been unable to make the decisions required to accomplish the necessary organizational restructuring. Its political parties have decayed, interest groups concentrate on increasing government benefits for their members, and the resolution of hard distributional choices (Thurow's allocation of losses) has devolved upon the courts as elected officials shun political controversy in pursuit of reelection. The United States lacks crucial public policies, such as an incomes policy to control inflation, an industrial policy to stimulate growth, regulatory policies to allocate the costs and benefits of achieving public goals, and training and retraining policies to develop human capital. Revitalization of political institutions and processes so that adaptive policies can be adopted is Reich's solution.

Essentially, Reich's position is that the United States is suffering from organizational ridigity brought about by its own past successes. The necessary organizational restructuring is being prevented by a conservative pattern of interest-group politics that has rendered government ineffective. Here Reich appears to provide additional support for the Olson thesis. However, in a review of Olson's *Rise and Decline*, he attacked its omission of the social dimension in interest-group politics. Reich argued that although interest groups do obstruct economic change they also serve as vehicles for democratic participation and as checks on the power of the state. More important, "Through the group experience a social morality is defined and refined."[39] According to Reich, the best way to avoid or overcome the obstacles to economic change posed by interest groups is through a democratized system of economic planning that equitably allocates the costs and benefits of that change.

Four of the five explanations of America's inability to deal effectively with its recent economic problems place substantial blame on its political system. The inability of Thurow's zero-sum society to allocate the losses resulting from public policy, the unrestrained pursuit of growth deplored by Wolfe, the economic overextension at home and abroad that Calleo attacks, and Reich's structural rigidities are due in large part to a fragmented political system that is dominated by organized interests and is incapable of adopting necessary corrective policies. Interestingly, all four studies stress the inseparability of economics from politics and all urge some form of political revitalization. However, none offers a program for accomplishing that elusive goal. Finally, all argue that ultimate solutions lie in the pursuit of social justice rather than reliance on market forces. The fifth explanation, Newton's polemic against the Fed, blames a single government institution for impairing the operation of market forces so extensively that the economy has been severely if not permanently damaged.

Great Britain

Explanations of Britain's economic decline range from general studies of politics and policymaking such as Samuel Beer's *Britain Against Itself* and Douglas Ashford's *Policy and Politics in Britain* to the memoirs of two former high-level economic policymakers: Sir Leo Pliatzky, a career official, and Joel Barnett (now Lord Barnett), a Labour Member of Parliament who served as chief secretary to the Treasury in the Wilson-Callaghan government of 1974–1979.[40] Among the other explanations examined were an economist's analysis of economic policies and reasons for their failure in the period 1964–1977;[41] a descriptive account of economic policymaking;[42] an analysis of public expenditure control in the early 1970s by two American political scientists;[43] two socialist-oriented critiques of British economic policy;[44] and an analysis that emphasized institutional domination of policy and policymaking by the Treasury and the financial community.[45]

Three principal explanations of Britain's economic decline and the limited success of its economic policies emerge from this diverse array of studies: (1) overextended foreign and domestic policy commitments; (2) institutional and structural weaknesses in government and the economy; and (3) the negative effects of British politics on economic policy.

Foreign policy—related explanations criticize Britain's maintenance of imperial responsibilities and pretensions such as military spending second only to that of the United States among Western countries as a percentage of GNP, defense of sterling as a reserve currency, and a sizable foreign aid program.[46] The major argument is that long after the British economy lost the capacity to support an imperial role for Britain in world affairs, governments of both parties have insisted on playing such a role. The consequence has been that the investment that would have kept the economy modern and competitive has been insufficient. Capital has been directed overseas when it should have been put to work in Britain. Domestic policy explanations argue that the commitments of the welfare state have outstripped the capacity of the economy to keep them either because politicians have overpromised or because investment and economic growth have been neglected.[47]

The institutional-structural approach cites the influence of governmental and external forces in shaping economic policy. The primary government institutions and influences are the Treasury, the Bank of England, and the higher civil service. The major external structures and forces are the financial markets (the City of London, or the City). William Keegan and Rupert Pennat-Rea maintain that there is a cycle of influence over economic policy based on the party in power and the time since the last election.[48] Under governments in the 1970s, the unions and the City at various times held considerable sway while inside the government the Treasury and the Bank exercised the greatest influence over the cabinet on economic policy issues. However, Keegan and Pennant-Rea attribute no undesirable consequences to the role played by the Treasuy and the Bank.

Hugh Heclo and Aaron Wildavsky, in a study of expenditure control during the early 1970s, maintained that policy was made by a small private political administrative community at the center of British government. They found that community to be dominated by Treasury civil servants because politicians were weak and uncreative.[49] Like Keegan and Pennant-Rea, Heclo and Wildavsky did not blame this coterie of officials for Britain's economic difficulties.

Sidney Pollard and Michael Meacher, in separate studies, also identified an influential group of higher civil servants centered in the Treasury. They claim, however, that these officials have been excessively sensitive to the needs of the City. Pollard asserts that the Treasury has consistently placed foreign trade and overseas investment (the concerns of the financial community) ahead of home investment, economic growth, and expanded productivity. He accuses both the officials and the City of having a "contempt for production" that has caused much of Britain's economic distress.[50]

Meacher claims that the higher civil service, with determinative power over policy based on its continuity and control of information, is linked to the business and financial power structure. The result of this alliance is the emergence of the state as the "guardian and protector of the economic interests that predominate it." The use of this concerted power to serve the interests of the dominant class, even when the effects are contrary to the national interests, "constitutes the central impediment that has brought about, and prevents escape from Britain's persisting economic decline."[51]

Undoubtedly the Treasury and the civil service are an independent force shaping economic policy. But evidence that they are partners with the City in a conspiracy that has driven Britain to the wall for private gain is not persuasive. If it were, what then could one say about unions, political parties, elections, and the process of responsible democratic government? Surely they amount to more than a social fraud that only a few perceptive observers, with the aid of particular ideological insights, have been able to discover.

The power of Britain's unions is also cited as a cause of economic decline and the inability of governments to stop it. Pollard notes the traditional resistance of British unions to technological innovation and the drive of the unions to reduce the rate of output of their workers rather than to maximize it. Keegan and Pennant-Rea, while not holding that unions are too powerful for the good of the economy, maintain that union influence is cyclical and conclude that unions have had both strong positive and negative effects on the economy. Certainly governments have found that they cannot successfully implement an incomes policy without union cooperation. Samuel Brittain argues that unions are more powerful in Britain than in other industrial democracies and that they make extensive demands on economic policymakers and complicate their task.[52] Beer views the British labor scene as self-defeating: the unions are too highly organized for market forces to prevail but not organized enough to yield overall sensible and lasting bargains with employers and government."[53]

The explanation of Britain's economic difficulties in terms of the pattern of party and interest-group politics is highlighted in studies by Beer and Ashford. Other analysts, such as Michael Stewart, also attribute determinative importance to it. Beer describes the British political system as afflicted with a "pluarlistic stagnation" that has "paralyzed public choice."[54] Numerous well-organized interests are committed to defending the status quo, or at least to retarding the adoption of new policies that they regard as threatening. Attempts by governing parties to implement radical policy departures are severely constrained and often defeated by the consensus that pluralism supports. However, efforts to implement solutions that fall within the boundaries of consensus, such as an incomes policy or curbs on the growth of public expenditures, are also defeated by pluralism. Governments are immobilized by real and anticipated backlash from "both the electoral power of consumer groups and the syndicalist power of producer groups."[55] Pluralistic stagnation has prevented the mobilization of social consent, which Beer claims is essential to the adoption and implementation of new policies.[56]

Electoral competition between the two major political parties contributed to Britain's economic problems by pushing up social spending and public expectations of improved living standards to levels that exceeded the economic capacity of the country. Interest groups then used their power to defend the benefits and subsidies they had gained. Governments' efforts to curtail spending, curb rising wages and prices, and eliminate economically unjustified subsidies failed or had limited success. The British political system had become what Pollard calls a "collective trap in which each pursuing his own rational self-interest contributes to harming everyone, himself included, and in which no individual way out is possible."[57]

Michael Stewart also blames the party system for the cycle of stop-and-go economic policies since 1964 and for retarding Britain's economic growth. According to Stewart, the heart of the problem lies in the role of the Opposition. In pursuit of electoral victory, the Opposition attacks unpopular decisions, however necessary they may be, and proposes radical alternatives. The all too frequent result is that "the Government is deflected from the path of responsible action by the need to protect its flank . . . and when the Opposition in due course becomes the Government, it is committed by its conduct and promises in opposition to reversing many of its predecessor's policies, however sensible, and pushing through new measures of its own, however silly and irrelevant."[58] Stewart's party-politics explanation complements Beer's more comprehensive pluralist-stagnation approach. Pollard maintains, in contrast to Stewart, that there is no real competition between parties on economic matters and that both parties follow a pattern of increasing spending as elections approach, a political business cycle explanation.[59]

Ashford attributes Britain's inability to solve its economic problems through public policy to a pattern of "unrestrained adversarial politics" at the highest levels of decisionmaking.[60] The adversarial behavior, which is supported by a solid elite and social consensus, is "heavily geared toward generating and maintaining support for the system." The consensus permits the concentration of power in a small elite group at the center of govenment. That group, claims Ashford, insulated from the political and economic environment by the consensus, manages the adversarial struggle with little regard for the consequences of the policies it pursues. In this situation British policymakers have been slow to identify changes in the environment and to adapt their policies to it. The slowness and ineffectiveness of policy responses to change are, Ashford concludes, primarily due to a refusal to alter the adversarial process.[61] That refusal is grounded in the closely integrated elite and social consensus. The solution, as Ashford sees it, is restructuring the consensus so that policymaking processes can be broadened, opened, and the participants made more sensitive and adaptive to environmental change. He is concerned, however, that the inability of adversarial politics to deal effectively with new problems such as economic decline may result in a radical restructuring of the consensus with a resulting loss of the restraint and moderation that makes it possible. Like most of the studies reviewed here, Ashford's diagnosis of the ailment is incisive but his prescribed remedy is elusive and vague.

These diverse studies of Britain's economic decline and efforts to reverse it yield various and sometimes conflicting explanations. They are of particular interest because the problem confronted Britain sooner and has been more persistent there than it has been in other industrial democracies. Essentially, the studies argue that overextended policy commitments at home and abroad have led to neglect of investment, slow economic growth, and relative economic weakness. Institutional and organizational structures in government and the economy and the pluralistic pattern of interest-group politics and an adversarial party politics have contributed to economic decline and led to the adoption of dysfunctional policies or the inability to act at all. When constructive action has been taken, it has frequently been delayed and diluted by political bargaining.

Canada

Canada's economic difficulties and Canadian ecnomic policies have not been studied as extensively as those of the United States or Britain. Students of the Canadian political economy have devoted relatively little attention to explaining economic decline or the inability of traditional fiscal and monetary policies to reverse it. Nor have they grappled extensively with questions of governability or whether the country has been afflicted with "the British disease." Canadian analysts appear to have been more concerned with the impact of political institutions on policy than with the pattern of politics.[62] The principal institutional factors cited as influences on economic policy are the organizational arrangements for managing and coordinating policy and federal-provincial relations.

Since the coming to power of the Trudeau government in 1968, Bruce Doern observes, "there has been a visible and increased concern about the aggrandizement of prime-ministerial power, about the unwieldiness of a huge Cabinet, and about the degree to which central agencies . . . are held accountable both to ministers and . . . Parliament."[63] The Trudeau era, which ended in June 1984, was characterized by extensive efforts to manage and control policy, including the creation of new departments and central agencies, the establishment of planning processes, and frequent shifting of responsibility for various policy instruments between ministries and agencies. Indeed, reorganization itself was often used as a governmental response to environmental changes.

There was during the Trudeau era, in Colin Campbell's words, "a fascination with coordination." He writes that the "government has treated each new approach or technique as if it had the potential to account for all the undesirable variance in spending. Each analytic fact has merited full bureaucratic incarnation by the establishment of new branches, even secretariats."[64] The result was uncertainty and confusion over which neither minister nor central agency has primary responsibility for managing various economic policy instruments and for overall policy coordination. This led to intense bureaucratic conflicts at the center of government between individuals and organizations.

Federal-provincial relations are of particular importance in Canadian policy making because of the relatively high degree of provincial autonomy in the areas of fiscal, resource, and regulatory policy.[65] Provincial authorities are capable of frustrating federal policies. The provinces play a major role in battles over taxing and spending, with provincial premiers often negotiating directly, individually or as a group, with the government. In addition, the federal government has made a strong commitment to eliminate regional economic disparities.

There is an important structural factor in the Canadian economy that affects its operation and governmental attempts to solve economic problems: the domination of Canadian industry and finance by American businesses and investors. This factor has become a major political issue. The dependence of Canada on resource-extractive industries in which American interests have invested heavily and strong American demand for their products gives the United States enormous influence. That influence is enhanced by the close relationship and interaction between Canadian and American financial markets. Canadian banks and corporations borrow frequently and extensively in the United States and Canadian interest rates closely follow those in the United States. Some Canadians believe that American influence has prevented the diversification of their economy and impeded the investment necessary for its growth and for increased productivity and competitiveness.[66] It is also argued that the United States government, on behalf of American business interests, has pressured the Canadian government to make unwise changes in some of its policies.[67]

In contrast with Britain, labor unions in Canada apparently had little impact on economic policy, at least during the Trudeau era. Canadian labor organizations are even more decentralized and fragmented than their American counterparts. the Canadian government's difficulty in dealing with economic decline is, however, partly a consequence of the pattern of Canadian politics. According to Robert Presthus, Canadian political and business leaders are closely linked through a politics of "elite accommodation."[68] Campbell claims that Trudeau consistently "followed elite accommodation in pursuit of economic policy, all along giving disproportionate weight to business."[69] French argues that the development of effective policies is constrained and complicated by a "pluralistic and heterogeneous" political economic framework.[70] Phidd and Doern maintain that sufficient economic consensus and commitment, nationally and in specific industries, are lacking because of such factors as industrial structure, union fragmentation, and federal-provincial conflicts. According to John McCallum, Canada lacks the underying social consensus and institutions such as "good" labor-management relations that helped countries such as Japan and West Germany to contain inflation.[71]

Assertions that Canada lacks the underlying social consensus necessary to sustain successful economic policies reflect basic patterns in Canadian society. There is a deep cultural division between English and French Canadians and regionalism is strong. As in the United States and Britain, the dominant political ideology in Canada is liberalism with its individualistic values. But there are strong egalitarian forces, as manifested in the political strength of the socialist New Democratic party, and at the same time there is a strong conservative tradition that is lacking in the United States.

The dominant political pattern, as in the United States and Britain, is pluralism. The presence of multiple social, economic, and governmental interests quite strong enough to exercise a veto over policies, but lacking the power to impose their own solutions, and the necessity of balancing economic stabilization with other goals through bargaining among business, labor, agricultural, and governmental interests is characteristic of pluralistic politics. The constraints that pluralism imposes on Canadian economic policymaking are restricted, however, by elite accommodation and by elements of corporatism. Canadian corporatism is not, according to Schmitter, highly developed, but there are corporatist features present in Canada such as the Social and Economic Planning Council. (Whether liberal-social corporatism can overcome the weaknesses of liberal pluralism will not be addressed here.)

Canadian politics since 1970 have not involved major shifts in economic policy following a change in the party in power. The short-lived Conservative government of Joe Clark in 1979 fell when, in its first budget, it cut spending and tried to increase taxes on gas and fuel oil. The Trudeau governments of the period pursued policies similar to those of the United States and Britain. The Conservative Mulroney government, which took office in September 1984, has abandoned its predecessor's nationalistic policies toward energy and foreign investment but retained the essentials of its macroeconomic policies. The deleterious impact of the Opposition noted in Britain by Stewart has not been manifested in Canada, nor have there been dramatic reversals in policy such as the Heath and Callaghan U-turns of 1972 and 1975. And the political-business cycle has not been as apparent as in the United States. Yet, the government adopted policies in the early 1980s that contained the essentials of Thatcherism and Reaganomics.

It is difficult to suggest the factors that explain Canada's economic problems or the failures of economic policy on the basis of the analyses reviewed here. For the most part, these studies have concentrated on intragovernmental politics and organizational responses. They do not suggest that Canada has overreached itself through imperial pretensions, and relatively few charge that it has become a profligate welfare state. Nor do the studies attribute Canada's economic problems to the power of specific institutions or the higher civil service. If there is a convenient scapegoat, it is the pervasive influence of the United States in all aspects of Canadian life. What is perhaps most distinctive about Canadian politics is the self-conscious attempt to establish a national identity in a bilingual-bicultural society. However, this Canadian dilemma does not appear to affect directly the choice of ecnomic policies.

Conclusion

It is with some trepidation that I attempt to summarize and synthesize what the American, British, and Canadian cases suggest about the causes of economic stress and decline in advanced industrial democracies and the factors that appear to limit the effectiveness of their policy responses. Three caveats are in order. First, the three economies, while similar in many respects, differ with respect to size, structure, and their international role. There are overlapping similarities between two pairs of the three countries—the importance of agriculture in the United States and Canada and of financial markets and the reserve role of the currency in the United States and Britain—that complicate comparison. Second, although the three countries share a common political heritage—liberalism, due process, civil liberties, and majority rule—and have similar institutions and processes, they have distinctive political systems of their own. Third, I am aware that three for-instances do not prove a case and that the conclusions reached here are necessarily suggestive and speculative.

The point I wish to make is that cross-national comparison of these three distinctive but similar political economies does not lend itself to hard, conclusive data-based analysis. The number of cases is too small, the variances are often minor, and overlapping similarities between pairs of countries tends to raise as many questions as it answers. Perhaps it would have been easier to have added several more countries, but that has already beeen done (by Andrain) and it was not my purpose.

The economic stress and decline experienced by the United States, Britain, and Canada in the period 1970–1982 affected all industrial democracies. It was particularly severe in the three Anglo-Atlantic democracies, certainly more so than in Japan, West Germany, Switzerland, and until recently France. Two principal factors apparently contributed to the severity of economic problems in the United States, Britain, and Canada: inability of the government and the economy to adapt adequately to changes in their environments and overextended commitments of public policies made by past governments. There are underlying causes of both factors.

Changes in the political and economic environments of the Anglo-Atlantic democracies since 1970 are well known: energy and other resource constraints, increased international economic interdependence, increased competition from the Japanese, Western European, and Third World economies such as Korea, Taiwan, and ASEAN countries, and rapid technological advances such as robotics. Generally, American, British, and Canadian responses to most of these changes were too little and too late. Underlying the inadequate adaptation to environmental change are organizational and structural rigidities in the economy and the government and the inertia of established policies, both of which are due to a pattern of politics best characterized by Beer's term "pluralistic stagnation."

Organizational rigidities in the economies of the three countries include (1) the ability of unions to obtain and maintain pay settlements that exceed gains in productivity and to resist changes in production that reduce employment, and (2) the ability of business to maintain or raise prices in the face of falling demand and to resist government regulatory efforts in pursuit of various policy goals. Economic interests in the three countries have access to governmental decision makers who control policies that affect them and with whom they have informal alliances. Those alliances enable them to obtain benefits, services, and protection through public policy. Organized interests have also been quite successful in distributing the costs of public policy so that they receive more from the government than they contribute. As long as economies were growing rapidly, this was not a problem; everyone each year enjoyed a larger piece of the pie. But the slowing down, and at some points the reversal, of growth has increased sharply political conflict over allocating the costs of public policy. This has made the negative effects of pluralism quite manifest: each interest has the ability to veto governmental action adverse to it, but no interest, acting alone or in concert with others, is able to initiate action that will benefit the country as a whole.

Once public policies have been adopted, they tend to develop a vitality that makes it difficult to change or end them. Organized interests defend policies that benefit them through mutually beneficial exchanges of support. Politicians and political parties seeking votes promise to institute and maintain specific policies. And career officials in government bureaucracies fight to expand or at least preserve those policies. The result is a policy inertia that delays and limits the ability of governments to respond and adapt to environmental change.

The overloading of the American, British, and Canadian governments by public policy commitments that overextend their financial capacities is also due substantially to pluralism. In all three countries, welfare-state programs and various subsidy programs for business and agriculture have grown rapidly and often continue to expand automatically with support from organized clientele interests. Attempts to curtail the growth of programs, reduce the level of benefits, or to terminate programs generally have but limited success because of interest-group opposition and electoral competition. Overextension of imperial commitments is not a problem in Canada, but in the United States and Britain it has been sustained by a combination of nationalistic pride and elite consensus.

The operation of the factors that lead to economic stress and decline in the Anglo-Atlantic democracies can be portrayed as a rough causal model (see figure 5.1). Policy responses to economic stress and decline in the United States, Britain, and Canada in the period 1970–1982 were similar, though not identical in content and in their limited degree of effectiveness. Pluralistic politics appears to have been the principal factor affecting the use and effectiveness of fiscal, incomes, and industrial policy instruments, but it did not affect monetary policy in the same way.

Initially, all three countries responded to economic decline with fiscal policy measures designed to increase aggregate demand. This has been the traditional response of the left for the past fifty years. However, Keynesian stimulation of aggregate demand under conditions that prevailed in the 1970s and early 1980s had limited success. (The massive fiscal stimulation applied to the American economy under the Reagan administration in the form of tax cuts and a sustained military buildup is either an exception or an indication that policymakers in the 1970s did not apply sufficient stimuli to achieve their goals). The politically asymmetrical nature of fiscal policy—spending is difficult to cut and taxes are difficult to raise—made it an ineffective weapon against inflation. Using fiscal policy to expand demand and reduce unemployment, while politically feasible, seemed only to increase inflation. Electoral and interest-group pressures to continue the expansion of spending and to adjust taxes to take account of inflation (either by indexing or cutting the rates) have resulted in fiscal ineffectiveness. In all three countries there are fears that continuing high deficits and government borrowing will ultimately stifle the economic recovery and growth that have been experienced since 1983.

In the late 1970s the limitations of fiscal policy contributed to increased reliance on monetary policy which has traditionally been advocated by the right. The United States, Britain, and Canada successfully used monetary policy, targeted on the money supply, to bring inflation down to tolerable levels. This was accomplished, however, at the cost of a severe recession in each country. The effectiveness of monetary policy has been impaired by the persistence of high inflationary expectations in the financial markets. Those expectations stem, at least in part, from concern over the impact of government borrowing to finance deficits on interest rates and the effects of the deficits on aggregate demand once recovery has been achieved. There is a persistent conflict between fiscal policies, which for political reasons have expansionary effects, and monetary policies. When monetary policies are expansive, hyperexpansive fiscal poli-

FIGURE 5.1
Causes of Economic Stress and Decline

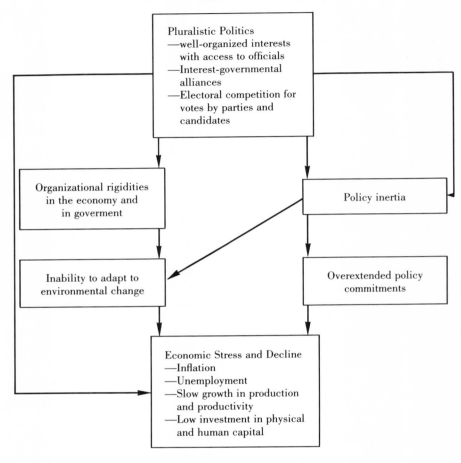

cies, such as the United States and Canada have pursued since 1982, threaten recovery by enhancing inflationary expectations. The effectiveness of monetary policy for expansionary purposes was demonstrated in the recovery that began in late 1982 after it was relaxed in each of the three countries.

It remains to be seen whether high levels of public borrowing in the United States and Canada to finance deficits will abort the economic recoveries there by refueling inflationary expectations. (Britain has done a much better job of coordinating monetary and fiscal policy in the 1980s. Its fiscal policy has not been nearly as expansionary as that of the United States and Canada). Political support for monetary policy is limited, however, to business and financial interests. They see monetary policy as beneficial to them as a means of aggregate economic management without taxation or government regulation. Because the effects of monetary policy cannot be targeted so as to benefit specific groups and sectoral and regional interests, it does not tend to acquire a strong supportive constituency. Nor, because of its broad impact that cuts across organized political and economic interests, does it lend itself readily to pluralist bargaining in policy and electoral politics.

According to most analyses, an incomes policy is the most effective means of controlling inflation. Even though it has been employed successfully in the United States, Britain, and Canada, incomes policy has not been established as a permanent instrument of economic management. The reasons for the reluctance of governments to use an incomes policy on a regular basis are clear: neither business nor labor is willing to surrender free collective bargaining in exchange for wage and price stability. Each distrusts the other and fears that in the long run the government's wage and price decisions will be disadvantageous to itself. Pluralism, with its denial of a general public interest, is incompatible with wage and price controls except as an emergency measure.

A comprehensive industrial policy is currently attracting considerable support in the United States, Britain, and Canada among politicians, economists, and some business executives and labor leaders. So far, however, none of the three countries has adopted one. Each country has elements of an industrial policy, some of which have been in effect for a long while, such as America's antitrust policy, loans and loan guarantees to failing firms in the United States and Britain, and tariffs and trade regulation to protect specific industries in each country. The main reason a comprehensive industrial policy appears unlikely to be adopted in any of the three countries, at least for the time being, is the absence of the necessary supportive consensus. The obstacles to developing such a consensus are formidable. Powerful business, financial, and labor interests all would have to consent. The particularistic goals of organized interests, each with an effective veto, would have to be reconciled before a policy with the general goal of modernizing the economy could be pursued. Although all interests could readily support such a goal, they would disagree sharply over the choice of means to achieve it. Moreover, an industrial policy that is developed through compromise and bargaining is unlikely to be much more effective than the separate and nonintegrated elements of industrial policy that are now in place. The limiting impact of pluralistic policy and party politics is again manifested.

It is appropriate before concluding this discussion to make some observations regarding the apparent effects, or lack of effects, of some of the other explanatory approaches that have been examined here. Statism does not provide much explanatory leverage because evidence that the state is an autonomous actor shaping society is limited and somewhat contradicted by the conflicts that exist within government and the framework for political choice in each country. If the state is weak, as is the case in the United States, Britain, and Canada, and constrained by internal conflicts and external pressures, then a statist approach is beside the point. What matters is the pluralist pattern of interest-group participation and influence in policy and electoral politics.

Corporatism does not contribute much to increased understanding, either. Schmitter's claim that a low degree of societal corporatism is associated with a high level of fiscal ineffectiveness has not been disproved or confirmed. But his argument is at odds with assertions that corporatist arrangements between business, labor, and government are a cause of economic distress and the ineffectiveness of policies adopted to overcome it.[72] All three countries have had corporatist features in their political economies for much of the twentieth century, but their economic policies reflect pluralist accommodation and compromise rather than syndicalist collaboration. It is not, then, inconsequential that the United States, Canada, and Britain ranked low on Schmitter's index of societal corporatism.

Analysts in all three countries have attributed determinative influence to specific governmental institutions and processes. For example, in the United States the Federal Reserve is blamed for economic problems and policy failures, in Britain the Treasury is asserted to have been unduly responsive to the City and to have shaped economic policies in accordance with the interests of the financial community, and in Canada the Department of Finance and other central agencies are sometimes regarded as overly responsive to the business and financial elite. There is no reason to believe, given the use of similar policy instruments with roughly equivalent results in each country, that institutional factors such as the independence of the Fed or the extensive financial management responsibilities of the Treasury or the Department of Finance have had a strong positive or negative effect on the American, British, or Canadian economies. (Since 1982, however, the independent Fed has pursued monetary policy that has often been at odds with the fiscal policy of the Reagan administration, wherea the Thatcher government has more effectively been able to coordinate monetary and fiscal policy).

Neither differences in public expenditure control processes, the status and perceived influence of civil servants, nor the pattern of intergovernmental relations appear strongly to have affected policy choice and effectiveness. At most, cross-national differences in government institutions and processes provide different terrains and rules of the game on which social forces contend. The pluralistic pattern of politics that characterizes the mobilization of social and economic forces appears to be a more important determinant of public policy and its effectiveness than institutional arrangements such as federalism, separation of powers, and a competitive, disciplined, responsible party system.

A word on political party systems is in order. True to the traditional American position, all but one of the studies of the United States' economic difficulties and problems examined here call for a political reorganization in which stronger political parties are a central feature. Interestingly, none of the British or Canadian studies advocates political restructuring. In fact, Ashford and Stewart believe that the adversarial competition between parties is a major cause of Britain's problems. It would appear that a strong, disciplined system of responsible party competition, as manifested in Britain and Canada, is no guarantee of effective economic policies. Nor does the weak, fragmented, nonresponsible American party system necessarily seem to have been a major contributor to the economic problems of the United States or the ineffectiveness of its economic policies.

These conclusions provide support for the pluralist model of politics and for Olson's economic theory of group behavior. They also support the view that factors exogenous to the political system—in this case, social and economic forces—can more satisfactorily account for the choice of economic policies and the limited effectiveness of those policies than the endogenous institutional and structural factors in the three political economies examined here. This is not to argue that organizational factors do not matter; I have always been convinced that they do. But the question of the extent to which political institutions and processes reflect social and economic forces and the degree to which they act upon them requires further study.

Notes

1. Charles E. Andrain, *Politics and Economic Policy in Western Democracies* (New York: St. Martin's Press, 1980); Arnold J. Heidenheimer, Hugh Heclo,

and Carolyn Teich Adams, *Comparative Public Policy: The Politics of Social Choice in Western Europe and America*, 2d ed. (New York: St. Martin's Press, 1983).

2. James G. March and Johan P. Olsen, "The New Institutionalism: Organizational Factors in Political Life," *American Political Science Review* 78 (March 1984), 734–49.

3. "Economic and Financial Indicators 1," *The Economist*, April 25, 1987, p. 97.

4. The growth data were obtained from *U.S. News and World Report*, October 8, 1984, p. 33.

5. If nothing else, the last fifteen years have revealed the limitations of economics as an all-purpose social scientific guide to policy making. That economists are at loggerheads over such a fundamental question as the nature of inflation— whether it is a consequence of excessive demand, escalating costs, or expectations of rapid growth in the money supply—illustrates the difficulty of relying on economics as a guide to policy.

6. Fritz W. Scharpf, "The Political Economy of Inflation and Unemployment in Western Europe: An Outline," discussion paper, Berlin: International Institute of Management, 1981.

7. Stephen D. Krasner, *Defending the National Interest: Raw Materials Investment and U.S. Foreign Policy* (Princeton, N.J.: Princeton University Press, 1978).

8. Theda Skocpol, "Bringing the State Back In," *Items* 36 (1982), 1–18.

9. Krasner, *Defending the National Interest*, p. 6.

10. Ibid., p. 20.

11. Ibid., p. 31.

12. Mancur Olson, *The Rise and Decline of Nations: Economic Growth, Stagflation, and Social Rigidities* (New Haven, Conn.: Yale University Press, 1982), pp. 217–18.

13. Ibid., p. 233.

14. Scharpf, "The Political Economy of Inflation," p. 6.

15. Phillipe C. Schmitter, "Interest Intermediation and Regime Governability in Contemporary Europe and North America," in *Organizing Interests in Western Europe*, ed. Suzanne Burger (New York: Cambridge University Press, 1981), pp. 285–327.

16. Ibid., p. 288.

17. Ibid., p. 293.

18. Ibid., p. 292.

19. Ibid., pp. 310, 312.

20. James E. Alt and John T. Wooley, "Reaction Functions, Organization, and Politics: Modelling the Political Economy of Macroeconomic Policy," *American Journal of Political Science* 26 (November 1982), 726–27.

21. Scharpf, "The Political Economy of Inflation," pp. 10–15.

22. Ibid., p. 14.

23. Edward R. Tufte, *Political Control of the Economy* (Princeton, N.J.: Princeton University Press, 1978), p. 143.

24. Heidenheimer, Heclo, and Adams, *Comparative Public Policy*, p. 151.

25. Richard Rose and B. Guy Peters, *Can Governments Go Bankrupt?* (New York: Basic Books, 1978), p. 7.

26. Ibid., p. 39.

27. Ibid., p. 202.

28. Ibid., p. 232.

29. Ibid., p. 109.

30. Maxwell Newton, *The Fed* (New York: Times Books, 1983); Robert Reich, *The Next American Frontier* (New York: Times Books, 1983); Lester C. Thurow, *The Zero-Sum Society* (New York: Penguin Books, 1981); Alan Wolfe, *America's Impasse* (New York: Pantheon Books, 1981); David P. Calleo, *The Imperious Economy* (Cambridge, Mass.: Harvard Univeristy Press, 1982).

31. For a more restrained assessment of the Fed's influence, see Robert J. Shapiro, "Politics and the Federal Reserve," *The Public Interest* 66 (1982), 119–39. He argues that the Fed has always acted to support the political objectives of the adminstration in power.

32. Thurow, *The Zero-Sum Society*, p. 11.

33. Wolfe, *America's Impasse*, pp. 230, 246.

34. Joseph A. Schumpeter, *Capitalism, Socialism, and Democracy*, 3d ed. (New York: Harper & Row, 1962), pp. 80–83.

35. Calleo, *The Imperious Economy*, p. 194.

36. Reich, *The Next American Frontier*, p. 194.

37. Ibid., p. 129.

38. Ibid., p. 139.

39. Robert Reich, "Why Democracy Makes Economic Sense," *New Republic*, December 19, 1983, p. 28.

40. Samuel H. Beer, *Britain Against Itself* (New York: W. W. Norton, 1982); Douglas E. Ashford, *Policy and Politics in Britain: The Limits of Consensus* (Philadelphia: Temple University Press, 1981); Leo Pliatzky, *Getting and Spending* (Oxford: Basil Blackwell, 1982); Joel Barnett, *Inside the Treasury* (London: Andre Deutsch, 1982).

41. Michael Stewart, *The Jekyll and Hyde Years: Politics and Economic Policy Since 1964* (London: J. M. Dent, 1977).

42. William Keegan and Rupert Pennant-Rea, *Who Runs the Economy: Control and Influence in British Economic Policy* (London: Maurice Temple Smith, 1979).

43. Hugh Heclo and Aaron Wildavsky, *The Private Government of Public Money: Community and Policy Inside British Politics* (Berkeley and Los Angeles: University of California Press, 1974).

44. Andrew Gamble, *Britain in Decline: Economic Policy, Political Strategy and the British State* (Boston: Beacon Press, 1981); Michael Meacher, *Socialism With a Human Face: The Politicl Economy of Britain in the 1980s* (London: Allen & Unwin, 1982).

45. Sidney Pollard, *The Wasting of the Britisch Economy: British Economic Policy 1945 to the Present* (New York: St.Martin's Press, 1982).

46. Ibid., p. 137; Gamble, *Britain in Decline*, p. 144.

47. See generally, Barnett, *Inside the Treasury*; Gamble, *Britain in Decline*; Pollard, *The Wasting of the British Economy*.

48. Keegan and Pennant-Rea, *Who Runs the Economy?* pp 210–11.

49. Heclo and Wildavsky, *The Private Government of Public Money*, p. 376.

50. Pollard, *The Wasting of the British Economy*, pp. 71–89.

51. Meacher, *Socialism With a Human Face*, pp. 32, 36.

52. Samuel Brittain, *The Economic Consequences of Democracy* (London: Maurice Temple Smith, 1977).

53. Beer, *Britain Against Itself*, p. 50.

54. Ibid., pp. 17, 19.

55. Ibid., p. 29.

56. Jack Hayward has attributed Britain's inability to act rapidly and effectively to economic change to an institutional inertia that is "linked with the twin practices of pluralism and incrementalism." See "Institutional Inertia and Political Impetus in France and Britain," *European Journal of Political Research* 4 (1976), 341–59. According to Hayward, pluralistic politics in Britain involves conflict between the government, which attempts to mobilize support in furtherance of "community purposes" and powerful private interests. Each of those self-governing groups has mobilized a sectoral interest and is able to resist attempts to subordinate those interests to the public interest as defined by the government.

57. Pollard, *The Wasting of the British Economy*, p. 113.

58. Steward, *The Jekyll and Hyde Years*, p. 244.

59. Pollard, *The Wasting of the British Economy*, p. 160.

60. Ashford, *Policy and Politics in Britain*, p. 264.

61. Ashford maintains (ibid., 295) that the policymaking process suffers from three handicaps: a small number of leaders handle a wide range of complex and intricate problems and decisions; crucial decisions are made secretly and with much information and serious discussion of alternatives kept from the public and Parliament; and the autonomous power of the civil service which even keeps ministers in the dark much of the time.

62. Richard W. Phidd and G. Bruce Doern, *The Politics and Management of the Canadian Economy* (Toronto: Macmillan of Canada, 1977); G. Bruce Doern and Peter Aucoin, eds., *Public Policy in Canada* (Toronto: McClelland and Stewart, 1979; Colin Campbell, *Governments Under Stress: Political Executives and Key Bureaucrats in Washington, London, and Ottawa* (Toronto: University of Toronto Press, 1983).

63. Doern, *Public Policy in Canada*, p. 37.

64. Colin Campbell, "Political Leadership in Canada: Pierre Elliott Trudeau and the Ottawa Model," in *Presidents and Prime Ministers*, ed. Richard Rose and Ezra N. Suleiman (Washington, D.C.: American Enterprise Institute for Public Policy Research, 1980), pp. 50–93.

65. Richard D. French, *How Ottawa Decides: Planning and Industrial Policy-making 1968–1980* (Toronto: Lorimer, 1980), p. 90.

66. Glen Williams, *Not For Export: Toward a Political Economy of Canada's Arrested Industrialization* (Toronto: McClelland and Stewart, 1983).

67. Stephen Clarkson, *Canada and the Reagan Challenge* (Toronto: Lorimer, 1982).

68. Robert Presthus, *Elite Accommodation in Canadian Politics* (Toronto: Macmillan of Canada, 1973).

69. Campbell, "Political Leadership in Canada," p. 80.

70. French, *How Ottawa Decides*, p. 89.

71. John McCallum, "Wage and Price Controls Would Help," *Canadian Forum* (September 1982), pp. 8–9.

72. Meacher, *Socialism With a Human Face*, pp. 31–32.

PART III

Focus on Britain:
Adversity and Decline

CHAPTER 6

The Changing Administrative Culture

of the British Civil Service

Richard A. Chapman

THE ROLE of British civil servants in relation to politicians and the power apparently in their hands has received increasing attention in the twentieth century. The constitutional position, as described in textbooks of the past (and also some elementary textbooks of the present) does not seem to reflect contemporary experience. Some politicians and commentators, especially those wishing to advance radical policies, have suggested that reforms should be introduced to ensure that politicians have the dominant role in government and that civil servants are servants. Others have drawn attention to particular cases and raised questions about the accountability of civil servants; ideas of responsibility have been reconsidered and attempts have been made to formulate codes of practice. Writers on administrative theory have increasingly focused on philosophies of administration, the effects of socialization and ethics in public administration. There have been recurring debates about power relationships in British society and, in particular, about the ways in which dominant social groups seem to maintain their position—with questions being raised specifically about the representativeness of the civil service and with demands for radical changes in procedures and criteria for recruitment, training, and promotion.

Until comparatively recently these debating topics and demands for reform appear to have made little impact. Whatever changes have been introduced, the civil service seems to have remained much the same. Even the last major commission of inquiry into the civil service, the Fulton Committee, which reported in 1968 with an opening chapter which amounted to a broadside attack on the civil service, really made little impact on the civil service. Although many of its most important recommendations were implemented in one way or another, their intended results have not been achieved. However, the situation may now have changed dramatically. The Thatcher government has not set out to introduce a program of civil service reforms, but the pursuit of certain of its policies may have fundamental effects on the position of civil servants in the British system of government and will also influence power relationships in British society. Some of these effects will take some time to mature and their implications may not yet be evident. Furthermore, the changes that have been introduced may owe as much to the British people's ignorance and/or lack of interest in their system of government as they do to the determination of a forceful, hard-working, very able and politically astute prime minister.

Given this background, this chapter has two related purposes. The first is to consider aspects of the present internal structure and organization of the British civil service and to offer comments on how higher civil servants achieve positions of leadership within it. The second, which follows from this, is to consider the role of civil servants in reforming the structure and organization of government.

Civil Servants in the British System of Government

Not only do civil servants have no general powers under the British constitution, until recently the civil service as an institution in British government did not formally exist. There are two main reasons for this.

First, "powers" in the British system of government are given to ministers through acts of Parliament. Legal power ultimately resides in Parliament and nowhere else. Indeed, there is still no written constitution for the United Kingdom, though there are from time to time serious discussions about whether one should be drawn up—this possibility has in recent times often been raised in connection with demands for a bill of rights and discussions about regional government.[1] Consequently, it is hardly surprising that unlike almost any other major power in the modern world Britain has no Civil Service Act which embodies in a legal document the powers and duties of civil servants with details of their conditions of service and how they should be organized in departments of state. The only legal definitions of "civil servant" are, in fact, those contained in Superannuation Acts,[2] though the standard description contained in the Report of the Tomlin Royal Commission on the Civil Service (1931) continues to be widely used in textbooks of public administration.[3] Therefore it is hardly surprising that sooner or later questions should be raised about the allegiance of civil servants. Civil servants see themselves as servants of the queen, though at the present time fundamental questions are being raised, as a result of the case involving Clive Ponting, about whether their line of allegiance is through ministers or through Parliament.

Second, in practice, civil servants are the servants of ministers and work in departments each of which is directly or indirectly the responsibility of a minister of the crown. This means that even today, despite the creation of the Civil Service Department in 1968 and its abolition in 1981, civil servants are more likely to feel that they belong to a "department" rather than to "a service." They can be sacked by ministers, called to account by Parliament (through accounting officers, the Public Accounts Committee and other parlimentary committees), and can be personally surcharged for unauthorized spending or gross mismanagement. Most departments deal with a distinctive client group, and this in turn fosters attitudes, relationships, and patterns of behavior which are different from those of other departments. One consequence of these features is the development of what Lord Bridges called "the departmental view"[4] or what Peter Self has called "the agency philosophy."[5] As Bridges put it: "Out of each department's store of knowledge and experience a 'practical philosophy' takes shape. Every civil servant going to a new job finds himself entrusted with this sort of inheritance. The good official will improve and mould his inheritance, but it is something he will ignore at his peril." Furthermore, because civil servants in Britain are permanent in the sense that they do not change with governments, they are career officials in line with one of the most important characteristics of Max Weber's ideal-type bureaucracy.

While many people may point to the advantages of this system, with permanency and nonpartisanship regarded as a more acceptable feature than the spoils system that operated in Britain in earlier times and still operates in many other countries, it may also give rise to criticisms about slowness, lethargy, and suggestions that the British civil service can be likened to Michel Crozier's *Bureaucratic Phenomenon.*[6] For example, Mrs. Shirley Williams, formerly a minister in Labour governments and now one of the leaders of the Social Democratic party, recently described the civil service as a "beautifully designed and efficient braking mechanism."[7]

Civil servants nevertheless must frequently exercise delegated authority because government today is so wide in scope as well as technically complex that officials have to make many decisions on behalf of their ministers—including decisions about which the minister can never expect to know the details. Because of their experience in these areas of government, they also have an important advisory role, not only on matters of detail but also on matters of policy. They are not expected to provide partisan advice, but their political neutrality is only in a party sense and does not mean that they have no power. This was well expressed by Professor John Porter, writing about Canada in the 1960s, who said that "the sheer growth of governmental operations over the last half-century has created within civil services . . . a new and relatively autonomous system of power and decision making."[8] Lord Allen of Abbeydale recently made a similar point in the United Kingdom: "Officials cannot constantly keep going back to busy Ministers to make sure that what is now proposed in a particular case is strictly in line with approved policy, but some of these decisions may of themselves amount to policy decisions."[9]

In practice these essential features of the British civil service have in recent years led to numerous criticisms and/or questions about the position of civil servants in the British system of government. These criticisms have come from politicians including ex-ministers and from academic and journalist commentators as well as, on a few occasions, civil servants themselves. Some examples will illustrate this. Brian Chapman in 1963 wrote, "Nobody really believes that senior civil servants are faceless, pliable, sexless creatures without fixed ideas, or intellectual eunuchs impartially proferring advice with all deference and humility to the great man in the minister's office."[10] Brian Sedgemore, in 1977, wrote: "We regard the resolution of the struggle for power between the executive, by which we basically mean the Cabinet, and the bureaucracy, by which we mean those top civil servants who claim to be policy advisers, in favor of political power and authority and against bureaucratic power and authority as the central need of our age."[11] Sir William Armstrong, referring to his service in the Treasury, said in the *Times* (15 November 1976): "We . . . had a framework for the economy basically neo-Keynesian. We set the questions which we asked ministers to decide arising out of that framework, so to that extent we had great power. . . . We were very ready to explain it to anybody who was interested, but most ministers were not interested, were just prepared to take the questions as we offered them, which came out of that framework without going back to the preconceptions of them."

In modern Britain, not only do civil servants have a legal and constitutional position different from that of their equivalents in every other country, but also their position is now the focus of considerable debate. The questions being raised are numerous and fundamental. They encompass the proposals for a written constitution which make provisions for regional government and a bill of rights, a code of ethics for civil servants, demands for freedom of information and more open government, new management techniques to enable ministers to exercise greater control over their officials, and numerous questions about the misuse of official information or the exercise of official power to the point where questions verge on allegations of corruption—as, for example, when senior officials who are by no means badly paid and can expect to receive very attractive and substantial retirement pensions are appointed to outstandingly lucrative appointments outside the civil service in companies or other organizations with which they had close contacts in their official life.[12]

In the past, complacency may have led commentators to overlook some of the most important questions that are only now beginning to receive attention. This earlier attitude is illustrated by the important litle textbook written in 1948 by Wilfrid Harrison, one of Britain's shrewdest commentators and a leading scholar of government and politics in the United Kingdom since the Second World War. He wrote:

We can take for granted the trustworthiness of our Civil Service: even so, we can appreciate to what an extent Ministers must often rely upon the advice of Civil Servants in order to distinguish the possible from the merely desirable, and to what an extent also they must always be dependent, for the time they have in which to consider any problems, upon Civil Servants dealing with other problems of which they, the Ministers, never hear. By the same token, the integrity of Civil Servants must also very often be left to determine whether Ministers hear about all the questions they ought to settle.[13]

In comparison to other countries or other public services, there may indeed be much that can still be taken for granted—but this should not discourage students asking why this may be so, or from considering aspects of the structure and organization of the British civil service afresh and from a variety of perspectives. It now seems unjustifiably self-satisfied to assume, without proper examination, that arrangements and standards of conduct in the British civil service are the best possible.

The most important question may not be whether civil servants exercise real power in our society because we know they do, within the meanings of power already mentioned. Previous approaches and explanations that emphasized the leadership role of politicians and stressed that civil servants, however progressive they might be, are servants, are now misleading and anachronistic.[14] Nor may it be helpful in this discussion to rehearse old arguments about who ultimately has the last word, because we know that the circumstances change from time to time and from case to case. No one can doubt that in the last resort Parliament can, if it wishes, make new laws almost without limitation. The most important questions today may instead be about persons in the civil service who exercise power and the ways in which they use it, how they are recruited and achieve senior positions, what their attitudes are and how their attitudes and judgments may be affected, and whether current procedures and practices are acceptable as they are or whether they should be reformed. Was Tony Benn right when he said that "the power, role, influence and authority of the senior levels of the Civil Service in Britain . . . have grown to such an extent as to create the embryo of a corporate state"?[15]

Leadership in the British Civil Service

Historians have written of great men as leaders and psychologists have written about types of leadership qualities observed in individual leaders. Political scientists have written about theories of leadership and the personalities of leaders; they have also written about political leaders in both central and local government. In addition, some have focused on the administrative style of politicians, but there has been no systematic and/or comparative analysis of how officials have assumed leadership roles within bureaucracies or the leadership qualities they have deployed in making important decisions in their senior positions. Indeed, few writers have been concerned in any way with leadership in relation to official hierarchies in the British public services.

There are various reasons for this. One important reason is that there is relatively little research material with which to work. Unlike politicians, civil servants do not usually keep papers for posterity or for the record, and the important papers on which civil servants work are generally found in the official files which are subject to rigorous weeding, often by persons without much training for the work and often with little or no appreciation of what future historians are likely to regard as worth preservation. Furthermore, the anonymity of higher civil servants in Britain means that they are as individuals almost unknown to the public at large, even by name alone, and this makes them unattractive as subjects for publishable biographies because their anonymity jeopardizes the marketability of such biographies. Marketability is even more difficult if a book is written about someone largely unknown during his working life and for whom the research sources do not become available until long after his death. In addition, the whole position becomes more complex and the role and achievements of a particular individual become difficult to isolate in an environment like the civil service, where collegiality is the norm in decision making.

This means that there are special difficulties in writing about public administrators as leaders. Because of the constitutional position of civil servants in the United Kingdom, the achievements of top civil servants are more likely to be the result of their influence than the exercise of formal powers. Nevertheless, a detailed study of the influence of a particular official may be revealing about the sort of person who gets satisfaction from working in a relatively secretive and anonymous manner in a senior position in government service. What sort of person, one might ask, is attracted to work where satisfactions arise from situations known only to a very small group of colleagues and where the details may never be recorded? In the British civil service, with its nonpartisan ethos, such individuals must be either lacking a strong ideological commitment or have the capacity to conceal it effectively if it exists. Indeed, does this mean that selectors at the recuitment stage should ideally be looking for rather introverted and secretive people who can hide their personalities behind the sort of sociable and friendly facade that may suitably impress a selection board?

The literature on leaders and leadership provides many definitions. All leaders are individuals who attain senior positions in the hierarchy, but not all people at the top are necessarily regarded as leaders. Recent writers have defined leaders as "persons or groups who can mobilize human, material, and symbolic resources towards specific ends"[16] and leadership as "a role that is understood in terms of the social and cultural context within which it is embedded and which shapes the particular forms it takes in any society."[17] "Leadership may be defined as the behavior of an individual while he is involved in directing group activities."[18] "Leadership is the process by which one individual consistently exerts more impact than others on the nature and direction of group activity . . . the leader is the one who 'makes things happen that would not happen otherwise.' "[19] "Leaders, in contrast to heads, are accorded their authority spontaneously by group members who, in turn follow because they *want* to rather than because they *must*."[20]

As far as the British civil service is concerned, these definitions are not very helpful for reasons that encompass the constitutional position of civil servants and the collegiality of decision making. Management in the civil service is different from management in other contexts, such as the armed forces or business, and consequently it is not easy to isolate particular individuals as leaders or to separate their personal achievements from the contributions of others to particular projects. Nevertheless, leaders may be seen in this context as individuals who achieve positions of leadership and who make a significant impact within the civil service. In practice, there are two important stages for leaders achieving their positions that should be considered in some detail. These are recruitment and promotion, though they also involve intermediate processes that encompass education, training, and socialization.

Although the Open Structure in the British civil service (the top six grades in the administrative hierarchy) includes a significant proportion of officials who joined in the pre-Fulton executive, clerical, or specialist classes, most of the top civil servants who, by generally acceptable definitions of leadership, reach positions where they can be called leaders actually joined the civil service as assistant principals or administration trainees. Furthermore, those who were promoted by limited competitions or as internal candidates at open competitions would have been assessed in terms of the criteria used in selecting assistant principals or administration trainees. Hardly any leaders in the British civil service joined as late entrants or by special procedures requiring the civil service commissioners to issue certificates under Regulation 11a of the General Regulations 1983 (or its predecessors).[21] Therefore it seems reasonable, as far as entry selection criteria are concerned, to focus on the qualities assessed in the administration trainee competitions.

In the Civil Service Selection Board (CSSB) rating scale printed in an appendix to the report of the Davies Committee, *The Method II System of Selection (for the Administrative Class of the Home Civil Service)*, the list of qualities comprised the following: penetration, fertility of ideas, judgment, written expression, oral expression, personal contacts, influence, drive and determination, emotional stability, and maturity.[22] Candidates are, however, only assessed by CSSB if they have passed the qualifying tests, which are written examinations designed to assess such qualities as intelligence, numeracy, comprehension of written words, and ability in writing English. Furthermore, candidates must have or be expected to achieve a good honors degree. These qualities do not, of course, determine whether candidates necessarily have leadership qualities, but the competition determines who shall be given the opportunity to show such leadership qualities as they might have and be given the opportunity to rise to the highest levels in the civil service; in normal circumstances the opportunities are rare for potential leaders to enter by other means and reach the top.

Once in the civil service, the potential leader advances by means of promotions. For good candidates these are likely to occur at reasonably predictable intervals for the first few promotions, but after that a lot may depend on opportunities arising from good fortune and being in the right place at the right time. Promotion below the grade of undersecretary is settled departmentally, though departments are required to consult the head of the civil service before promoting to the undersecretary grade itself. Promotions to grades above underscretary are made after the prime minister has been consulted by the head of the Home Civil Service, who takes the advice of a selected group of senior colleagues serving as a small committee known as the Senior Appointments Selection Committee. No forms or formalized criteria are used for assessment above the level of assistant secretary. This means that officials who are promoted to leadership positions in the British civil service get there as a result of a complex interaction of various factors. These include the advantages of social background and schooling (often related), university education, performance in examinations, postentry experience, contacts, and personal achievements. In this procedure some of the most important elements are related to and arise from socialization. The opportunity for postentry education and qualifications is small, and even if qualifications are obtained they are not generally rated highly in the civil service. Training courses also do not play much part in the careers of officials at these senior levels in the hierarchy.

A great deal depends on the administrative culture of the higher civil service.[23] This is the aggregation of the attitudes and standards, values, beliefs, and assumptions of individuals. The result of this culture is apparent in a set of patterns and guidelines of behavior. It is a variable phenomenon that changes from time to time although, as one might expect of a bureaucracy, it is esentially conservative and consistent with the social backgrounds, education, and life experience of the groups in society from which the individuals are drawn.

This administrative culture has numerous important effects on the careers of leaders in the civil service. For example, it seems to have an influence on who succeeds in the initial selection processes. However careful the Civil Service Commission is in safeguarding the fairness and justice of its selection procedures, there will always be scope for the judgment of individuals on selection boards at various stages in the selection procedure—whether at the CSSB or the Final Selection Board. From time to time there is particularly strong competition to get into the civil service; at those times, when numerous well-qualified candidates are being considered, judgments may be very marginal and certainly not purely objective. After the appointment of a candidate, early promotions and postings may be particularly significant, partly because they may open up new opportunities but also partly because the higher civil service in Britain receives little formal training, and postentry education is virtually discouraged. Consequently, the reasonably frequent postings of fairly junior civil servants in the elite groups of entrants means they are quickly socialized into the ethos of generalist administration. They adjust to the administrative processes in the civil service, learn how things are done primarily from experience, and acquire an appreciation of the ambiance and ethics of the higher civil service. As civil servants who are regarded as "high fliers" progress in their careers, the objective elements determining their career progression become less and less important. As has already been mentioned, there are no forms or structure for promotion to the highest levels; indeed, they are not thought necessary in the environment of the Whitehall village community where so many civil servants at the most senior levels know each other fairly intimately because the group in which they work is so small and the opportunities for interaction are so significant.

Perhaps it should be emphasized at this point that no judgment is being offered or implied about either the socialization process in the British civil service or the administrative culture of the higher civil service. The line of discussion is quite simple. It has been shown in the first section of this chapter that civil servants in modern Britain have considerable scope for exercising power and making important contributions to policymaking. It is naive to state at the present time, as so many textbooks have done in the past, that the civil service is simply the organization in central government that implements the policies formulated and agreed by politicians. This may have been the situation in the nineteenth century when the state had a much less positive role; but in the 1980s it has been shown beyond doubt that civil servants have power as well as influence. It has also been shown that leaders in the British civil service reach their positions as a result of recruitment at a fairly early age and progress by processes of socialization and promotion in circumstances where the closeness of the Whitehall society can be easily demonstrated. The third section of this chapter is therefore concerned primarily with administrative reform of selected aspects of the British civil service—in particular, those aspects of considerable importance in the appointment and development of leaders and in relation to the powers and influence they exercise.

Administrative Reform, Leadership and Efficiency in the British Civil Service

The twentieth-century history and literature on the British civil service is not only the story of criticisms of its structure and organization, but also the story of attempts at reform of its management and culture. Criticisms of civil service admissions procedures and the educational backgrounds of successful candidates date back to the MacDonnell Royal Commission (which reported in 1912) and books like Donald Kingsley's *Representative Bureaucracy: An Interpretation of the British Civil Service*, published in 1944.[24] Kingsley argued that the British civil service was representative because it represented the dominant forces in British society. His thesis was based on careful research and was persuasively argued. What may be important now is whether the representative nature of the civil service is suited to contemporary needs and whether any adjustments need to be made. Recent criticisms of the civil service have not been completely different from the criticisms heard previously. Perhaps the time has come for a study parallel to Kingsley's but focusing on the 1980s and asking not only questions about the representative nature of the British civil service but also questions about the administrative culture.

In the late 1960s the Fulton Committee made recommendations that, whether intentionally or unintentionally, were relevant to changing the administrative culture.[25] The first chapter of the report was meant to be provocative, eye-catching, and to rally people behind its proposals. Second, the report made proposals for fundamental changes in the structure of the civil service by recommending a Civil Service Department and measures to undermine the dominant role of the Treasury. Third, it made recommendations for a wider graduate entry, for the dilution of the role of generalists and more flexibility for the promotion of specialists by changing the class structure, and for a large program of training and education, to be led by the new Civil Service College, which it also recommended. For several reasons the administrative culture has nevertheless remained largely the same and the opportunity for affecting such important reforms was lost. Had the Fulton Committee been less pioneering and more in tune with the mood of the time, there would probably have been some sort of orchestrated protest when the main recommendations that had been implemented were largely reversed. In fact, there was very little concern expressed when the Edinburgh centre of the Civil Service College closed in the mid-1970s and hardly any interest, let alone protest, in 1981 when the Civil Service Department was abolished. Although many of the recommendations of the Fulton Committee were implemented, they had little effect on the administrative culture or style of government.

In contrast, the Thatcher government is having a more sustained impact on the administrative culture of the higher civil service, from a more radical and possibly also a more ideological perspective. This is especially remarkable because the government did not set out to change the administrative culture: the changes that have been introduced are therefore the unintended but not unacceptable consequences of particular policies. For example, the government's radical approach has ruthlessly reduced the number of civil servants, introduced more monetarist guidelines into government decision making and introduced new management techniques including MINIS, Financial Management Initiatives, and Rayner scrutinies. In addition, there have been suggestions in the press that the prime minister has been taking a more positive interest than her predecessors in the backgrounds and attitudes of individuals appointed to the top posts in the civil service. Together, these and related measures are likely to have a much greater impact on leadership in the British civil service than the much discussed but largely ineffectual changes of the previous quarter of a century. This is partly because the recent changes have been more evident and well publicized, but it is also because instead of being part of a program of administrative reform they are the by-products of other policies. Furthermore, they are likely to have effects far into the future. Primarily because civil servants in Britain do not change with changes in governments, the appointees in whom Mrs. Thatcher seems to have taken some interest are likely to hold leading positions and have an important part to play in policymaking and decision making for some time after Mrs. Thatcher has ceased to be prime minister—unless, of course, there are revolutionary changes in the civil service.

There are at least two reasons why the changes introduced by the Thatcher government have not been unacceptable. The first reason is that they are not unacceptable in terms of general public attitudes and opinions. In Britain people are not highly educated in their system of government, nor are they greatly interested in what happens in the civil service unless developments occur that affect them personally. But the well-publicized goal, for which the government seems to be on target, to drastically reduce the size of the civil service, is always likely to be popular. People generally are simply not very concerned about issues like the future or demise of the Civil Service Department, and they seem to be quite content to accept that a Civil Service College to provide education and training for officials is not really indispensable. Indeed, if civil servants themselves do not have much belief in the value of such opportunities, why should a less well-informed member of the public hold a contrary opinion?

Second, the British civil service has itself not been particularly sympathetic to the earlier programs of administrative reform, directed towards making the civil service more "professional." C. H. Sisson put the proposition well when he drew attention to the reasoning behind selection for the administrative class: "It is as if it did not matter what one knew as long as one could explain clearly what it was." He added:

It is small wonder if . . . the British administrator travelling abroad is shocked to discover that many countries are administered by men who read books about public administration. . . . The British Civil Servant does not want to suppress books of this nature. With his professional tolerance, he is not altogether against their being read in this country by other people. The real turpitude is for people engaged or about to engage in administration to read them. Such people are committing the crime of learning from books something one just *does*.[26]

This attitude of mind—well illustrated by Sisson from the civil service in which he served for many years—seems not uncharacteristic of the British civil service and also seems quite acceptable to the society outside it. Even if one absolves the civil service from any responsibility for Britain's decline since the Second World War—a line of thinking adopted by many citizens apparently ignorant of the British system of government—the future may hold more problems than the recent past and the problems may not so easily be resolved by officials with traditional civil service backgrounds. The danger is that real problems may be developing beneath the surface to become evident only in the more distant future.

One argument that could be put forward is that the Thatcher government's concern with efficiency in the administrative machine, partly related to the introduction of new management techniques, should result in the beneficial effects the Fulton Committee envisaged would be achieved by its proposed reforms. However, there are three more likely effects. First, the result of reducing the size of the administrative machine must concentrate power in fewer hands which consequently become more powerful. Indeed, one of the main effects of staff cuts is to make administration less sensitive to individual needs and the peculiarities of particular clients: economies result in rougher justice. Second, the emphasis on quantification and an approach to efficiency that puts a premium on cost-cutting means that qualitative elements, which are often associated in the minds of citizens with democratic ideals, have only secondary importance. This is quite a contrast to what Sir William Armstrong saw as one of his tasks at the Civil Service Department: "to carry out a programme of reforming the Civil Service, with the object of improving its efficiency and its humanity . . . both humanity as between the Civil Service as a whole and the public which it serves, and humanity as between the management of the Civil Service and the civil servants who are managed."[27] Third, candidates recruited to the higher civil service are being increasingly selected from those with privileged social and educational backgrounds, and present political leaders seem to be playing a more positive role in choosing top officials. These top officials then help to set the tone of the whole service as their ideas permeate down within it. In some respects, therefore, civil service leaders may be more unrepresentative than they were only a few years ago. The recent changes in the civil service may not be simply changes in the nature and direction of the administrative culture or changes focusing the power base more sharply and making the administrative culture more concentrated, but changes in the direction of making the civil service more powerful from a management-oriented perspective.

There may continue to be little public concern about what goes on beneath the surface of the administrative system until a serious issue leads to a public inquiry—indeed, it is through the evidence gathered by public inquiries that most details have emerged in the twentieth century about methods of work in the administrative system. In the future, however, it may not just be an administrative issue that leads to revelations at a public inquiry but a change in the focus of power within the political system. If a Conservative government can influence the civil service in one particular direction, another government might in the future be as radical but in a different way. The issues being raised here therefore involve not only the power and influence of officials and their degrees of representativeness and ethical practices but also the relationships of ministers and officials within the system of government. One aspect of this was well expressed by Mr. Melford Stevenson, QC, one of the lawyers appearing at the Crichel Down Inquiry in the early 1950s, who asserted that while officials concerned in the case had no corrupt motive, "they derive great satisfaction from the exercise of personal power" and declared, "There is a time when the public administrator can become, if not drunk, unfit to be in charge of his personal power."[28] The time may, indeed, be opportune for a reconsideration, in the widest possible context, of aspects of the administrative system which include details of how people achieve positions of leadership and also how they exercise their powers when occupying those positions. It is not good enough to acquiesce in the approaches accommodated within the administrative culture and uncritically (and often ignorantly) to agree that the United Kingdom's is the best civil service in the world. It may well be that in Britian it is the civil service that holds the residue of power and ultimately exercises checks and controls to safeguard the constitution—much as the army appears to do in certain Third World states. Perhaps there is a salutary lesson in the final sentence of Ellen Wilkinson's annex to the report of the Committee on Ministers' Powers: "Nothing is so dangerous in a democracy as a safeguard which appears to be adequate but is really a facade."[29] One might add that in the modern world there may be nothing so undermining in a democracy as a people who have little interest in their political system.

Notes

1. For example, *Towards a New Constitutional Settlement*, Second Report of the Joint Liberal/SDP Alliance Commission on Constitutional Reform, London, 1983.

2. The question is discussed in the Appendix to the *Eleventh Report from the Expenditure Committee, Session 1976–77, The Civil Service*, vol. 1: *Report*, HC 535-1 (London: HMSO, 1977).

3. *Royal Commission on the Civil Service, 1929–31, Report*, Cmd. 3909 (London: HMSO, 1971).

4. Sir Edward Bridges, *Portrait of a Profession* (Cambridge: Cambridge University Press, 1950).

5. Peter Self, *Administrative Theories and Politics* (London: Allen and Unwin, 1971).

6. Michel Crozier, *The Bureaucratic Phenomenon* (London: Tavistock, 1956).

7. Shirley Williams, "The Decision Makers," in Royal Institute of Public Administration, *Policy and Practice: The Experience of Government* (London: RIPA, 1980).

8. John Porter, *The Vertical Mosaic* (Toronto: University of Toronto Press, 1965), p. 418.

9. Lord Allen of Abbeydale, in Royal Institute of Public Administration, *The Home Office* (London: RIPA, 1982), p. 35.

10. Brian Chapman, *British Government Observed* (London: Allen and Unwin, 1963), p. 39.

11. *Eleventh Report from the Expenditure Committee*, p. lxxix.

12. *Treasury and Civil Service Committee Session 1983–84, Acceptance of Outside Appointments by Civil Servants*, HC 302 (London: HMSO, 1984).

13. Wilfrid Harrison, *The Government of Britain*, 5th ed. (1948; rpt. London: Hutchinson, 1985), p. 40.

14. Sir Warren Fisher, Foreword to W. J. Brown, *The Civil Service: Retrospect and Prospect* (London: W. J. Brown, 1943).

15. Tony Benn, "Manifestos and Mandates," in Royal Institute of Public Administration, *Policy and Practice: The Experience of Government*.

16. David M. Rosen, "Leadership Systems in World Cultures," in *Leadership: Multidisciplinary Perspectives*, ed. Barbara Kellerman (Englewood Cliffs, N.J.: Prentice-Hall, 1984), p. 42.

17. Ibid., p. 39.

18. Barbara Kellerman, "Leadership as a Political Act," in *Leadership*, ed. Kellerman, p. 70.

19. Ibid.

20. Ibid., p. 71.

21. Civil Service Commission, *Annual Report, 1983* (London: CSC, 1984). See also earlier years.

22. *The Method II System of Selection for the Administrative class of the Home Civil Service*, Cmnd. 4156 (London: 1969), p. 100.

23. This is explained further in Richard A. Chapman, *Leadership in the British Civil Service* (London: Croom Helm, 1984).

24. Donald Kingsley, *Representative Bureaucracy: An Interpretation of the British Civil Service* (Yellow Springs, Ohio: Antioch Press, 1944).

25. *The Civil Service*, vol. 1: *Report of the Committee, 1966–68*, Cmnd. 3638 (London: HMSO, 1968).

26. C. H. Sisson, *The Spirit of British Administration* (London: Faber and Faber, 1952), p. 28.

27. Sir William Armstrong, "The Civil Service Department and Its Tasks," *O and M Bulletin* 26 (May 1970), 63–79.

28. See R. Douglas Brown, *The Battle of Crichel Down* (London: Bodley Head, 1955), p. 102.

29. *Committee on Ministers' Power, Report*, Cmd. 4060 (London: HMSO, 1932).

CHAPTER 7

Demystifying Whitehall:
The Great British Civil Service Debate,
1980s Style

Peter Hennessy

THEY BEGAN their official lives believing that everything was achievable. (Lord Bancroft, former head of the Home Civil Service, describing the generation of senior civil servants recruited after World War II, 1984)[1]

Senior civil servants have been engaged in a twenty-five year campaign with scarcely one significant victory to punctuate steady retreat; . . . it is almost inevitable that a bureaucracy of this kind, blamed too much for our post-war failures, should close its ranks against advice, criticism or reform. (Sir John Hoskyns, former senior policy adviser to Mrs. Thatcher, 1982)[2]

When Sir Winston Churchill died in January 1965, the British did one of the things they do best and laid on a state funeral of immense dignity and style. Some of the 350 million people viewing the spectacle across the world may have noticed a line of statesmen standing, that freezing January Saturday, on the steps of Saint Paul's Cathedral as the old warrior's body was carried by guardsmen back to its gun carriage when the service was over. There were, to British eyes at least, famous, familiar faces from World War II and after, the former prime ministers Eden and Macmillan, a very frail Attlee perched on a chair, Menzies from Australia, and the military men Slim and Portal. Between Menzies and Portal stood two gray, tired-looking figures to whom very few people could have put a name. They were Edward Bridges and Norman Brook, Churchill's two cabinet secretaries, the dominant figures of their Whitehall generation.[3] Within

four years both were dead, their lives shortened by the punishing administrative regime of the war and immediate postwar years. *Their* passing—in
1967, in Brook's case, and in 1969 in Bridge's—was scarcely noticed
outside Whitehall and establishment circles, apart from a pair of weighty
and respectful obituaries in the *Times*.[4]

They were very different characters. In the 1940s, the Economic Section of the Cabinet Office coined the phrase, "Bridges is the best of poetry
of the Civil Services, Brook the best of the the prose."[5] Bridges was the
more outward-looking of the two. He delivered what became a collector's
item, the Rede Lecture at Cambridge Univerity in 1950, "Portrait of a
Profession," in which he chided his fellow administrators for their reti-
cence in the face of press and public. "The tendency of many civil
servants," he said, "is . . . to hedge or confine themselves to what has
already been said. This disease is so endemic that we have had to call in
gentlemen from Fleet Street to help us out of our difficulties. I see no
remedy for it, unless it be accustoming the younger generation of civil
servants to face the rigours of the press from their earliest years."[6]

Brook, by constrast, was both the supreme practitioner and arch apos-
tle of closed government. In 1958, James Margach of the *Sunday Times*
asked Brook to come as his guest to the annual lunch of the Westminster
Lobby Correspondents. Brook declined with these words:

I have always thought it best, in my capacity as Secretary of the Cabinet, I
should avoid direct personal contact with the Press. I am conscious that, by
following that principle, I have deprived myself of many pleasant contacts; but I
believe that, even so, it has been the wiser course for me to follow. I recognize
that you may have asked me in my other capacity as Head of the Civil Service;
but I must take account of the fact that I still remain Secretary of the Cabinet.
And, that being so, I feel that I must ask you to excuse me from accepting this
invitation."[7]

Sir Norman Brook was a zealous fundamentalist when it came to
preserving the confidentiality of the cabinet. That same year found him
threatening Lord Hankey, his predecessor but one as cabinet secretary,
with the Official Secrets Act if Hankey published *Supreme Command*, his
account of World War I.[8]

For most of the post-1945 period, Brook's philosophy, rather than the
more liberal attitude of Bridges, prevailed. Indeed, it was welcomed by
his colleagues. Shortly after volume 1 of the Crossman diaries had driven
a coach and horses through the thirty-year rule for official papers, Dame
Evelyn Sharp, Crossman's permanent secretary at the Ministry of Housing

and Local Government, declared in her forceful fashion: "This would never have happened in Norman Brook's time."⁹

In the two decades following Churchill's death, the discreet, private world of Bridges and Brook crumbled, piece by piece. It was not just a matter of leaks that drove successive prime ministers to distraction. The successors of Bridges and Brook, starting with the late Lord Armstrong of Sanderstead, permanent secretary of the treasury 1962–1968 and head of the Home Civil Service 1968–1974, adopted a more forthcoming attitude towards the press. Almost exactly twenty years to the day after Bridges and Brook watched their old chief carried down the steps of Saint Paul's, Sir Robert Armstrong, Mrs. Thatcher's secretary of the cabinet, broadcast twice inside a month, an activity unthinkable in their time.

To be sure, it was pretty feeble stuff. His careful evasions on civil service morale and relationships with Mrs. Thatcher and her ministers did nothing to raise his standing with his troops, though they can hardly have expected much else.¹⁰ On the first occasion, January 21, 1985, he was interviewed by Paul Greengrass of Granada Television's *World in Action* at the other end of a sofa from Lord Gowrie, Mrs. Thatcher's minister for the civil service: "I don't find," he said, "that ministers respect you any more for trimming advice . . . advice to what you think they want to hear. On the contrary, ministers that I deal with, and the prime minister, respect advice given which is independent and clear."¹¹ On BBC Radio on February 13, 1985, Sir Robert conveyed what his questioner, Hugo Young, described as an air of "continuing timelessness" when he said:

I'm not sure that the underlying requirements of the civil servant have changed really in four hundred years. When Queen Elizabeth I appointed Sir William Cecil to be her Secretary of State in 1558, she said: "This judgement I have of you, that you will not be corrupted by any manner of gift, and that without respect of my private will, you will give me that counsel that you think best."

I think that summed it up pretty well. I think that is what we still expect of our civil service and I think it's what we still get of it. And I have every confidence that it will continue to provide a good public service, an outstanding public service, on that basis.¹²

For all his carefully prepared, prepolished utterances, Sir Robert Armstrong in 1985 was presiding over a profession in ferment. Two days before he had exhumed William Cecil for Hugo Young, an Old Bailey jury had acquitted Clive Ponting, a senior civil servant at the Ministry of Defence, of charges that in passing information to an MP on the deliberate misleading of Parliament about the sinking of the Argentine cruiser, *Gen-*

eral Belgrano, during the Falklands War, he had breached section 2 of the Official Secrets Act.

The Ponting affair was but the latest in a long line of events—not least the stunning economic decline of Britain in relation to other Western nations—which since the deaths of Bridges and Brook had changed the climate in which their cherished civil service operates almost beyond recognition. Their profession had become, for the first time, the object of intense scrutiny, public criticism, and debate.

For the most of the thirty-five years since Bridges painted his "Portrait of a Profession," criticism and comment about the machinery of government and the "production engineers of the parliamentary process," as William Armstrong liked to call his fellow civil servants,[13] had been almost wholly confined to a small slice of the political nation. Even then the critics had a pronounced tendency to fish for red herrings such as the timeless preoccupation with the social and educational origins of the old administrative class. Each year the annual report of the Civil Service Commission would be scoured for the Oxbridge/red brick, public/state school statistics and the figures blazoned by the antielitists as if they had discovered, for the first time, the key to Britain's decline.

Occasionally some commentator would leap out of the rut and ask sensible questions about the self-image and performance of the senior civil servants, as happened in Thomas Balogh's celebrated 1959 essay, "The Apotheosis of the Dilettante," which still bears rereading.[14] Balogh was active in the Fabian Society, whose 1964 pamphlet, *The Administrators*, caught the reforming tide of the first Wilson government.[15] When Wilson commissioned the Fulton Committee on the Civil Service in 1966, some of the Fabian pamphleteers were included among its membership.

The Fulton Committee was intended to do for the mid-twentieth-century civil service what Northcote and Trevelyan had done for the mid-nineteenth. It failed. Its impact was minimal even on its chosen ground of greater managerialism, an enhanced role for specialists, and the dissolution of grade barriers. Wilson skewed its terms of reference to keep it out of anything affecting ministerial responsibility which, in effect, meant all the important and interesting questions about the relationship between ministers and officials and the relative power of appointed people and elected people. In 1968 Wilson swiftly accepted nearly all the main recommendations.[16] (The most important casualty was "preference or relevance" in the degree subjects of candidates presenting themselves for the Assisting Principal Competition—Wilson, a scholarship boy, an economist and statistician, was a true traditionalist on civil service matters). He lost interest as the 1970 general election approached. Whitehall reform was abandoned by the only patron that counts—the prime minister. Therefore, the senior civil service was able to pick off with ease any of the many Fulton reforms it did not care for.[17]

Edward Heath, who replaced Wilson in No. 10 in June 1970, made a brave if doomed attempt to tackle a set of genuine machinery of government problems. In opposition, he had commissioned a Public Sector Research Unit[18] to prepare plans for what the Conservative manifesto proclaimed as a new style of government.[19] Heath's object was to streamline the cabinet machine created by David Lloyd George and Maurice Hankey in World War I and to lighten the burden on overloaded ministers. The strategy contained three distinct elements: big conglomerate departments to reduce the size of cabinet and to curb the flow of decisions referred to it; a new system of policy audit known as Programme Analysis and Review; and a new capability unit for the cabinet as a whole, which became known as the Central Policy Review Staff. By June 1983, all three remedies had been jettisoned.[20]

The Labour governments of 1974–1979 were largely in the business of crisis management.[21] Institutional reform, a priority in 1964 reflected in a clutch of new ministries (most notably the Department of Economic Affairs), was off the agenda a decade later,[22] though James Callaghan did toy with the idea of breaking up the Treasury and placing its expenditure divisions alongside the personnel groups of the Civil Service Department in a new ministry of management and budget.[23]

Yet the mid-seventies saw the construction of the launch pad that was to project the great British civil service debate to unprecedented heights in the eighties and to lift it beyond the arcane circle of machinery-of-government buffs. The process began in 1975. As the Wilson cabinet grappled with hyperinflation in the mid-twenties, the great inflation-proof pension scare was invented—with the shadow chancellor, Sir Geoffrey Howe, making much of the running. With public service pensions linked to the retail price index by the Superannuation Act of 1971, introduced by the Heath government, the feeling was fostered that senior civil servants had somehow managed to protect themselves from the consequences of their own incompetence. The attacks enjoyed an immediate vogue in the popular press and the public imagination and managed to distill the antibureaucratic prejudice that runs deep in the United Kingdom.

On a more elevated level, the political nation enjoyed itself hugely in 1975 as it witnessed Wilson's attempt to prevent publication of Richard Crossman's *Diaries of a Cabinet Minister*.[24] The first Crossman volume was serialized in the *Sunday Times* and widely read by two gifted caricaturists, Antony Jay and Jonathan Lynn. They saw the dramatic possibilities of the very first entry, Thursday, October 22, 1964. For a start it gave them their title:

They know how to handle me. Of course they don't behave *quite* like nurses because the civil service is profoundly deferential—Yes, Minister! No, Minister! If you wish it, Minister![25]

And it gave them their first sketch:

I turned to my private secretary, George Moseley, and said, "Now you must teach me to handle all this correspondence! And he sat opposite me with his owlish eyes and said to me, "Well, Minister, you see there are three ways of handling it. A letter can either be answered by you personally in your own handwriting; or we can draft an official answer." "What's an official answer?" I asked. "Well, it says the Minister has received your letter and then the department replies. Anyway, we'll draft all three variants, and if you just tell us which one you want." "How do I do that?" "Well, you put all your in-tray into your out-tray, and if you put it in without a mark on it then we deal with it and you never see it again."[26]

When *Yes, Minister* appeared on British television screens in January 1980, it was an instant success. At its peak it was attracting 9 million viewers. A tiny handful would have recognized it as a tarted-up version of Crossman's battles with Lady Sharp. But for millions it was their first encounter with the question of civil service power. Jim Hacker, the minister, and Sir Humphrey Appleby, his permanent secretary, became household names. It was the favorite program of the real permanent secretaries (among them, Sir Robert Armstrong) and of Mrs. Thatcher, who has each episode videotaped for weekend viewing. Most important of all, it transformed the nature of Whitehall coverage on radio and television current affairs programs. The subject and appropriate specialist could be introduced at the drop of a cliche or the screening of a clip. The issue became familiar and mainstream. It is the most enduring legacy of Crossman's laborious compilation of his diary. Of even greater significance, Mrs. Thatcher herself subscribes to the caricature view of the senior civil service. And it is her practice to mobilize prejudice.

Mrs. Thatcher's Handbag

I am always amazed by the contempt with which permanent secretaries treat junior ministers. One junior minister at the Ministry of Pensions in the early 1960s never forgot. (An undersecretary, 1985)[27]

She cannot see an institution without hitting it with her handbag. (Julian Critchley, MP, 1982)[28]

The Civil Service is a great rock on the tide-line. The political wave, Labour or Conservative, rolls in, washes over it and ebbs. The rock is exposed again to the air usually virtually unchanged. But Mrs. Thatcher has been applying sticks of dynamite to that rock. (Clive Priestley, chief-of-staff, Prime Minister's Efficiency Unit, 1979)[29]

The best intelligence on the anti–civil service bias Mrs. Thatcher brought with her to Downing Street comes from a commentator who shares it. "She was, already, when she came into office," according to Patrick Cosgrave, "profoundly suspicious of the civil service. A friend asked her in 1980, "Do you hate all institutions?" She frowned and replied, "Not at all. I have great respect for the Monarch and Parliament." But for the City, the trade unions, the civil service, and the Church of England she has a dislike that some would call hatred and certainly veers regularly over into contempt.[30]

Cosgrave was, in opposition days, in a position to assess her attitude at first hand:

This ferocious attitude to the civil service which she rarely bothers to justify in terms of greater efficiency or savings made, is one she has held for a long time. I recall an occasion in 1977 when I was helping her to prepare a speech in which there were to be a number of references to Churchill. I told her that when I had been working on a book on Churchill some years previously I had interviewed General Sir Ian Jacob, in 1940 a Deputy Military Secretary to the War Cabinet. I knew from the papers I had read that Sir Ian had been highly critical of Churchill before he became Prime Minister, and highly supportive afterwards. I asked him if there was any particular time when he had changed his mind. "Yes. It was the thirteenth of May 1940. I saw a permanent under secretary in a corridor in Whitehall in his shirtsleeves, *running*. Then I knew that Churchill could shake up the machine," he replied. The anecdote gave her enormous pleasure.[31]

Her dislike of the official culture she encountered at the Department of Education and Science during the Heath administration is well known. But *the* formative experience dates from a decade earlier, shortly after Mrs. Thatcher had entered Parliament, when Harold Macmillan appointed her parliamentary secretary at the Ministry of Pensions. The memory of the occasion could bring on an attack of the "iron ladies" twenty years later as her friend, Sir Laurens van der Post, discovered when he interviewed her in 1983. Speaking of official advice, Mrs. Thatcher remembered:

I saw it vary from minister to minister. I used to sit there sometimes and say, "That's not what you said to the last minister. You are giving him totally different advice. Why?" And gradually they said, "Well, the last one wouldn't have accepted that advice." I said, "Well, you're now trying it on with the present one."[32]

Mrs. Thatcher is a great believer in the "guilty men" theory. In her demonology, it is the protagonists of the failed Keynesian-Beveridgite consensus who have brought Britain low. And those with the biggest horns are the "permanent politicians," the senior civil servants who assisted at the birth of that consensus and who had succeeded in capturing every cabinet, Labour or Conservative, for its cause from the mid-forties until May 1979. Always ready to exempt those who have served her closely and personally, Mrs. Thatcher nonetheless detests senior civil servants as a breed. She does not believe people of flair and enterprise should sign up for jobs in the public service.

Her attitude was quickly apparent in the spring of 1979 and the word spread fast through the Whitehall grapevine. Within a year, a balanced and seasoned senior official was telling me over lunch that "to be told by politicans that they don't want whingeing, analysis or integrity—that we must do as we are told and that they have several friends in the private sector who could do the job in a morning with one hand tied behind their back—is a bit much. It seems to be injudicious to attack the people on whom you rely." In Cosgrave's judgment, "That official gave Hennessy a very fair picture of the Prime Minister's attitude to the civil service in general."[33]

From this deep pool of prejudice flowed Mrs. Thatcher's intervention in top civil service appointments which led to claims that she had broken the post-Northcote-Trevelyan conventions and had taken the first steps to a politicized civil service. From this sprang what senior men came to call their "four-minute rule." (At a briefing in No. 10 you have four minutes in which to sum up the policy, display the options, and make a recommendation—however complicated the issue. If her eyes glaze over and you continue, you are deemed unhelpful and promotion prospects can suffer.) Such phenomena may be exaggerated but they indicate serious morale problems if nothing else. An assessment of Mrs. Thatcher's disturbance of the private world of the Senior Appointments Selection Committee (SASC), the group of permanent secretaries who advise her and her cabinet ministers on promotions within the top three grades, is difficult to make. She has her favorites certainly. And some of them fly higher faster because of her patronage. Sir Peter Middleton was her choice to succeed Sir Douglas Wass at the Treasury. If SASC had been left to its own devices, the mantle would have fallen most likely on Sir David Hancock (who went to Education) or possibly Sir Brian Hayes (who moved to Trade and Industry).[34] Middleton is a convinced monetarist and has a sparky style that appeals to his patroness.

Yet if one examines the case of another beneficiary of the Thatcher largesse, Sir Michael Quinlan, permanent secretary at the Department of Employment, he had no known views on trade union power or reform before being sent to Caxton House. He had made his mark advising on strategic nuclear weapons as head of the Ministry of Defence's holocaust desk. She liked his style, too. Sir Clive Whitmore, Mrs. Thatcher's former principal private secretary, became permanent secretary at the MOD at the (by Whitehall standards) early age of forty-seven. But he would have got there later rather than sooner with another incumbent in No. 10. The top appointments spectrum among the career officials can be interpreted either way, Middleton at one end of the spectrum and Quinlan at the other.

It is in the recruitment of outsiders to top posts, however, that the most significant changes have occurred. And one appointment in particular, that of Peter Levene from the chairmanship of the United Scientific Holdings to the MOD's Procurement Executive, has become a test case of the Gladstonian ground rules as laid down along Northcote-Trevelyan lines. Levene had already had a spell in Whitehall as a special adviser to Michael Heseltine, the secretary of state for defense. But his appointment to the Procurement Executive at £95,000 a year (some 40,000 above the going rate) very nearly precipitated the resignation of another Trevelyan— Dennis, first civil service commissioner and the man responsible for keeping Gladstone's creation clean and healthy.[35] Sir Robert Armstrong had informed Trevelyan of the Levene appointment the evening before it was announced. (There are signs that Sir Robert himself had only just heard of Heseltine's intention). The civil service commissioners had not been asked to arrange an open competition for the post, held by a career incumbent with time to run. Nor had they been asked to provide a certificate establishing the probity of Levene's preferment as is possible under the Civil Service Order in Council (1982) when an appointment involving rare and special qualifications is involved. The five commissioners came very close to resignation en masse. They chose to remain, letting their disapproval be known, informally initially and shortly after publicly, in an opening statement to their one hundred eighteenth report which thought it "useful" to issue a reminder of the "endemic inefficiency" that had existed in the days of unfettered ministerial patronage prior to the establishment of the Civil Service Commission in 1855. In language worthy of Northcote and Trevelyan, the 1985 commissioners declared, in what was regarded as their most significant annual report in living memory:

Our fundamental task remains as it was in the middle of the nineteenth century—to select candidates on merit, according to our independent judgement (in respect of which we are answerable only to Your Majesty) by means of competitions that are open to all candidates who are suitably qualified.[36]

After reminding ministers that the civil service commissioners were answerable solely to the monarch, the commissioners pointed out that fostering their traditional standards should be an important element in the current drive for improved efficiency—adding, just in case the absence of a direct reference to the Levene case left any illusions—that the principles underlying the Order in Council must apply at all levels of recruitment, including the most senior.

The Levene appointment and general uneasiness about Mrs. Thatcher's activism on top appointments fueled a debate inside the First Division Association, the senior officials' trade union. Its 1985 annual conference instructed its executive to examine a set of options for regularizing the position ranging from the status quo (a smattering of ministerial special advisers with the status of temporary civil servants) to a deliberate politicization of the top three grades.[37] The Levene appointment also set ticking a time bomb beneath the government which went off just before the parliamentary recess in the summer of 1985.[38] The Top Salaries Review Body recommended that the remuneration of senior career officials be brought closer into line with those of Peter Levene and Anthony Wilson, recruited from Price Waterhouse to the Treasury to head the Government Accountancy Service at £75,000 a year. All hell broke loose when the government accepted the recommendations and authorized, in the most notorious case, a staged rise of 46 percent for Sir Robert Armstrong at a time when stern restraint was being applied to the rest of the public sector. A large proportion of the government's parliamentary support was outraged and its majority was reduced on the issue to seventeen, the lowest since the 1983 general election. (The current state of the parties gave the Conservatives a supremacy of 138 seats in the Commons.)

Mrs. Thatcher's taking her handbag to the status, culture, views, and promotion of Whitehall's policymaking bureaucrats triggered a protracted debate in the press, in Parliament, within the civil service, and among the public service unions. A senior figure in the civil service unions commented that things had come to a pretty pass when he and his colleagues appeared in the role of Mr. Clean and guardians of tradition.[39] Surprisingly, they were joined by Neil Kinnock, leader of the Opposition, some of whose National Executive Committee were keen on a future Labour government staffing the senior bureaucracy with its political sympathizers

(Ken Livingston, leader of the Greater London Council claimed with pride that his activities at County Hall had shown how this should be done). Kinnock would have none of it:

What I don't like . . . is Mrs. Thatcher's system of stuffing the top of the civil service and massively increasing the Cabinet Office with assorted kinds of political favorites. I think that's against British tradition. I think it's against the best system of the British Civil Service and that's a process I want quickly to bring to an end.[40]

Kinnock, however, in the same television interview with Peter Jay, struck a somewhat contradictory and threatening note about the most senior career officials. Asked if he would sack some permanent secretaries, he replied:

I don't know about the permanent secretaries. We obviously have to examine the degree of enthusiasm and loyalty that they are prepared to demonstrate in support of a Labour government and in the implementation of the policy of that government. I'm prepared to work on . . . the conventional basis, which has stood us in good stead in Britain, about the way in which civil servants are prepared to work.[41]

Despite the caveats, Kinnock's words were warmly seized upon by Sir Robert Armstrong in a public lecture a few weeks later. "I welcome his statement," Sir Robert said. "He can be sure that . . . the civil service would serve the government of which he was the head with no less loyalty, energy and goodwill than they have served the present government and its predecessors."[42] The snag about Sir Robert's reassuring words is that the anti–career service politicians in the two major parties based their critique on the claim that loyalty, energy, and goodwill are precisely the qualities that have been lacking in the permanent bureaucracy in recent times.

Just how sharp were the divisions on the politicization of Whitehall in the summer of 1985 can be gauged from Sir Robert's speech to the chartered accountants in Brighton and an article in the *Political Quarterly* a month later by Sir Douglas Wass. Wass and Armstrong had shared the leadership of the Home Civil Service between 1981 and 1983. They had sat together on the Senior Appointments Selection Committee. One had entered the Treasury in 1946, the other in 1950. They had been colleagues for a generation. Yet the distance between their positions on Mrs. Thatcher's record on politicization yawned. Take, first, Armstrong in Brighton on top civil service appointments:

There is no question of political considerations entering into the choice. The prime minister is ultimately responsible for the appointment of permanent and deputy secretaries, and she takes a keen interest in them. She attaches much importance, as I do, in making recommendations to her, to skill and effectiveness in management as well as in the traditional role of policy advice. She is not concerned with, and I can vouch for the fact that she does not seek to ascertain the political views or sympathies (if any) of those who are recommended. Nor do I. She wants, as I want, to have the best person for the job.[43]

Wass in the *Political Quarterly* linked the issue of politicization with the Ponting affair and adopted a strikingly different tone from that of his friend and former colleague:

Many commentators with no particular party political bias have seen in Mrs. Thatcher's recent top promotions evidence of the "politicization" of the service. Outsiders have been appointed to key posts with, on one case at least, little apparent regard for the proprieties of open competition. . . . What is being questioned today is nothing less than the issue which Northcote and Trevelyan were thought to have settled for good and all, that is to say that the Civil Service should be a strictly meritocratic institution, a career service based on open competitive recruitment, with advancement free from political interference, and a staff who gave undivided and unquestioning loyalty to the ministers they served.[44]

There was another fundamental issue where the Wass and Armstrong approaches veered apart—the need for a rethink of the loyalty question after the acquittal of Clive Ponting. Armstrong, with the approval of his fellow permanent secretaries, circulated on February 25, 1985, a note entitled *The Duties and Responsibilities of Civil Servants in Relation to Ministers*. It made not the slightest concession to the Ponting defense that, in certain circumstances, an official has a higher loyalty to Parliament as a whole. The Armstrong canons were uncompromising and were meant to be the last word on the subject:

Civil servants are servants of the Crown. For all practical purposes the Crown in this context means and is represented by the government of the day.

The civil service as such has no constitutional personality or responsibility separate from the duly elected government of the day.

The duty of the individual civil servant is first and foremost to the Minister of the Crown who is in charge of the department in which he or she is serving.

There is and must be a general duty upon every civil servant, serving or retired, not to disclose . . . any document or information or detail about the course of business which has come his or her way in the course of duty as a civil servant.[45]

Sir Robert laid out a clear path for the cvil servant of tender conscience who must, in all circumstances, keep secret the cause of his dissent even to the grave:

A civil servant who feels that to act or to abstain from acting in a particular way, or to acquiesce in a particular decision or course of action, would raise for him or her a fundamental issue of conscience, or is so profoundly opposed to a policy as to feel unable conscientiously to administer it . . . should consult a superior officer, or in the last resort the Permanent Head of the Department, who can and should if necessary consult the Head of the Home Civil Service. If that does not enable the matter to be resolved on a basis which the civil servant concerned is able to accept, he or she must either carry out his or her instructions or resign from the public service—*though even after resignation he or she will still be bound to keep the confidences to which he or she has become privy as a civil servant.*[46]

At first glance, Wass's rejoinder seemed a model of that evenhandedness which thirty years in Whitehall can bring. First he defended his old colleague—"Much of the criticism of Sir Robert Armstrong is in my view unfair. To say that he is seeking to model the civil servant on the Vicar of Bray is to ignore completely the consequences implied by a permanent career civil service."[47] But Wass went on to state that "public disquiet about the civil service stems in part from anxiety about the public accountability of its members and is unlikely to disappear with the soothing assurances they and their former colleagues may offer."[48]

As if to underline his totally different reading of recent developments, where Armstrong had repressed the traditional verities of closed government, Wass argued for openness—"a Freedom of Information Act would go far towards making devious behaviour difficult to conceal."[49] Where Armstrong had laid down a conscience-clause which kept the secret in the family, Wass called for an inspector-general to hear appeals from concerned officials with "the power to require the minister to correct his statement or face a report to the relevant Select Committee of the House of Commons."[50] Far from Armstrong's post-Ponting note being the last word, Wass recommended a Royal Commission to examine civil service appointments, loyalty, and accountability.[51] The great Whitehall debate had come home with a vengeance.

Clive Ponting, ironically, had been awarded an OBE on the recommendation of Mrs. Thatcher for his performance as a new-model civil servant. So impressed had she been with his Rayner scrutiny on provisioning the armed forces that he was invited to make a presentation to the cabinet. Lord Rayner regarded him highly and, bravely, set a glowing testimonial for use in his Old Bailey trial. Rayner and his "ism" became the subject of debate from the moment he was summoned from Marks and Spencer in May 1979 to root out waste in Whitehall. Would he succumb to the mandarin's embrace? Would he go for the big targets or confine himself to forays in the foothills? Would he simply camouflage a cuts program in the language of efficiency?

Painting a clear portrait of Raynerism is difficult even after six years. A profile of the man himself is easy enough—big, cheerful, unstuffy, energetic, and far from a hard Thatcherite. He is one of her few close advisers (perhaps the only one) who could serve without difficulty a government of a different stripe. Rayner returned to M&S in 1983 and was succeeded as head of the Prime Minister's Efficiency Unit by Sir Robin Ibbs of ICI who had led the Central Policy Review Staff from 1980 to 1982. Sir Robin's office will cheerfully release the statistics of achievement since 1979. In the spring of 1985 this was the tally:

Some 250 efficiency scrutinies completed.

Savings identified: 275 million pounds per annum; 30,000 staff.

Savings achieved so far: 275 million pounds per annum; 20,000 staff.

(Overall shrinkage of the civil service 1979–1984, 108,000 or 15 percent).

Running cost of central government had been stabilized: it climbed 2.7 percent, from £13.4 billion in 1984–1985 to £13.9 billion in 1985–1986, less than the rate of inflation.

The new Financial Management initiative, devolving power and responsibility
    deep down the line, was being progressively implemented.

Substantial reforms of personnel management and training were under way. The
    experimental introduction of merit pay had started.

Succession plans were drawn up to ensure that key posts were filled by officials
    with experience in managing manpower and money. [52]

It was a matter of pride that, by making use of talent available in the departments themselves when appointing scrutineers, the Efficiency Unit had got this far on a staff of seven and an annual budget of £400,000 compared to the Grace Commission's 2,000 outside executives, 161 task forces, and 47 volumes. [53]

Yet, there was an air of unfinished business, a sense of considerable distance to travel before phrases like "Rayner Revolution" could be coined with confidence. The man himself reviewed his "ism" in a little-noticed lecture in November 1984. Significantly, Lord Rayner chose as a title "The Unfinished Agenda." [54] His lecture bore the linguistic hallmarks of his partnership with Clive Priestley, first chief of staff in the Efficiency Unit, by this time director of special projects at British Telecom. Their philosophy of the well-managed states "as a higher policy in its own right" was restated. The indispensability of prime ministerial backing, the "unique political imperative," was acknowledged as "support for the initiative was not extensive among other ministers or at the higher echelons of the civil service." There was a sideswipe at Grace. "Goliath should be matched with David, not with a smaller version of himself." The scrutiny approach, "the power of facts," was defended. And one important failure was acknowledged:

I also wanted a more specific and comprehensive recognition of and response to the quality of the talent available at more junior level; . . . it seemed to me that a large part of this recognition must consist in ensuring that staff had the right equipment and the right conditions in which to give of their best and that any other course was a false economy. I cannot claim that this part of my program had much success.[55]

In sketching his future agenda, Rayner pitched for bipartisanship— "The first need is for ministers and indeed politicians in all parts of Westminster to accept that good and effective management should be a prime policy in its own right." But he concentrated his fire on the civil service, "a mixture of superb talent and commitment to the public good on the one hand; and an able coterie of cynics on the other." If they were to be seen as a profession with a conscience, they had to give a lead. "In the state we are all, or should be, managers, now." Outside commentators, including the author, had stated frequently that the real test of Raynerism would come when the political imperative from No. 10 disappeared with a change of administration. Would the permanent secretaries ask the new PM to sustain the post-Rayner management systems? In his lecture, Rayner was doubtfully agnostic:

I have to ask myself in conclusion whether the assumption I made in 1979 that the service could and would reform itself is correct. The answer is, "yes and no." "Yes" to the extent that the capacity and the willingness are undoubtedly present and much has already been achieved. "No" to the extent that, if the influence of individuals now vigorously active were removed, *it is still doubtful whether the collective, professional conscience of the higher civil service would spring to replace it with a driving commitment and ambition of its own.*[56]

In 1984–1985, as second-term problems and the difficulty of managing backbenchers liberated by the huge Conservative majority weighed down the PM, the feeling grew inside Whitehall and out that the crucial political imperative was becoming ever more diluted, that Raynerism with the novelty wearing off was losing steam. Sir Robin Ibbs, a retiring man, avoided the high public profile that came naturally to Rayner. And the suspicion was voiced by two insiders allowed to publish under license,

Sue Richards and Les Metcalfe (Civil Service College lecturers who had spent time in the Treasury and the Efficiency Unit, respectively), that Raynerism was itself an impoverished concept of management, facing great problems in cracking Whitehall's disbelief system.[57] More significant still were the growing number of critics who claimed that Mrs. Thatcher's good-housekeeping approach to Whitehall reform was hopelessly inadequate for dealing with what Lord Rayner himself called the "weaknesses . . . bred out of the fatigues and disappointment of the British political and economic systems."[58] And the panoply of critics included some surprising people.

The Critical Panoply

The problem arises from the fact that the civil service sees itself as being above the party battle, with a political position of its own to defend against all comers, including incoming governments armed with their philosophy and program. (Tony Benn, 1980)[59]

My impression of the British Civil Service [is that] it is a beautifully designed and effective braking mechanism. It produces a hundred well argued answers against initiative and change. (Shirley Williams, 1980)[60]

The first thing to realize about civil servants is that few, if any, believe that the country can be saved; . . . the present system of career politicians and career officials is a failed system. (Sir John Hoskyns, 1982)[61]

When Mrs. Shirley Williams, a favorite figure among the closet Butskellites of the senior civil service, took to the lecture halls within a year of holding cabinet office, the spectrum of criticism was complete. However, the radical, free-market right had to wait a couple of years to find their wordsmith in Sir John Hoskyns. Britain had long been what one permanent secretary called an alibi society with each group in society sloughing off responsibility for the nation's decline onto another.[62]

By the mid-1980s the politics of scapegoating had settled into a fixed pattern. For the Thatcherites the guilty parties were the trade unions, nationalized industries, left-wing academics, progressive clergy, the center-left Keynesian consensus, and the civil service. For the Labour party, culpability lay with the financial markets, multinationals, monetarists, and the civil service. For the Liberal-SDP Alliance, those who had brought Britain low were the two old, class-based parties, private- and public-sector monopolies, and the civil service (with especial venom, in the case of David Owen, reserved for the Foreign Office). Significantly, the one ingredient of decline upon which most political activists could agree was Whitehall. Such attacks did more than merely contribute to a downward spiral of morale inside the civil service. They stimulated the permanent politicians, particularly those who had recently retired, to take to the lecture halls themselves. Sir Kenneth Berrill, the former chief economic adviser to the Treasury, marked his departure from the leadership of the Central Policy Review Staff[63] with a survey of the overload problem in Whitehall. His targets were the prime minister, the chancellor of the exchequer, and the foreign secretary: "The cohesion of this troika is crucial; . . . the troika is the center and the center has to hold."[64]

Berrill's particular focus was the premiership and the three forces bearing down upon it: preserving the balance between strategy and departmental interest, the media's identification of the government with the prime minister whatever the issue, and the growing burden of summitry in international affairs. He found the personal support system for the British prime minister meager in comparison to those of other Western leaders. Though aware of the constitutional pitfalls, Berrill pressed the case for a prime minister's department: "Our competitors have, by and large, faced this issue and come to some structured solutions which have put rather more resources into the area than we have been prepared to do; . . . of one thing I am sure: we *do* need strength at the center if as a nation we are to find a way out of our troubles."[65]

Sir Kenneth's contribution to the lecture circuit was essentially technocratic. Rebutting the more personal attacks on the civil service was left to others after the first Hoskyns onslaught. Another ex–permanent secretary who concentrated solely on structure was Sir Kenneth's friend and bureaucratic partner, Lord Hunt of Tanworth, who, as Sir John Hunt, had served four prime ministers (Health, Wilson, Callaghan, and Thatcher) as secretary of the cabinet. On election day in June 1983, he treated a conference of accountants meeting in Eastbourne, a seaside resort on the south coast of England, to the most authoritative disquisition to have come from a holder of this pivotal post in the British system.

Lord Hunt traced the development of cabinet government in its modern form from the founding period of Lloyd George and Maurice Hankey, through its Attleean apogee and into the era when "doubts began to creep in":

In the absence in our system of a chief executive with his own supporting staff a "hole in the center" of government was perceived which an overworked cabinet seemed incapable of filling. It was widely felt that the decentralization of so much cabinet business to a whole lot of cabinet committees made a coherent strategy much more difficult. It was suggested that the hard grind of a subject through the cabinet committee system led not only to unnecessary delay but also to unsatisfactory compromises resulting from a tendency to accommodate every point of view.

It was also argued that the public expenditure survey did more to illustrate the inflexibility of public spending programs than to provide ministers with clear alternative choices: and furthermore that the subsequent public expenditure arguments in cabinet were settled by muscle rather than by their relevance to the government's strategy.

None of these criticisms was fully justified: but in aggregate they led to a feeling in some ministers and former ministers—a feeling shared by some officials—that they were in danger of becoming prisoners of the system instead of its master.[66]

Hunt himself clearly shared several of these reservations about the performance of British government. Like Berrill, he tracked the forces bearing down on the system: media pressure making governments feel they have to respond to everything, a job that usually falls on the prime minister; a wider span of departmental activities (he singled out those associated with Britain's membership in the EEC); summitry; a breaking down of the Treasury's near-monopoly of economic policymaking.

True to his old calling, Lord Hunt rehearsed the familiar solutions—a PM's department, a beefed-up Cabinet Office, a strengthened CPRS, an expanded Prime Minister's Office—adding, "I am not myself strongly wedded to any particular solution." But the official whom Joe Haines, Wilson's Downing Street press secretary, called the most powerful man in Whitehall,[67] placed reform of the cabinet system itself firmly on the agenda when he confessed:

I have little doubt that there *is* a problem and that we have not entirely solved it yet. I accept that cabinet government must always be a somewhat cumbrous and complicated affair and that this is a price well worth paying for the advantage of shared discussion and shared decision—provided the system can keep up with the demands put upon it. I have however often been worried that we are imposing more and more on a system of collective ministerial decision-taking that was designed for a quite different era.[68]

Completing what Sir Kenneth Berrill might have called a "troika" of retired practitioners disturbed by the performance of cabinet government, Sir Douglas Wass, former permanent secretary of the treasury, returned to the theme in his 1983 Reith Lectures on BBC Radio. Like Berrill and Hunt, Wass had been at the epicenter of the economic crises which afflicted the Wilson and Callaghan cabinets of the 1970s, of which the negotiation of an IMF loan in 1976 (which took twenty-six cabinet meetings to resolve)[69] was the most traumatic. Like them, he bewailed a lack of grip in what is, according to constitutional theory, supposed to be the highest decision-taking body in the land:

> Ministers in cabinet rarely look at the totality of their responsibilities, at the balance of policy, at the progress of the government towards its objectives as a whole. Apart from its ritual weekly review of foreign affairs and parliamentary business, cabinet's staple diet consists of a selection of individually important one-off cases or issues on which the ministers departmentally concerned are unable to agree.[70]

Retired permanent secretaries cannot shake off the habits of a lifetime. Wass, in his turn, launched upon a Cook's tour of options for reform—a peacetime version of the small "high command" war cabinet of 1916 and 1939, a streamlined cabinet system with cabinet review committees for economic affairs and other important slices of policy, a new-style CPRS locked firmly into the public expenditure cycle and not distracted by peripherals like the reform of the diplomatic service.

For the bulk of Mrs. Thatcher's senior colleagues, reform of the cabinet system is not an issue.[71] The prime minister herself does not deem it so. It is, perhaps, expecting too much from people at the pinnacle or even on the upper slopes of a system, the ascent of which has made them famous, to question its construction. Such a line of inquiry, if pushed too far, might raise some awkward personal questions. Very few politicians have the stature of Aneurin Bevan, who told Richard Crossman: "There are only two ways of getting into the cabinet. One way is to crawl up the staircase of preferment on your belly; the other way is to kick them in the teeth."[72]

The colleagues they left behind in Whitehall have not thanked Hunt and Wass for their public speaking.[73] The customary common front in the face of hostility had failed to materialize. And hostility the permanent secretaries certainly sensed when Sir John Hoskyns, fresh from No. 10 where he had been Mrs. Thatcher's senior policy adviser, took his place at the lectern. He addressed the question "Why do governments fail?" Among the reasons he listed was how ministers and officials think and work. He proceeded to take both apart.

Sir John described the failure systems that trapped both breeds. First of all, the ministerial culture:

> Politicians, even more than the rest of us, don't know what they don't know. If, as a minister, you are then surrounded by highly intelligent but deferential civil servants, you can quickly start to feel infallible.
> The pressures on ministers are such that precedent and the ritual of office

tend to carry them through each hectic day; . . . a minister's intelligence tends
to be used up in self-defense; . . . the survivor is a relic from the more stable
past. In a time of discontinuity the country cannot survive being ruled by survivors.[74]

Life with ministers, according to Sir John, had pushed the senior bureaucracy into a cycle of underachievement:

As each government retired exhausted after another few years of fire fighting,
the service had somehow to continue with the next. It has done so, I believe, by
lowering its metabolic rate in order to conserve its energy and persuading itself
that the problem was insoluble in order to conserve its self-respect. . . . It is
almost inevitable that a bureaucracy of this kind, blamed too much for our
postwar failures, should close ranks against advice, criticism or reform.[75]

The Hoskyns remedies included a substantial transfusion of new blood
into Whitehall of politically appointed officials on contracts at proper
market rates. He recommended that public money should be used to fund
political parties in opposition to enable them to maintain shadow teams of
officials and something like a prime minister's department of one to two
hundred people to guard government strategy.

Almost a year later Hoskyns returned to the attack at the annual
dinner of the Institute of Directors (whose director-general he became in
1984). This time his prime target was the British political class and, most
of all, the party whose leader he had so recently served:

Conservative MPs (and probably MPs of other parties) are uninterested in
method. This is, I believe, because they are at heart, romantics. They see Britain as a canvas on which the young MP, a sort of Dick Whittington figure, can
paint his political self-portrait; making his way in the world until he holds one
of the great offices of state; and finally retiring full of honor and respectability.[76]

In a sustained burst of blunt language, he said "a country of 55
million people is forced to depend on a talent pool which could not sustain
a single multinational company." The remedies were a system that allowed the appointment of ministers from outside Westminster; a Whitehall
machine reorganized for strategy and innovation; the transfusion of high-quality outsiders; and a reduced ministerial workload.

For his pains, Hoskyns was criticized from all quarters, from Mrs.
Thatcher, in private, to permanent secretaries and the press who accused
him of wanting a businessman's government. David Owen was just about
the only senior politician who rallied to his defense. For Owen, a longtime
establishment basher, "The call for fresh thinking by Hoskyns is utterly

right and it is typical of the club that they have grouped together so stridently to denigrate and denounce Hoskyns and all his works."[77]

There were echoes of Hoskynry from the left of center too, from Tony Benn and some of the people around him. Indeed, their call for political appointees in the upper reaches of Whitehall predates the Hoskyns thesis. After the 1979 election defeat, Labour's National Executive Committee estabished a working group on the machinery of government under Eric Heffer, MP. It recommended that incoming ministers should have the right to remove top officials and to determine promotions in the top three grades.[78] The NEC document, which was endorsed by the party's annual conference, reflected the thinking of Benn's former parliamentary private secretary, Brian Sedgemore, whose views on the senior civil service had been radicalized by a spell as an assistant principal in the Ministry of Housing in the mid-1960s. Sedgemore's animus against his former White-hall colleagues was brutally expressed in 1977 in his unsuccessful amend-ment to a Commons expenditure report on the civil service: "There is, as should be, no role in our society for people with little to offer in a practical way but civil servants have got round this stumbling block by inventing a role for themselves. The role that they have invented for themselves is that of governing the country."[79]

Benn delivered his critique, with his usual blend of radical ideas and courtesy towards those individuals whose philosophies he was rubbishing, in the RIPA's series of winter lectures, 1981–1982. He described, in general terms, how successive governments of all colors had succumbed to Whitehall's consensus view and, in specific terms, how an alliance of senior civil servants and his own PM had undone him and the manifesto policies he had espoused at the Department of Industry in the mid-1970s.[80] The Benn remedies were a freedom of information act, stronger parliamentary control, a "constitutional premiership," and making the most senior officials in each department more responsible to the ministers whom they serve.[81]

Shirley Williams was not the only centrist politician to contribute to the panoply of criticism in the 1980s. Edmund Dell, trade secretary in the Callaghan administration, in that same series of RIPA lectures took on two canons of the constitution—the myth of collective cabinet responsibility that is not believed,[82] and the requirement that ministers be drawn solely from the Houses of Parliament,[83] a view seized upon with relish by Sir John Hoskyns when he took to the boards at the Institute of Fiscal Studies two years later. Dell's heterodoxy led to a good deal of private scuttlebutt to the effect that old Edmund was a nice, intelligent chap but too much of a technocrat who had never really fitted in at Westminister. Such is the fate under contemporary British conditions of even those with insider experience who try to create an agenda for change.

The Reform Agenda

Parties came into power with silly, inconsistent and impossible policies . . . because in opposition they have scrambled back on the ideological kites where they feel happiest. (Sir Adam Ridley, 1985)[84]

Our system of government was designed for an age of deference and authority. It will not do for these more democratic, sometimes anarchic, times. (Report of the Fabian Society, 1982)[85]

Interest in the intestines of the political process is a very British pastime. (Ralf Dahrendorf, 1982)[86]

What does the accumulated detritus of the lecture hall and the seminar room amount to in 1985? Very little by the way of a clear program for change. The nearest any group has come to that are the Fabians. Under David Lipsey, a former Labour special adviser at the Department of the Environment, the Foreign Office, and No. 10, a group of experienced insiders and amphibians produced a well-drafted report in 1982. They attacked all the key points: the quality of policymaking in opposition, the relationships between ministers and civil servants, the power of the PM vis-à-vis the cabinet, relationships between Whitehall and the outside world, and more open government—the last being their indispensable solvent to remove bureaucratic rigidities and to unfreeze communications with Westminister, the governing party, the opposition, and the outside world.[87] Even the Fabians could not agree. They differed over the premier's powers, the extent of freedom of information, and the degree of politicization of senior posts. Instead they offered a menu of reforms and ways of initiating a process of change rather than a blueprint.[88]

In midsummer 1985 there was yet more work in progress. After William Plowden, the highly respected director-general of the RIPA had taken Whitehall by surprise in a Royal Society lecture in February 1985 by noting a long-term trend toward greater political control of the civil service, and adding that such a trend is necessary and desirable, the RIPA had a working group on politicization under David Williams taking evidence.[89] A small all-party group of politicians (Tim Eggar, MP, for the Conservatives, Lord Donoughue for Labour, and Tom McNally for the SDP), assisted by management consultants, journalists, and former officials, were working on the idea of "contract" for those on whom the country depended for a well-managed state. Their motivation was twofold: a fear that the Rayner reforms were running out of steam and a belief that efficiency and effectiveness in government should be a priority in any party program given pressure of manpower and money in the foreseeable future.[90]

As for Mrs. Thatcher, there was no sign that she was prepared to buy any of the reform packages, other than the efficiency and effectiveness program already in the train. The crucial factor determining whether the mid-1980s reform agenda faced a more promising future than becoming yet another footnote in British administrative history would be its ability to project itself into the 1987 election campaign as a priority issue of practical politics. Of active politicians, Owen ("One vital element is to force reform of Whitehall and Westminster on to the political agenda") and Benn ("The relationship in practice between different parts of the Constitution is a legitimate—indeed essential—subject for public discussion and understanding") clearly wished to do.[91] It was possible that Kinnock might make a restoration of probity in civil service appointments a minor theme in his campaign. But one thing was certain. The combined effect of *Yes, Minister*, consistent newspaper attention, the Fabians, and the tyros of the lecture halls meant that if an opposition party wished to avoid Sir Adam Ridley's strictures, on machinery of government matters at least, they had within their grasp the raw material for a considered reform program and a public opinion well placed to comprehend it. It could just be that fascination with the intestines of the political process is about to become rather more than a very British pastime.

Notes

1. Lord Bancroft, "The Art of Management," "II Whitehall and Management: A Retrospect," in Three Cantor Lectures, Royal Society of Arts, January 30, 1984.

2. Sir John Hoskyns, "Westminster and Whitehall: An Outsider's View," Institute for Fiscal Studies Annual Lecture, October 12, 1982.

3. The photograph is reproduced in Harold Wilson, *A Prime Minister on Prime Ministers* (London: Michael Joseph, 1977), p. 300.

4. *Obituaries from The Times, 1961–70* (Newspaper Archive Developments, 1975), pp. 99, 590–91.

5. Private communication.

6. Michael Cockerell, Peter Hennessy, and David Walker, *Sources Close to the Prime Minister* (London: Macmillan, 1984), p. 53.

7. Copy of a letter dated November 17, 1958, given to the author by the late James Margach.

8. Maurice Hankey, *The Supreme Command, 1914–1918*, 2 vols. (London: Allen & Unwin, 1961).

9. At a meeting of the St. Albans Baconian Society, March 9, 1975.

10. Private communication.

11. Granada Television, "Civil Unrest," *World in Action*, January 21, 1985.

12. "The Vanishing Mandarins," *Analysis*, BBC Radio 4, February 13, 1985.

13. Private communication.

14. Thomas Balogh, "The Apotheosis of the Dilettante," *The Establishment*, ed. Hugh Thomas (London: Anthony Blond, 1959), pp. 83–129.

15. *The Administrators: The Reform of the Civil Service* (London: Fabian Tract no. 355, 1964).

16. *The Civil Service*, vol. 1: *Report of the Committee*, Cmnd 3638, HMSO 1968.

17. Peter Kellner and Lord Crowther-Hunt, *The Civil Servants: An Inquiry into Britain's Ruling Class* (Macdonald, 1980), chs. 4 and 5.

18. David Howell, "The Demanding Mistresses," *The Quality of Cabinet Government*, BBC Radio 3, July 11, 1985.

19. *A Better Tomorrow*, Conservative Central Office, May 26, 1970.

20. Andrew Gray and Bill Jenkins, "Policy Analysis in British Central Government: The Experience of PAR," *Public Administration* 60 (Winter 1982) 429–50; Peter Hennessy, Susan Morrison, and Richard Townsend, *Routine Punctuated by Orgies: The Central Policy Review Staff, 1979–83*, Strathclyde Papers on Government and Politics, no. 30, 1985; Peter Hennessy, "The Quality of Cabinet Government in Britain," *Policy Studies* 6, no. 2 (October 1985).

21. Peter Shore, "Crisis Management," *The Quality of Cabinet Government*, BBC Radio 3, July 18, 1985.

22. Lord Wilson of Rievaulx, "Smoking Is Not Compulsory," *The Quality of Cabinet Government*, BBC Radio 3, June 27, 1985.

23. Private communication.

24. Hugo Young, *The Crossman Affair* (London: Hamish Hamilton, 1977).

25. Richard Crossman, *The Diaries of a Cabinet Minister*, vol. 1: *Minister of Housing 1964–66* (London: Hamish Hamilton and Jonathan Cape, 1975), p. 21.

26. Ibid., p. 22; Jonathan Lynn and Anthony Jay, *The Complete Yes Minister*, BBC, 1984, p. 33.

27. Private communication.

28. *Times*, June 21, 1982.

29. Clive Priestley, seminar at St. George's House, Windsor, The Adam Smith Institute, May 1–2, 1984.

30. Patrick Cosgrave, *Thatcher: The First Term* (London: Bodley Head, 1985), p. 169.

31. Ibid., p. 170.

32. Hennessy, "From Woodshed to Watershed," *Times*, March 5, 1984.

33. Cosgrave, *Thatcher*, p. 71.

34. Private communication.

35. Private communication.

36. *Civil Service Commission Hundred and Eighteenth Report* (Basingstoke: Civil Service Commission, 1985), p. 7.

37. Richard Norton-Taylor, "Senior Civil Servants Ask for Complaints Body," *Guardian*, May 17, 1985.

38. See the British press, July 24, 1985.

39. Private communication.

40. Interview with Peter Jay, *A Week in Politics*, May 24, 1985.

41. Ibid.

42. Sir Robert Armstrong, speech presented at the Chartered Institute of Public Finance and Accountancy Centenary Conference, Brighton, June 18, 1985.

43. Ibid.

44. Douglas Wass, "The Civil Service at the Crossroads," *Political Quarterly* 56, no. 2 (1985), 227–41.

45. Sir Robert Armstrong, *The Duties and Responsibilities of Civil Servants in Relation to Ministers*, Cabinet Office, February 25, 1985.

46. Ibid.

47. Wass, "Civil Service at the Crossroads," p. 234; the reference to the Vicar of Bray is an allusion to a charge made by F. F. Ridley, "Jawohl, Herr Minister," lecture at RIPA, June 4, 1985.

48. Ibid., p. 241.

49. Ibid., p. 235.

50. Ibid.

51. Ibid., p. 241.

52. Conversation with the Prime Minister's Efficiency Unit, March 22, 1985.

53. Peter Hennessy, "Politics of Scapegoating," *Times Higher Education Supplement*, August 2, 1985, p. 12.

54. Lord Rayner, "The Unfinished Agenda," the Stamp Memorial Lecture, University of London, November 6, 1984.

55. Ibid.

56. Ibid.

57. Les Metcalfe and Sue Richards, "The Impact of the Efficiency Strategy: Political Clout or Cultural Change," *Public Administration* 2, no. 4 (1984), 439–54; J. L. Metcalfe and S. Richards, *Improving Public Management* (London: Sage, 1985).

58. Rayner, *Unfinished Agenda*.

59. Tony Benn, "Manifestos and Mandarins," *Policy and Practice: Experience of Government* (London: RIPA, 1980), p. 62.

60. Shirley Williams, "The Decision Makers," *Policy and Practice*, p. 81.

61. Hoskyns, "Westminster and Whitehall."

62. Private communication.

63. Hennessy, Morrison, and Townsend, *Routine Punctuated by Orgies*, pp. 43–47.

64. Sir Kenneth Berrill, "Strength at the Centre—The Case for a Prime Minister's Department," the Stamp Memorial Lecture, University of London, December 4, 1980.

65. Ibid.

66. Lord Hunt of Tanworth, "Cabinet Strategy and Management," Joint Chartered Institute of Public Finance and Accountancy/Royal Institute of Public Administration Conference, June 9, 1983.

67. Joe Haines, *The Politics of Power* (London: Cape, 1977), p. 97.

68. Hunt, "Cabinet Strategy and Management."

69. Peter Hennessy, "The Quality of Cabinet Government in Britain," *Policy Studies* 6, no. 2 (October 1985).

70. Douglas Wass, "Cabinet: Directorate or Directory?" Reith Lecture no. 2, BBC Radio 4, November 16, 1983.

71. Private communication.

72. Crossman, *Inside View* (London: Cape, 1972), p. 46.

73. Private communication.

74. Hoskyns, "Westminster and Whitehall."

75. Ibid.

76. Sir John Hoskyns, "Conservatism Is Not Enough," Annual Institute of Directors Lecture, September 28, 1983.

77. David Owen, "We Have Had Enough of Conservatism with a Small 'c,'" *Political Quarterly* 55 (January–March 1984), 20.

78. "A Wind of Change in Whitehall?" *Economist*, February 12, 1982, p. 25.

79. Brian Sedgemore, *The Secret Constitution: An Analysis of the Political Establishment* (London: Hodder, 1980), pp. 229–35.

30. Tony Benn, "Manifestos and Mandarins," *Policy and Practice*, pp. 27–48.

81. Ibid., p. 77.

82. Edmund Dell, "Collective Responsibility: Fact, Fiction or Facade," *Policy and Practice*, pp. 27–48.

83. Sir Adam Ridley, "Policy-Making in Opposition," RIPA seminar, May 15, 1985.

84. Ibid.

85. David Lipsey, ed., *Making Government Work* (London: Fabian Tract no. 480, 1982), p. 23.

86. Ralf Dahrendorf, *On Britain*, BBC, 1982, p. 162.

87. Lipsey, ed., *Making Government Work*.

88. Ibid., pp. 2, 23.

89. William Plowden, "What Prospects for the Civil Service?"; *RIPA Report* 6, no. 2 (Summer 1985), 1.

90. Private communication.

91. Owen, "Conservatism with a Small "c," p. 17; Benn, "Manifestos and Mandarins," p. 58.

CHAPTER 8

The Rise and Fall and Rise
of the Department of Trade and Industry

૨૦

Brian W. Hogwood

This chapter covers a twenty-five-year period beginning at a time when interest in government intervention in the British economy was about to undergo an upturn.[1] Specifically, 1959 saw a number of changes in departmental responsibilities for industries, marking one of a series of such rounds over the following twenty-five years.

One of the purposes of this chapter is not merely to document the changes in responsibility that have taken place but to analyze how the basis of that responsibility has changed. A good starting point for any such analysis is Gulick's classic four competing principles of organization: the purpose served, the processes employed, the persons or things dealt with, and the area covered—that is, functional, process, client, and territorial principles.[2]

None of these fully describes the allocation of industrial policy responsibilities in Britain at any stage, but the picture in 1959, to a much greater extent than in 1984, was a client-based one, with a number of departments acting as "sponsors" for a set of "production" industries.[3] This concept of sponsorship is of considerable importance in understanding the relationship between government and industry from the 1940s to the 1960s. Sir Maurice Dean explains it as follows:

There is often doubt about the meaning of the word sponsorship. The system started in the last war when manufacturers needed permits from Whitehall for labour and materials. As a result, every industry was allotted to a particular Whitehall department. With the end of controls, sponsorship has come to mean much less but the words "sponsor department" still signify to a particular industry its main point of contact with the government machine. It is, however, not an exclusive point of contact and firms are free to deal with departments other than their sponsor department for special needs.[4]

Sir Richard Clarke suggests that the concept of sponsorship became used in a slovenly way, with confusion between the roles of departments as advocates for the demands of an industry and as links between government and industry, providing the channel through which government policy is created and communicated to industry and industry's views are communicated to government. Clarke suggested in 1975 that "the continuing use of the word 'sponsorship' in the Whitehall vocabulary must take its share of odium for the lack of clarity in the relationship between government and industry in the last 20 years."[5]

Clarke pointed to two snags in the allocation of industries to sponsoring departments. First was the frequency of changes, leading to possible confusion on the part of firms and officials in departments. Secondly, fragmentation of responsibilities for individual industries meant that they tended to be treated as separate enclaves, with responsibility for relationships with individual industries being separated from the responsibility for the government's policy toward industry as a whole.[6] The study of government departments responsible for the shipbuilding industry in the 1950s and 1960s confirms the validity of both these points.[7]

By 1964 the meaning of sponsorship varied widely from one industry to another: "Thus in the case of agriculture where the State was handing over 300 million pounds annually in subsidies, sponsorship clearly meant a great deal. In the case of the chemical industry, fully able to look after itself and relying little on the State, it meant little. So sponsorship meant much or little according to the subject sponsored."[8]

For most "sponsoring" departments in 1959, their responsibility for a set of industries was only part of a broader range of activities. In some cases, the departments had become responsible for an industry because it was a major customer: this was the case with the Ministry of Supply, which was responsible for aircraft production and procurement; the Admiralty, which was responsible for shipbuilding; the Ministry of Health, which was responsible for surgical and health goods and most pharmaceuticals (though not at that stage for proprietary pharmaceuticals, which remained with the Board of Trade); and the Ministry of Works, which had responsibilities for civil engineering and construction.

Other departments had sponsoring functions because of the relationship of those industries with other major functions. Thus, the Ministry of

Agriculture, Fisheries, and Food was responsible for the food processing industry which, as J. W. Grove points out, even then employed many more than farming itself.[9] The Ministry of Power, in addition to dealing with the nationalized energy industries, also dealt with iron and steel, which following nationalization and subsequent denationalization in the early 1950s was now managed indirectly through the Iron and Steel Board.

The nearest approximation to an industry department at this time was the Board of Trade, which had an ancient duty to "care for domestic industries and manufactures."[10] The department had broad functional responsibilities for overseas trade and for commercial regulation, including the relatively recently acquired responsibility for monopolies and restrictive practices legislation. The board had a responsibility, together with the Ministry of Housing and Local Government, the Treasury, and the Ministry of Labour, for administering the government's distribution of industry policy (that is, regional policy). The board was responsible for a number of functions applying to industry generally, including productivity, some research and development functions (but see discussion of R&D below), standards, and industrial statistics.

As far as individual industries were concerned, the Board of Trade was the sponsoring department for all industries not covered specifically by some other department (about half of production, measured by both value and employment). However, it did not actively intervene in them except when crises arose.[11] In other words, it was a reactive rather than a positively intervening department. As result, the board had regular dealings with problem industries such as textiles, motor vehicles, machine tools, and the film industry. It had a particular interest in a number of other industries because of their foreign exchange implications, either because they were major foreign exchange earners, such as electrical engineering and tourism, or large dollar spenders, such as the tobacco industry.

Changes in responsibility in 1959 affected two specific industries. Responsibility for aircraft production and procurement was taken from the disbanded Ministry of Supply and combined with aviation, taken from the Ministry of Transport and Civil Aviation, to form a new Ministry of Aviation. This was one of several changes in responsibility for aircraft production in an attempt to resolve the dilemma of whether responsibility for aircraft production could be separated from defense procurement. Responsibility for shipbuilding, ship repairing, and marine engineering was transferred from the Admiralty to the Ministry of Transport. Again, this was one of a series of changes in departmental responsibility for shipbuilding over the years, but this particular change marked a move away from the "customer as sponsoring department" principle.[12]

The other changes in 1959 affected ministerial responsibility for research and science, including research and development of interest to industry. These formed part of a labyrinthine series of changes in responsibility for these matters both before and after 1959. In October 1959 a new post of minister of science was established. This official took the place of the lord president of the council as chairman to the five Privy Council committees for scientific research; took over responsibility for atomic energy research from the prime minister (who had taken it over from the lord president of the council in 1957); and assumed the supervision of space research. A small Office of the Minister of Science was created, effectively superseding the responsibilities of the Office of the Lord President of the Council. However, this change was less than it seemed, since the lord president of the council up to 1959 became the minister for science (and in July 1960 again took up the post of lord president of the council in addition).[13]

Developments 1959–1964

There were a number of relatively minor changes in ministerial responsibility on industrial policy matters in between 1959 and 1964. For the most part these were ad hoc, but many of them symbolized the increasing interest of the Conservative government in economic planning.[14]

In July 1962 the Ministry of Works was renamed the Ministry of Public Building and Works and given additional responsibilities for studying the problems of the building industry. Over subsequent years various changes increased the roles of the department both as supplier to other government departments and as a sponsor for the building industry as a whole.

One development of interest was the formation of a Scottish Development Department within the Scottish Office in June 1962, taking over responsibility for the work of the old Scottish Home Department on electricity, roads, and industry, together with local government responsibilities from the old health department. Although the "new" department had few industrial responsibilities apart from overseeing the nationalized electricity industry in Scotland, the change signified the Conservative government's increased interest in economic planning at both national and regional level, as well as illustrating how that the territorial principle of allocation of responsibilities does enter into the picture. In January 1963 the lord president of the council was asked to advise the cabinet on means of reviving economic activity in the northeast of England, though with no departmental responsibilities for implementing policy.[15]

In October 1963, the new Conservative prime minister, Sir Alec Douglas-Home, established the new office of secretary of state for trade, industry, and regional development, a position held by the minister who headed the Board of Trade. The minister was to be responsible for coordinating the work of all ministers responsible for regional development. The new office carried with it no new implementing administrative powers, but, together with developments such as the setting up of the National Economic Development Office and the National Incomes Commission in 1962 symbolized the Conservative government's increased inclination toward intervention in the economy.

Shortly before losing office in 1964, the Conservatives made yet another set of changes in responsibilities for research and development, with the Department of Education and Science taking over the responsibilities of the office of the Minister for Science (with the minister for science, Quinton Hogg, becoming the "new" secretary of state for education and science). It was announced in February 1964 that the Department of Scientific and Industrial Research would be disbanded, though this did not take place before the Conservatives lost office. The issue of responsibility for industrial research and development was argued out in the context of a vigorous discussion about the roles of government in promoting scientific research and higher eduction rather than the industrial policy aspects as such, though the Labour Opposition placed particular emphasis on the importance of technology.[16]

The Development of the Ministry of Technology 1964–1969

The return to power of a Labour government at the 1964 general election was accompanied by a flurry of departmental reorganizations, including a number relating to industrial policy. In particular, the Labour Party Manifesto promised to establish a "Ministry of Economic Affairs, with the duty of formulating, with both sides of industry, a national plan," and a "Ministry of Technology to guide and stimulate a major national effort to bring advanced technology and new processes into industry."

With the advantage of hindsight, we can see that the major enduring feature of departmental reorganizations under the Labour government 1964–1970 was the establishment and subsequent development of the Ministry of Technology. The development of this ministry has been characterized in Orwellian phraseology by Sir Richard Clarke, its permanent secretary from 1966 to 1970, as divisible into first Mintech (1964–1967), second Mintech (1967–1969) and third Mintech (1969–1970). However, an examination of the proposals of the incoming Labour government regarding the new ministry and the piecemeal history of its reorganizations provides a much less neatly structured picture. However, in retrospect the first permanent secretary at the Ministry of Technology has claimed, "Our object was to develop it as a Ministry of Industry, particularly of the high technology industries, and to leave to the Board of Trade that vast area of commercial responsibilities which, in so many countries, is handled by a Ministry of Commerce."[17]

Ironically, given the eventual disbandment of the Department of Economic Affairs (DEA) and the continuing accretion of functions by the Ministry of Technology, it was the DEA which was the better prepared proposal, though its proposed functions were not clearly defined.[18] The DEA was intended to focus on planning and the physical side of the economy, in contrast with the Treasury's concern with financial matters. A combination of limited direct executive powers for the DEA, combined with political obsession in the government with financial issues such as the balance of payments and the exchange rate, ensured that the DEA never could fulfill the expectations held for it. The DEA had an Industrial Policy Division, but, as its permanent secretary noted, "The most important distinguishing feature of the Department of Economic Affairs is that unlike others, for example the Board of Trade or the Ministry of Labour, it has no executive responsibilities towards those involved in practical terms in the problems with which it deals."[19] Much of the work of the Industrial Policy Division involved working with the National Economic Development Council and the newly created Economic Development Committees or individual industries, but these bodies in turn had no executive powers.

By initial contrast, the responsibilities of the proposed Ministry of Technology had been so poorly thought through that it took some months before staff were transferred to it and its initial limited responsibilities clarified.[20] Indeed, according to the account given by its first permanent secretary, the Ministry of Technology had something of a struggle for survival in its first few months.[21] It was difficult to define a department around a *process* such as technology that pervaded the economy and therefore the interests of a large number of other departments, in contrast to a broad *function* of government such as overseeing agriculture or trade.[22] The department was also hampered politically by the fact that its first minister, Frank Cousins, had a trade-union rather than a parliamentary background, and at the time of his appointment did not even have a seat in the Commons. The initial allocation of responsibilities was that in addition to being responsible for industrial R&D (including responsibility for the NRDC taken from the Board of Trade and for atomic energy), the Ministry of Technology was made the sponsoring department for computers, machine tools, electronics, and telecommunications. Despite this fragile launch, the Ministry of Technology developed to form the core of what is now (again) the Department of Trade and Industry, indicating that clear remit and a well-prepared launch are *not* preconditions for organizational growth and survival.

As part of the 1964 reorganizations, shipping and shipbuilding were transferred from the Ministry of Transport to the Board of Trade. For shipbuilding this was to be a temporary resting home, since in November 1966, at a crucial stage in government involvement in the industry, responsibility was transferred to the Ministry of Technology.[23]

The overall effect of these 1964 changes was to increase the number of major government departments with functions cutting across industries, one concerned with economic planning (though with virtually no coercive powers) and one concerned with the promotion of technology.

It appears to have been envisaged from the start that the Ministry of Technology would gradually acquire additional functions. The prime minister announced in December 1965 that responsibility for sponsoring the electrical and mechanical engineering industries and for engineering standards and for weights and measures would be transferred to the Ministry of Technology from the Board of Trade. The actual transfer took place in February 1966. Shipbuilding was transferred from the Board of Trade in November 1966. The transfer of engineering to the Ministry of Technology removed the problem whereby "in a triangular situation with Mintech responsible for spreading the technological gospel and BOT as sponsor department, a situation of frustration was inevitable."[24] The Ministry of Technology had tried to get all of engineering from the start and the fact that they did not until later "was something of an embarrassment."[25]

There was a hiatus before the Ministry of Technology acquired aircraft procurement and manufacturing functions from the disbanded Ministry of Aviation in February 1967. Civil aviation functions had been transferred from the Ministry of Aviation to the Board of Trade in June 1966, but there was a delay while it was decided whether the aircraft procurement responsibility should go to the Ministry of Defence or remain linked with sponsorship of aircraft manufacturing and go to the Ministry of Technology. The latter solution was adopted (only for the issue to be confronted yet again in 1970). Although the Ministry of Technology "took over" these aerospace activities, these new responsibilities were actually bigger in staff and expenditure terms than the Ministry of Technology's existing functions, and there was some concern that the political and administra-

tive burdens might swamp the original technological focus.[26] The acquisition of responsibility for aerospace made the department's already existing
responsibility for electronics more meaningful, since the aerospace industry was the major customer for electronics.

This marks the establishment of what Clarke has described as "second
Mintech."[27] It can be seen from the narrative above that the transformation from "first Mintech" into "second Mintech" represents the accumula-
tion of responsibilities over a period of months rather than a single event.
At this stage, the Ministry of Technology combined a set of cross-industry
responsibilities for research, standards, and technology with sponsorship
of a number of engineering and electronic industries.[28]

The transformation of "second Mintech" into "third Mintech" in October 1969 did consist of a single large-scale set of reallocations. The
Ministry of Technology absorbed the Ministry of Power, which in addition
to the nationalized fuel industries was responsible for iron and steel. At
the same time, the Ministry of Technology took over responsibility for the
IRC and industrial planning from the disbanded DEA and responsibility
for regional policy, chemicals, textiles, and mineral extraction from the
Board of Trade. According to the ministry's permanent secretary at the
time:

This time the change in the machinery of government did not arise at all from
the needs of Mintech, which had quite enough on its plate already. It was part
of a definite policy by the Prime Minister . . . to concentrate greater areas of
departmental responsibility within the field of operations of individual ministers,
and to establish a clearer line of authority for new priorities in industrial policy.[29]

Although the Ministry of Technology, in its evolution into "second
Mintech" in 1966–1967, was acquiring direct responsibility for engineering and related sectors, the DEA was itself acquiring an important additional industrial policy function, not because of the transfer of sponsorship
for particular sectors, but because it was the department responsible for
the new Industrial Reorganisation Corporation (IRC). The Ministry of
Technology would, however, claim to have taken the lead in a study which
"played certainly an important and probably a decisive part in the decision of the Government to form an Industrial Re-organization Corporation."[30] The IRC formally came into existence at the end of December
1966, although it had been informally established by summer 1966 (this
presumption of parliamentary approval is normal in Britain). It was given
the role of promoting or assisting the reorganization or development of any
industry, based on the assumption that British firms were often too

small.[31] The IRC was given considerable discretion and powers to carry out this role and a budget ceiling of £150 million. It played a role in promoting, facilitating, or encouraging a number of mergers in the late 1960s, as well as acting as the government's agent in a number of rescue cases.

The relationship between the IRC and its sponsoring department, the DEA, and the government more broadly were initially tense, since the IRC did not appear to be as activist as had been hoped. However, after the IRC's role in promoting the merger between two major electrical engineering companies, GEC and AEI, the relationship became more harmonious.[32] There continued to be fluctuations in the IRC's relationship with its sponsoring department, including the period after the Ministry of Technology became the sponsoring department in 1969 with the disbandment of the DEA.

When the IRC came under the DEA, the Ministry of Technology and other departments concerned with industrial policy nevertheless had a number of links in terms of personnel and overlapping interests.[33] One of the IRC's initial board members was an industrial advisor at the Ministry of Technology; the chairman of the IRC, Lord Kearton, was a member of the Ministry of Technology Advisory Committee. Although the Ministry of Technology had been given responsibility for the engineering industry, the DEA was looking at the problems of the heavy engineering industry at the start of 1967, and this was one of a number of problem industries which the DEA passed on to the IRC. The IRC carried out studies on behalf of a number of departments in 1967 and 1968, including the Ministry of Technology. In 1968 the Ministry of Technology asked the IRC to investigate the nuclear power construction industry, and subsequently to carry out its recommendations. The IRC itself approached departments for information, especially the sponsoring sections of the Ministry of Technology (and prior to that of the Board of Trade). Young reckons that the more technologically complex the industry, the more likely that the IRC was to seek information from the Ministry of Technology.[34]

The IRC's most regular contacts with another government department were with the Board of Trade (and after October 1969 with the Department of Employment and Productivity) over monopolies and restrictive practices. These were in an attempt to iron out conflict between legislation which sought to restrict monopolies and mergers on the one hand, and the role of the IRC in actively promoting mergers.

Responsibility for coordinating this web of contacts fell to the sponsoring department, initially the DEA. Much of the consultation was informal, but there was also an interdepartmental committee. There was a major interdepartmental dispute in 1968–1969, initially over monopolies policy but later broadening out into the whole question of monitoring the private sector.[35] The Ministry of Technology also provided something of a coordinating role for the industries for which it was responsible.

The relationship between the IRC and other government departments and agencies developed over time. The IRC "was growing increasingly closer to MinTech than to the DEA, even before the latter's dissolution led to the former being given the sponsorship role."[36]

When the Labour party was defeated at the 1970 general election, it left behind a Ministry of Technology that in terms of sponsorship of industries and cross-industry functions was a de facto ministry of industry. Trade and regulatory functions were, however, split between the Board of Trade and the Department of Employment and Productivity as a result of the transfer of responsibility for monopolies, mergers, and restrictive practices from the former to the latter in October 1969. The then permanent secretary at the Ministry of Technology subsequently indicated his reservation about this last round of reorganization:

The weakness of this plan was not in the creation of this "giant" department, but in the fact that it left the Board of Trade to carry its responsibilities for overseas commercial policy and export promotion without direct responsibilities for "sponsorship" of manufacturing industry; and this was made worse by the transfer of responsibilities for monopolies and mergers to the Department of Employment and Productivity.[37]

The idea of merging the Ministry of Technology with the Board of Trade was apparently considered but not pursued by Prime Minister Harold Wilson.[38]

Although the Labour government had started out with quite different stated intentions, the net effect of its reorganizations was to establish "industry," rather than research or technology or planning, as a broad function that provided a basis for departmental structure. Despite continuing substantial reorganizations since then, "industry" has continued to be recognized as a "function" providing the basis for a major department of state.

Developments Under the Conservatives 1970–1974

When the Conservatives took office in 1970, they undertook a major consolidation of industrial policy organizations by merging the Ministry of Technology and the Board of Trade (together with monopolies, mergers, and restrictive practices reclaimed from the Department of Employment and Productivity) into a Department of Trade and Industry (DTI). The formation of this "giant" department was only one of a series of departmental mergers which should be seen in the context of (1) ideas or proposals already considered by the previous Labour government;[39] (2) thinking among some senior civil servants about the machinery of government;[40] and (3) proposals for a "new style of government" developed by the Conservatives in opposition.[41] The latter two sets of ideas overlapped in their emphasis on the role of giant departments in promoting the formulation and implementation of an explicit set of objectives for related activities of government and in enabling comparisons to be made about public expenditure allocations to a smaller number of large departments. Departments were to be reorganized on the "functional principle."[42] This approach was further articulated in a white paper, "Reorganisation of Central Government" issued by the Conservative government within four months of taking office.[43]

Although many of these aspirations evaporated when political and economic crises emphasized the continuation of a reactive style of government in practice, the establishment of the DTI did provide an organizational container for more coherent industrial policies. In a sense, it removed the organizational excuse for ineffective policies.

The formation of the DTI received less widespread approval than the formation of the other main "giant" department, the Department of the Environment. The Labour Opposition criticized the DTI as too large and too heterogeneous and some senior civil servants considered the DTI's functions too miscellaneous.[44]

The aerospace functions of the Ministry of Technology were temporarily allocated to a Ministry of Aviation Supply while the relationship between responsibility for civil aerospace and defense procurement was again examined. The Gordian knot was at last cut, and procurement was allocated to a procurement executive within the Ministry of Defence, and civil aerospace sponsorship went to the DTI (though the procurement executive acted as the DTI's agent in the management and execution of the civil aerospace program).[45] The permanent secretary of the DTI at the time was less than enthusiastic at taking on this additional responsibility.

The resolution of responsibility for aerospace left pharmaceuticals and health equipment (Department of Health and Social Security) and the construction industry (Department of the Environment) as the only major industries still sponsored on a "customer as sponsoring department" principle.

Given the frenetic pace of constant reorganizations between 1964 and

1969, the absence of major reallocations to or from the DTI between 1971 and the end of 1973 might appear to mark a period of stability. However, this apparent stability conceals a change of emphasis in the work of the DTI and an important internal reorganization. While it is possible to exaggerate the extent to which there was a U-turn from nonintervention in 1970 to intervention in 1972, the Industry Act of 1972 represented a systematic framework for government support and intervention for both national and regional reasons. Associated with this change of emphasis, an industrial development executive was established within the DTI, including accountants and people with financial or industrial experience. This development was interesting, in that it involved the establishment of a unit within a government department rather than in a separate statutory body. A further development within the DTI was the appointment in 1972 of a second cabinet minister at the DTI with responsibility for prices and consumer affairs as well as trade. This signified the more interventionist stand of the Heath government on prices and incomes.

The organizational grand design of 1970 began to unravel as departmental change was used as a response to political crisis. With the institution of direct rule in 1972, a Northern Ireland Office was established; this made relatively little difference to London's involvement in Northern Ireland industrial affairs since major industrial policy decisions had already involved Whitehall, and even under direct rule the Northern Ireland departments retained a considerable degree of autonomy in administering policy and proposing policy changes.[46] Northern Ireland industrial policy matters were not handed over to the DTI.

A combination of the oil price rise and the miners' strike made energy policy a highly salient political issue in 1973. Accordingly, in January 1974, weeks before the Conservative government lost office, a Department of Energy was carved out of the DTI. This split was strongly opposed by the DTI, with the secretary of state threatening resignation.[47] The DTI still remained a very large functional department. It is worth noting that the organizational change in response to the energy crisis was very much simpler in Britain, where energy functions were already consolidated within the DTI, than in the United States, where energy functions had to be consolidated from a number of existing departments and agencies.[48]

Despite the carving out of the Department of Energy, the DTI remained a very large department organized around the industrial policy "function," now redefined to exclude energy. That there was nothing immutable about such an arrangement was quickly made clear by the incoming Labour government in 1974.

The Dissolution of the DTI: Changes Between 1974 and 1979

The carving out of the Department of Energy from the DTI was rapidly followed by a much more dramatic splitting of its responsibilities into three departments: Industry, Trade, and Prices and Consumer Protection. Thus what had been one giant department was split four ways within a matter of months. Pollitt suggests that the splitting up was due to three considerations: (1) the need to balance DTI portfolios among different political positions within the Labour leadership, especially over the Common Market; (2) the salience of inflation as a political consideration leading to a separate department; and (3) Labour's view, noted earlier, that DTI was too large and heterogenous.[49] A possible, more personal, consideration is that Harold Wilson may have considered it undesirable to give a large department to Tony Benn to administer.[50]

One element of consolidation did take place. The Ministry of Posts and Telecommunications, which had been set up when the Post Office (then including what is now British Telecom) ceased to be a government department in 1969 and was transformed into a public corporation, was disbanded. Responsibility for posts and telecommunications was transferred to the Department of Industry, and broadcasting came under the Home Office. A move of this sort had been expected at some stage, since the Ministry of Posts and Telecommunications was a small department with a narrow remit, and its merger had been advocated by Clarke.[51]

The DTI set up only in 1970 therefore appeared to have been completely dismembered by spring 1974. But, in fact, such a total dismemberment did not take place. Although strangely uncommented on (for example, not mentioned by the definitive work on changes in British government departments),[52] the common services of the Departments of Industry, Trade, and Prices and Consumer Protection were maintained intact, although the Department of Energy did become largely separate. The "Departments of Industry, Trade, and Prices and Consumer Protection Common Services" is an example of what I have elsewhere called an "interdepartment,"[53] the other major example of which is the common services of the Departments of Environment and Transport, which were split in 1976. The common services covered staffing and finance, economics and statistics, legal services, accountancy services, and information services. A common staffing structure was maintained—an important point if the issue of socialization of staff into "departmental views" is considered significant.

The regional offices also continued to be integrated. Initially, these were nominally under the Department of Industry, though continuing to carry out trade work and reporting on that to the Department of Trade. However, when personnel restraints become fierce in the early 1980s, the Department of Industry objected to having trade work in regional offices being counted against its personnel targets, and the regional offices were nominally reallocated to common services, though this did not affect their operation or lines of responsibility. (The regional offices also carried out, and still do, work for the Department of Energy, which does not have its own regional office structure.)

The significance of this continuing common service element in personnel terms can be seen from the figures for 1975 (they are not provided for subsequent years). Out of a total listed for the Department of Industry of 10,239 "more than 4,000" staff (not including the regional offices) were in common services.[54] By comparison, figures for the Department of Trade were 7,303 and for Prices and Consumer Protection 347. Thus, even without the inclusion of the regional offices, the common services element was over 20 percent of the combined staff of the departments and was of the same order of magnitude as the two main departments drawing on the common services.

Thus, rather than unwind all the integration efforts of the previous four years on the assumption that the new arrangements were permanent, the civil servants arranged for a continuation of the existing common services. What this effectively meant was that there was a "shadow DTI" in operation throughout the 1974–1983 period.

In the context of concern about the rise of nationalist parties in Scotland and Wales and the limitation of devolution to proposed assemblies, the Labour government announced increased decentralization of the administration of regional and employment policy.[55] The Scottish and Welsh Offices were given responsibility for the administration of selective regional financial assistance (but not automatic assistance). They were also given a role in responsibility for manpower policy, though this did not actually give them any direct executive responsibility. Another important development was the establishment of the Scottish and Welsh Development Agencies (largely based on existing organizations) under the Scottish and Welsh Offices, respectively. From the perspective of overall British industrial policy, these arrangements were of relatively minor significance. However, they did place a greater emphasis on the territorial principle of the allocation of responsibilities. More important, they served to emphasize that the Scottish and Welsh Offices had a role to play in industrial and regional policy. Thus, while the Department of Industry was clearly the "lead" department in all British-wide industrial and regional policy matters, it became accepted that the Scottish and Welsh Offices had a legitimate role to play in the formation of policy changes and in guidelines for implementation throughout Britain and not simply in terms of administration within their own countries.

One development that began in the late 1970s and only later became significant in terms of interdepartmental allocation of responsibilities was that the Urban Programme administered by local authorities developed less of a social emphasis and more of an economic one. This was symbolized by the transfer of responsibility for the Urban Programme from the Home Office to the Department of the Environment (and the Welsh Office) in June 1977. This changing direction of the Urban Programme raised the possibility of overlap with the Department of Industry both in terms of the focus on industry and on an "urban" rather than "regional" definition of policy.

The Labour government of 1974–1979 in splitting up the DTI might appear to have undone the thrust of much of the reorganization of the preceding Conservative government. However, a basically functional definition of allocation of industrial responsibilities was maintained. The continuation of joint common services also meant that the departments formerly making up the DTI were clearly identified as a set of organizations with something in common.

The DTI Reincarnated: Developments 1979–1985

The incoming Thatcher government, though committed to substantial changes in policy, had relatively little interest in institutional rejigging of government departments. One of the few changes which was made by the incoming government was the merging of the Department of Prices and Consumer Protection, already small and with no envisaged continuing role in price control, with the Department of Trade. The Department of Trade thereby again became responsible for a wide range of regulations affecting companies.

Although no changes in formal responsibility were involved, there were interesting developments in the responsibilities of the Departments of Industry and the Environment arising from a mixture of ministerial personalities and changing policy emphases on the territorial focus on economic problems. The secretary of state for industry, Sir Keith Joseph, did not believe in direct government involvement in industry, though circumstances constrained him to continue such involvement.[56] Michael Heseltine at the Department of the Environment, by contrast, developed a style of taking actual or apparent initiatives. He also became genuinely concerned about the economic condition of many inner-city areas, which he was made aware of as a result of his responsibilities for the Urban Programme and local authorities more generally. Normal Whitehall practice would be to leave an initiative to the department most obviously responsible, or at a minimum engage in extensive interdepartmental consultation regarding the initiative. However, Heseltine, without consulting the Department of Industry, launched an initiative to promote local enterprise agencies, which would enable local businesses to assist the promotion of job opportunities in their area. This and other developments on the urban economic front led to strains between the two departments at both the national and the regional level. The tension was resolved by a document referred to as the "concordat," sent to the relevant deputy secretary at the Department of the Environment by the Department of Industry. This peace treaty set out the procedures to be adopted in both Whitehall and the regions in dealing with such matters as applications for urban development grant for industrial assistance. The Department of Industry reclaimed responsibility for local enterprise agencies.

When the Conservative government was returned in 1983, there were again few departmental changes, but again industrial policy departments were affected. The Departments of Trade and Industry were merged, with the exception of aviation and shipping, which were transferred from the Department of Trade to the Department of Transport. The Department of Transport thus came full circle in our story, ending up in 1983 with the same responsibilities the Ministry of Transport and Civil Aviation had had before the 1959 changes. The "new" DTI also acquired responsibility for radio frequency regulation from the Home Office, a minor change in itself but significant in the context of developing telecommunications markets.

Some internal reorganizations followed the reestablishment of the DTI, but the task of integration was obviously made easier by the fact that the departments already shared common services. At first the DTI continued with two permanent secretaries (top civil servants), one on the trade side and one on the industry side, but in March 1985, the permanent secretary on the trade side was asked to retire a year early and the remaining permanent secretary took responsibility for the entire department.

It soon became clear that the remerger of the Department of Trade and Industry was not to be a final or even long-term arrangement, but was merely an interim stage in the continuing flux of policy fashion and personalities. A minor change occurred in December 1984, with the Scottish and Welsh Offices being given responsibility for administering regional development grants in addition to their existing responsibility for selective regional assistance. Given the earlier decisions to give the Scottish and Welsh Offices a role in regional policy administration, this change, which coincided with a revamping of regional policy, represented a rationalization of administration, with a further strengthening of the territorial dimension of administration.

A much more important change occurred in September 1985, when the DTI's responsibility for small firms and tourism was moved over to the Department of Employment, together with the junior minister responsible for them. Thus size of firm was to be added to functional and territorial definitions of industrial policy responsibilities. The DTI officials fought a rearguard action to minimize the definition of small firm responsibilities to be transferred. That the DTI has not accepted the change as the new status quo is symbolized by the continued publication by the DTI of a newsletter, *In Business Now: News for small and growing businesses from the Department of Trade and Industry*. The DTI's ability to fight the loss of responsibilities was hampered by the fact that the change coincided with a ministerial reshuffle so that the previous minister, Norman Tebbit, had no continuing interest in the fate of the department.

Two important features of the change can be identified. The first is the government's increasing concern with unemployment as a political issue; given the association the government made between small firms and service industries and job creation, the change symbolized the government's concern. Second, the personal standing of the new Secretary of State, Lord Young, in the prime minister's eyes is important in understanding the department's new roles. Just as Harold Wilson had strengthened the Department of Employment and Productivity to give Barbara Castle a department with strengthened responsibilities, so nearly two decades later Margaret Thatcher had done the same for Lord Young to that department's successor. Lord Young, formerly chairman of the Manpower Services Commission, had been appointed as a minister without portfolio in 1984 and had been responsible for a new "Enterprise Unit" set up in the Cabinet Office. Lord Young took the unit with him to the department. One of the unit's main concerns had been to reduce the regulatory burdens which the government imposed on firms, particularly small firms. Thus the Department of Employment effectively became the Department for Deregulation, while the DTI remained the Department for Regulation. Proponents of the idea of creative tension can expect an interesting test of whether it can produce positive results. More jaded commentators will expect two departments working at cross-purposes, with the occasional episode of direct combat.

Political fashions and personalities will change, and so will the responsibilties of the Departments of Employment and of Trade and Industry.

Conclusions

If one were to examine simply the 1959 "before" and the 1984 "after" positions, one would note the decline of fragmented "sponsorship" departments and the consolidation of a wide range of sponsorship and cross-industry functions in a single Department of Trade and Industry. One might assume that this must have come about by an expansion of the functions of the Board of Trade, since it dealt with many of these matters in 1959. The Department of Transport seems similar to the Ministry of Transport and Civil Aviation of 1959, and the Department of Energy is similar to the Ministry of Power without iron and steel (though with important new responsibilities related to North Sea oil). Yet as the narrative in earlier sections shows, there was a long and winding set of roads to journey from the 1959 structure to the 1984.[57] There has been a considerable element of "rediscovering the same solution." Guy Peters and I argue that there is a particular danger of reinventing the same "solution" when there is a rapid sequence of policy successions.[58]

So just as striking as the emergence of the "functional" principle for structuring departments that deal with industrial policy has been the sheer frequency of changes. Whatever the disadvantages of any given structure at any given time, these disadvantages are at least in part outweighed by the costs of change. It takes time for restructured departments to begin to operate smoothly.[59] Arguably, in the period 1964–1970 there was inadequate time between changes to evaluate the advantages and disadvantages of any given arrangement. At the same time, change itself produced disruption—though occasionally also an initial sense of exhilaration among those participating in a new venture.

This chapter has concentrated on changes to ministerial departments, and has mentioned other bodies, such as the IRC, only when they are relevant to an understanding of changes in departmental responsibilities. The scale and pace of organizational change would be further emphasized if it had been possible to cover the establishment and abolition of bodies such as the Shipbuilding Industry Board and the formation and subsequent transformation of the National Enterprise Board.

To reiterate a point already well understood in the literature on organizational change in government: many reorganizations have a symbolic rather than largely instrumental purpose. The establishment of new bodies, or the replacement of old, serves to emphasize a government's commitment to, say, technology or planning or the reinvigoration of the Scottish economy, even if such bodies are not necessarily given the resources necessary to substantially implement such commitment.

While it would be wrong to attribute an underlying purpose to the overall collection of changes, it would also be wrong to see the consequences as simply random. Reorganizations affect the channels through which issues are processed and therefore how such issues will be characterized as well as affecting the option chosen for dealing with them.

This chapter has for the most part discussed changes in individual departments, but as some of the discussion has shown, industrial policy has been the concern of a number of different, and necessarily interacting, organizations. Reorganization has affected the membership of this network and how those members interact. In some ways, then, the network of industrial policy departments should be seen as our unit of structure when analyzing the implications of change. During the period under consideration, the types of interaction have included that between functional departments (such as the old Board of Trade) and sponsoring departments, between departments with different functional emphases (technology and planning, or industrial policy and urban economic policy), and especially since the mid-1970s between a functionally defined department like the DTI and territorial departments like the Scottish and Welsh Offices.

At the opposite extreme—the detailed responsibilities and how they are transferred within and between departments—there is no basic organizational unit of British government usable between industries or functions or across time. As I have shown in the case of responsibility for the shipbuilding industry,[60] a responsibility that is transferred between departments may in between be mixed in with a bewildering range of other activities, so that there is no separate unit that can be tracked. (Changes in *internal* structures of departments have not been discussed in this chapter: that would reveal a continuing orgy of reallocation). A narrative type of analysis of change at this level is practicable, but the lack of a suitable basic unit of analysis poses problems for the quantitative analysis of change over time in British government. There is no clear self-contained unit of transfer. The existence of "interdepartments" further muddies the waters.

This chapter, purportedly about changes to British government departments dealing with industrial policy matters, concludes by emphasizing that analysis of change must be focused on levels above and below the individual department if the significance of reorganization is to be understood.

Notes

1. Samuel Brittan, *Steering the Economy: The Role of the Treasury* (Harmondworth, Middlesex: Penguin, 1971); Jacques Leruez, *Economic Planning and Politics in Britain* (London: Martin Robertson, 1975).

2. Brian W. Hogwood, "The Regional Dimension of Industrial Policy," in *The Territorial Dimension in United Kingdom Politics*, ed. Peter Madgwick and Richard Rose (London: Macmillan, 1982), pp. 55–64; Guy B. Peters, *The Politics of Bureaucracy: A Comparative Perspective* (New York: Longman, 1978), pp. 109–24.

3. J. W. Grove, *Government and Industry in Britain* (London: Longman, 1962).

4. Sir Maurice Dean, "The Machinery for Economic Planning: IV. The Ministry of Technology," *Public Administration* 44 (1966), 51.

5. Sir Richard Clarke, "The Machinery of Government," in *The Modernisation of British Government*, ed. William Thornhill (London: Pitman, 1975), p. 79.

6. Ibid., p. 80.

7. Brian W. Hogwood, *Government and Shipbuilding: The Politics of Industrial Change* (Farnborough, Hants: Saxon House, 1979), ch. 9.

8. Sir Maurice Dean, "The Formation of the Ministry of Technology," lecture at the University of Strathclyde, May 19, 1967.

9. J. W. Grove, *Government and Industry in Britain* (London: Longman, 1962), p. 93.

10. Ibid., p. 87.

11. Ibid., p. 88.

12. Hogwood, *Government and Shipbuilding*, ch. 9.

13. D. N. Chester and F. M. G. Willson, *The Organization of British Central Government* (London: Allen and Unwin, 1968), p. 372.

14. Ibid., ch. 10; Christopher Pollitt, *Manipulating the Machine: Changing the Pattern of Ministerial Departments 1960–83* (London: Allen and Unwin, 1984), ch. 4.

15. Brian W. Hogwood, "The Regional Dimension of Industrial Policy," in *The Territorial Dimension in United Kingdom Politics*, ed. Peter Madgwick and Richard Rose (London: Macmillan, 1982), pp. 34–66.

16. Chester and Willson, *The Organization of British Central Government*, pp. 372–75; Pollitt, *Manipulating the Machine*, pp. 28–33; Dean, "The Formation of the Ministry of Technology," pp. 3–8.

17. Sir Maurice Dean, seminar on Machinery of Government Changes, University of Strathclyde, Nov. 12, 1970, p. 10; H. Wilson, *The Labour Government* (London: Michael Joseph, 1971), pp. 8, 62.

18. Pollitt, *Manipulating the Machine*, pp. 51–62; Leruez, *Economic Planning and Politics in Britain*, ch. 6; Brittan, *Steering the Economy*, pp. 310–24.

19. Sir Eric Roll, "The Machinery for Economic Planning: I. The Department of Economic Affairs," *Public Administration* 44 (1966), 1–11.

20. Pollitt, *Manipulating the Machine*, p. 56; Sir Richard Clarke, "Mintech in Retrospect," *Omega*, 1 (1973), pp. 28–29; Dean, "The Machinery for Economic Planning," pp. 58–59.

21. Dean, "The Formation of the Ministry of Technology."

22. Pollitt, *Manipulating the Machine*, p. 57; Dean, "The Machinery for Economic Planning," pp. 58–59.

23. Hogwood, *Government and Shipbuilding*, pp. 244–45.

24. Dean, "The Formation of the Ministry of Technology," p. 16.

25. Ibid.

26. Ibid., p. 30.

27. Clarke, "Mintech in Retrospect."

28. Peter Self, *Administrative Theories and Politics* (London: Allen and Unwin, 1972), p. 58.

29. Clarke, "Mintech in Retrospect," p. 35.

30. Dean, "The Formation of the Ministry of Technology," p. 28.

31. Stephen Young and A. V. Lowe, *Intervention in the Mixed Economy* (London: Croom Helm, 1974), chs. 4–10.

32. Ibid., pp. 93–95.

33. Ibid., pp. 96–105.

34. Ibid., p. 99.

35. Ibid., p. 102.

36. Ibid., p. 106.

37. Clarke, "Mintech in Retrospect," p. 36.

38. Pollitt, *Manipulating the Machine*, pp. 60–61.

39. Ibid., ch. 5.

40. Sir Richard Clarke, *New Trends in Government*, Civil Service College Studies, no. 1 (HMSO, 1971).

41. David Howell, *A New Style of Government* (London: Conservative Political Centre, 1970); Pollitt, *Manipulating the Machine*, ch. 6.

42. Pollitt, *Manipulating the Machine*, p. 87.

43. Cmnd 4506, "Reorganisation of Central Government," London: HMSO, 1970.

44. Pollitt, *Manipulating the Machine*, pp. 94, 98.

45. Ibid., p. 196.

46. Hogwood, "The Regional Dimension of Industrial Policy."

47. Pollitt, *Manipulating the Machine*, p. 105.

48. Brian W. Hogwood and B. Guy Peters, *Policy Dynamics* (New York: St. Martin's Press and Brighton: Wheatsheaf, 1983), pp. 94–95.

49. Pollitt, *Manipulating the Machine*, pp. 108–09.

50. Wyn Grant, *The Political Economy of Industrial Policy* (London: Butterworths, 1982), p. 30.

51. Clarke, *New Trends in Government*; see also Pollitt, *Manipulating the Machine*, pp. 111–12.

52. Pollitt, *Manipulating the Machine*.

53. Brian W. Hogwood and P. D. Lindley, "Variations in Regional Boundaries," in *Regional Government in England*, ed. Brian Hogwood and Michael Keating (Oxford: Oxford University Press), p. 25.

54. *Civil Service Statistics 1975*, p. 21.

55. Hogwood, "The Regional Dimension of Industrial Policy"; Brian W. Hogwood, "In Search of Accountability: The Territorial Dimension of Industrial Policy," *Studies in Public Policy*, no. 82 (Glasgow: Centre for the Study of Public Policy, University of Strathclyde, 1982).

56. Sir Keith Joseph, "At Least Make the Framework Sensible," in *Allies or Adversaries? Perspectives on Government and Industry in Britain* (London: Royal Institute of Public Administration, 1981).

57. Cf. Clarke, "Mintech in Retrospect," p. 30.

58. Hogwood and Peters, *Policy Dynamics*, p. 264.

59. Clarke, *New Trends in Government*; Hogwood, *Government and Shipbuilding*, and "Analysing Industrial Policy: A Multi-perspective Approach," *Public Administration Bulletin* 29 (1979); Pollitt, *Manipulating the Machine*, pp. 146–49.

60. Hogwood, *Government and Shipbuilding*.

PART IV

Other National Experiences

CHAPTER 9

Administrative Reform and
Theories of Organization

❧

Johan P. Olsen

Challenges of the Public Revolution

Since 1945 the growth and diversification of the public agenda has been so extensive that it amounts to a public revolution.[1] Likewise, changes in the organization of the administrative apparatus have been substantial. Two interrelated developments stand out. First, the number of nondepartmental bodies "at the margin of the state" has grown. Administrative functions have been entrusted to semiautonomous governmental or quasi-private agencies.[2] Second, there has been an extensive and complicated interpenetration of governmental agencies and organized interests. Public policymaking and the administration of public programs have been turned over to a network of collegial bodies in which civil servants, experts, and the representatives of organized interests have been the major participants.[3]

The development has not been the result of explicit design based on an administrative doctrine: nor has it generated a coherent body of justifications post hoc. The process has rather been an example of what Skowronek names patchwork and Johnson calls opportunistic pragmatism. A result is that the actual working of the administrative apparatus has become more complex and more obscure. It is difficult to say precisely who influences the administrative apparatus, to whom it is accountable, and with whom it identifies, but it is often documented that there are loose connections between elected political leaders and governmental agencies.

The situation is a challenge to theories of representative and responsible government, and especially to the parliamentarian doctrine of ministerial responsibility. The ideas that ministers head unified bureaucracies, that the administrative apparatus is a tool for implementing the policies of elected political leaders, and that ministers are responsible to a parliament for its actions, seem to capture the realities of everyday administrative life only to a limited extent. While it has always been difficult to reconcile democratic theories and bureaucratic realities, today the need for a reconstruction rather than a marginal updating of our theories is more pressing than ever.

The situation is also a challenge to political leaders, and in many countries the government now gives high priority to administrative reform. Aspirations are high. It is believed that a comprehensive review and reorganization of the administrative apparatus will facilitate the achievement of political goals. Reform objectives include the usual concerns of reorganization efforts—economy and efficiency. But more important, programs of reorganization also involve discussions of the proper role of the state and politics in society, the ethical base and legitimacy of government, and attempts to redesign the public agenda. What is labeled a "modernization" of the administrative apparatus may amount to a reconstitution rather than patchwork.

This chapter focuses on such reorganization attempts. My primary interest is in the organization of the links between central political authorities and various agencies. Sometimes efforts are made to tighten these relations in the name of ministerial responsibility. But sometimes central governments argue for more loosely coupled relations.[4] Why should any government want to give agencies more autonomy? Considering this question may help us place ideas of numerical democracy, majority rule, and minsterial responsibility within a wider framework of democratic theory. It may also illuminate the possibilities and limitations of political leadership through administrative reform.

The next section summarizes some possible lessons from empirical studies of organizational decision making and change. Reorganization efforts are based on explicit or implicit assumptions about formal organizations—how they are formed and changed, how decisions are made within and between them, and what effects they have. Thus studies of formal organizations may contribute to more realistic underpinnings of democratic theory, as well as of theories of political leadership and administrative reform. Then I will outline four different models of state governance, each of which links ideas about the proper role of the state and specific agencies to assumptions about organizational properties. The two final parts illustrate how this framework may be helpful in analyzing some recent administrative reforms in Norway, and discuss why it is difficult to establish stable relations between central political authorities and agencies of government.

Theories of Organizational Choice and Change

Students of organizations have often put a damper on the enthusiasm of administrative reformers. They have argued that traditional democratic theory has provided a flawed model of administrative management of the public sector,[5] that hopes for a firm theoretical basis for organizational design have been mostly unfulfilled,[6] that prescriptions for organizational design tend to be contradictory,[7] and that advice is often given without making explicit the assumptions and the methods used.[8] But despite the difficulties involved in understanding and controlling the structure of formal organizations and institutions, attention to the organizational factors in human behavior and to organizational design has increased in recent years.[9]

The thrust of this chapter is that the weaknesses of the ministerial-responsibility doctrine and the sovereign-state model to a large extent coincide with the weaknesses of classical theories of organizational choice. Both emphasize decision making as the product of rational choices made on the basis of prior objectives; both see organizational forms as instruments for making those choices; and both regard reorganization as a way of making those instruments more effective and efficient.

Empirical studies of decision making in formal organizations have over the past thirty years contributed to a gradual relaxation of the idea of willful choice as the basic model of organizational behavior and change.[10] Thus, the recent study of organizations has been linked to one of the most honored traditions in political theory—the role of intentions, reflection, and choice in the development of political institutions.[11]

Cognition

A first major criticism of the rational-choice model and thus the ministerial-responsibility model is that it makes extraordinary time and information demands on decision makers—although it takes time to gather information, information and time are treated as freely available resources.[12] As it has become more generally accepted that the complexity of decision making often overwhelms the cognitive abilities and the time budgets of ministers and other organizational leaders, it has become more usual to build models of governance that acknowledge bounded rationality. A result is increased interest in models which assume that leaders have ambiguous preferences, do not completely understand causal connections, and are sometimes part-time participants.[13]

Conflict

A second major criticism was that organizations cannot be viewed as unitary actors with simple, consistent, and stable preferences. Nor may it be assumed that conflicting preferences are managed by some prior agreement like a coalition contract or an employment contract. Rather, an important feature of organizations is that they exist, and that officials make decisions, despite significant unresolved conflict. Strategic action and coalition formation are central features of organizational choice and change.[14] Consequently, standard political models have become more relevant in studies of organizations.[15]

Appropriateness and Legitimacy

Organizations are institutions as well as instruments for leaders.[16] Norms, rules, and standard operating procedures modify the consequences of bounded rationality and conflict. They limit the scope of, and systematically bias, decision making. Decision making in this approach is a search for appropriate actions within established structures of meaning and norms rather than choice among alternatives on the basis of rational expectations. Rationality is constructed after the fact to make sense of behavior that has already occurred. As a consequence, students of organizational decision making have relaxed the assumption that the primary outcome of a decision process is the substantive decision, or who-gets-what. More attention is focused on organizations as interpretive and symbolic systems, where the development of meaning, including concepts of appropriateness and legitimacy, are central outcomes.[17]

Contextuality

Theories of organizations have become more contextual, and empirical studies describe environments as less understood and less controlled than assumed by models of rational choice. One major branch of studies has interpreted environments as deterministic and viewed surviving organizations and decision rules as the result of environmental, evolutionary selection.[18] Students of decision making have been more inclined to view environments as an ecology of games rather than deterministic—an approach we will return to.[19]

Four Models of Governance and Autonomy

We do not expect any single model to apply to all government agencies in all situations. The task is to match models to situations, that is, to clarify where the different models are applicable.[20] The four kinds of models can be ordered along two dimensions. First, we distinguish between voluntaristic and deterministic explanations of decision making, that is, whether explanations are based on assumptions about rational actors who make decisions about the future or assumptions about the causal impact of environmental or situational factors—"forces" that make organizational actors irrelevant as explanatory variables.[21] We differentiate between models that assume that conflict is solved a priori, so that decisions are made with reference to shared goals or norms, and models that assume conflict and self-interested behavior.[22]

The resulting four (ideal-type) models are summarized in table 9.1. Each relaxes one of the crucial assumptions underlying the doctrine of ministerial responsibility and the model of the sovereign, society-forming state as a goal-directed, rational, unitary, and sovereign actor. First, the *sovereign, rationality-bounded state model* views rationality as problematic. It assumes that the state is sovereign, but that rationality is limited and that time and energy are scarce resources for political leaders. Second, the *institutional state model* views legitimacy as problematic. It assumes that behavior is driven by standard operating procedures, and that the main concern of the state is the development and maintenance of norms and meaning—including ideas about the proper sphere for politics and majority rule. Third, the *corporate-pluralist state model* views power as problematic. It assumes that the state is an arena for resolving conflicts between self-interested public and private actors. Fourth, the *supermarket state model* views the environment as dominating the state. It assumes that the state is an epiphenomenon, formed by "objective," social forces.

This chapter will argue that each model is based on a different view of the proper role of the state, the public, and government agencies, and that these views are linked to (1) ideas about how organizations are formed and changed, (2) the criteria or standards used in assessing organizations, (3) beliefs about the most adequate organizational form for specific agencies and for the networks they are embedded in, (4) the justification for agency autonomy, and (5) predictions about when change will take place.

The Sovereign, Rationality-Bounded State

In this model, the role of the state is to adapt society to political preferences, plans, and visions of the good society. The perspective is managerial. Winning public elections gives political leaders the necessary authority, legitimacy, and power to act as the architects of society. The public is viewed as voters subordinate to the state. The administration is a neutral instrument and its task is to implement political goals and programs.

TABLE 9.1
Four Models of Governance

	Decisions are voluntary and reflect the goals and expectations of rational actors	*Decisions are determined and respond to environmental forces*
	Sovereign Rationality-Bounded State Model	*Institutional State Model*
The organization's role in the state	The state is the architect of society; the agency is a neutral instrument implementing political goals; the public are voters subordinate to the state.	The state develops and maintains political and moral order; the agency protects the order and individual rights; the public are citizens with rights and duties defined by the system.
Formation of organizations	Organizations are designed by political leaders; autonomy is delegated.	Organizations develop over time in a natural, historical process.
Criteria used to assess organizations	Organizations are judged by their political effectiveness.	Organizations are judged by their effects on structures of meaning and norms.
The organization's form and place in a network	The organization is a departmental agency embedded in a hierarchy.	The organization is an independent court embedded in a moral order.
Reasons for an organization's autonomy	Autonomy is justified by rationality and expertise; it relieves political leaders and avoids embarrassment	Autonomy is justified by shared norms of noninterference.
Reasons for change in an organization	Change depends on changes in political leaders, elections, coalition formation and breakdown.	Change depends on the historical process, mostly influenced by changes in the government.
	Corporate-Pluralist State Model	*Supermarket State Model*
The organization's role in the state	The state is an arena for bargaining and conflict resolution; the agency defends special interests; the public are members of formal organizations.	The state is a service provider and "bookkeeper for the great necessities"; the agency facilitates service delivery; the public are sovereign consumers or clients.
Formation of organizations	Organizations develop out of bargaining and political struggles among interests.	Organizations are formed by environmental pressures, "evolutionary" selection.
Criteria used to assess organizations	Organizations are judged according to who gets what.	Organizations are judged according to their economy, efficiency, flexibility, and survival.
The organization's form and place in a network	The organization is a collegium with interest representation embedded in a corporate-pluralist network.	The organization is a corporation embedded in a competitive market.
Reasons for an organization's autonomy	Autonomy is justified by realpolitik, or the distribution of interests and power.	Autonomy is justified by the ability to survive.
Reasons for change in an organization	Change depends on changes in power, interests, and alliances.	Change depends on the rate of stability or change in the environment.

Decisions are made among actors with shared goals or norms

Decisions are made among actors with conflicting interests

Political leaders design the administrative apparatus to make it more effective and efficient. The standard organizational model is the departmental agency, embedded in a hierarchy of influence, responsibility, and control, and insulated from other influences. If an agency achieves autonomy from central control, it is by leadership choice or *delegation*. Leaders delegate decisions because they are embarrassing, unimportant, or routine. They also accept that certain tasks demand special skills, experience, working methods, and organizational forms that cannot easily be combined with the standard departmental form. Thus, leaders face a dilemma. Tightly controlled agencies often show little initiative—they become impotent and formalistic. Less tightly controlled agencies, on the other hand, may allow self-interest or special interests to take priority, rather than the politically defined national interest.[23] Leaders prefer loosely coupled relations in situations where they are heavily dependent on an agency's energy and expertise, and where differences in interests, definitions of the situation, and identifications are modest. In such cases, agencies or boards of experts are given a central role in public policymaking.

The degree of autonomy from central governance given to an agency is a question of ranking decisions in terms of their importance and attractiveness for leaders, and stipulating the role of experts. Loose coupling is the result of leaders' choice, because they see it as a means of achieving their goals. Leaders may be ignorant about causal effects, but they have the authority or power to make choices. Thus, changes in organizations primarily follow changes in political leadership, such as when government loses an election, or when coalitions break down and new ones are formed.

The Institutional State

In this model the state is viewed as a political and moral order, and as a collection of long-lasting standard operating procedures—reflecting values, principles, and beliefs that are shared by the population. The primary task of the state is to guarantee the political order and the autonomy of various institutional spheres of society. Political leaders are "gardeners" more than architects—their duty is to support rather than to direct society. They are obliged to defend uniform and collective standards of appropriateness and justice, with a reference to what is best for society as a whole. Such standards rank higher than numerical democracy and cannot be changed arbitrarily through majority decisions. The public is viewed as citizens with system-defined rights and duties.

Governmental agencies are not neutral instruments in the institutional state. They are cultural systems and carriers of missions, values, and identities. They are unlikely to adapt automatically to any attempts of influence—including those of political leaders.[24] Organizations are not designed, they develop slowly and imperceptibly over time through a "natural," historical process.[25] The long-run development is less a product of intentions, plans, and consistent decisions than incremental adaptation to ever changing problems with available solutions within gradually evolving structures of meaning. Reorganizations formalize developments that have already taken place. They are symbolic and rhetorical events that educate the public and change the climate of opinion. Reorganization processes facilitate the maintenance, development, and transmission of cultural norms and beliefs, and they keep concepts, theories, and proposals alive.[26]

Agency autonomy is based not upon leaders' choice, but upon a shared norm of noninterference and an appeal to higher and more stable values than numerical democracy, majority decisions, and ministerial responsibility. The standard form of organizations in the institutional state is the independent court embedded in a political and moral order. The term of the major actors is indefinite. They exercise authority in a way that reflects the history and the future of the institution without reference to the interests of a specific constituency—that is, without reflecting or adjusting to the demands of a current set of elected political leaders, voters, consumers, employees, or owners. There may be substantial conflict between the immediate self-interest of current constituencies and the long-run interest of future constituencies. The independent-court model assumes that it is possible to identify or train incorruptible judges capable of perceiving the long-run logic of the institution. The model also assumes that it is possible to induce the public to accept, a posteriori, actions in the name of the institution that they would not necessarily have chosen a priori.[27] Like Ulysses, they are willing to tie themselves to the mast in order to avoid the Sirens' song about short-term interests and benefits.[28]

Thus, we would not expect elections or shifting governmental coalitions to create major changes in the organization of the administrative apparatus. Reforms will be slow and incremental, reflecting the development of the wider political culture. Where party leaders or experts are the judges (or "high priests") of the political order, change will follow the development of shared understanding among such groups.

The Corporate-Pluralist State

In this model the state is involved in a political struggle between self-interested, powerful, organized actors. Elected leaders do not have the power assumed by the sovereign state model. In Rokkan's terms—votes count, but resources decide. Winning elections gives one a place at the bargaining table, but the formal administrative hierarchy is just a minor part of the real structure of control. The public is viewed as members of a variety of self-interested formal organizations.

While historical studies have been primarily interested in struggles between the state and social actors like the church and the business corporation, or in fights between the constitutional powers, the contemporary literature on bureaucratic politics focuses upon the administrative apparatus as a collection of agencies with different models of the world, loyalties, and resouces.[29] Agencies are unlikely to be neutral instruments for elected leaders. They act strategically and take part in various coalitions of public and private interests.

Political leaders are unable arbitrarily to design or reform the administrative apparatus. Reorganizations result from struggles over the control of organizations, and organizational structures are the results of previous political fights.[30] To be effective, the reorganization process must reflect the heterogeneity of interests, beliefs, and power that surround public policymaking.[31] Agency autonomy from central governance is the choice of a winning coalition.

In this model the standard organizational form is a collegium with interest representation, embedded in a network of government boards and committees.[32] Conflicting preferences are resolved by bargaining between representatives of the major interests and then forcing a compromise on the members. No single actor can decide unilaterally and force all the others to abide by a decision. Threats and sanctions are used, but normally all parties will be better off if a compromise is reached. The contending interests are well defined and organized. They have access to public policymaking, and they are committed to the results of collective bargaining. The main concern of the participants is who-gets-what: including the allocation of substantive benefits and future positions.

Changes in the organization of the administrative apparatus is a result of changes in constellations of interests, resources, and alliances. Elections and renegotiation of government coalitions have an impact, as do changes in the relative position of agencies, professional groups, experts, and organized interests in society.

The Supermarket State

In this model the state is a service provider—an epiphenomenon of technological, economic, demographic and physical forces outside the explicit control of any actors. Political leaders are the "bookkeepers of the great necessities."[33] Agencies are supposed to perform services in the most efficient way and to adapt to changing needs and circumstances. The public is viewed as sovereign consumers or clients.

Administrative reforms mirror attempts to make agencies adapt better to environmental forces. However, explanations of organizational patterns are based on environmental, evolutionary selection, not on the ability of leaders to make rational choices.[34] There is no need to build into the model assumptions about actor rationality and motives because organizational forms that are inconsistent with environmental contingencies are selected out and disappear. Only the most adaptable forms survive.

Survival, flexibility, economy, and efficiency become the key values for assessing organizational forms. Flexibility of an organization depends on acquiring good intelligence about external changes and upon its capacity to process this information and make appropriate responses. This implies a need for delegating decisions to those who have the necessary information and expertise.[35] Agency autonomy from central political authority is the result of environmental necessities.

The standard organizational model is the corporation embedded in a competitive market. A government agency is just one among many market actors. The assumptions of the supermarket state model are those of the perfect market. Quality, price, and quantity are determined in the usual competitive market way. The market is characterized by perfect information, easily available alternatives, and ease of entry. There is little friction. A basic idea is that history is efficient. Problems move rapidly to solutions determined by current environmental conditions, and thus are independent of the historical path that is central to the institutional state mode.[36]

Changes in the organization of the administrative apparatus depend upon the rate of change in the environment. In turbulent societies or turbulent times, administrative patterns change rapidly. In rigid societies the administrative apparatus will be highly stable, independent of shifts in governments or ruling coalitions. Competition is the main factor in securing flexibility, adaptability, and innovation.

Recent Reforms: The Norwegian Case

Each of the four models represents a form of governance that is, under some specified set of circumstances, politically efficient. That is, if implemented under certain conditions, each system will be able to discover viable solutions reliably and with minimum administrative costs.[37] Further work is needed to specify the models better and to specify the conditions under which they are politically efficient and the conditions under which a state or an agency shifts from one model to another. More work is also needed to analyze how different models enter the political debate as ideological sterotypes used to decribe the governmental system or to establish norms for administrative reforms. While this chapter is a part of a larger study,[38] we concentrate on using the four models to illustrate briefly some recent administrative reforms, and programs for reforms, in Norway.

The Norwegian case may be of some general interest because the Nordic welfare state model has for some time been viewed as a success story, combining an active welfare state with a welfare society. The last decade has seen the emergence of a less optimistic mood, and more doubt about the present situation and future possibilities.[39] Governments in all the Nordic countries have become more interested in exploring the possibility of administrative reform. The question has been repeatedly raised whether a large welfare state necessarily makes a better society. Governments are searching for new visions of the role of the public sector in future society. And the situation seems to have a potential for major modifications of the administrative apparatus.

The transformation from a liberal-democratic state with a modest public agenda to the present welfare state required a reconciliation of the new activities with existing institutions.[40] Of special importance in Norway was a cadre of civil servants primarily trained in law, with lifelong, protected careers in public administration; with their primary loyalty toward an impersonal system of laws; with an independent court and the objective, impartial judge as role models—and thus with strong elements of the institutional state model of governance.[41]

The growing agenda made it necessary to transfer a substantial amount of discretion to the administrative apparatus. Political leaders had to be relieved from administrative burdens, new types of expertise had to be used, and it was crucial to encourage initiative and flexibility in public administration.[42] An administrative apparatus based on the procedures of the independent court model would not have the capacity, expertise, or flexibility needed for many of the new tasks of the state. But there were strong disagreements over the amount of discretion to be transferred and how it should be controlled.[43]

The transferred discretion had three significant consequences. First, the number of nondepartmental agencies grew faster than the number of departmental agencies.[44] Second, civil servants became key players in public policymaking—as defenders of different institutions, agencies, values, and clients. Their views and behavior are formed by the tasks they are responsible for, by the agencies and professions to which they belong, and by the parts of the environment they interact with. Their most usual role perception is as negotiators or mediators—not impartial judges.[45] Third, organized interests claimed—and achieved—direct, integrated participation in the formation of public policy and administration of public programs.[46] As ideas about workplace democracy and codetermination spread from the private to the public sector, the associations of civil servants also became major participants.[47]

Martin Heisler and Robert Kvavik described Norway as the archetype of the "European polity model." That is a modern welfare state which has institutionalized a stable political process characterized by the following: a declining role given to parliaments, ideological parties, and the public; the delegation of authority to a network of boards and committees where bureaucrats and organized interests are the main participants; the absence of broad ideological issues; a political agenda dominated by technical issues; a low level of conflict; and an emphasis on compromise.[48]

In terms of the four models, Norway took a large step toward becoming a corporate-pluralist state. Political, economic, cultural, and social spheres became more integrated. The participation of organized interests made hierarchical governance based on sheer votes more problematic. The role of the market was modified, as was the significance of institutional and constitutional rules. The tendency was to view such rules as instruments of majority governance, rather than as constraints on government.[49] It became more difficult for courts and courtlike institutions to assert themselves because so much discretion was transferred to collegial decision-making organs acting without clear regulations or standards. While all four models were still relevant for capturing parts of administrative reality, their relative importance certainly changed. Recent reforms can be seen as an attempt to turn Norway away from the corporate-pluralist state.

The administrative reform program of the conservative-center government reveals a strong belief in the relevance of organizational design. It assumes that the organization of the administrative apparatus has a significant impact upon the content of decisions made; that an administrative policy is important; and that government has the right and the ability to design the administrative apparatus in order to facilitate the implementation of political goals.

The political debate has focused upon questions of privatization and deregulation. Certainly the program aspires to push back frontiers of public regulation, control, and expenditures, and to expose governmental agencies to more competition. But the program also includes ideas about restoring governance based on numerical democracy and a renewed emphasis on the institutional state.

The corporate-pluralist state is seen by reformers as too expansive and expensive. It is too rigid and sectorized—unable to change its own structures, work processes, and priorities. Its ability to reallocate goods is doubted. The corporate-pluralist state also makes society less innovative and enterprising, as well as less flexible and able to adapt to technological and economic necessities. Special interests are too powerful in public policymaking. Professions act in self-interested ways, not as experts driven by codes of ethics and the needs of citizens. Elected leaders and individual citizens have problems asserting their rights, and while the main tendency since 1945 has been to integrate organized interests, and thus social conflicts, into the administrative apparatus,[50] the key argument now is that the state, in order to govern, needs a certain distance and independence from the various interests. The lines of responsibility between public authorities and organized interests should be drawn more clearly. Consequently, the number of collegial bodies will be reduced. Government will be more reluctant to allow organized interest to participate; alternatively, weakly organized interests or commonweal organizations will be given participation rights to balance the sector-oriented interests dominating the system today. The government also emphasizes that workplace democracy must not constrain the operation of political democracy. In sum, the very basis of the corporate-pluralist state is questioned.

The solution to the problem is not to establish a sovereign state—to collect all power in the hands of government. That would be against the government's ideology and principles of decentralization and power sharing. It would also be unrealistic because hierarchical channels have limited capacity and are cumbersome to use. Thus, the task is to relieve central government for most decisions, to increase the integrative capacity and the ability to establish general goals, frameworks, and principles for decisions to be made elsewhere.[51]

Within such broad frameworks, state agencies are promised more autonomy. That is, more autonomy from central, political control will accompany more influence for the public as consumers and clients. The ideas of the sovereign consumer, the private corporation, and the competitive market are to be given a more central place in public administration. A powerful bureaucracy is to become more productive and more directed toward the public's needs and preferences. Where marketlike conditions cannot be established, the incentive structure should be constructed to simulate markets.[52]

The reform program is also concerned with the traditional issues of the institutional state. Democratic governance needs: (1) a sense of community, joint interests, shared loyalties, identification, a sense of justice, due process, and predictability, and (2) institutional spheres beyond political intervention and majority rule that guarantee citizens' rights and protects private initiative. The concern for the value base of society and political life is viewed as increasingly important because Norwegian society is moving from a unitary Christian-humanitarian culture to a more pluralistic culture. Among the organizational implications are to give the (state) Church of Norway more autonomy from political intervention and to establish more nonpolitical appellate institutions, independent courtlike agencies, similar to the present ombudsmen and the Insurance Court.[53]

In sum, the reform program of the Norwegian government is negative toward the corporate-pluralist state model. It is positive toward the three other models. Reformers will study the eighty central administrative, nondepartmental agencies in an attempt to simplify and coordinate their organizational structures and systems of governance. A fundamental promise of the program is that it will be possible to define the division of labor and responsibility more clearly between society and state; between institutional spheres of political, economic, social and cultural activities; and between different types of governmental tasks.[54] Corporations and organized interests should get out of politics. Public corporations should be treated like private firms and should compete on equal terms. Business and service agencies will be given more autonomy where competition can be established. Public monopolies will not be given autonomy.

The model of organization and governance should be a function of the substantive content of decisions to be made or work to be done. The sovereign rationality-bounded state model should be used where the task is to establish basic frameworks for social life. The institutional state model should be used where the task is to secure citizens' rights and other values ranking over majority governance. And the supermarket state model should be used where the task is to provide public services with the highest possible productivity and flexibility.

The intentions of the administrative reform program has been followed up in recent reorganizations. Since 1981 the number of governmental boards and committees has been reduced by more than 200. Partly this reduction is cosmetic—a result of updating statistical records more than changing patterns of representation. But partly the reduction is real, and a break with the trend since 1945. Government has also stayed out of central bargaining over salaries and wages. Participation in such processes is seen as costly and unproductive.[55]

A central theme in the reorganization of the state oil company (Statoil), the central health administration, the Water Resources and Electricity Board, and the Telegraph Service, has been to separate political, administrative, expertise, and businesslike functions; to distinguish between those functions that are exposed to competition and those that are not; and to let organizational designs and systems of governance be a function of the distinctions drawn.

While the ideals of the corporation and the competitive market have been obvious in most reorganizations, the importanct of strengthening political control has also been emphasized in the reorganization of the health service,[56] the administration of aid to developing countries,[57] the state oil company, and the Bank of Norway.[58] The granting of autonomy based on institutional arguments has been most obvious in the case of the Church of Norway.

Temporal Structures, Ambiguity, and Governance

It remains to be seen whether the reform program will succeed and a "new Nordic model" will develop. Clearly, there is no simple solution to the organizational problems of the welfare state. None of the four models specified above, nor any other single model of governance, can alone guarantee representative and responsible government. At present, almost no one advocates growth of government[59] and the weaknesses of the corporate-pluralist state model are emphasized. It would be a mistake to forget what an active welfare state and governance based (primarily) on the corporate-pluralistic model has accomplished over the last four decades— for instance, in the Nordic countries. For students of politics and organization the challenge is to specify better alternative organizational forms, to clarify the assumptions they are based on, to document the effects of alternative forms upon democratic values, and to consider the possibilities and limitations of using administrative reform as a political means.

In terms of the four constraints on the rational-actor model, the Norwegian government seems to be little concerned about institutional and constitutional constraints and authority and power constraints. The government *is* concerned about the need to adapt to environment constraints and the need to improve available theories and data about the actual working of the administrative apparatus. How realistic are such assumptions?

Over the last four decades, institutional and constitutional constraints on administrative reforms have declined in importance.[60] The attention given to reorganizations by political leaders has varied.[61] Where reorganizations have been given top priority, ordinary routines have been by-passed, and political leaders have often succeeded.[62] However, such cases have been restricted to reforms of specific agencies. Large-scale reorganizations may be derailed more easily and may attract more opposition.[63] The international tendency seems to be that the public does not evaluate government organizations according to their congruence with classic democratic norms of representativeness: they appear to judge them by their performance in delivering services. Yet in Norway political traditions, as well as present configurations of power, make it a reasonable guess that a coalition demanding reforms of the administrative apparatus will collect more support than a coalition aiming at extensive privatization and more use of competitive markets.

Knowledge about the causal effects of organizational forms may be a limiting factor. Case studies show that even when the government controls reorganization processes and achieves a favored solution, neither the objectives nor the effects of organizational changes are clear. Reorganizations may focus on solving personnel problems or aim at creating a balance between participating parties in a governing coalition. Typically governments have been accused of ill-considered reorganization decisions. Problems, goals, alternative organizational forms and their consequences are badly specified and analyzed. Little is done afterward to collect data about actual effects.[64]

There are no theoretical reasons for assuming one-to-one relationships between organizational forms and various outputs, like decision-making content.[65] Organizational forms interact with a great number of other factors. Thus, interaction between variables may modify the effects of an organizational form from one context to another. Likewise, environments are often ambiguous and give conflicting implications for organizational design.[66] Organizational adjustments to environments are not instantaneous or efficient, and equilibrium between environmental contingencies and organizational structures are rare.[67] This view implies that the government may overestimate contextual constraints on administrative reforms.

The less understood the causal structure, and the less effort invested in exploring actual effects, the more likely that reorganizations will be merely symbolic. Organizational forms will be used to symbolize values, beliefs and loyalties; "reorganization" becomes a code word symbolizing a general frustration with bureaucracy and governmental intrusion in private lives.[68] Since it is often difficult to establish legitimacy by showing that decisions accomplish appropriate objectives, legitimacy depends on the appropriateness of the process as much as it does on the outcomes. Structural, process, or personnel measures are treated as surrogates for outcome measures and it becomes vital for organizations to use normatively approved forms.[69]

It is beyond the scope of this chapter to enter into the details about the factors that drive or constrain administrative reforms. My final remarks are restricted to a problem the Norwegian reform program shares with most reorganization efforts. It is very difficult to impose clear distinctions between different categories of organizational and individual actors, and between different tasks and decisions, and to maintain a stable matching of actors and tasks/decisions.

A common observation in the study of public management is that nearly any issue at any time may be politicized.[70] Political and administrative roles are fundamentally unstable and agency autonomy is affected by the level of politicization and conflict.[71] To separate a decision-making process into two phases—one where conflicts are solved (politics), and another where decisions are implemented—is problematic. All phases of decision making have elements of strategic action and conflict resolution.[72] Thus, restoring clear divisions of labor, authority, and responsibility is a Sisyphian job. Distinctions between politics and administration, or expertise, or implementation, or economics are unstable because the definitions of issues and decisions are so.

Most decision makers are part-time participants in the process, and their attention to goals and decisions is sequential. Governmental agencies will act will act with long periods of inattention from the minister, interrupted by brief periods of intensive monitoring and attempts of influence—usually as a result of a political crises. Management by exception means that as long as there are no complaints or visible failures, the superordinate authority does not intervene.[73] Typically, reorganization efforts have difficulty sustaining the attention of major actors.[74] Reorganizations are also occasions where the rationale for existing structures are rediscovered. Reformers setting out to solve a problem may redesign the organizational structure, only to discover afterward that the organization is doing worse, by some criteria unnoticed during the reorganization.[75]

Students of decision making in organizations describe behavior as unfolding, sequential, and variable. Preferences and meaning develop in the process as new participants are activated. New participants are involved as the definition of a choice changes. The short-run course of action is heavily influenced by the ways in which relatively autonomous flows of choice opportunities, problems, solutions, and participants are associated in terms of their simultaneous availability. Sometimes temporal structures are more important than forecast consequences, and decisions are turned into "garbage cans" for participants, problems, and solutions.[76]

Reformers typically try to eliminate the temporal order of "garbage-can" situations. They do their best to clarify goals, specify chains of ends and means, and to control the access to decisions for participants, problems, and solutions. Essentially, such attempts, and their concomitant organizational models are based on stimulus-response theory. Organizational behavior is understood in terms of antecedent stimuli—the preferences, norms, or power of the actors or exogenous forces and situational contingencies.[77] While the stimulus-response view, with its emphasis on clarity and order, has so far exerted a dominating influence on reformers of public administration, students of decision making in organizations argue that it may be unwise, as well as difficult, to eliminate temporal orders and ambiguity.

Messy processes have their virtues. Acknowledging ambiguity reflects an intelligent modesty about the adequacy of one's guesses about future wants and needs, and facing up to ambiguity is part of a sensible effort to manage the tendency for one's preferences to become inappropriate.[78] Ambiguity allows preferences to develop through action.[79] Vague and imprecise goals tend to give new and innovative ideas a chance.[80] Coexisting definitions and concepts can facilitate rapid change.[81]

Ambiguity also affords protection from the misuse of rational argument.[82] For instance, if politicians commit themselves to clear goals or plans, bureaucrats with superior information can more easily act strategically.[83] Removing ambiguity also deprives politicians of a means of direct influence. For instance, defining a decision as an administrative or a technical issue makes it easier for a minister to stay out of the decision. Defining a choice as political can be used to restrict access for bureaucrats and experts.[84]

Thus, the art of managing and changing networks of large-scale organizations may not depend on the ability to remove ambiguity, crosspressures, and conflicts, like those arising from multiple sources of accountability,[85] but to be able to live with such tensions or to exploit them for reform purposes.

Notes

1. Richard Rose, *Understanding Big Government* (London: Sage, 1984); Daniel Tarschys, *Den Offentliga Revolutionen* (Stockholm: Liber, 1984).
2. Anthony Barker, *Quangos in Britain* (London: Macmillan, 1982); D. C. Hague, W. J. M. Mackenzie, and Anthony Barker, *Public Policy and Private Interests, The Institution of Compromise* (London: Macmillan, 1975); Brian Hogwood, "The Tartan Fringe: Quangos and Other Assorted Animals in Scotland," manuscript, University of Strathclyde, 1979; Grant Jordan, "Hiving Off and Departmental Agencies," *Public Administration Bulletin* 21 (1976), 37–51.
3. Martin O. Heisler and Robert B. Kvavik, "Patterns in European Politics:

the 'European Polity' Model," in *Politics in Europe*, ed. Heisler (New York: David McKay, 1974), pp. 27–89.

4. B. Guy Peters, "The Machinery of Government: Concepts and Issues," manuscript, Political Science Department, University of Pittsburgh, 1984.

5. Martha W. Weinberg, *Managing the State* (Cambridge, Mass.: MIT Press, 1977).

6. Harold Seidman, *Politics, Position and Power: the Dynamics of Federal Organization* (New York: Oxford University Press, 1980).

7. Herbert Simon, *Administrative Behavior* (New York: Macmillan, 1957); Herbert Kaufman, "Reflections on Administrative Reorganization," in *Setting National Priorities: The 1978 Budget*, ed. J. A. Pechman (Washington, D.C.: Brookings, 1977).

8. Fritz W. Scharpf, "Does Organization Matter? Task Structure and Interaction in the Ministerial Bureaucracy," in *Organization Design: Theoretical Perspectives and Empirical Findings*, ed. Elmer Burack and Anant Negandhi (Kent, Ohio: Kent State University Press, 1977), pp. 149–67.

9. Morten Egeberg, *Organisasjonsutforming: Offentlig Virksomhet* (Oslo: Aschehoug, 1984).

10. James G. March, "Decision in Organizations and Theories of Choice," in *Assessing Organizational Design and Performance*, ed. Andrew Van de Ven and William Joyce (New York: Wiley, 1981).

11. Alexander Hamilton, John Jay, and James Madison, *The Federalist Papers* (New York: Pocket Books, 1964); John Stuart Mill, *Considerations on Representative Government* (South Bend, Ind.: Gateway Press, 1962).

12. Herbert Simon, *Models of Man* (New York: Wiley, 1957), and *Administrative Behavior* (New York: Macmillan, 1957).

13. Michael Cohen, "Artificial Intelligence and the Dynamic Performance of Organizational Designs," in *Ambiguity and command: Organizational Perspectives on Military Decision Making*, ed. James G. March and Robert Weissinger-Baylon (White Plains, N.Y.: Pitman, 1986).

14. James G. March, "The Business Firm as a Political Coalition," *Journal of Politics* 24 (1962), 662–78; Richard M. Cyert and James G. March, *A Behavioral Theory of the Firm* (Englewood Cliffs, N.J.: Prentice-Hall, 1963).

15. Samuel B. Bacharach and Edward J. Lawler, *Power and Politics in Organizations* (San Francisco: Jossey-Bass, 1980).

16. Philip Selznick, *Leadership in Administration* (New York: Harper, 1957).

17. Martha S. Feldman and James G. March, "Information as Signal and Symbol," *Administrative Science Quarterly* 26 (1981), 171–86.

18. Howard E. Aldrich, *Organizations and Environments* (Englewood Cliffs, N.J.: Prentice-Hall, 1977).

19. N. Long, "The Local Community as an Ecology of Games," *American Journal of Sociology* 44 (1958), 251–61.

20. Dennis A. Hayes and James G. March, "The Normative Problem of University Governance," Graduate School of Business, Stanford University.

21. John Child and Alfred Kieser, "Development of Organizations Over Time," in *Handbook of Organizational Design*, ed. Paul C. Nystrom and William H. Starbuck (Oxford: Oxford University Press, 1981).

22. James G. March and Herbert Simon, *Organizations* (New York: Wiley, 1958).

23. S. N. Eisenstadt, "Bureaucracy and Bureaucratization," *Current Sociology* 7 (1958), 99–164.

24. James B. March, "Footnotes to Organizational Change," *Administrative Science Quarterly* 26 (1981), 563–77.

25. Edward McChesney Sait, *Political Institutions—A Preface* (New York: Appleton-Century-Crofts, 1938).

26. James G. March and Johan P. Olsen, "Organizing Political Life: What Administrative Reorganization Tells Us About Government," *American Political Science Review* 77 (1983), 281–97.

27. Hayes and March, "The Normative Problem of University Governance."

28. Jon Elster, *Ulysses and the Sirens* (Cambridge: Cambridge University Press, 1984).

29. Graham T. Allison, *Essence of Decision* (Boston: Little, Brown, 1971).

30. March, "The Business Firm as a Political Coalition"; Jeffrey Pfeffer, *Organizations and Organizational Theory* (Boston: Pitman, 1981).

31. Francis Rourke, "The Politics of Administrative Reorganization," *Journal of Politics* 19 (1957), 461–78.

32. Jorolv Moren, *Den Collegiale Forvaltning* (Oslo: Universitetsforlaget, 1974).

33. Jens Seip, *Teorien om Det Opinionsstyrte Eneveldet* (Oslo: Universitetsforlaget, 1958).

34. Michael T. Hannan and John Freeman, "The Population Ecology of Organizations," *American Journal of Sociology* 82 (1977), 929–64.

35. Child and Kieser, "Development of Organizations Over Time."

36. James G. March and Johan P. Olsen, "The New Institutionalism: Organizational Factors in Political Life," *American Political Science Review* 78 (1984), 734–49.

37. Hayes and March, "The Normative Problem of University Governance."

38. Johan P. Olsen, "Statsstyre, Fristilling og Organisering," manuscript, Institute of Public Administration and Organization Theory, University of Bergen, 1985.

39. Erik Allardt et al., *Nordic Democracy* (Copenhagen: Det Danske Selskab, 1981).

40. Douglas E. Ashford, *Political Development of the Welfare State*, manuscript, Political Science Department, University of Pittsburgh, 1985.

41. Forvaltningskomiteen, *Innstilling fra Komiteen til a Utrede Spjersmolet om mer Betryggende Former for den Offentlige Forvaltning* (Krager: Naper, 1958).

42. Wilhelm Thagaard, "Den Offentlige Administrasjon Under et System med Statsregulert naeringsliv," *Nordisk Administrativt Tidsskrift* 26 (1946), 156–71.

43. Francis Sejersted, *Hoyres Historie 3. Opposision og Posisjon* (Oslo: Cappelen, 1984); Sejersted, *Demokrati og Rettsstat* (Oslo: Universitetsforlaget, 1984); Rune Slagstad, "En ny Statsskikk? Striden om Fullmaktslovene etter 1945," *Samtiden* 2 (1984), 39–45.

44. Paul G. Roness, *Reogranisering av Departementa–eit Politisk Styringsmiddel?* (Bergen, Norway: Universitetsforlaget, 1979).

45. Per Laegreid and Johan P. Olsen, *Byrakråti og Beslutninger* (Bergen, Norway: Universitetsforlaget, 1978); Laegreid and Olsen, "Top Civil Servants in Norway: Key Players—on Different Teams," in *Bureaucrats and Policy Making*, ed. Ezra N. Suleiman (New York: Holmes and Meier, 1984).

46. Morten Egeberg, *Stat og Organisasjoner* (Bergen, Norway: Universitetsforlaget, 1981).

47. Per Laegreid, "Medbestemmingsretten i den Offentlige Sektor og det Politiske Demokrati," *Deltakerdemokratiet* (Oslo: Universitetsforlaget, 1983).

48. Heisler and Kvavik, "Patterns in European Politics," p. 24.

49. Slagstad, "En ny Statsskikk?"

50. St. meld nr. 83, 1984–85, Langtidsprogrammet, pp. 300–06.

51. Ibid., p. 299.

52. Ibid., p. 311.

53. Ibid., p. 300.

54. Ibid., pp. 303, 397.

55. Sejersted, *Hoyres Historie 3. Opposision og Posisjon*, p. 338.

56. Tom Christensen, "Styrt Endring og Planlagte Konsekvenser. En Organisasjonsanalyse av omorganiseringen i den sentrale Helseforvaltning 1982–83," manuscript, Institutt for Samfunnsvitenskap, Tromso, 1985.

57. Katrine Kloster, *U-hjelpsforvaltningen: En analyse av (re) organiseringsprosessen, og en drofting av mulige konsekvenser av reorganiseringen for politikkens innhold* (Oslo: Institutt for Statsvitenskap, Hovedoppgave, 1984).

58. Olsen, "Statsstyre."

59. Klaus von Beyme, "The Role of the State and the Growth of Government," *International Political Science Review* 6 (1985), 11–34.

60. Olsen, "Statsstyre."

61. Egeberg, *Organisasjonsutforming i Offentlig Virksomhet.*

62. Christensen, "Styrt Endring og Planlagte Konsekvenser."

63. March and Olsen, "Organizing Political Life."

64. Christensen, "Styrt Endring og Planlagte Konsekvenser"; Ingunn Gjerde, *Planleggingssekretariatet—en Studie av Etablering og Virkemate* (Bergen, Norway: Institutt for Offentlig Administrasjon og Organisasjonskunnskap: Hovedoppgave, 1983).

65. Scharpf, *Policy Failure and Institutional Reform.*

66. Child and Kieser, "Development of Organizations Over Time."

67. March and Olsen "The New Institutionalism."

68. Seidman, *Politics, Position and Power.*

69. John W. Meyer and Brian Rowan, "Institutionalized Organizations: For-

mal Structure as Myth and Ceremony," *American Journal of Sociology* 83 (1977), 340–63.

70. David G. Garson and E. Samuel Overman, *Public Management Research in the United States* (New York: Praeger, 1983).

71. Bengt Jacobsson, *Hur Styrs Forvaltningen—myt og Verklighet Kring Departementenes Styrning av Ambetsverken* (Stockholm: EFI—Studentlitteratur, 1984).

72. March, "Decision in Organizations and Theories of Choice," p. 221.

73. Renate Mayntz, "Public Bureaucracies and Policy Implementation," *International Social Science Journal* 31 (1979), 632–45.

74. March and Olsen, "Organizing Political Life."

75. Johan P. Olsen, "Reorganisering som Politisk Virkemiddel og Statsvitenskap som Arkitektonisk Disiplin," *Statsviteren* 4 (1982), 1–20.

76. Cohen, "Artificial Intelligence and the Dynamic Performance of Organizational Designs"; Michael Cohen and James G. March, *Leadership and Ambiguity: The American College President* (New York: McGraw-Hill, 1974).

77. Pfeffer, *Organizations and Organization Theory.*

78. James G. March, "Bounded Rationality, Ambiguity, and the Engineering of Choice," *Bell Journal of Economics* 9 (1978), 587–608.

79. Michael Cohen and Robert Axelrod, "Coping with Complexity: The Adaptive Value of Changing Utility," *American Economic Review* 74 (1974), 30–42.

80. John W. Kingdon, *Agendas, Alternatives, and Public Policies* (Boston: Little, Brown, 1984), p. 192.

81. Child and Kieser, "Development of Organizations Over Time," p. 52.

82. March, "Bounded Rationality, Ambiguity, and the Engineering of Choice."

83. Daniel Tarschys and Maud Eduards, *Petita: Hur Svenska Myndigheter Argumenterar for Hogre Anslag* (Stockholm: Liber, 1975), p. 91.

84. Christensen, *Styrt Endring og Planlagte Konsekvenser,* p. 72.

85. Richard Rose, "Accountability to Electorates and the Market: *The Alternatives for Public Organizations,*" manuscript, Centre for the Study of Public Policy, University of Strathclyde, 1985.

CHAPTER 10

The Centralization-Decentralization
Tug-of-War in the New Executive Branch
૨**

Michael G. Hansen and Charles H. Levine

IF THERE is any one proposition that students of public administration can agree on, it is probably that there is no consensus about the best way to organize and manage the U.S. federal government. Unlike the thirties, forties, and fifties, when the Brownlow and Hoover Commissions articulated clear and widely accepted doctrines of administrative practice, for the past three decades there has been no consensus in the field of public administration regarding basic principles of public management. As nature abhors a vacuum, the Reagan administration has stepped forward with the avowed purpose of resolving these issues of organization and management in the direction of greater presidential control and streamlining governmental operations. However, the changes already instituted and the administration's proposals for further change have not been accompanied by any overarching articulated theory of governance or of public management. The result may well be to confuse the issue further by leaving practice unguided by any consistent doctrine. Critics of the Reagan administration's management practices have also charged that this strategy has further weakened the administrative capacity of the permanent federal work force.

This chapter will review the following argument: (1) In the United States the career civil service suffers from problematic legal standing and weak political legitimacy that leaves it vulnerable to political incursions and ideological shifts. (2) Given the Reagan administration's success in creating an "administrative presidency," conservative proposals for even greater change in this direction would have the effect of transforming parts of the bureacracy into a weak "technocracy."[1] (3) These reforms, if fully implemented, run counter to the needs of modern complex government. (4) Thus the long-term result may well be a passive bureaucracy unable to implement policies without high error rates, low productivity, and excessive delays.[2]

To evaluate this line of argument, it is necessary to explore several of these assertions in greater depth. The discussion is organized around the following questions: What is the "legitimate" role of career public employees in the federal government and how has this changed in the past three decades? How has the Reagan administration organized and managed the executive branch? What proposals have been made for further transforming the bureaucracy? How do these changes and proposals compare to the organization and management needs of the federal government and contemporary private-sector theory and practice? And what are the long-term implications of these proposals, and of the changes already implemented, for the capacity and performance of the federal government?

Legitimacy of the Bureacracy

Perhaps the key to understanding what is happening to the American federal bureaucracy is to understand why it has so little legitimacy. David Easton has defined "legitimacy," as applied to a government or organization, as "the conviction on the part of the member that it is right and proper for him to accept and obey the authorities and to abide by the requirements of the regime. It reflects the fact that in some vague or explicit way he sees these objects as conforming to his own moral principles, his own sense of what is right and proper in the political sphere."[3] While Easton is speaking of the political system as a whole, the same ideas are applicable to subsystems like bureacracies; their existence and actions are granted more or less legitimacy by their clients, elected officials, and the general public.

The legitimacy of the bureaucracy in the United States is made problematic by its uncertain legal standing and its week position in the nation's political system. Legally the Constitution barely hints at the existence of administrative agencies and does little to clarify their relationship to the three main branches of government—Congress, president, and Supreme Court. The Constitution merely gives the president the right to request written opinions from the heads of departments and, if Congress agrees, to appoint such inferior officers in government as necessary. On this slim constitutional peg, the American civil service developed largely without constitutional status for most of our history. Lacking constitutional clarity, the role of bureaucracy in the governmental system has been defined gradually through legal precedent on a case-by-case basis. According to Peter Strauss:

Bits and pieces of history contribute to our assumptions about the place of agencies in government; . . . the important fact is that an agency is neither Congress nor President nor Court, but an inferior part of government. Each agency is subject to control relationships with some or all of the three constitutionally named branches, and those relationships give an assurance—functionally similar to that provided by the separation-of-powers notion for the constitutionally named bodies—that they will not pass out of control. Powerful and potentially arbitrary as they may be, the Secretary of Agriculture and the Chairman of the SEC for this reason do not present the threat that led the framers to insist on a splitting of the authority of government at its very top. What we have, then, are three named repositories of authorizing power and control, and an infinity of institutions to which parts of the authority of each may be lent. The three must share the reins of control; means must be found of assuring that not one of them becomes dominant. But it is not terribly important to number or allocate the horses that pull the carriage of government.[4]

Strauss goes on to observe that perhaps the most difficult aspect of the task of firmly anchoring agencies in one or another part of government involves "accommodating theory to the accepted present . . . given the highly political and informal cast of important presidential and congressional relationships with the agencies. Thus, a basic difficulty in writing about the president's legal authority over the affairs of government lies precisely in the infrequency with which that authority is tested in a legal rather than a political arena."[5]

If the principle of separation of powers creates theoretical problems of accountability, these problems are compounded by operational difficulties arising out of the present institutional allocation of authority between the executive, legislature, and bureaucracy. Instead of a clean division of powers, the lines have become increasingly and hopelessly blurred. In what is no doubt an overstatement, Lawrence Dodd and Richard Schott contend that we have witnessed the rise of a "runaway bureaucracy":

The administrative state is in many respects a prodigal child. Although born of congressional intent, it has taken on a life of its own and has matured to a point where its muscle and brawn can be turned against its creator. Over the past several decades, the federal bureaucracy has come to rival the president and the Congress, challenging both for hegemony in the national political system. Protected by civil service tenure, armed with the power to issue orders and rules that have the force of law, supported by strong clientele and interest groups, and possessing a wealth of information, knowledge, and technical expertise, it goes forth to battle its institutional rivals on equal, and sometimes superior terms. And, though occasionally defeated, it rarely returns home repentant.[6]

Even though the bureaucracy has a certain legal legitimacy stemming from initial congressional grants of authority, Dodd and Schott suggest that it often exceeds congressional intent and therefore is invariably on legal, if not political, thin ice. Congress itself may have contributed to this problem by consistently delegating its authority to the president in areas such as reorganization, spending, and appointment power. In doing so, it may have created more ambiguity that order. In the interregnum that exists, the bureaucracy has sought to add strategies of organizational preservation and growth to those provided by program statute. According to Nelson, this has been caused by the unusual history of the development of the federal government:

In the United States . . . the establishment of democratic political institutions *preceded* the establishment of administrative ones. The latter which were resisted strenuously in the Continental Congress and scarcely mentioned in the Constitution, have remained somewhat illegitimate in American political culture even since. From the start, this has forced bureaucratic agencies to build independent political bases to provide sustenance to their pursuit of organizational goals, an endeavor encouraged by the constitutional system of divided political control. The development of political skills," writes Rourke, "was part of the process by which executive agencies adapted to their environment in order to survive in the egalitarian democratic society in which they found themselves."[7]

To explain—and justify—this delegation of authority to administrative agencies, in the late nineteenth and early twentieth centuries there developed a normative theory of bureaucracy based on the separation of politics from administration. In this theory, elected officeholders determine policies and civil servants apply the most efficient means to implement them. Yet even as it was being written, the theory of a "political-administrative dichotomy" was being eroded as either a valid description of reality or a normative ideal by the increased intrusion of government in complex policy areas and the attendant delegation of greater authority to the bureaucracy. Nevertheless, the doctrine of a dichotomy persisted for two reasons. First, the theory served as a defense of the legitimacy of the bureaucracy. According to Rourke, the theory "made the expansion of bureacracy much less threatening to American democracy than it might otherwise have appeared to be."[8] Second, there was no other theory to explain and justify the roles of civil servants in the policy process other than as neutrally competent executors of laws passed by Congress and signed by the president.

Although the empirical validity of the theory of totally separate political and administrative roles has been soundly assaulted since the mid-1930s, no other justification for the legitimacy of bureaucracy in the policy process has commanded either academic or popular assent. Dwight Waldo has written in the introduction to the reissue of his classic work, *The Administrative State:*

Centrally, what is problematic here is the nature and roles of politics and administration. *In essence,* we neither live with or *without the distinction, realistically separate the two nor find an agreed, proper joining.* Western history, our Constitutional structure, our political experience, and our institutional development combine to present us with a problem that cannot be solved in any definitive sense. . . . But the problem must, nevertheless be dealt with: it is *there.* The emergence of a new synthesis . . . now seems remote.[9]

Given its frail legal and theoretical standing, the role of the career civil service in the policy process during much of the past fifty years has come to be determined on other grounds that were not much affected by theory. As government grew and became more complex from the 1930s onward, more bureaucrats were needed to staff and manage programs. The practical necessity of running an extended government apparatus meant that no matter what their legal or theoretical status, career civil servants would have an important role to play in the policy process. In this context, the politics of professionalism and the legitimacy of claims of expertise have come to dominate the debate about the proper role of the civil service.

The Politics of Expertise

Above all else, bureaucracies are hierarchically organized divisions of labor based on specialization of function and expertise. Knowledge of programs, laws, regulations, and clients is finely broken down and lodged in cadres of experts throughout government. Historically, it has not been reasonable to assume that politically appointed executives will have a full understanding of the technical information, language, politics, and management of specific programs and agencies. As a consequence, they have needed to rely on the permanent civil service for much of this specialized information and expertise.

In recent years, however, this balance of power has changed somewhat, for two reasons. First, as more outsiders housed in interest groups and policy research centers (or "think tanks") have gained greater knowledge of programs, people who can at least be considered "semiexperts" stand ready to take over the reins of program management when an administration changes hands. Second, the authority of experts and the value of their specialized information has eroded both because of disagreements within the expert community as to what constitutes valid knowledge and more generally as a result of the popular skepticism surrounding the "expertise" of the policy professions. This is perhaps stated most succinctly by Hugh Heclo, who notes that policy debates tend to produce

more experts making more sophisticated claims and counterclaims to the point that the non-specialist becomes inclined to concede everything and believes nothing that he hears. The ongoing debates on energy policy, health crises or arms limitation are rich in examples of public skepticism about what "they," the abstruse policy experts, are doing and saying. While the highly knowledgeable have been playing a larger role in government, the porportion of the general public concluding that those running the government don't seem to know what they're doing has risen rather steadily. [10]

Heclo's observation, which has been buttressed more recently by Lipset and Schneider and others,[11] stands in marked contrast to those who only two decades ago proclaimed that knowledge would displace politics as the dominant source of public policy—that is, would promote an "end of ideology" in policy formulation.[12] One such theorist was Robert Lane who in 1966 wrote:

If we employ the term "ideology" to mean a comprehensive, passionately believed, self-activated view of society, usually organized as a social movement, rather than a latent half conscious belief system, it makes sense to think of a domain of knowledge distinguishable from a domain of ideology, despite the extent to which they overlap. Since knowledge and ideology serve somewhat as functional equivalents in orienting a person towards the problems he must face and the politics he must select, the growth of the domain of knowledge causes it to impinge on the domain of ideology; . . . the characteristics of a knowledgeable society may be thought to reduce ideological thinking . . . through the reduction of dogmatic thinking. Following Rokeach, we may conceive of dogmatic thinking as a selection and interpretation of information so as to reinforce a previously established creed, dogma, or political ideology. Information is used not so much to understand the world as it really is, but as a means of defending against conflict and uncertainty. The knowledgeable society is marked by a relatively greater stress on the use of information verididically, relying on its truth value and not on any adventitious defense, popularity, or reinforcement value. This should be associated with a decline in dogmatic thinking. The decline of dogmatism implies the decline of ideology, in the narrow sense of the term used here. [13]

While hindsight affords the best view for assessing trends and events, and while it is easy to ridicule Lane's limited powers of foresight, the more interesting question is "what went wrong?" The convenient and often invoked answer is that perceived "policy failures and political fiascos" of the 1960s and 1970s such as the Vietnam War, the Great Society, and Watergate undermined confidence in government. However, there is an antecedent explanation, one rooted in the position of experts and professionals in American society and government.

Consistent with Lan's idea of knowledge occupying a legitimate influence in policymaking, others have observed that scientists, experts, and professionals in general occupy a socially determined sphere of influence.[14] Speaking of science, Kenneth Boulding asserts that it occupies a "sociological niche," the boundaries of which are "very largely determined by the image of science in the minds of nonscientists. . . . If this image changes unfavorably, the niche will begin to close.[15] Similarly, Robert Friedman in his analysis of professionalism, expertise, and policymaking presents a broad hypothesis regarding professional influence in government:

A professional group with high self-esteem and substantial prestige can play a major part and exert great influence over public policy within areas closely associated with its own expertise. The influence can transcend the technical findings of the group so long as the style of the group does not lead it to encroach upon policy matters perceived to be beyond its skills. In policy matters that are redistributive, regulatory, or highly salient to society, the influence of the group will diminish but remain greater for those groups that have "high" professional standing than for those that have "low" professional standing.[16]

In other words, Americans grant authority to experts and professionals on a provisional basis. They can therefore take back or shrink this domain of legitimate authority when any one of three conditions are present: first, when the knowledge base upon which claims of expertise rest comes under scrutiny in the aftermath of policy failures; second, when experts claim authority to speak to controversial issues in policy areas where their expertise has no obvious application—as for example, when physicists speak out on foreign policy issues; and, third, when their expertise rests on a weak base of scientifically grounded knowledge that is accessible to many people with little effort. These three points have special implications for the profession of public administration, especially the third.

Professional occupations are generally considered to have the following attributes: (1) the application of a skill based on theoretical knowledge; (2) advanced education and training; (3) competence tested through examinations or other testing methods; (4) membership in a professional association; (5) adherence to a code of conduct; and (6) espousal of altruistic service.[17] Occupations that are relatively high on most or all of these measures are considered highly "professionalized." Medical doctors, lawyers, and highly trained scientists are usually considered advanced professionals, without much argument, but beyond medicine, law, and advanced science there can be controversy over what is to be accepted as a "profession." Hal Rainey and Robert Backoff have observed, "College professors, engineers, accountants, and sometimes social workers are often placed in the professional category, but there is sometimes disagreement over whether some of these, and especially certain less-developed specializations such as librarians and computer programmers should be considered semi-professions, emerging professions, or less-professionalized occupations."[18]

Although professions may vary along these dimensions (for example, doctors can be weak on "ethical obligation" and those considered only semiprofessionals can be strong on any or all of them), advanced or professionalized occupations would presumably tend to have more members with high levels of many of these attributes. In government, many of these attributes obviously conflict with the bureaucratic imperatives of hierarchy and accountability to elected officials, but these potential conflicts have been largely buffered by the sizeable domain of authority granted the more highly professionalized occupations, the protection of their professional organizations, and the tendency to recruit political appointees responsible for supervising these professionals from among the ranks of the professions themselves. Thus, the National Institutes of Health is run by doctors, the Justice Department by lawyers, the Forest Service by foresters, etc.

There are some obvious problems in applying this conception of professionalism to government. First, not all government occupations are covered by the dimensions of professionalization. Indeed, many government jobs cannot even remotely be considered semiprofessions. Second, members of some occupations are distinctly government workers or predominantly so (such as military officers, foreign service officers, social workers, schoolteachers, and librarians) and they vary in the extent to which they are "professionals." Third, there exist many generalist public administration managers whose expertise relates directly to program management (such as the staff functions of budget, personnel, and grants management) rather than to any other professional field of expertise like medicine, law, or a specific "hard science" such as physics, chemistry, or biology. Even though they may take their "professionalism" seriously by obtaining advanced degrees and espousing a commitment to public service and "neutral competence," there is little evidence that they have ever been granted the legitimacy accorded the "hard sciences" or the medical and legal professions.

There are several reasons for this. First, the knowledge base of profes-

sional public management is not very advanced, sophisticated, or codi-
fied.[19] Success as a government manager depends much more on knowledge of government institutions, regulations, and organizational memory
than on a "science of public administration." Second, although public
managers place some value on autonomy from the political environment,
by law they must recognize the legitimacy of congressional intervention
through oversight and presidential direction in their work. Third, they are
likely to identify less with their profession (public administration) than do
other professionals. This occurs largely because of their commitment to
their agency and the more particularistic knowledge base underlying
agency practices and programs. As result, public managers are less likely
to seek technical and intellectual recognition by their fellow professionals
outside their agency. Fourth, the commitment to the "calling" of public
service as a profession is weakened by the vagueness of the professional
skills involved in public management and the truncated hierarchy in
which they work, which dictates that they can advance only to that level
where the political level of management begins. Finally, the regulation
and maintenance of professional standards of conduct is part of the government's administrative law system and is not established or maintained by
professional groups outside the government.

Given these limitations, it is easy to understand why career public managers have been so easy to exclude from the policymaking process. Neither
their independent legal standing nor their claims of expertise rooted in a
profession of public management have provided enough legitimacy to allow
them to withstand the political challenges of the Nixon, Ford, Carter, and
Reagan administrations. This has been especially true in domestic agencies
whose missions have come under criticism and where the government's role
in society has been challenged.[20] Perhaps more significantly, the sociological niche of authority granted to public managers and other professionals
during the period of relative political consensus following the New Deal and
lasting through much of the 1960s has contracted as the conditions that
underpinned that consensus—perceived affluence and confidence in the
solvability of public problems—have changed. The slowdown in economic
growth during the 1970s, policy failures, and political embarrassments have
eroded public confidence in all government professions, not just career
public managers. The result has been a rejection, by a large part of the
general public, of the New Deal ideology that government is benign and is the
best tool for allocating resources and resolving society's problems. Instead of
the "knowledgeable society" based on a broad consensus about extending
government's role in society that Lane wrote so optimistically about less than
two decades ago, we have had a resurgence of conservative ideology based on

the tenets of the marketplace and calling for a contraction of the federal government's role in society. This philosophical shift has been summarized most succinctly by Chester Finn:

The Reagan revolutionaries . . . started with the assumption that of course there are problems—but efforts by the Federal government to solve them are more likely than not to create new and at least equally serious problems. . . . What really troubles them are the social costs of government actions . . . [and] the belief that when Washington sets out to solve problems it often creates worse ones.[21]

When taken to the extreme, the conservative view is that the problems caused by government can, in large part, be traced to the entrenched career bureaucracy. Therefore, the proper working relationship between political appointees and career civil servants should result in a very circumscribed role for the career executive. This position has been articulated most clearly by Michael Sanera of the Heritage Foundation, who argues that these relationships should be characterized by "jigsaw puzzle" management:

Control over the process [of implementing a planned agenda or formulating a new one] must be retained by the political executive and his immediate political staff. Very little information will be put in writing. Career staff will supply information, but they should never become involved in the formation of agenda-related policy objectives. Similarly, once controversial policy goals are formulated, they should not be released in total to the career staff. Thus, the political executive and his political staff become "jigsaw puzzle" managers. Other staff see and work on the individual pieces, but never have enough of the pieces to be able to learn the entire picture.

By operating in this fashion, the political executive maintains control over his political agenda and his political opponents can only guess what the political executive is after.[22]

Although Sanera advocates a balance in this policy of information control—that is, it should be applied in full only for truly controversial policies—his advice to political appointees in general is clear: unless political appointees gain control over the centrifugal forces of bureaucratic ideology, numerous traditional management tools, and the self-interest of individual bureaucrats, they will be frustrated in their attempts to change the scope and direction of government to achieve conservative goals. Therefore, political appointees can implement their conservative mandate only by limiting the discretion and policy input of career personnel. To control career personnel, policy goals and implementation objectives should be clear and the arena of their action should be tightly delineated. If the policies and goals that are to be implemented are controversial, Sanera advises that the overall goals should be kept from the career staff to "keep them guessing."[23]

Clearly, in this view, whatever legitimacy the civil service has accumulated for its participation in the policymaking process is based on very circumscribed grounds. But this is not a wholly idiosyncratic interpretation. Even supporters of a stronger career civil service have to admit that neither legal grants of authority nor claims of expertise and neutral competence legitimate bureaucratic participation in policymaking. Because of this weak legitimacy, the past four administrations (under Nixon, Ford, Carter, and Reagan) have moved to narrow the participation of the career civil service in policy formulation and to reduce the elements of partnership that existed between career and political appointees, particularly in those agencies whose mission these administrations opposed. How this is being done by the Reagan administration is the subject of the next section.

The Reagan Administration's Organization and Management Strategy

President Reagan's report to Congress, *Management of the United States Government: Fiscal Year 1986*, begins by reiterating the promise of his first inaugural address to "limit government to its proper role and make it the servant, not the master, of the people."[24] Reflecting widely perceived public discontent with both the scope and effectiveness of American government, during its first term the Reagan administration developed a governance strategy with five key features:

Restriction of the central agenda. The strategy was to limit the range of subjects in which the president was personally and politically involved.

Centralization of executive decision making. Mechanisms included a highly centralized budget process, a tightly structured White House–dominated policy management team, a network of cabinet councils, and an elaborate procedure for regulatory clearance and review.

Improved political mobilization. The president's own media efforts were augmented by a White House legislative strategy group and an extensive public relations operation.

The administrative presidency. There was a primary emphasis on administrative rather than legislative changes to implement policy, with close White House supervision of the appointments process.

Pragmatism. An effort was made to balance staff members whose principal concern was allegiance to the central policy agenda with others whose principal concern was to maintaining a workable measure of support within other centers of political power like Congress.[25]

Basic to the centralization of executive decision making and the administrative presidency were several discrete management initiatives. The first is what came to be known as Reform '88. According to Joseph Wright, deputy director of the Office of Management and Budget, Reform '88 is an umbrella concept for a set of initiatives to reform federal management and administrative systems. There were ten initial, or "Phase I," objectives mostly aimed at reducing costs and enhancing revenue collection and management. The ten goals were to: (1) upgrade federal cash management systems; (2) increase collection of debts owed the government; (3) encourage the sale of surplus government property; (4) foster efficient, effective management and eliminate fraud and abuse through strengthening internal accounting and administrative controls; (5) identify unliquidated obligations on agency books; (6) recover funds owed agencies as results of audits; (7) reduce nondefense workers by 75,000 full-time equivalents during the period 1982–1984; (8) limit wasteful spending on government periodicals, pamphlets, and audiovisual products; (9) achieve significant savings through systematic reform of procurement practices; and (10) reduce government paperwork and, thereby, limit costs to individuals, private organizations, and state and local governments.[26]

The Reform '88 emphasis on increased economy, efficiency, and accountability in government is both complementary to and consistent with other executive and legislative mandates such as OMB Circular A-123 on internal control systems (October 23, 1981), the Federal Managers' Financial Integrity Act (September 8, 1982), and the Deficit Reduction Act of 1984 (PL 98-369). According to results published in the president's management report to Congress for fiscal year 1986, which was mandated by the Deficit Reduction Act of 1984, many of the initial Reform '88 goals have been achieved. In fact, work has already begun on nine "Phase II" projects that include: (1) budget automation; (2) development of a standard governmentwide financial data base; (3) improvement of agency accounting systems to General Accounting Office standards; (4) development of standard payroll and personnel systems with a high degree of automation in both areas; (5) streamlining administrative payment centers across the country; (6) intensifying automation and using private-industry techniques in both credit and cash management; (7) expansion of an electronic telecommunications system between the White House and major agencies; and (8) upgrading automated data processing hardware and software to an efficient and effective level as demonstrated within the private sector.[27]

While the projects of Reform '88 became a centerpiece of the administration's intention to make the government more efficient, cost-effective, and businesslike, other elements were incorporated into the strategy. Administration efforts to minimize agency fraud, waste, and mismanagement are coordinated through the President's Council on Integrity and Efficiency. Established by executive order in March 1981, the council is composed of all statutory inspectors general, the deputy director of OMB, the deputy attorney general, the director of the Office of Personnel Management, and other key enforcement officials.[28] Like other administration initiatives, the council is a structure imposed on preexisting entities to promote better communication among participating individuals and offices, to provide more policy consistency governmentwide, and to provide a mechanism for direct presidential influence.

A second presidential council, the President's Council on Management Improvement, consists of agency assistant secretaries for administration. The council oversees and coordinates management improvement projects and formulates additional long-range plans to promote improved federal management systems. As is the case with the Integrity and Efficiency Council, coordination of the management improvement council is provided by the management branch of the Office of Management and Budget.

Overall guidance for the management reform efforts of the first Reagan administration was provided by the Cabinet Council on Management and Administration (CCMA). Established eighteen months into Reagan's first term (September 1982), the council was intended to bridge policy and implementation concerns by serving as a linking organization between the White House and top agency officials.[29] The CCMA, an integral part of the White House policy apparatus, functioned like all the other cabinet councils. The councils facilitated the coordination of secondary-level domestic policy development, interpretation, and implementation; they did not provide general policy direction. The councils were preoccupied with the details required to carry out the Reagan agenda.[30] The CCMA was the White House funnel and filter for initiatives promoted by agencies, the Office of Management and Budget, the Council on Integrity and Efficiency, and the Council on Management improvement. These devices together provided a rather effective means for structural coordination and control for implementing the president's administrative strategy. Whereas the White House focus has been on overall management policy coordination, the OMB focuses more directly on implementation. It continues to be oriented toward contralization, cost reduction, and control-oriented management improvement. It emphasizes controlling the scope and cost of government through a series of tightly focused internal control systems and initiatives. The management arm of OMB has become the principal monitor of the Grace Commission recommendations, Section 2901 of the Deficit Reduction Act, and Reform '88 initiatives.

Certainly the most visible Reagan administration management improvement initiative has been the President's Private Sector Survey on Cost Control (PPSSCC), better known as the Grace Commission, after its chairman, J. Peter Grace. The Grace Commission was composed of task forces headed by 161 top private-sector executives. The commission, in a forty-seven-volume report to the president issued in January 1984, recommended program and management changes in thirty-six areas of the federal government; 2,478 recommendations were made that promised savings of $424 billion over a three-year period after implementation. Nearly a year after submission of the controversial report, however, fewer than a fifth of the recommendations had been implemented and the estimated cost savings remained in dispute.[31] Dispute over the Grace Commission report continues unabated among commission sponsors, government officials, and academics.[32]

Inherent in the Grace Commission's recommendations are ideas that are consistent with the thrust of Reform '88 (or already included within that umbrella initiative) as well as the intentions of the CCMA and the President's Councils for Integrity and Efficiency and Management Improvement. They are: (1) to control the growth of government by selectively limiting funding through the budget process and controlling personnel levels to promote efficiency and enhance productivity; (2) to identify waste and fraud in what remains of the funding provided; (3) to improve agency management to further reduce costs and make better use of remaining funds; (4) to develop improved governmentwide management systems; and (5) to improve program delivery systems.[33]

Despite the controversy surrounding the assumptions underlying the Grace Commission's report and the accuracy of its data and projected savings, the report and its recommendations remain very much on the public agenda. This has occurred for two reasons. First, its chairman, J. Peter Grace, has campaigned indefatigably to win public support for the commission's recommendations through the media, personal lobbying, and Citizens Against Waste, a citizen's organization formed to promote the commission's reform proposals. Second, official consideration of the Grace Commission's recommendations is required by the Deficit Reduction Act of 1984, which authorized a review of the implementation of the commission's recommendations in the president's management report to Congress.

The FY 1986 report also served as an update on the Reform '88 management improvement initiatives and a report on government progress toward cost savings in the management area.

The mechanism to promote recommended improvements is the management review process that is now an integral part of the budget process. Fiscal 1986 reviews were intended to be a rigorous, full-scale review of managerial systems and practices and to monitor implementation of all approved Reform '88, Grace Commission, and FY 1985 recommendations. All agencies were to formulate management improvement plans consistent with their FY 1986 budget requests to the president.

In summary, the Reagan administration, through its first-term management and administration cabinet council, president's councils, Reform '88 programs, and the Grace Commission, provided an infrastructure for cross-cutting executive branch management coordination and reform. It is highly centralized in nature and looks to the private sector for appropriate management tools and techniques. This emphasis complements previous control-oriented management reforms passed by Congress such as the Paperwork Reduction Act of 1980 (PL 96–511), the Prompt Payment Act of 1982 (PL 97–177), the Debt Collection Act of 1982 (PL 97–365), and the Single Audit Act (PL 98–502) as well as the Federal Manager's Financial Integrity Act of 1982 and the Deficit Reduction Act of 1984.[34]

As announced in the president's FY 1986 management report to the Congress, the second Reagan administration planned to alter somewhat its strategy with respect to management improvement and control. The administration intended to further its management reform agenda by proposing legislation to Congress in six categories: (1) productivity improvement; (2) reorganization; (3) fraud prevention; (4) payment integrity; (5) procurement; and (6) reductions in regulation and paperwork.[35]

To achieve these reforms, the Reagan administration acknowledged that it must work more closely with Congress than it had done. This realization echoed a 1983 recommendation of the General Accounting Office (GAO) which advocated closer administration and congressional cooperation in the management area. The GAO report asserted that a key benefit of such cooperation would be better administration follow-through:

Although not a guarantee of success, the legislative process ensures there will be considerable debate and compromise over any reform effort. That debate extends the base of the interest and commitment to reform measures and may lead to a general consensus among affected parties about what needs to be done. . . . Congressional oversight of legislated initiatives can be helpful in providing much needed continuity to sustain progress.[36]

The GAO report concluded by noting that the only broad management initiatives that have remained on the government's management agenda over the past decade are those to which the Congress has committed itself through legislation. Thus, there appeared to be some need for the executive and legislative branches to work together in the area of management improvement if the Reagan administration and Congress were to make lasting changes.

Reactions to the Reagan Administration's Approach to Management Reform

By the end of its first term, the Reagan administration had been largely successful at putting together a centralizing administrative strategy that Richard Nathan has labeled an "administrative presidency." This strategy was originally designed by John Ehrlichman for Nixon's second term as a way to centralize power by overcoming the resistance of the bureacracy to White House policy initiatives and the "normal" centrifugal tendencies of the departments and agencies to go their own way.[37]

While Nathan applauds this general strategy and finds it quite compatible with notions of strong presidential leadership and accountability in a democratic system, not everyone agrees that this strategy is the best way to administer the executive branch or to achieve effective policy implementation. Hale Champion has noted the critical reception it has received from other actors in the policy process. For the General Accounting Office, for example, the concept of public management reform extends beyond cost control and efficiency goals basic to the president's program to include broader organizational and personnel management changes aimed at improving program productivity and effectiveness. For Congress, public management remains something different for each member, often "depending on the interests of his or her district and the jurisdiction of the committees and subcommittees on which he or she serves." For the media, public management largely provides opportunities for exposing episodes of fraud, waste and abuse, and/or examples of indifference to human concerns.[38]

There have been various responses to the administration's strategy for public management reform from past and present members of the career service and those who focus on its contribution to government. The National Academy of Public Administration's (NAPA) 1983 report, *Revitalizing Federal Management*, asserts that the recent accretion of control systems has produced a situation in which procedure overwhelms substance.[39] Administrative systems and increasingly centralized and detailed administrative procedures have produced a managerial overburden that has become a barrier to the responsiveness and cost effectiveness of government, in the academy's view. NAPA recommends an enhancement of the federal managers' roles and an appropriate amount of flexibility and discretion to allow them to meet their responsibilities adequately. Such recommendations are clearly at odds with the current thrust of the administration's efforts at centralization.

Some public employee groups and organizations have used legal and political means to oppose some of the Reagan administration's management decisions. For example, employees dismissed following reorganizations of the Department of Energy in 1982 lobbied Congress for special legislation to provide some mobility support to fired and downgraded Senior Executive Service (SES) personnel and employees of the Community Services Administration appealed to the courts and the Merit System Protection Board to restore them to their jobs once the agency's functions had been shifted to the Department of Health and Human Services. Unsurprisingly, public employee unions and professional associations have been active and outspoken in their opposition to the administration's personnel policies. The major federal unions were among the first organizations to endorse Walter Mondale for president and contributed heavily to his campaign through their PACs. Several organizations of federal, executive, the professional employees issued position papers on federal management and pay and compensation that were clear challenges to the administration's orientation and proposals. All of this activity added up to a powerful lobby pressuring Congress to halt or at least slow down many of the Reagan administration's management initiatives.

Heclo speculates whether the growing strain between political executives and civil service personnel approximates more closely a "government of enemies" than the "government of strangers" he described in his classic 1978 study. Quoting evidence presented before the House Post Office and Civil Service Committee hearings on the SES in 1984, he notes that 40 percent of those who entered the SES in 1979 had left government by March 1983; 22 percent of current career executives said that they were planning to leave; and 72 percent of career executives would not recommend a career in the federal government to their children. Heclo argues that this is a negative change from patterns of recent history.[40] The hearings, under Democratic leadership, also presented results of surveys conducted by the Federal Executive Institute Alumni Association, testimony, and other supporting documentation to reinforce the perception that administration initiatives have had a negative effect on the career service.

The administration's management strategy has been severely criticized from an institutional point of view. Although the impact of the Reagan administration's initiatives on the civil service has been mixed, the future ability of the career service to perform effectively is threatened, according to Edie Goldenberg, who argues that civil service is less appealing today than at any time in recent years.[41] One reason she gives is that the administration has displaced many high-ranking career executives with political appointees by making extensive use of its authority to make appointments of noncareer appointees to the Senior Executive Service and also through the use of Schedule C political appointees at lower levels.[42] Goldenberg observes, "What is especially striking . . . is that the increases in the number of political appointees under President Reagan have occurred primarily in the very domestic agencies where the total number of career employees has declined. That is, in those agencies targeted for major shifts in program priorities, the ratio of political to career employees appears to be significantly higher than before.[43] Institutional capacity could suffer, she asserts, because reliance on political appointees to the exclusion of career staff in program planning and management could leave agencies vulnerable to the relatively frequent turnover of political appointees. If organizational memory and communication between political appointees and career employees erodes, she believes that in a relatively short time employees may become confused about their agency's mission and direction, causing a deline in performance. Furthermore, Goldenberg argues that by stressing privatization and contracting out, while weakening the career staff, the administration may have created a bureaucracy increasingly unable to oversee effectively those third-party implementors who are receiving an increasing portion of the federal budget.

Chester Newland follows a similar line of reasoning in his critique. While admitting that similar problems were widespread in the Carter administration, Newland labels the Reagan administration's approach "ideological political administration," which he says deinstitutionalizes and politicizes key management and agency offices. He argues that loyalty defined in personal and partisan terms is contrary to informed continuity and the long-term responsibility basic to effective or "excellent" management. Such a partisan approach, Newland contends, also seeks to delimit essential congressional and judicial involvement in the process.[44]

In what is perhaps the most negative academic assessment of the administration's management approach, Salamon and Lund conclude that in its efforts to reverse the growth of government and reduce its role in society, the Reagan administration has taken actions that have weakened more than strengthened the more permanent institutions of presidential management, has undermined the morale of the civil service, has taken a narrow auditing approach to improving management in the executive branch, has done little to encourage competent professionals to serve in the federal government, and has overlooked opportunities to strengthen existing partnership arrangements between the federal government and other institutions at the state and local level and in the private sector.[45]

What should be done? Champion argues that experienced, committed public managers have to be brought back into the rooms where legislation is written and where policy decisions are made.[46] Comptroller General Bowsher believes that a strategy based on problem solving through the powers of central management agencies is fundamentally flawed. A balance needs to be struck between the legislative and executive branches.[47] A review of the 1984 House of Representatives SES hearings concludes with the observation that the hearings disclosed again that the U.S. government is one of shared powers and that this must be understood to achieve improvements in public management.[48] In short, the need for balance, cooperative linkages among governmental branches, and a concern for the capacity of government institutions are common themes of those critical of the administration's management strategy.

It is important to note that not every well-informed academic observer of the federal government has reacted so negatively to the Reagan administration's management initiatives. For example, in the concluding pages of *The Administrative Presidency*, Nathan observes that the roles and relationships among career and political executives are difficult to delineate and problematic in practice, but when faced with a choice of how to allocate responsibility, he would opt for a constricted role for career professionals:

The tensions between appointed political officials and the bureaucracy in the Reagan and Nixon periods come down to a basic question involving the role of politicians in defining the scope and tasks of government versus the application of more academic analytical techniques of problem identification and problem solving on the part of professionals. No conclusive answer can even be given as to which group should dominate, nor is it possible to provide a specific delineation of the proper roles of politicians and bureaucrats.

Under Reagan, this issue has come to the fore in many subtle ways. Critics of the administration claim that its approach is demoralizing for the bureaucracy because of its confrontational tactics and that this undermines the capacity of government to operate efficiently. My own view is that there is a need to strike a new balance between planning and management in the government service. In essence, this means going back toward the original meaning of the idea of "neutral competence."[49]

Also, while generally critical of how the administration has handled relationships between career and political appointees, Newland praises several of the administration's management improvement efforts, particularly those aimed at improving management information systems, those used for coordinating management policy such as the cabinet councils, and several of the initiatives contained in Reform '88.[50]

Finally, Lynn stresses the positive aspects of the leadership structure that the Reagan administration has used for managing the executive branch and cautions critics that "failure to understand the Reagan experiment in public management will mean that a valuable lesson for future administrations— administrations which may have more positive views of government—will be missed. That lesson is that loyal and competent supporters in key executive positions can be a potent tool of administrative leadership."[51] In Lynn's view, one should not underestimate the importance of combining a reasonably coherent philosophy of government's role with: (1) the institutional apparatus of OMB to give it operational meaning; (2) the appointment of appropriately skilled cabinet and subcabinet officials who share the presidents' visions; (3) the delegation of authority over execution of the presidents' philosophy to these appointees subject to oversight by the executive office; and (4) the education of these appointees.

Lynn observes that though President Reagan's appointees have performed unevenly, on balance all have moved the government in directions consistent with his policies. He concludes:

Ronald Reagan is changing the character of the American government because he is making intelligent use of his own abilities and those of his subordinate managers to carry out his vision. Future chief executives will have different visions, but they will be well advised to study carefully how Reagan pursued his vision. He gave his managers a role to play, and play it they did.[52]

To summarize, the sparring over the Reagan administration's management strategy can be understood as a debate between those who believe that relationships between career employees and political appointees is out of productive balance and those who do not. In general, proponents of the administration's policy agenda and some who believe in a strong presidency support the centralization tactics it has pursued in the management area, while many supporters of the civil service have expressed their opposition. The intensity of the debate and the importance of the stakes involved suggests that this issue will be on the public and academic agenda for some time.

Toward Building a Successful Balance

Experience has demonstrated that the successful management of the federal government depends on a balance of several factors. Two are especially notable: presidential control must be in reasonable balance with agency flexibility, and technical efficiency must be balanced against democratic responsiveness. In addition, finding a legitimate niche for career civil servants in agency management and in the policy process is an issue that will not go away; it remains a problem that continues to beg for a solution.

The first issue that needs to be addressed is the balance between presidential control and agency flexibility. The reality of management in the federal government is that "government needs a sense of purpose, a sense of leadership, and a sense of coherence; and often it needs to be told which way to go. Hence the president and the White House aides must go about their jobs of asking tough questions, making hard decisions, and prodding people to do a better job."[53] But too much centralization in the relationship between the White House and agencies is problematic because "the more the White House usurps responsibilities from their proper home in the departments, the more the White House undermines the goal of competent departmental management."[54] Thus a balance must be struck between White House direction and agency autonomy in order to produce a healthy and productive executive-agency relationship.

It is not surprising that the Reagan administration's definition of management improvement as cost-cutting, centralization of management policy-making, and control through auditing and other accountability-oriented management systems is particularly controversial among experienced public managers. This control-oriented approach to managing federal programs is in sharp contrast with demands on managers that emanate from a variety of other, often contradictory, sources. These can be summarized using four factors or discrete "frames" that delimit the management task: (1) A *structural* frame emphasizing rationality, task acomplishment, structural clarity, and formal goals and objectives; (2) A *human resource* frame emphasizing the best use of personnel and effective responses to human needs; (3) A *political* frame emphasizing the organization as a coalition of competing subsystems and preoccupied with power, conflict, and the problems of resource allocation; and (4) A *symbolic* frame emphasizing organizational culture and cohesion through shared values, symbols, myths and ceremony.[55]

Using these frames, Lee Bolman and Terrence Deal argue that in healthy, high-performing organizations, these four factors need to be aligned with one another in order to provide support for organizational goals and objectives. Attending to the dynamics inherent in each frame as well as coordinating and balancing the dynamics among them requires discretion in both policymaking and implementation.

Environmental circumstances further complicate the task of management. For instance, the literature on management thinking in the United States chronicles an increasing recognition of the impact of fragmentation, randomness, and chance on the achievement of formal organizational goals. This literature argues that organizational environments are often ambiguous and prone to chance occurrences that negate a programmed approach to management. Rigid, top-down control will, it is argued, limit the ability of managers to attempt alignment and adaptation of their organizations to meet unexpected contingencies.[56]

The Reagan administration's goal of redirecting the size, scope, and focus of the federal government creates some management problems by its very nature. In addition to the problems of employee morale and organizational coordination that arise in a cutback situation,[57] decision making and management strategy are affected. James Thompson and Arthur Tuden have observed that decision making is a function of the degree of consensus about the facts and values surrounding a problem.[58] Where consensus exists, programmed decision making with an emphasis on tight accountability and control is likely to be effective. However, if there is a lack of consensus over facts or values, *and power is shared*, the actors involved (for example, the White House and the Congress) must either negotiate compromises or one party must dominate its opposition in order to reach a decision. The conflict between the White House and Congress over facts and values surrounding many domestic programs, suggests that conditions do not exist for using management strategies more appropriate for situations where consensus exists. If strategies appropriate for consensus situations are used to tackle problems surrounded by conflict, the management literature suggests that organizations will be error-prone.[59]

Schmidt and Abramson add that the debate over the facts concerning an agency's performance is often really a debate over the value of an agency's mission. When management performance problems are confused with problems of political consensus, the effectiveness of government almost certainly suffers.[60] Recent critiques of certain Grace Commission recommendations illustrate this problem. Numerous examples of waste were cited by the commission that, upon closer examination, reflected its displeasure with the substance of certain policies rather than with how they were administered.[61]

In sum, much of public management occurs in a complex, fragmented system which can only partially be accommodated to a tight, centralized model of control.[62] Attempts to impose such a model of centralized executive management in situations characterized by value and policy conflict can exacerbate that conflict. From this perspective, what may appear to be individual cases of bureaucratic recalcitrance, disloyalty, or incompetence may be explained by systemic causes.

In a broader context, the government's pursuit of technical rationality and efficiency through the selective embrace of approaches, tools, and techniques from the private sector is especially anomalous and problematic to many federal employees and management theorists. They argue that centralization militates against the structural trend in business demanded by what Michael Maccoby calls the new "technoservice system." In Maccoby's view, as business firms move into areas based on new technologies, greater international competition, and demands for greater productivity and better products and services, they will have to abandon the bureaucratic layering and the control orientation of the traditional industrial management structure in favor of greater decentralization, because the traditional structure is becoming increasingly burdensome and costly.[63] This same theme is expressed in Thomas Peters's and Robert Waterman's best-selling book on the top American corporations, *In Search of Excellence*.[64] Hugh Heclo observes that if applied to the public sector, the Peters and Waterman ideas would result in the following changes: those responsible for implementation would help to decide policies (counter to the policy-versus-administration dichotomy); any presumption of a we-versus-they relationship would be obliterated (with the exceptions of innovative change from on high and mute responsiveness from below); and topside staff would be "lean" and composed of persons with a long-term commitment to the organization's core values.[65] Heclo views the emerging system of public management in the federal government as going in exactly the opposite direction. But this is hardly a unanimous verdict. For example, Donald J. Devine, former director of the Office of Personnel Management, has argued:

It would be foolish to separate [the roles of career civil servants and political appointees] into airtight compartments. . . . Even this administration . . . does not come in with a full list of precisely what it wants to do. And even in terms of what it thinks it wants to do, it needs very much the advice of the career civil servant who knows how the system really works, and the problems (the appointee) may have in instituting the program that he is executing in the name of the people through the election. So there are two separate fields of primary importance but those must overlap. . . . I would consider it the height of folly not to involve the career expertise that we have. . . . The political appointee cannot survive if he doesn't know the facts, and the only repository of that institutional memory is the career service.[66]

This division of opinion between Heclo and Devine illustrates why the definition and evaluation of the roles, responsibilities, and legitimacy of the U.S. civil service remains an important and problematic issue. In part, this is because these relationships can take various forms, as evidenced by cross-national research on the role of the civil service in other democracies and our own history.[67] And, in part, because the career civil service in the United States enjoys such little status. For over fifty years systematic studies of the civil service have demonstrated that the American people hold little esteem for public employment or public employees.[68] In spite of the government's spectacular success in promoting agricultural productivity, rural electrification, and space exploration—to cite just three out of hundreds of examples—most civil servants are still viewed as "the hired hands of the public" who are to be given authority on a limited and provisional basis with a considerable degree of skepticism and some suspicion.[69] The frustration of many career civil servants over their status and the general dissatisfaction of the American people with government and its employees suggests that we need a new normative theory or doctrine of public administration that deals with the legitimacy issue. Such a doctrine, if developed, is likely to encompass differences between employment in the public and private sectors, between higher civil servants and other public employees, and between alternative models of accountability in the executive branch. Such a theory or doctrine can be best developed through a widespread public dialogue. With such a dialogue, perhaps at last, a workable theory may emerge that will allow the design of federal administrative systems with a clear conception of the role that civil servants should play in our complex system of governance and public policy.

Notes

1. The concept of an "administrative presidency" has been extensively outlined in Richard P. Nathan, *The Plot that Failed: Nixon and the Administrative Presidency* (New York: John Wiley, 1975); and in Nathan, *The Administrative Presidency* (New York: John Wiley, 1983).

2. See for example, Bernard Rosen, "Effective Continuity of U.S. Government Operations in Jeopardy," *Public Administration Review* 43, no. 5 (September/October 1983), 343–92.

3. David Easton, *A Systems Analysis of Political Life* (New York: John Wiley, 1965), p. 278.

4. Peter L. Strauss, "The Place of Agencies in Government: Separation of

Powers and the Fourth Branch," *Columbia Law Review* 84, no. 3 (April 1984), 579–80.

5. Ibid., p. 580.

6. Lawrence C. Dodd and Richard L. Schott, *Congress and the Administrative State* (New York: John Wiley, 1979), p. 2.

7. Michael Nelson, "A Short, Ironic History of American National Bureacracy," *Journal of Politics* 44, no. 3 (August 1982), 775.

8. Francis E. Rourke, *Bureaucracy, Politics, and Public Policy*, 3d ed. (Boston: Little, Brown, 1984), p. 36.

9. Dwight Waldo, *The Administrative State*, 2d ed. (New York: Holmes & Meier, 1984). p. 1.

10. Hugh Heclo, "Issue Networks and the Executive Establishment," in *The New American Political System* ed. Anthony King (Washington, D.C.: American Enterprise Institute, 1978), pp. 118–19.

11. S. M. Lipset and William Schneider, *The Confidence Gap* (New York: Free Press, 1983).

12. See, for example, Daniel Bell, *The End of Ideology* (New York: Collier Books, 1961).

13. Robert Lane, "The Decline of Politics and Ideology in a Knowledgeable Society," *American Sociological Review* 31, no. 5 (October 1966), 660.

14. See, for example, Yaron Ezrahi, "Utopian and Pragmatic Rationalism: The Political Context of Scientific Advice," *Minerva* 18 (Spring 1980), 111–31; and Ben L. Martin, "Experts in Policy Processes: A Contemporary Perspective," *Polity* 6, no. 2 (Winter 1976), 149–73.

15. Kenneth E. Boulding, "Science: Our Common Heritage," *Science*, February 22, 1980, pp. 832–33.

16. Robert S. Friedman, *Professionalism: Expertise and Policy Making* (New York: General Learning Press, 1971), pp. 13–14.

17. See Hal G. Rainey and Robert W. Backoff, "Professionals in Public Organizations: Organizational Environments and Incentives," presented at the National Conference of the American Society for Public Administration, Detroit, Michigan, April 12–15, 1981.

18. Ibid., p. 4.

19. For a critique of the status of the "science" of public administration, see Herbert Kaufman, "Reflections on Administrative Reorganization," in *Setting National Priorities: The 1978 Budget*, ed. Joseph A. Pechman (Washington, D.C.: Brookings, 1977), pp. 391–418.

20. See Richard E. Schmidt and Mark A. Abramson, "Politics and Performance: What Does It Mean for Civil Servants?" *Public Administration Review* 43, no. 2 (March/April 1983), 155–60.

21. Chester E. Finn, Jr., "The Reagan Revolutionaries: Budget-Cutting Fervor—And More," *Chronicle of Higher Education*, June 29, 1981; rpt. in *Current Issues in Public Administration* ed. Frederick S. Lane (New York: St. Martin's, 1982), p. 460.

22. Michael Sanera, "Implementing the Mandate," in *Mandate for Leadership*

II: Continuing the Conservative Revolution, ed. Stuart M. Butler, Michael Sanera and W. Bruce Weinrod (Washington, D.C.: Heritage Foundation, 1984), pp. 514–15.

23. Ibid., p. 515.

24. Executive Office of the President and the Office of Management and Budget, *Management of the United States Government: Fiscal Year 1986* (Washington, D.C.: GPO, 1985), p. 1.

25. See Lester M. Salamon and Alan J. Abramson, "Governance: The Politics of Retrenchment," in *The Reagan Record*, ed John L. Palmer and Isabel V. Sawhill (Cambridge, Mass.: Ballinger, 1984), pp. 41–48.

26. See John D. R. Cole, "Joe Wright on Reform '88," *The Bureaucrat* 12, no. 2 (Summer 1983), 7–11.

27. Ibid.

28. See Charles L. Dempsey, "Managerial Accountability and Responsibility," *Bureaucrat* 12, no. 4 (Winter 1983–84), 17–23.

29. See Chester A. Newland, "Conclusions and Observation," *The Bureaucrat* 12, no. 4 (Winter 1983–84), 35–37.

30. See Chester A. Newland, "Executive Office Policy Apparatus: Enforcing the Reagan Agenda," in Lester Salamon and Michael S. Lund, *The Reagan Presidency and the Governing of America* (Washington, D.C.: Urban Institute, 1984), pp. 135–68.

31. See Robert Rothman, "Few Grace Commission Suggestions Adopted," *Congressional Quarterly*, November 24, 1984, p. 2990. A more favorable report on implementation results is contained in EOP and OMB, *Management of the United States Government: Fiscal Year 1986*, pp. 93–106.

32. For discussions of the activities and recommendations of the Grace Commission, see: President's Private Sector Survey on Cost Control, *War on Waste* (New York: Macmillan, 1984); J. Peter Grace, *Burning Money* (New York: Macmillan, 1985); Charles Goodsell, "The Grace Commission: Seeking Efficiency for the Whole People?" *Public Administration Review* 44, no. 3 (May/June 1984), 196–204; Steven Kelman, "The Grace Commission: How Much Waste in Government?" *The Public Interest*, Winter 1985, pp. 62–82; Congressional Budget Office and General Accounting Office, *Analysis of the Grace Commission's Major Proposals for Cost Control* (Washington, D.C.: GPO, February 28, 1984); and Comptroller General of the United States, *Compendium of GAO's Views on the Cost Savings Proposals of the Grace Commission* (Washington, D.C.: GAO/OCG-81-1, February 9, 1985).

33. See EOP and OMB, *Management of the United States Government: Fiscal Year 1986*, esp. Appendix B, "Status Report on the Recommendations of the President's Private Sector Survey on Cost Control," pp. 93–106.

34. See Charles A. Bowsher, "Building Effective Public Management," *The Bureaucrat* 13, no. 4 (Winter 1984–85), 26–29.

35. See EOP and OMB, *Management of the United States Government: Fiscal Year 1986*, pp. 63–74.

36. U.S. General Accounting Office, *Selected Government-Wide Management*

Improvement Efforts—1970 to 1980 (Washington, D.C.: GAO/GGD-83-69, August 8, 1983), pp. 40–41.

37. Nathan, *The Administrative Presidency*, pp. 43–55.

38. Hale Champion, "A New Doctrine of Reform," *The Bureaucrat* 13, no. 4 (Winter 1984–85), 12–16.

39. National Academy of Public Administration, *Revitalizing Federal Management: Managers and Their Overburdened Systems* (Washington, D.C.: NAPA, November 1983).

40. See Hugh Heclo, "A Government of Enemies?" *The Bureaucrat* 13, no. 3 (Fall 1984), 12–14.

41. See Edie N. Goldenberg, "The Permanent Government in an Era of Retrenchment and Redirection," in *The Reagan Presidency and the Governing of America*, ed. Salamon and Lund, pp. 381–404.

42. For example, between September 1980 and September 1982, the percentage of executive appointees who were noncareer or limited grew from 7 to 18 percent in the Consumer Product Safety Commission, from 35 to 40 percent in the Department of Education, from 33 to 50 percent in the Federal Home Loan Bank Board, from 5 to 19 percent in the General Services Administration, from 5 to 23 percent in the Federal Trade Commission, and from zero to 8 percent at the National Aeronautics and Space Administration (ibid., p. 369).

43. Ibid.

44. See Chester A. Newland, "A Midterm Appraisal—The Reagan Presidency: Limited Government and Political Administration," *Public Administration Review* 43, no. 1 (January/February 1983), 1–21.

45. Lester M. Salamon and Michael S. Lund, "Governance in the Reagan Era: An Overview," in *The Reagan Presidency and the Governing of America*, ed. Salamon and Lund, p. 23.

46. Champion, "A New Doctrine of Reform."

47. See Bowsher, "Building Effective Public Management," pp. 26–29.

48. See Robert C. Taylor, "Improving Management in the Federal Government: 1984 Senate Hearings," *Public Administration Review* 45, no. 1 (January/February 1985), 262–66.

49. Nathan, *The Administrative Presidency*, p. 86.

50. Chester A. Newland, "Federal Government Management Trends," *The Bureaucrat* 12, no. 4 (Winter 1983–84), 3–13.

51. Lawrence E. Lynn, Jr. "Manager's Role in Public Management," *The Bureaucrat* 13, no. 4 (Winter 1984–85), 20.

52. Ibid., p. 25.

53. Thomas E. Cronin, "Presidential-Departmental Relations," in *Current Issues in Public Administration*, 2d ed., ed. Frederick S. Lane (New York: St. Martin's Press, 1982), p. 91.

54. Ibid., p. 89.

55. Lee G. Bolman and Terrence E. Deal, *Modern Approaches to Understanding and Managing Organizations* (San Francisco: Jossey-Bass, 1984).

56. For example, see Jeffrey Pfeffer, *Organizations and Organization Theory* (Boston: Pitman, 1982); W. Richard Scott, *Organizations: Rational, Natural and Open Systems* (Englewood Cliffs, N.J.: Prentice-Hall, 1981); James G. March and Johan P. Olsen, *Ambiguity and Choice in Organizations* (Bergen, Norway: Universitetsforlaget, 1976); and G. David Garson and E. Sam Overman, *Public Management Research in the United States* (New York: Praeger, 1983).

57. For discussion of the problems of managing public organizations during retrenchment, see Charles H. Levine, ed., *Managing Fiscal Stress* (Chatham, N.J.: Chatham House, 1980).

58. James D. Thompson and Arthur Tuden, *Comparative Studies in Administration* (Pittsburgh, Pa.: University of Pittsburgh Press, 1959).

59. Russell Stout, *Management or Control: The Organizational Challenge?* (Bloomington: Indiana University Press, 1978).

60. Schmidt and Abramson, "Politics and Performance," pp. 155–60.

61. For example, see Kelman, "The Grace Commission," pp. 62–82.

62. Dann H. Fenn, Jr., "Finding Where the Power Lies in Government," *Harvard Business Review*, September/October 1979; and Walter G. Held, "Decision-Making in the Federal Government: The Wallace W. Sayre Model," in *Current Issues in Public Administration*, ed. Lane; and Martin Landau, "Redundancy, Rationality, and the Problem of Duplication and Overlap," *Public Administration Review* 29, no. 4 (July/August 1969), 346–58.

63. Michael Maccoby, "A New Way of Managing," *IEEE Spectrum*, June 1984, pp. 69–72.

64. Thomas J. Peters and Robert H. Waterman, Jr., *In Search of Excellence* (New York: Harper and Row, 1982).

65. Hugh Heclo, "A Government of Enemies?" *The Bureaucrat* 13, no. 3 (Fall 1984), 14.

66. Donald J. Devine, "Career-Political Interface," *The Bureaucrat* 11, no. 3 (Fall 1982), 40.

67. See Joel D. Aberbach, Robert D. Putnam, and Bert A. Rockman, *Bureaucrats and Politicians in Western Democracies* (Cambridge, Mass.: Harvard University Press, 1981); and Bruce L. R. Smith, ed., *The Higher Civil Service of Europe and Canada: Lessons for the United States* (Washington, D.C.: Brookings, 1984).

68. This is the response to the biannual question: "Do you think that people in the government waste a lot of money we pay in taxes, waste some of it, or don't waste very much of it?" Since 1970 around 95 percent of those surveyed have responded either "waste a lot" (65–78 percent) or "waste some" (18–30 percent) (American National Election Studies, Center for Political Studies, Institute for Social Research, University of Michigan).

69. See Reinhard Bendix, *Higher Civil Servants in American Society* (Boulder: University of Colorado Press, 1949), p. 112.

CHAPTER 11

Organizational Change in the Canadian Machinery of Government: From Rational Management to Brokerage Politics

Peter Aucoin

IN HIS comparative study of the central executive systems of the United States, Britain and Canada, Colin Campbell describes the Canadian system of the early 1980s in the following manner:

> Turning to Canada, we find the most institutionalized system of cabinet committees. As well, the most highly differentiated central agencies support ministers' efforts towards collective decision-making. Thus the Canadian arrangements come much closer than the others to fulfilling the canons for institutionalized executive leadership.[1]

By 1985, however, "this most institutionalized system of cabinet committees" with its "most highly differentiated central agencies" had been substantially changed. It has been substantially changed in at least two major respects. First, a number of structural alterations have been made; parts of the system have been dismantled and some others have been simplified and streamlined. Second, there has been a shift in power at both the political and administrative levels of the central executive system.

These changes have been effected primarily as a consequence of the coming into office of new prime ministers: first, John Turner as the Liberal party leader who replaced Pierre Trudeau; and, second, Brian Mulroney as the Conservative party leader whose party defeated the short-lived regime of Turner.[2] As Canadian and comparative studies on executive government have made clear, changes in the central machinery of government invariably follow changes in chief executive offices as new political leaders seek to mold structure and process to their personal philosophies of leadership, management styles, and political objectives.[3] In some instances, changes in structure and process are minor and incremental; in other cases, they are major and substantial. These changes in positional policy are adopted in order to affect the arrangement of power and authority in the central executive system and thus have an essentially political character. Questions of administrative efficiency and effectiveness need not be absent in such attempts, but they are secondary considerations.

The Canadian machinery of government since the departure of Pierre Trudeau as prime minister has been subject to a major assault on the executive system most clearly identified with his regime. On the one hand, John Turner concluded that his predecessor's system was not only "too elaborate, too complex, too slow and two expensive" but it also and most importantly had "diffused and eroded and blurred" the responsibilities of ministers.[4] On the basis of this assessment, he took steps to dismantle and simplify what was in place when he assumed office. He viewed these initial steps as but part of a process of organizational change, a process that the electoral defeat of his government abruptly ended. His changes were not repudiated by Brian Mulroney, however. A further consolidation, simplification, and streamlining of the central-executive machinery was effected by his new government. In addition, and of greater significance, Mulroney has sought to alter the structure and processes of the central-executive system in ways that are designed to enhance both the role of the prime minister and the functions performed by explicitly "political" officials within his government.

In some respects the most important alterations of the Mulroney government recall a number of developments initiated by Trudeau himself when he first came to power in the late 1960s. Yet, in other respects, Prime Minister Mulroney's philosophy of leadership, his management style, and his political objectives are clearly in sharp contrast to those of Trudeau. The latter's philosophy, style, and objectives constituted a "paradigm" of executive leadership that was characterized as one of "rational management."[5] In the case of Mulroney, his style, objectives and philosophy are perhaps best described as a paradigm of "brokerage politics." Each of these paradigms has different organizational implications for the structure and process of the central machinery of government.

This chapter will outline these different paradigms, examine their organizational implications, and assess their respective capacities to cope with the challenges to execute leadership inherent in the complexities of our modern administrative state.[6] This case of organizational change at the center of the Canadian system illustrates not only the significance of the prime minister's prerogatives with respect to this government machinery, but also the limits imposed by the very complexity that organizational change is meant to address. This case of organizational change involves a comparison of two regimes: one that lasted a decade and a half and the other in office for just over two years. For obvious reasons, this analysis must be tentative in some important respects.

At the same time, the basic features of a political regime under the parliamentary form of government are nonetheless shaped by the organizational paradigm of the prime minister and, while these can be subject to some evolution and adjustment over time, the evidence, both Canadian and comparative, indicates that change is first and foremost a function of political leadership. This is not surprising. At the same time, however, it indicates that organizational analyses must be as precise as possible about the paradigms of political leaders, and the fit between these, the organizational design adopted by leaders, and the political and organization context within which leadership is exercised.[7] The degree of precision that can be applied in organizational analysis is limited, of course, by a number of factors, not the least of these is the fact that the philosophies, styles, and objectives of leaders—their paradigms—are not easily captured as independent variables. But like the effect of ideas in public policy analysis generally, to ignore what is not easily defined and measured is to ignore what are the most significant determinants of policy.[8]

The Trudeau Paradigm of Rational Management

As Bruce Doern noted in his initial work on the policy philosophies of Canadian prime ministers, the fact that Trudeau had written explicitly on his personal political theory prior to his entry into elective office made the task of identifying his philosophy of leadership much simpler than is usually the case.[9] Trudeau's philosophy was "rationalist" in that reason, he argued, should take precedence over all forms of "emotionalism" in governing. Within the framework of what he, along with several of his intellectual associates, considered to be a "functionalist" approach to politics, he advocated a nonideological, even nonpartisan, model of governance. His oft-quoted reference to a future in which the science of cybernetics would prevail captures this philosophy succinctly; in the "world of tomorrow," he wrote:

the state . . . will need political instruments which are sharper, stronger and more finely controlled that any based on mere emotionalism: such tools will be made up of advanced technology and scientific investigation, as applied to the fields of law, economics, social psychology, international affairs, and other areas of human relations; in short, if not a pure product of reason, the political tools of the future will be designed and appraised by more rational standards than anything we are currently using in Canada today.[10]

As several observers have stressed at length, this philosophical orientation was not mere rhetoric; rather, Trudeau did believe that knowledge would increasingly become the basis for political power. He was not alone in this belief, of course, either within his own provincial milieu in Quebec or within the more cosmopolitan universe which he considered his intellectual home. His vocation, if not his profession, was that of a political philosopher. As an elected politician in the late 1960s this may have made him unique among his peers, especially in Canadian party politics of that time, but he stood for both a major tradition in Western political thought as well as a current fashion in international political and intellectual circles. His functional rationalism merged well with the tenets of the technocracy of state planning in an era that posited the "end of ideology" in modern political life.

In and of itself, however, Trudeau's functional rationalism would not perhaps have had as profound an influence on his role as prime minister were it not for the fact that his personal style of leadership also placed great emphasis on the essentially liberal concept of the interplay of ideas in the practical realm of decision making. What functional rationalism was to the search for knowledge through political science, the interplay of ideas was to the application of knowledge in political practice. For Trudeau, as for other liberals, "The theory of checks and balances . . . translates into practical terms the concept of equilibrium that is inseparable from freedom in the realm of ideas. It incorporates a corrective for abuses and excesses into the very functioning of political institutions."[11]

This style of liberal leadership demands a collegial approach to political decision making. The fact that it is easily incorporated within the cabinet system of executive government is essentially fortuitous. This style demands a collegial approach precisely because knowledge is best applied to practical concerns when ideas are freely expressed by more than one leader in order that the interplay of ideas thus obtained can serve to produce an equilibrium—a process that avoids the abuses and excesses of a monopoly of ideas advanced by a single authority. The theory of checks and balances, however, requires collegiality primarily to conduct decision making as an intellectual exercise. It presumes conflict, at least in the realm of ideas. As a style of management, a style advocated and practiced by Trudeau, it does not seek consensus as a managerial norm or ideal. Rather, collective decisions are to be based upon rational debate wherein some ideas prevail and others do not. A consensus may be achieved as a matter of course, but a consensus is not sought as an end in itself. It follows, accordingly, that this management style is not that of a manager of a "team." In this sense, there was no logical contradication between Trudeau's collegial management style and the fact that "people management" was not his forte. [12]

The political objectives that Trudeau brought to his prime ministership were determined in part by his political philosophy and management style and in part by his assessment of the prevailing situation with respect to the practice of government. With regard to the latter, three conditions, in his view, required attention. First, and most generally, his government had to overcome the tendency by which public policy decision making was determined primarily by partisanship on the one hand and incremental drift on the other. Intense partisanship, as illustrated most clearly in the Diefenbaker-Pearson era, had to be countered by the insertion of rationality into public policy debate. Incremental policy drift, on the other hand, had to be corrected by a commitment to comprehensive policy planning and evaluation.

Second, the relative chaos in cabinet decision making, in part a function of the minority government situation that prevailed during the Pearson regime, had to be brought under control if a more rational approach to governing was to be implemented and if policy drift was to be checked. This required giving greater priority to the collegial dimension of cabinet decision making, a priority that demanded both an increased measure of corporate discipline and a greater formalization of the roles and responsibilities of cabinet committees. The abuses and excesses of individual ministerial autonomy had to be replaced by a rigorous system of checks and balances within the cabinet as a collective executive.

Third, the influence of the bureaucracy had to be countered to ensure that the organization interests of departments and agencies did not take precedence over required policy innovation and policy coherence. In part this was to be achieved by the assertion of the role of cabinet as a collective executive. As Richard French has noted, it was "the Prime Minister's often expressed conviction that cabinet is less easily captured by the bureaucracy than are ministers operating independently."[13] In part, this was also to be achieved by the expansion of bureaucratic "counterweights" in the form of the central agencies of the prime minister and cabinet. Trudeau's objective in these two regards did not derive from partisan considerations, however. As a functional rationalist, he clearly supported the ideal of an expert, knowledgeable, and professional bureaucracy as a prerequisite to effective and efficient public administration. As a Liberal prime minister coming to power in the late 1960s, moreover, he had little to fear in terms of the "partisanship" of the federal bureaucracy. Yet at the same time, given his prior administrative and ministerial experience, he was well aware of the degree to which bureaucratic "mandarins" had been able to manipulate the decision-making system in the service of their views of "sound government." As a matter of general principle as well as in the pursuit of several specific policy changes, Trudeau insisted on countering the influence of such bureaucratic forces in order to introduce new perspectives on national priorities.

It was the combination of Trudeau's philosophy, style, and objectives that makes it possible and plausible to refer to a "paradigm of rational management." As Doern and others have noted, there was in fact a certain evolution in the executive machinery of government from Pearson to Trudeau. At the same time, however, the latter's position was that major and not incremental innovations were required of this machinery. This he set out to accomplish.

The Organizational Instruments of Rational Management

Trudeau inherited from Pearson a system of cabinet committees that enabled him to implement his paradigm of rational management without having to introduce a great deal of structural change per se. His approach to the actual operations and processes of decision making did require significant change, however. First and foremost, the committee system had to be managed with a great deal more discipline. This meant increased formalization and more rigid rules and procedures. The rationale for such changes was not primarily to use the committee system for the administrative purposes of increasing specialization and delegation of authority and thereby reducing the span of control of the full cabinet— although each of these administrative purposes was served; rather the intention was to effect a system of checks and balances in accordance with Trudeau's paradigm. This system of check and balances was meant to ensure that individual ministerial autonomy was countered by the collective authority of cabinet committees. In addition, the sectoral policy committees of the cabinet were themselves to be subject, on the one hand, to the direction of the Priorities and Planning Committee that was to provide overall integration and coherence, and, on the other hand, to the supervision of specialized coordinating committees such as the Federal-Provincial

Relations Committee, the Legislation and House Planning Committee, and the Treasury Board. This matrix arrangement of committees with its checks and balances and multiple reporting relationships conformed perfectly to the principles of rational management.

Second, the cabinet committee system also had to be transformed from an arrangement that merely facilitated the processing of an increased volume of cabinet business to a forum for increased attention by ministers to policy planning. Policy planning was considered essential if policy drift was to be overcome and thus the practice of disjointed incrementalism was to be avoided. This meant of course that ministers would have to spend more time not only in committee meetings but also in preparation for them. For this to occur the process and procedures for individual ministerial submissions to cabinet committees had to require that such submissions both set out alternatives and provide comprehensive analyses of them. Ministers were to engage in policy planning; they were not simply to give or withhold final approval to a single proposal from one of their colleagues. In so doing, the design was meant as much to control the influence of departmental officials on their respective ministers as it was to control individual ministers themselves.

In organizational terms, in short, the collegial character of cabinet decision making had to be enhanced. In the strict constitutional sense, individual ministerial responsibility remained insofar as the development and administration of departmental policies and programs was concerned, but individual ministerial autonomy was to give way to an increased diffusion of power and authority among the collectively that is the cabinet and its system of committees.

To support the increased attention given to the management of cabinet decision making and planning processes, the roles of central agencies were expanded and their capacities strengthened.[14] Given the importance of checks and balances within the decision-making system, it was logical that central agencies would have a critical role to play in providing the prime minister and cabinet with independent analyses of departmental proposals prepared for submission to cabinet committees. In addition therefore to the traditional secretarial functions required of central agencies, especially the Privy Council Office (PCO) and Treasury Board Secretariat (TBS), there had to be greater assurance that departmental proposals were assessed in reference to the cabinet's policy priorities and plans. Second, the importance attached to planning as part of cabinet decision making demanded that central agencies manage the process and framework of departmental submissions so as to ensure that policy options were developed and analysis of them provided. This required increased attention by central agencies to the substance of submissions for cabinet consideration. Finally, central agencies had to promote among departments a greater appreciation of the need for interdepartmental coordination in policy planning and development. In this sense they were to be among the chief promoters of rational management with its emphasis on the integration of the total policy system.

This organizational design required that the capacities of the PCO and the TBS be strengthened. The PCO was reorganized, in particular to be better able to provide policy advice. To achieve this, an additional level of hierarchy was added, responsibilities were made more specialized, and a planning unit was created. Within the TBS a planning branch was also created. As well, TBS management of the budgetary process was reoriented to focus more on the relationship between it and the other policy processes of the cabinet committee system.

In a somewhat similar fashion, the Prime Minister's Office (PMO) was strengthened and reorganized. The number of advisers was increased, greater policy specialization introduced, and regional responsibilities differentiated by way of the "regional desks." The PMO also was to coordinate the activities of ministerial staff to promote adherence to the political objectives of the government as a corporate body. In short, even these political/partisan functions were to conform to the paradigm of rational management.

These were among the most important organizational instruments in the redesign of the central machinery of government immediately after Trudeau became prime minister. The changes that took place constituted a coherent organizational framework—coherent, that is, with respect to the principal elements of Trudeau's paradigm. For the decade and a half that Trudeau was prime minister, this paradigm prevailed. Although structural and process changes were introduced as the system was elaborated upon, at the end of his tenure the central machinery of government had not departed from the paradigm of rational management.

The most important elaborations of this framework were threefold. First, there was the creation of a new type of coordinating portfolio and agency: the minister and ministry of state. Second, there was the closer integration of policy and budgetary decision making with what is now known as the policy and expenditure management system (PEMS). Third, there was increased organizational differentiation with the establishment of new central agencies.

Ministers and ministries of state were established as coordinating portfolios and agencies to give both ministerial and administrative attention to what were called "priority problems" that did not fall exclusively or even primarily within the scope of an existing portfolio but cut across the mandates of several. As Richard French and I described this organizational innovation in 1974:

The ministers of state would be faced with a novel task. The organizations that would serve them would not be departments in any traditional sense, but rather ministries whose initiatives would inevitably and consistently involve the responsibilities of other ministers. Fundamental to the notion of a Ministry of State is the idea that the activities of research and policy analysis can provide an adequate basis for successful policy formulation and coordination. The logic underlying such a ministry derived from the "knowledge is power" hypothesis: i.e., that research, information and analysis will carry the day in Cabinet and Cabinet committees against the traditional sources of political and bureaucratic power. [15]

The two agencies first established according to this new design were the Ministry of State for Science and Technology and the Ministry of State for Urban Affairs.

The second and third organizational innovations of greatest significance were related to each other in an important way and, as well, partly developed on the basis of the initial ministry of state experience. The increased integration of decision making on policy and expenditures developed in response to a number of factors, but two in particular were critical. On the one hand, the program, planning, and budgeting system (PPBS) that was meant to relate policy and expenditure decision making through the matrix arrangement of sectoral policy committees of the cabinet, the Priorities and Planning Committee, and the Treasury Board, as well as their respective central agencies, had not entirely lived up to the expectations of its designers. It had tempered the worst excesses of disjointed incrementalism, perhaps, but it did not prevent individual ministers and departments from pursuing independently their own objectives and priorities. On the other hand, as recession and restraint took their toll on the Canadian economy, government revenues and thus expenditures, the deficiencies of the decision-making system were brought to a head. In an attempt to impose even greater discipline on the cabinet committee system, the machinery of government was refined further in terms of structure and process. In the system that emerged, the major sectoral cabinet committees were to allocate resources from sectoral expenditure "envelopes" when they approved policy proposals under the policy and expenditure management system (PEMS) that replaced PPBS. [16] To assist these committees, new central agency structures were created for the major sectors of economic development, social development, and foreign and defense policy. In the case of the first two sectors, new ministries of state were established and headed by ministers of state who chaired their respective sectoral cabinet committees. In the case of foreign and defense policy, the secretary of state for external affairs was assisted by a central agency group lodged within the reorganized and enlarged portfolio of External Affairs.

The basic framework of this structure and process was put in place with the establishment of a cabinet committee for economic development along with a minister and ministry of state for this sector prior to the defeat of the Trudeau government in 1979.[17] The short-lived Conservative government of Prime Minister Joe Clark did not disband but rather further developed this innovation as the model for all sectors.[18] The elaboration of the system after Trudeau's return in 1980 provided the basis for the final addition to his "most institutionalized system." In 1982, a major reorganization included redesigning the economic development sector to extend the responsibility for regional economic development to all ministers of the cabinet committee for economic development and creating within the ministry of state serving this committee (the Ministry of State for Economic and Regional Development, or MSERD), a system of regional offices in provincial capitals headed by federal economic development coordinators. This "decentralization" of MSERD was a first for the central agency apparatus of the federal government. As a consequence, the central agency role, heretofore confined to Ottawa, was now extended to the field, introducing an additional element in the complex pattern of authority and responsibility. These coordinators were to advise the cabinet committee served by MSERD, to assist the regional minister for their provinces, and, among other things, to facilitate coordination between the regional offices of line departments and agencies in the development and implementation of their policies and programs.[19]

Assessment: Rational Management in Perspective

In his assessment of Trudeau's "institutionalized executive leadership," Campbell concludes that "the major difficulties with the Canadian system appear in the nature and organization of officials support of the prime minister and the cabinet."[20] In this regard he singled out in particular the following features of Trudeau's system: (1) the "access to cabinet committees enjoyed by Canadian public servants far exceeds that of their opposite numbers in the United States and the United Kingdom"; (2) the "proliferation" of central agencies "overly fragments support to the cabinet in the very process that attempts to integrate and co-ordinate its efforts";

and, (3) "the one explicitly political operation in the centre, the Prime Minister's Office, has yet to develop units that can play sustained independent roles in critical policy decisions."[21] Although Campbell suggested a number of ways of addressing these difficulties, what he did not suggest was that they were, to a significant extent, the logical consequence of Trudeau's paradigm of rational management.

Public servants enjoyed access to cabinet committees precisely because the committee system by design was "bureaucratic." When the prime minister wanted this system to work and thus paid close attention to its operation, it did work and worked quite well. But when the prime minister did not provide the required leadership and hence discipline, however, one of two organizational pathologies tended to occur. On the one hand, some ministers would attempt "end-runs" around the system and take their proposals directly to Priorities and Planning and thus to the prime minister. Or, on the other hand, the formalities of the process were observed but departmental officials carried the ball for ministers who found better things to do with their time than spending it in committee. The innovations from 1978 onward, with the elaboration of PEMS, improved matters because sectoral policy committees had important powers regarding expenditure allocations.[22] Nonetheless, in the latter years of the Trudeau regime even these changes were undermined by several factors, the most important of which was the disintegration of cabinet collegiality as the race to succeed Trudeau took place.

The basic limitation inherent in the Trudeau design of cabinet committees was that as organizational mechanisms to promote both checks and balances and collective ministerial planning, they depended greatly upon a strong prime ministerial presence. In some measure this was acknowledged. But it was also assumed that, because of the principle of collective responsibility underlying the cabinet system of responsible government, the norm of cabinet solidarity could be transormed into a system of collegial decision making wherein ministers would accept direction from other ministers in their own areas of responsibility, given the increased interdependence of government policies and programs. It presupposed further that because ministers function within a corporate executive headed by a first minister, who is more than a first among equals, he could in essence "delegate" powers to certain ministers to effect the desired degree of control and coordination within cabinet committees.

The fundamental flaw in this design was that it was too optimistic about the collegiality of ministers—that is, their willingness, in the absence of a strong prime ministerial presence, to compromise their personal objectives and departmental ambitions in pursuit of coherent corporate policies. As with any prime minister, Trudeau had a limited range of personal policy interests and thus his presence could not always be assumed. Accordingly, substantive priorities and the policies proposed to effect them were too often driven by individual ministerial and departmental ambitions. The structures and processes of rational management could not alone ensure that checks and balances and planning followed prime minister's paradigm. Nor, in these circumstances, could cabinet committee chairmen, even after the introduction of ministers of state as chairs of the major sectoral committees, fill the void. They could not function as "deputies" of the prime minister for their sectors simply because they had been given mandates to effect policy coordination. They required prime ministerial support and intervention to be effective. In many instances too little was forthcoming.

The fact that the paradigm of rational management stressed the importance of policy advice and planning to the decision-making system meant not only that central agencies would be important within the Trudeau regime but that the limitations of this paradigm would find their expression at this level as well. In several respects, the influence of central agencies, wherein the "superbureaucrats" were housed, was significant. Central agency officials were able to frustrate the ambitions of individual ministers to a degree that heretofore was not the norm. There were two reasons for this. First, cabinet decision making by its very character encouraged a greater bureaucratization of the cabinet. The central agency official most identified with the Trudeau paradigm, namely, Michael Pitfield, clerk of the Privy Council and secretary of cabinet, said it all when he stated: "My own view is that dealing with the governmental problems of which so many Canadians complain is a matter of process and machinery more than it is a matter of personalities and philosophies."[23] Given that ministers tend to focus on the latter factors and not the former, it is little wonder that central agency officials had considerable influence under Trudeau. Second, as noted, most ministers had neither the time nor the inclination to act "collectively." Their natural inclination was to let their colleagues have their own way in their own portfolio domains, except when local/regional implications or ideological differences required them to seek either bilateral compromises or collective showdowns with their colleagues. In most instances, therefore, control and coordination became, as much by default as by design, the role of central agency officials at the pre–cabinet committee process of interdepartmental relations, or within cabinet committees themselves, or both.

The flaw in this aspect of the design was that it depended too much on the capacities of highly differentiated central agencies to give the prime minister and cabinet committees integrated policy advice. Although intended to serve as a counterweight to line department bureaucracies, the complex central agency system also experienced competition from within. This was the case even before 1978 when the major contenders numbered only three—PCO, TBS, and the Department of Finance.[24] After the creation of PEMS, three new major contenders were added—MSERD, the Ministry of State for Social Development (MSSD), and the reorganized External Affairs central staff—and the competition intensified accordingly. In the absence of integrated or coordinated policy advice, ministers soon learned that they could essentially ignore most of the substance if not the framework of the strategic plans developed by these new central agencies even if they agreed in committee to the general (and usually imprecise) priorities for their sector. As the system unfolded (or, as some would describe it, unraveled), Finance—because of its central role in setting the fiscal plan under PEMS, including the determination of major new expenditures—reemerged as a major force. It did so largely because the central agency system failed to provide for coordination among the agencies themselves. As one senior official put it: "It must . . . be noted that in a system dependent on different subsystems with different lead agencies, immense problems or coordination can arise. The result can be an apparent lack of overall direction in government policy, as if the government had jumped on its horses and ridden off in all directions."[25]

Finally, it needs to be noted that the Prime Minister's Office, which at the outset of Trudeau's regime appeared to have taken on a major role, did not become the powerful political force in public policymaking that many assumed it would. Its influence was not insignificant throughout the Trudeau period, although it had its peaks and valleys in terms of influence, but three related factors kept its role a limited, albeit at times a strategic, one. First, its policy advisory staff was limited to less than a handful; thus much depended on the personal capacities and stature of a very few individuals. Of necessity this meant a very narrow span of attention to strategic policy issues—strategic, that is, in terms of the prime minister's personal policy agenda. Consequently, much of the ongoing agenda was given little or no attention. Second, throughout his tenure as prime minister Trudeau had a number of key ministers whose political judgment he respected highly. In this sense he could afford to have a lean office staff. Third, as noted, Trudeau's Liberal partisanship was not such that he distrusted the mandarins of the public service on the basis of any anti-Liberal bias on their part. A strong PMO was thus not necessary to counter the bureaucracy with partisan analyses. And, in any event, his paradigm stressed the importance of bureaucratic central agencies as counterweights to the bureaucratic ambitions of departmental officials. For this reason, among Trudeau's key policy advisors were officials from these bureaucratic central agencies, best exemplified by Michael Pitfield in the PCO and Michael Kirby in the Federal-Provincial Relations Office (the latter having also served in the PMO). Trudeau, in effect, obtained political advice from several quarters within government, only one of which was the PMO. The paradigm of rational management did not ignore political advice but it certainly downplayed purely partisan advice. For some (if not many) Liberals, this meant that they were excluded from the center of power as bureaucratic officials and that a handful of party technocrats were able to control access to the prime minister.

The Mulroney Paradigm of Brokerage Politics

Although much press attention was paid to what was seen as Brian Mulroney's lack of specific policy objectives when he became prime minister, other than a general preference for restraint in government and a greater dependency on the private sector to generate economic growth, his philosophy of political leadership was clear.[26] Mulroney's philosophy assumes that political leadership is about the accommodation of interests and not the interplay of ideas. Whereas Trudeau was most concerned with the role of knowledge and analysis in comprehensive planning for rational decision making, Mulroney has a much more political conception of ideal government, namely, the pursuit of compromise among competing interests. The difference of course is one of emphasis and degree, but it is critical insofar as it leads to different approaches to leadership. Trudeau's rationalism made his leadership no less political for his focus on ideas, and the more explicitly political conception of governing that Mulroney brings to his leadership makes him no less rational. But what constitutes rationality and politics is obviously interpreted differently within these two perspectives.

It is important to note that Mulroney's philosophy of leadership, while it contrasts with Trudeau's, is not simply or even primarily Mulroney's reaction to Trudeau. Moreover, although both Mulroney's and Trudeau's philosophies owe something to the tenor of the times in which they became political leaders, each was developed as a personal perspective on politics. Mulroney's philosophy of leadership was clearly developed prior to the rise of neoconservatism, increased skepticism about the efficacy of planning by government for state intervention, and the recognition of the limited power of the state to eradicate the conflicts of interests inherent in the political condition. However one interprets his ideological persuasion, on a scale of conservatism or even liberalism as they are traditionally understood, it is clear that Mulroney is in the tradition of both Robert Stanfield and Mackenzie King in his philosophy of political leadership with its emphasis on the need to accommodate political, social, and economic interests.[27]

It is not surprising, given his philosophy of political leadership, that Mulroney's leadership style is transactional rather than collegial. He prefers to deal with individuals on a one-to-one basis rather than collectively. The logic here of course is that this transactional style better facilitates the negotiation of compromises among differing points of view than does the collegial process where checks and balances more readily lead to stalemate if different views are strongly held. The contrast here with Trudeau is again obvious. Mulroney's philosophy assumes greater conflict over interests and thus different views as to their accommodation. It follows that Mulroney's style seeks compromise and does not promote checks and balances.

The leadership style of Mulroney with its emphasis upon personal transactions between the leader and his executive colleagues does not imply that Mulroney does not value consensus among his colleagues as a corporate executive. Indeed, as a strategy of management, a high priority is given to consensus as an end in itself. In this sense Mulroney's style requires that he be manager of a team and, accordingly, that "people management" be among his chief concerns as chief executive officer. As noted, however, the requirement does not demand collegial decision making in the Trudeau manner.

The political objectives Mulroney brought to his prime ministership were in some measure determined by both his philosophy and style. They were also partly determined by his assessment of the situation with respect to the practice of government at the time. At one level, Mulroney's political objectives upon taking office focused on the need for political leadership to effect a "reconcilation," as it was put, among the two orders of government in Canada on the one hand and major socioeconomic interests on the other. Mulroney's assessment of the legacy he inherited—an assessment widely shared, of course—was that both federal-provincial relations and government-business-labor relations so deteriorated that a major effort to reach new accords or accommodations was essential. More specific to the structures and processes of governing, although related to the first set of objectives, Mulroney's objective required that his government take the initiative in determining how to reach this reconciliation. Action rather than planning was to be the norm for political leadership, even if action was to involve much discussion with the affected parties. In some measure, or course, this focus on "action" was political rhetoric, but so too was Trudeau's focus on "planning." But it was also more than simply rhetoric as proved by the effort to ensure that the prime minister and his cabinet colleagues assert their authority over the administrative branch of government, including the "superbureaucrats" in central agencies.

The "bureaucracy bashing" that constituted a significant element in Mulroney's campaign for party leadership as well as in the national election campaign of 1984 was a function both of the perceived public opinion about bureaucracy that has become part of contemporary politics and of the fact that the Conservative party has played such a minor, almost negligible, role in the development of Canada's administrative state, and especially in the staffing of the senior mandarin ranks within the federal bureaucracy. Because of these two factors, there is an obvious similiarity between what Trudeau and Mulroney each set out to accomplish with respect to political control of the bureaucracy. At the same time, however, Mulroney as a Conservative in the mid-1980s was in a very different situation from Trudeau's in the late 1960s. Trudeau, as noted, did not confront a bureaucracy that was perceived to be an obstacle to the government in any partisan sense; Mulroney, in contrast, inherited a bureaucracy perceived to be such an obstacle, if not in terms of party partisanship then at least in terms of policy partisanship. Whereas Trudeau simply wanted to overcome bureaucratic resistance to policy innovation per se, Mulroney's objective was to overcome bureaucratic resistance to "conservative" policy innovations, innovations considered contrary not only to the bureaucracy's "liberal interventionist" policy preferences but also to bureaucratic interests in "big government" with all that these entail for the personal status of individual mandarins.

Because of Mulroney's philosophy, style, and objectives, as with Trudeau, it is possible and plausible to refer to a "paradigm of brokerage politics." This is not to suggest that this paradigm is unique to Mulroney. But this paradigm is sufficiently different from that of rational management as to require a radical change in the machinery of government in order that it may fit with and serve Mulroney's philosophy, style, and objectives.

The Organizational Instruments of Brokerage Politics

Prior to the 1984 national election that brought Brian Mulroney to office, John Turner presided as prime minister for several months. As noted earlier, he quickly proceeded to dismantle a good part of the machinery of government put in place by Trudeau. He eliminated three cabinet committees, three central agencies—MSERD, MSSD and the group that performed the central agency function in External Affairs—and the "mirror committees" of deputy ministers that had been chaired by the deputies of these three central agencies. In addition, among other things, he simplified the procedures of cabinet committees. It seems clear that these steps would likely have occurred with the coming to power of Brian Mulroney. Indeed, on assuming office, he immediately undertook a further rationalization of cabinet committees, a consolidation of the "envelopes" under PEMS, and a further simplification of the procedures of the cabinet decision-making system.

These organizational changes have diminished what Doern, in describing the early Trudeau changes, characterized as "the differentiation and bureaucratization of roles and organizations in the executive arena" and which he suggested "may, in the long run, constrain the Prime Minister's power."[28] In reducing the "formalization of policy organizations and procedures," the cabinet committee system under Mulroney was to be given less importance.[29] The cabinet's need to accommodate a variety of interests in public policy in accordance with Mulroney's philosophy, his transactional style of executive management, and his objectives of reconciliation have each in their own way required that the prime minister not be constrained by a tightly organized and collegial planning and decision-making process. Greater flexibility and thus uncertainty invariably enhance the power of the prime minister vis-à-vis his cabinet colleagues and thereby also give him more opportunities to empower certain ministers to deal with pressing priorities without requiring that their initiatives be put through numerous hoops of collective decision making.

The most important organizational implication of this approach is more power is concentrated under the prime minister. As such, the Priorities and Planning Committee assumes a greater role as well. This is not so much because it constitutes the apex of the cabinet committee hierarchy, which it does officially, but rather because it becomes, for most intents and purposes, "the cabinet"; those left out are, in effect, simply part of the "ministry." Even here, however, the prime minister must be able to exercise his powers with a considerable degree of autonomy in order to negotiate on a one-to-one basis with his key ministers.

This change is, of course, relative but by no means minor. The preeminence of the prime minister is inherent in the constitutional and political system but the Mulroney paradigm of brokerage politics demands that the prime minister's powers be exercised to the fullest. In this sense it involves more than simply prime ministerial presence to support collective decision making. It also involves significant personal intervention in those areas of priority to the prime minister and his government. The prime minister in this sense becomes the principal counterweight to ministerial ambitions that are not in accord with his policies, priorities, or strategy.

To assist the prime minister in this role, a deputy prime minister has been appointed with the stated intention that this minister should have "a substantial role and authority in the Ministry."[30] As minister responsible for "government communications" as well as vice-chairman of the cabinet and of the Priorities and Planning Committee, this minister is able to keep a firm hand on the behavior of ministers. This is a critical role, given that Mulroney has created the largest federal cabinet ever, with forty members at the outset, while recognizing that even within his cabinet's composition he had to seek the broadest possible accommodation of regional and other interests.

Mulroney's philosophy has also meant that machinery had to be established to solicit input to policy development from outside the regular administrative systems of the federal government. In addition to using his own network of personal outside advisors (some of whom were been brought into government), Mulroney established a special ministerial task force—an ad hoc cabinet committee—chaired by the deputy prime minister to review all government programs and, where necessary, to recommend their consolidation or termination.[31] This task force, accordingly, entailed a number of sub–task forces comprised of individuals approximately half of whom were seconded from the private sector and half from public service. Mulroney also initiated a major consultative process, culminating in a major conference, that involved individuals and groups from a comprehensive cross-section of Canadian society. To some extent both these initiatives were unique in the Canadian federal experience and added new wrinkles to the machinery of government. In other respects, they were contemporary versions of traditional brokerage politics. In any event, they represented the kind of innovations that are the consequence of the prime minister's philosophy of accommodation and his objective of reconciliation.

The task force also constituted an attempt to evaluate and control the bureaucratic establishment in its defense of programs established under a previous regime of a different partisan stripe. In a similar vein the Prime Minister's Office has been given the task of managing the change of personnel under the new regime. All appointments made under the prerogative of the crown, that is, by the prime minister, have been centralized in the PMO. This increased centralization of appointments has served to ensure that close attention be given to the personal allegiances and ideological dispositions of those considered for key administrative positions as well as to federal government boards, commissions, and councils.

The PMO has also played a central role in the selection of ministerial "chiefs of staff," an elevation of the rank of top ministerial political aides in line with the objective that ministers receive advice from political officials who are sensitive to the prime minister's objectives and priorities.

The Mulroney paradigm of brokerage politics has also meant that the PMO assume an enhanced role in government vis-à-vis the other central agencies that support cabinet decision making. The concentration of power under the prime minister, as a consequence of his transactional style and his emphasis on negotiation, requires a greater policy capacity within the PMO. Accordingly, the staff of this office was immediately increased by a third with a budget over 50 percent higher than that expended in Trudeau's last year in office. More important perhaps, the number of professional staff concerned with policy advice, broadly defined, went from three to four under Trudeau to over a dozen.

Giving the PMO greater importance and enlarging its policy capability was meant to have obvious implications for the roles of other central agencies, and in particular the Privy Council Office. In addition to the fact that the PCO was to have a reduced role in managing the decision-making process, since there is less complexity to manage, Mulroney's style has also downplayed its role as a center of countervailing policy advice. Its role is thus more strictly confined, relatively speaking, to that of a "process" secretariat. It is the PMO that is meant to assist the prime minister in ensuring that the policy proposals of ministers are in line with the prime minister's objectives and priorities. The Department of Finance and the Treasury Board secretariat have benefited from the elimination of the central agencies that served the sectoral policy committees of cabinet. Each of these institutions, however, is affected by the concentration of power under the prime minister. Both the fiscal budget and the expenditure budget are central policy instruments of brokerage politics with its emphasis on the distributive questions of who gets what and thus must be subject to the active involvement of the prime minister and his office.

Assessment: Brokerage Politics in Perspective

The paradigm of brokerage politics is clearly different from that of rational management in terms of philosophy, style, and objectives. Its organizational instruments differ as well. The implications of the latter for governing are not so easily assessed, however, especially as they relate in this case to a regime that was in power for just over two years. At the same time, nonetheless, both Canadian and comparative experiences suggest that the paradigm of a political leader does not change substantially even as political circumstances alter political priorities and strategies. Adjustments may be required, of course, but they are normally no more than incremental alterations.

The Mulroney paradigm of brokerage politics depends largely for its successful implementation upon two related factors. The first is the capacity of the prime minister to retain his preeminence as a chief executive officer who can intervene effectively in the domains of other ministers to accomplish his personal objectives. To date this intervention has been extensive and includes all major areas of government policy—fiscal policy, foreign policy, economic development policy, and social policy. Mulroney's reach has not only been extensive, it has also taken at least some of the ministers so affected by surprise. Given his personal style, however, such intervention is not surprising: his own policy agenda has been kept close to the vest and "uncertainty," as Doern notes, is part and parcel of this leadership style.[32]

In order to continue in this mode, however, the prime minister will have to keep his ministers, especially his senior ministers, on his side. This requires keeping his personal status high in public opinion, particularly in comparison to that of the leaders of the opposition parties. Personal credibility is essential both to his transactional style and to his philosophy of accommodation. Both his ministers and important socioeconomic interests must perceive him to be able to accomplish his objectives. In this sense the concentration of power under the prime minister must lead to effective government; the paradigm of brokerage politics depends upon it.

The record of just over two years is mixed on this criterion. Mulroney has intervened in a wide range of policy domains to be sure, but his government has been unable to avoid at least the appearance of contradictory statements of policy in a number of critical areas. In part, no doubt, this is merely evidence of a government learning as it goes. Trudeau's first years exhibit a pattern of "paralysis by analysis" and "getting ready to get ready." At the same time, however, this was perhaps expected of Trudeau's government, given its commitment to planning. In the case of Mulroney, with his commitment to action, indecision, or at least conflicting policy statements, is more critical. In any event, the record to date underscores the complexity of public policy and thus the limits on the efficacy of direct prime ministerial intervention. The fact that the Cabinet Committee on Foreign and Defense Policy had to be reestablished, after its initial takeover by Priorities and Planning, is but one indication of the limitations of centralized power.[33] The purely administrative demands of such a broad policy area require some delegation of authority even within the paradigm of brokerage politics.

The second factor that will determine whether the paradigm of brokerage politics is implemented successfully is the capacity of the Prime Minister's Office to provide not only political advice but also strategic policy advice. Both its enhanced organizational capacity and the support of the prime minister have enabled the PMO to extend its sphere of interest to a wide range of policy areas. With the prime minister's blessing, the PMO, for instance, was more intimately involved in the preparation of the government's first budget than is usually the case. The PMO, and in particular the Principal Secretary, Bernard Roy, have covered policy as well as political issues relating to Quebec with a comprehensiveness that probably exceeds even the practice of the Trudeau regime, notwithstanding its overriding concern with the place of Quebec in the federal system.

The concentration of power under the prime minister cannot in itself ensure that the PMO is an effective central agency, however powerful it might be. Its record to date does not provide much evidence that it has been able to manage and coordinate the decision-making system in ways that provide the desired prime ministerial leadership necessary for effective brokerage politics.[34] In most instances where Mulroney has intervened in the domains of other ministers—in fiscal, foreign, and economic development policies, for example—the intervention has been in reaction to ministerial or even cabinet decisions already taken and made public. This reactive interventionism may indicate a close monitoring of public opinion by the PMO but it hardly speaks highly of its capacity either to anticipate the political implications of policy decisions or to ensure that it is fully briefed on ministerial intentions.

In large part, the problems experienced by the PMO are due to the fact that the first years of a new regime inevitably overloads such a central staff agency. This has been compounded by the significant concentration of power under the prime minister with its obvious implications for the PMO. In addition, moreover, the senior staff of Mulroney's PMO are themselves new to government: the freshman prime minister has freshmen for his advisors. Finally, Mulroney's management style has led to a PMO that is organizationally larger and more complex than that of his predecessors, given the requirement that its staff specialize across a wider range of public policy concerns and are required to deal with the prime minister individually.

At the same time, it is now clear that Mulroney had not thought through carefully, despite the work of his transition team, just how to relate the concentration of power under the prime minister and his office to the operation of the cabinet decision making and the roles of the bureaucratic central agencies that support it. The cabinet committee system can be arranged, it is clear, to serve a number of different purposes depending upon the prime minister's paradigm of political leadership. Yet it is also clear that the complexity of the Canadian government requires that it at least serve to process the tremendous volume of public business that must be administered by ministers. In this sense, for administrative reasons cabinet government demands an efficient committee system even when power is concentrated under the prime minister. Secondly, bureaucratic central agencies are crucial to these operations if they are to be managed effectively even when the lead policy advisory role is assumed by political officials in the Prime Minister's Office. On both of these counts, and they are obviously interconnected, the design of the central government machinery, as effected during Mulroney's first year in office, was deficient. The result has been an overburdened prime minister and Priorities and Planning Committee with a relatively inoperative cabinet committee system on the one hand and an overworked Prime Minister's Office with an underutilized Privy Council Office on the other.[35]

Given these problems, the obvious challenge to the Mulroney government is to make more effective use of the cabinet committee system and its supporting central agency structure, if only to enhance the efficient management of government. The paradigm of brokerage politics does not preclude this possibility and the complexity of contemporary government requires that it delegate more responsibility to both cabinet committees and bureaucratic officials than has been the norm to date for Mulroney's government.

Conclusions

This chapter argues that the leadership paradigms of prime ministers—their philosophies of governance, their management styles, and their political objectives—are the chief determinants of the organizational design of central government machinery. In the Canadian case the prerogative powers of the prime minister provide more than sufficient authority for a prime minister to change the executive organization inherited from a previous regime to fit a new paradigm. As noted, such change may need only be minor or incremental but when required it can be major or radical. The changes introduced by Trudeau in the late 1960s were clearly of the latter character. It has been argued in this chapter that Mulroney's leadership paradigm has introduced equally major or radical changes in the structures and processes of the central machinery of government.

As also noted, however, the introduction of a new leadership paradigm by a new prime minister does not occur in an intellectual or political vacuum. However personal a prime minister's paradigm may be, it cannot help but be influenced by the intellectualy and political environment extant when a leader assumes office. The actual organizational design that is adopted to give effect to a new paradigm will therefore reflect in large measure the intellectual and political realities of the times. In the case of Trudeau, for instance, this was most evident. What is perhaps even more significant for the thesis advanced in this chapter is that his paradigm continued to be the driving force throughout his tenure as prime minister. Indeed, the organizational manifestation of his paradigm reached its zenith in his final design of 1982.

The intellectual and political environment of 1984, when Mulroney assumed office, provided more than sufficient support for the replacement of the paradigm of rational management. It is less certain, however, whether the paradigm of brokerage politics, expecially Mulroney's version, is the most appropriate replacement. In some respects—its transactional management style and its objective of political control over the administrative state—it is clearly in tune with the temper of these neoconservative times. In other respects, however, it is more problematic. This is particularly the case regarding to its philosophy of accommodation which gives priority to reconciliation of diverse interests and, in so doing, may undermine the perceived need for a major reordering of policy priorities away from the interventionism of the liberal welfare state. Accommodation and reconciliation, from the neoconservative perspective, too easily can lead to compromises of the policy priorities of neoconservatism. The experience to date confirms this tendency. In a number of important respects it is clear that Mulroney's paradigm is not entirely consistent with neoconservatism, and especially not with the version practiced by Ronald Reagan, Margaret Thatcher, or Bill Bennett. Mulroney may not be a "red Tory" in the strict definition of this Canadian conservative tradition, but his philosophy of governance is certainly more populist than that of his more conservative neoconservative contemporaries.

The implications of the above for Mulroney's operation of the central machinery of government as he and his government develop greater experience in governing cannot be predicted with any great certainty, of course. Both Canadian and comparative experiences would suggest, nonetheless, that his basic paradigm with its organizational design of the central machinery of government will prevail. As Campbell and others have demonstrated, paradigms and thus major organizational change occur only with new leaders. At the same time, nevertheless, this does not preclude adjustments and modifications within a basic framework of political and bureaucratic power. As noted, a more efficient and effective management of government requires that Mulroney make better use of both his cabinet committees and the central agencies of cabinet, particularly the Privy Council Office. The ultimate test of his paradigm, however, will inevitably be Mulroney's capacity and that of his office to provide coherent and coordinated political leadership and public policy. The final verdict on his regime's performance, of course, will depend upon a great deal more.

Notes

1. Colin Campbell, *Governments Under Stress* (Toronto: University of Toronto Press, 1983), p. 351.

2. For a description of these changes, see Ian D. Clark, "Recent Changes in the Cabinet Decision-Making System in Ottawa," *Canadian Public Administration* 28 (1985), 185–201.

3. In addition to Campbell, *Governments Under Stress*, see G. Bruce Doern, "Recent Changes in the Philosophy of Policy Making in Canada," *Canadian Journal of Political Science* 4 (1971), 243–63; and Harold Seidman, *Politics, Position and Power*, 3d ed. (New York: Oxford University Press, 1980).

4. Office of the Prime Minister, Ottawa, Canada, September 17, 1984.

5. See, for instance, G. Bruce Doern and Peter Aucoin, eds., *Public Policy in Canada* (Toronto: Macmillan of Canada, 1979).

6. The analysis in this study is restricted to the paradigms of Trudeau and Mulroney. This is not to imply that the changes introduced by either Joe Clark or John Turner were not based upon their personal paradigms. On Clark, for example, see G. Bruce Doern and Richard Phidd, *Canadian Public Policy* (Toronto: Methuen, 1983). By restricting the analysis to Prime Ministers Trudeau and Mulroney, however, it is possible to consider in some depth the relationships between their paradigms and their organization of the central machinery of government within the limits of a single chapter.

7. The Trudeau regime has been analyzed extensively by students of Canadian politics and public administration. My treatment draws upon these analyses. It is necessary, however, to consider the Trudeau regime at some length in order to look systematically at the effects of the three principal dimensions of his paradigm and to so not only with hindsight but also in contrast to another major paradigm.

8. See, for instance, Anthony King, "Ideas, Institutions, and the Policies of Governments: A Comparative Analysis," pts. 1–3, *British Journal of Political Science* 3 (1973), 291–313, 409–23.

9. Doern, "Recent Changes in the Philosophy of Policy Making in Canada."

10. P. E. Trudeau, *Federalism and the French Canadians* (Toronto: Macmillan of Canada, 1968), p. 203.

11. Ibid, p. xxiii.

12. See George Radwanski, *Trudeau* (Toronto: Macmillan of Canada, 1978).

13. Richard D. French, "The Privy Council Office: Support for Cabinet Decision-Making," in *The Canadian Political Process*, 2d ed., ed. R. Schultz et al. (Toronto: Holt, Rinehart and Winston, 1979), p. 365.

14. See G. Bruce Doern, "The Development of Policy Organizations in the Executive Arena," in *The Structures of Policy-Making in Canada*, ed. G. Bruce Doern and Peter Aucoin (Toronto: Macmillan of Canada, 1971), pp. 39–78.

15. Peter Aucoin and Richard French, *Knowledge, Power and Public Policy* (Ottawa: Science Council of Canada, 1974), p. 12.

16. See Richard Van Loon, "The Policy and Expenditure Management System in the Federal Government: The First Three Years," *Canadian Public Administration* 27 (1984), 348–71.

17. See Richard D. French, *How Ottawa Decides* (Toronto: James Lormier and Company, 1980), pp. 120–32.

18. Clark's use and elaboration of this innovation, it should be noted, was not to refine collegial decision making but rather to introduce greater control over government spending. As such, greater efficiency in government was to be achieved through control of cabinet and bureaucracy by his inner cabinet. See Doern and Phidd, *Canadian Public Policy*, pp. 194–96.

19. See Peter Aucoin and Herman Bakvis, "Regional Responsiveness and Government Organization: The Case of Regional Economic Development Policy in Canada," Peter Aucoin, ed., *Regional Responsiveness and the National Administrative State* (Toronto: University of Toronto Press for the Royal Commission on the Economic Union and Development Prospects for Canada, 1985), pp. 51–118.

20. Campbell, *Governments Under Stress*, p. 351.

21. Ibid., pp. 351–52.

22. See, again, Van Loon, "The Policy and Expenditure Management System in the Federal Government," and his chapter in Richard D. French, *How Ottawa Decides*, 2d ed. (Toronto: James Lormier and Company, 1984).

23. Michael Pitfield, speech to the Empire Club, Toronto, October 20, 1983, quoted in William A. Matheson, "The Cabinet and the Canadian Bureaucracy," in *Public Administration in Canada*, 5th ed., ed. Kenneth Kernaghan (Toronto: Methuen, 1985), p. 278.

24. See French, *How Ottawa Decides*.

25. Van Loon, "The Policy and Expenditure Management System in the Federal Government," p. 285.

26. See James C. Simeon, "Prime Minister Brian Mulroney and Cabinet Decision-Making: Political Leadership in Canada in the Post-Trudeau Era," presented at the annual meeting of the Canadian Political Science Association, Montreal, May 31, 1985.

27. On King's "accommodative" approach, see David E. Smith, "Party Gov-

ernment, Representation and National Integration in Canada," in Peter Aucoin, ed., *Party Government and Regional Representation in Canada* (Toronto: University of Toronto Press for the Royal Commission on the Economic Union and Development Prospects for Canada, 1985), pp. 1–68, esp. 20–25.

28. Doern, "The Development of Policy Organizations in the Executive Arena," p. 74.

29. Ibid.

30. News release, Office of the Prime Minister, Ottawa, Canada, September 17, 1984.

31. Ibid.

32. Doern, "The Development of Policy Organizations in the Executive Arena."

33. News release, Office of the Prime Minister, Ottawa, Canada, July 5, 1985.

34. The most incisive analysis of the effectiveness of the PMO during the first year of the Mulroney government has been provided by Jeffrey Simpson of the *Globe and Mail*. See, in particular, his "Problems in the PMO," *Globe and Mail* (Toronto), July 3, 1985.

35. See Jeffrey Simpson, "The Missing System," *Globe and Mail* (Toronto), July 4, 1985.

CHAPTER 12

Entrenching New Instruments for Government: The Case of Switzerland

Ulrich Klöti

For a long time after World War II, the Swiss system of government appeared capable of promoting the development of Switzerland as a modern welfare state. The combination of the essential features of this system promised social peace and economic success. The following structural features warranted such optimism:

1. The three-level federal organization implies a marked decentralization of powers and a shift of the implementation of federal laws to cantons and communes. Thus demands at the federal level, including demands on the federal government, are alleviated.
2. The institutions of direct democracy account for a highly stable government. Important questions that cannot be solved agreeably within the system of government can be decided, through the referendum, by the people. The popular initiative serves as an early warning system to identify unsolved problems and as a safety valve for citizens' concerns.
3. The two-chamber, nonprofessional federal Parliament mediates between diverse cantons and guarantees the proximity of government to the citizens. It therefore is effective in legitimating government decisions.
4. The nonparliamentary system of government further enhances the stability of the executive. The government is elected for an assured period of four years and, in reality, the members of government cannot be removed for a much longer time. Thus they are in, at least, a potentially strong position to govern effectively.
5. In the tradition of "consociationalism," the government has been com-

posed of the same four major parties since 1959. Those parties represent about 80 percent of the votes in Parliament, and are therefore well
established.

6. The principle of collegial organization of the Federal Council necessi-
tates a constant balancing of the forces involved, since there is no
head with special rights or the capacity to organize the work of the
council.

7. Since 1848, there have been seven members of the government. The
assurance of organizational continuity in the executive contributes to
an efficient and smooth-running administration.

The "Small Reform" of Government

Although assessments of the Swiss system of government by domestic
and foreign authors have been largely positive, skeptical views were expressed as early as the sixties.[1] Speaking of a "Helvetic malaise," Imboden in 1964 criticized the political system as undemocratic and inefficient
at the same time.[2] Various authors especially deplored the increasing gap
between the need for problem solving and the capacity to do so. Three
particular shortcomings of the activities of government and administration
were stressed.

First, a preponderance of the executive over Parliament was noted.
Massive cost overruns in the purchase of 100 French Mirage combat
planes triggered an extended debate on the lack of parliamentary control
over government administration.[3] The general diagnosis was to increase
the independence of government and the administration in policymaking
processes, and a reduction in the influence of Parliament on politically
relevant decisions.

Second, the inadequate direction of the administration by the political
executive—that is, the Federal Council—has been pointed out. The government seemed to succeed less and less in its supervisory function over
the administration. The following factors, among others, were held responsible for the Federal Council's difficulty in keeping a tight grip on the
administration: an unequal work load among different departments; too
many directly subordinated federal offices (see figure 12.1); and an insufficient number and strength of staff units.

Third, commentators have deplored the Federal Council's inadequate
fulfillment of the government function. According to the Swiss federal
constitution, the Federal Council is the "supreme governing and executive
authority" (Art. 95). Thus, it is not only an administrative institution, but
has tasks of directing and leading as well. In particular, it must discern

FIGURE 12.1

Organization of the Swiss Federal Administration

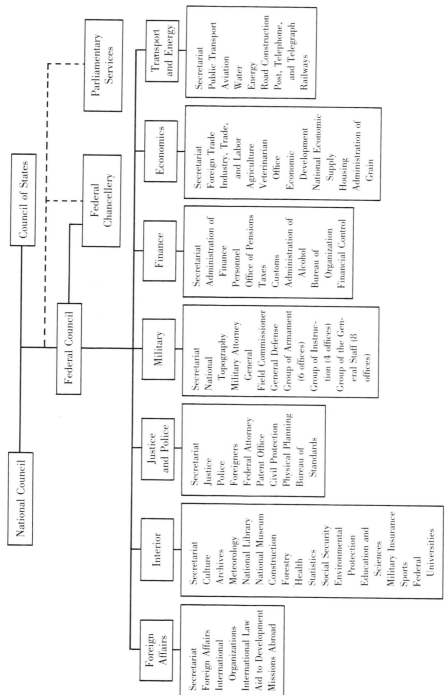

new developments in time and work out an active, conceptual, and coordinated policy. It was blamed for not fulfilling precisely this governing function due to an overload of daily administrative routine. Eichenberger noted in 1961 that already, but for a few exceptions, government functions were being carried out "as it were from week to week, empirically and according to opportunity."[4] The measures taken in the late sixties to counter these deficiencies are, in this chapter, summarized as "the small reform of government."

First, staff units were introduced or reinforced throughout the federal administration. This meant, as a first step, enlarging the role of the general secretariats of the departments. All members of the government were given a secretariat designed to assist them, as heads of departments, in their government functions. Each secretariat had the new task of coordinating the department's affairs and supporting the member of government in his work in the collegial body.

By the same token, the Federal Chancellery was upgraded from a bureau with administrative and translation tasks to a real staff unit of the government. The federal chancellor, a government official elected by Parliament, was entrusted with additional coordinating responsibilities. He became entitled to forward formal government propositions and chaired the conference of general secretaries performing administrative coordinating tasks. Finally, in 1968 Dr. Karl Huber was elected federal chancellor. With his extensive administrative experience in top positions at the Federal Department of Economy, he was charged with implementing this portion of the reform of government.

The second part of this reform consisted of the introduction of a new planning instrument for the Federal Council, the so-called *Guidelines for Government Policy*. Stemming from a 1968 parliamentary motion, a new provision was introduced in the law regulating parliamentary procedures. It read as follows:

After the beginning of a new legislative term the Federal Council submits a report of the guidelines for government policy to the parliament. These guidelines must in particular give information about the goals by which the Federal Council intends to be guided in fulfilling its constitutional tasks during the new legislative term; at the same time, an order of priorities for the pending tasks must be presented.[5]

To give the council a certain control over the *Guidelines*, it was added: "The Federal Council reports on the implementation of the guidelines at the last summer session before the legislative term expires."[6]

It was expected that the *Guidelines* would improve the planning of lawmaking, foster a coordinated and forward-looking policy, and increase the intelligibility of government activity. It was certainly no coincidence that the responsibility for preparing and formulating the new *Guidelines* was again entrusted to the newly elected federal chancellor and thus to the upgraded Federal Chancellery. This also underscored the intention of using the *Guidelines* to strengthen the government board and to reduce its directorial weakness.

The "small reform" of government comprising the introduction of new staff units and of the new planning instrument was implemented without much opposition at the end of the sixties. This chapter deals with its effects.

In the seventies, a more basic restructuring of Swiss government was proposed. In two reports by expert commissions and in a message of the Federal Council containing proposals for Parliament, the following points were discussed: (1) the question arose whether the size of the Federal Council itself was to be changed. For several reasons, things were left as they had been for more than a hundred years. Most important was the consideration that a larger government would make it impossible to maintain collegiality. (2) To relieve the federal councillors of their heavy administrative burden, the institution of state secretaries was proposed. The result of this discussion was modest. Two directors of important federal offices (Foreign Affairs and Trade) may hold the title of state secretary, which gives them more leverage in international negotiations. (3) Two other measures with the aim of narrowing the control span were discussed. In two civilian ministries a new hierarchical level between the department and the office should be introduced. In addition, the experts proposed a new assignment for twelve officials. (4) Finally, to get more flexibility, the power to organize and reorganize the federal administration, originally given to Parliament, was given to the Federal Council.

We might call the four reform proposals mentioned above the "big reform" of Swiss government. Although we will not discuss their effects in this chapter, we can say that only a small part of the "big reform" was implemented.

The Guidelines 1975–1979

This chapter will attempt to determine to what extent Switzerland's "small reform" of government has reached its goals. The assessment is based on an empirical evaluation of *The Guidelines* for the legislative term of 1975–1979. The *Guidelines 1975–1979* were already the third government program published by the Federal Council. In 1968 the government presented its first reports on such guidelines, after two months' preparation, but this was only a rather academic discussion of future questions. The second report, that of 1971, was heavily based on the "development perspectives of the Swiss national economy until the year 2000."[7] It contained the first moves toward a policymaking program, but it had to compete with a plan created by the four government parties, entitled "Goals for the Legislative Term 1971–1975," based on the model of a coalition agreement alien to the Swiss system of government. It was not until 1975 that the format for governmental planning was developed that essentially persists up to the present day.

When preparing the *Guidelines* in 1974, the government was faced with a difficult situation. The Federal Council had been obliged to "create the conditions for the coordination of the *Guidelines* for government policy in the legislation term 1975–1979 with middle-range financial planning."[8] This coordination of two kinds of planning had important implications for the method used in preparing the report.

The well-tried earlier methods no longer could be employed. First, the two planning instruments to be coordinated had different legal bases. Second, preparation of the *Guidelines* was a task of the Federal Chancellery, while financial planning was a task of the Finance Administration in the Federal Department of Finance. Third, the projected publication dates for the two reports were initially different, and consequently so were the schedules for their preparation.

Politically, the starting position was difficult for the Federal Council, because the relationship between its own forthcoming *Guidelines* and the competing "Goals for the Legislative Term" issued by the four government parties was not clear. The Federal Council had to fight off attacks from the parties, who demanded a say in the preparation of the *Guidelines*. It succeeded in retaining its exclusive authority for designing the program, but in turn was subjected to considerable pressure of expectations.

The economic recession following 1973 also occurred during the preparation time of the *Guidelines*. Following the increase in unemployment, the Federal Council was confronted with numerous demands for the state's stronger involvement in alleviating economic difficulties. It was all the more difficult for the Federal Council to satisfy these demands and expectations, since it was confronted with an extremely unpleasant financial situation. According to the budget laws then in effect, it expected a deficit of nearly 3 billion francs (around 15 percent of the budget). This massively reduced the freedom of action required for solving economic problems.

Because of these difficulties, a relatively complicated planning procedure was selected.[9] The main actor was the Federal Chancellery. First, it requested from the administration an extensive listing of policy problems.

These were then discussed with prominent and forward-looking scientists and politicians. Then, in cooperation with the departments, it drew up a catalogue of measures, directed the bargaining process through which these measures were reduced to a more manageable number, and so prepared the main decisions of the Federal Council.

Finally, the Federal Chancellery also edited the report. The Federal Council, for its part, approved the problem-oriented approach and discussed the contents in three sessions. Its essential decisions dealt with reductions and limitations of the program. For this, important conditions were also set by the Administration of Finance.

Thus, a tripartite *Guidelines* report was produced. The first section gave an account of conditions and limitations—that is, legal prerequisites, economic prospects, the financial situation, and political circumstances. The second main part contained the catalogue of measures: Subdivided into five chapters, it contained a total of 127 measures, mostly of a legislative nature, for solving pending problems. Of the 127 projects, 38 were given first priority. Finally, 24 so-called further projects were added, although they were not to be pursued in the next legislative term and so belonged to a third-priority level. Among the most important measures were a new distribution of tasks between the cantons and the federal government, fundamental fiscal reform, and new laws on physical planning and on environmental protection. The "further projects" were usually less important. They concerned, for example, the coordination of railways with major airports and new laws on hunting.

Besides the 127 projects, the *Guidelines* report contained additional planning elements. First, for the legislative projects it indicated when the government would submit the corresponding bill to the Parliament, thus implying a certain time planning. Furthermore, for projects with direct financial implications, the plan of finance listed their financial consequences. Finally, some projects were combined with a reservation: they were to be pursued only if a value-added tax were successfully promoted and implemented, securing the federal government considerably higher revenues than the existing turnover tax.

The *Guidelines 1975–1979* have been quite successful. Table 12.1 shows that over two-thirds of the projects (69 percent) were realized during the 1975–1979 legislative term. This, however, only means that the Federal Council had made its decision and in most cases submitted a bill to Parliament. Of the total of sixty-six constitutional and legal projects that are subject to popular referendum, fifty-eight were finally realized and enacted. No project failed in Parliament, but eight proposals were defeated in the referendum vote.

TABLE 12.1
Realization of Departmental Projects, 1975–1979

	Nonrealized Projects		Realized Projects	
	No.	% of Total	No.	% of Total
Foreign Affairs	3	50	3	50
Interior	8	40	12	60
Justice and Police	13	39	20	61
Military	0	0	13	100
Finance	1	12	7	88
Economy	8	27	21	73
Transport and Energy	6	33	12	67
Total	39	31	88	69

Approaches to Evaluation

This "small reform" was intended to rectify three shortcomings of the Swiss system of government. First, the executive needed to be in a better position again to perform its governmental function, and the system better able to solve current and future problems. Furthermore, a new balance between the executive and legislative branches was necessary. Finally, the direction of the administration by the government had to be improved and strengthened.

In this section, we will discuss the extent to which these goals were reached. This evaluation of the "small reform" of government is based, in part, on the empirical analysis of the content and the implementation of the *Guidelines for Government Policy 1975–1979* described above, and, secondly, on a close observation of the events around the appearance of the *Guidelines* and other coordination efforts within the staff units created in the early seventies—the markedly upgraded Federal Chancellery in particular.[10] This is only meant as a contribution from an empirical and practical point of view to the question of implementation and effects of structural reforms and new instruments for government and administration.

Perspectives for the Future and Strategies for Action

Both the introduction of the *Guidelines* as an instrument of political design and the organizational innovations regarding upper staff units occurred when there was much interest in planning. Consequently, the *Guidelines* in their first version of 1968 were seen as a part of an extensive discussion of the future. The Federal Council wrote then: "The promoters of the national fare of 1964 have courageously set out to acquaint our people with the problems of 'the Switzerland of tomorrow.' " Also, the " 'Guidelines for Government Policy' represent a discussion of questions of the future."[11] Such statements raised hopes for a new view of government matters. For many, the *Guidelines* was a new instrument with which to discern and tackle in time future problems. Strategies and instructions for action derived from an all-encompassing vision of the future would introduce a new set of policies that would settle problems, if not for good, for a long time at least.

According to prevailing ideas, strategies for various policy areas were to be based on a comprehensive overview of the situation.[12] Thus, the overall conception of transportation and energy issues were on the agenda of the 1975 *Guidelines*. Furthermore, overviews of mass media policy and environment policy were called for. In the more traditional realms of defense and agriculture policy, periodic reports and model designs were more meaningful than overall conceptions. The model designs of the Institute for Local, Regional and National Planning (ORL) and of the conference of top civil servants (CK-75) were used as the basis for the overall conception of physical planning. A fundamental conception for research policy was also in progress. According to the ideas of the time, these area-specific overall conceptions should have been assembled into a higher-level document by the *Guidelines*, with the Federal Council coordinating the different policy areas through its own program. Staff units were to have prepared the planning and coordinated the implementation.

The idea of the *Guidelines* as a vision of the future, yielding conceptual strategies for action, has remained attractive and current in political discussions in Switzerland. Every *Guidelines* report has led journalists and members of Parliament to demand more stringent goals, perspectives, and designs for action by the Federal Council.

Mostly representatives of the Independents, and especially the Social Democrats, criticized the *Guidelines* for their lack of bold new schemes. In 1984, the former mayor of Zurich and national councillor, Sigmund Widmer, blamed the Federal Council for avoiding a fundamental debate on the future of the country. Its taste for pragmatism, he said, bore the "seeds of narrow-minded jigsaw work" in it: "Every people need a vision for their future. Only in that way it can identify with the state it lives in."[13] The Social Democratic law professor from Berne, Richard Baumlin, went even further. He put down a motion in the National Council, not treated until the middle of 1985, demanding a more goal-oriented government policy and mandating the Federal Council. Among other things, such a policy was needed: "to base the government *Guidelines* in the future more on a coherent, critical analysis of the present national and international situation and the middle- and long-range terms of development [in which] existing prognostic studies . . . must be taken into more account and critically evaluated;" and "to develop and determine openly and argumentatively the relevant goals and priorities of government policy, and to design strategies that will place Swiss politics in the context of improved economic, social, and ecological chances of survival."[14] Those who expected from the *Guidelines* a vision of the future and far-reaching strategies, and from the organizational reforms a new kind of policymaking, must have been disappointed. This conclusion was repeatedly corroborated by the empirical analysis we conducted. The following arguments attempt to demonstrate this.

1. The Federal Council chose a problem-oriented approach for the preparation of the *Guidelines*. In the view of the advocates of a "goal-oriented government policy" it had, with this, already forfeited all chances of satisfying the demands of a future-oriented program. According to the planning theories of the early seventies and the flow-chart models frequently borrowed from industrial management, an improvement of government activity would have been possible only by setting superior goals, deriving intermediate goals, and then developing appropriate strategies on the level of interventions.[15] Such a procedure did not seem feasible in Switzerland. Rather, pragmatic and well-tried techniques were retained as much as possible.

2. Following a parliamentary request, the *Guidelines* and financial planning were combined, first in 1975. Thus, financial restrictions prevented from the start any carefree perspective of the future. It was hoped that greater freedom of action would result from *Guidelines*, but the opposite occurred, although only around half of the projects had financial implications.

3. The design of the *Guidelines* after projects encouraged a departmental perspective. The selection of issues and especially the setting of priorities shows an overlarge consideration for economic and financial matters. Yet no department was really slighted or even neglected (see table 12.2). Cross-references are exceptions in the *Guidelines* report, as are discussions of the interdependencies of programs. The composition of the report based on high-level problem complexes cannot conceal the fact that actual, positive, forward-looking coordination across policy areas was possible only in rudimentary fashion.

4. A total of 127 *Guideline* projects, among them even 38 of the first

TABLE 12.2
Departmental Projects, by Order of Priority

	First Priority	% of Total	Second Priority	% of Total	Further Projects	% of Total	Total No.
Foreign Affairs	1	16	5	83	0	0	6
Interior	7	28	13	52	5	20	25
Justice and Police	8	19	25	58	10	23	43
Military	6	40	7	47	2	13	25
Finance	4	50	4	50	0	0	8
Economy	10	32	19	62	2	6	29
Transport and Energy	2	9	16	69	5	22	23
Total	38	25	89	59	24	16	151

priority, constitute a conspicuously long list. Thus, the *Guidelines* do not deal with, for instance, the ten most important problems, but with an array of smaller detailed problems which, although their importance should not be underestimated, do not reach the scale of a visionary government policy.

5. The additive and incrementalistic character of the *Guidelines* planning is confirmed by the policy of the Federal Council to defer responsibility is demonstrable in various instances. For one, for 42 percent of the projects not even the intended date of completion is mentioned in the program. Furthermore, as figure 12.2 shows, the largest number of projects with an identified completion date are scheduled for the beginning or the end of the legislative term, while the actual completion of projects gradually declined during the term. Finally, out of thirty-nine projects not realized in the 1975–1979 term, twenty-two were transferred to the program of the subsequent period, or the *Guidelines* for 1979–1983. The planning as to time, then, rather reflects the state of affairs for each item than a serious attempt at coordination over time.

6. The most serious failure of the *Guidelines* was that the most important project—the introduction of a value-added tax—could not be realized. The most emphasized goal, balancing the federal budget, thus became unattainable.

In essence, the government *Guidelines* do not contain a vision for the future nor do they give sweeping strategies for coping with the "big" problems of our time. They remain a pragmatic platform for a four years' activity. The Federal Council acknowledged this; in its own words, the *Guidelines'* discussion of the future was "on the grounds of politics, the dealing with problems of concrete, compelling nature, not in the realm of

FIGURE 12.2
Guidelines Projects Planned and Realized, 1976–1979

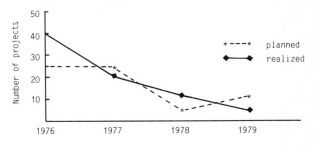

speculative and theoretical discourses. Ambitious and far-reaching ideas may step into the background in favor of a certain pragmatism, yet such a presentation of the government's intention is doubtless closer to the spirit of the Swiss and the Swiss referendum democracy."[16] The conclusion must be drawn that the Federal Council's *Guidelines* have contributed but little to shaping the future through bold designs. The "small reform" of government was apparently unable to help the Swiss system of government solve big and urgent problems in time.

Government Reform and Parliament

Every reform of political structures touches upon the relationship between government and Parliament. To assess the Swiss situation, one has to take into account that legally the government controls the classical resources like finance, personnel, and organization only to a limited extent. Parliament holds the budget authority. Most expenditures are earmarked by law. Revenues must be approved by the people and are therefore difficult to increase. The government's freedom of action in personnel matters is minimal as well. Since 1975, a rigid restriction on personnel expansion has imposed narrow quantitative limitations. Decisions for the appointment to a top position are rare, for there are no political officials besides the seven federal councillors and civil servants in general serve much longer than the members of government. With regard to organizational resources, the Federal Council's hands are particularly tied. The number of members of government is fixed by the constitution. The power for organizational arrangements is mostly in the hands of Parliament. Without its consent, the Federal Council can neither create a new federal office nor reassign one to another department. Hence, from a legal point of view, the council is hardly in a position to fulfill its leadership and managerial tasks.

It comes as no surprise, therefore, that the Federal Council, by introducing the *Guidelines* as a new planning instrument, intended not to be bound further but rather to retain the largest possible freedom of action toward Parliament. Even in the first *Guidelines* report it stated emphatically that the *Guidelines* were not legally binding. It also did not want to be politically committed either. Especially with changing circumstances, "The possibility must be preserved for us to divert from the *Guidelines* laid down here with regard to time or substance—except for the fundamental principles of the Confederation," the Council wrote in 1968.[17] The statement, in different wording, can be found in every *Guidelines* report since. This not only means that the Federal Council wants to remain free in the case of new situations. It also signals its intention to assert its claim for leadership toward the Parliament in lawmaking. This is evident where the Federal Council maintains, for example, that its *Guidelines* were intended to "call the other federal decision makers' attention to problems, connections, and consequences, insofar as they contain an invitation to Parliament, the people, and the parties to discuss the fundamental goals of our policy. For the Federal Assembly the *Guidelines* are an informative tool and a basis for discussion."[18]

Obviously, a parliament does not like limiting itself to the discussion of planning arrangements designed by another authority. Social scientists, as well as members of Parliament, have repeatedly demanded two things: a right to codetermination of policy instead of a simple acknowledgment of governmental reports by Parliament at the beginning of the legislative term; and increased participation of Parliament in the preparation of the *Guidelines*.[19] In 1976 and 1982, parliamentary interventions were made to this effect. The second motion, argued by State Councillor Binder (Christian Democrat, Aargau), stated the point clearly:

Political planning in today's state entails fundamental decisions and infringes upon the financial and legislative authority of Parliament. Therefore, such planning—besides legislation and supervision over the authorities—must become one of the prime powers of the Federal Assembly. Today's right only to be informed about the *Guidelines* for governmental policy does not suffice for Parliament to influence sufficiently future state—and finance—policy.

In our study we have analyzed to what extent the "small reform" of government has changed the relationship between the Swiss government and Parliament. The above-mentioned parliamentary motions indicate that Parliament has not succeeded in decisively influencing government planning.

Hence, the hypothesis is warranted that the reform of government, the introduction of the *Guidelines* device in particular, has tended to reinforce the position of the Federal Council. The following arguments empirically buttress this hypothesis.

1. Overall planning is not feasible without involving the government. The goals for the legislative term, agreed upon in 1971 by the parties and leading members of parliament, were no longer accepted in 1975 and have not reemerged since. The Federal Council did not even have to accept more influence on its government program by the parties or the parliament. Neither the preparation procedure nor the basic structure of the *Guidelines* report hass substantially changed since.
2. There is no influence of the Parliament on the selection of *Guidelines* items worth mentioning. In the period analyzed (1975–1979) only nineteen projects (15 percent) stem from parliamentary motions, although ninety-four motions, obliging the Federal Council to prepare legislation, were pending at the time of the preparation (late 1975) of the *Guidelines*. Almost half (48 percent) of the *Guidelines* projects, furthermore, cannot be related to a postulate, although around 800 postulates were pending in late 1975.[20] Hence, the Federal Council's program took account of parliamentary suggestions only marginally.
3. Parliament (and other external actors) had no influence on the selection of priorities and emphases in the program. They were quickly established by a small circle and were never questioned later on.
4. Both houses of Parliament have taken note of the *Guidelines* without appreciable opposition. When the report was discussed in 1976, no serious attempt was made to pin the Federal Council to a different political line.
5. The projects prepared on the basis of the *Guidelines 1975–1979* were well received and accepted by the Parliament. None was rejected. In the long run, 85 percent of the *Guidelines* projects that were submitted to Parliament have been approved and enacted. The rest failed in popular votes, not in Parliament.
6. During the legislative term, the Federal Council has not been mandated by the parliament to go substantially beyond its program. There were hardly any important bills not projected in the *Guidelines* report. Hence, the parliament could not induce additional legislative efforts of the Federal Council.

This list of arguments cannot and does not intend to demonstrate that because of the new instruments of the government Parliament has lost influence relative to the Federal Council. On the other hand, the above facts suggest that the "small reform" was not able to intensify the dialogue between Parliament and government regarding the political reshaping of Switzerland. Rather, the impression remains of two authorities involved in a balance of power carefully trying to define and possibly enlarge their own sphere of influence. According to our analysis, the Federal Council managed to keep a slight advantage in this reciprocal process. In this sense it has largely fulfilled its principal function in relation to parliament.

Reform of Government and the Administration

In relation to Parliament, the Federal Council has succeeded in maintaining, if not reinforcing, its leading role. Yet it has been repeatedly charged with a lack of leadership. The already mentioned criticism of the sixties regarding its incompetence in managing government administration and in guiding its course were in part triggering the "small reform."

Criticisms have persisted up to the present day. When the Federal Councillors, Rudolf Friedrich and later Alphons Egli resigned after only a short time in office for reasons of health, new motions were forwarded in both chambers of Parliament, demanding that federal councillors as heads of departments be relieved of petty tasks in Parliament and its committees. Thus the conditions should be created allowing the government to make better use of the leading and managerial functions of the council. "Essentially, the issue can only be to examine anew to what extent the possibilities of relief for the Federal Council—created by the new organization law—have sufficed to free them increasedly for their primary task and responsibility in the collegial conduct of government beyond the direction of their departments."[21] The "renewed examination" of the effects of the small reform of government was also the subject of our empirical analysis. It could not, however, clarify completely to what extent the instrument introduced by the reform was suitable and succeeded as a means of direction of the Federal Council toward its own administration. Some arguments rather favor a positive assessment of the reform, others rather suggest minimal or even negative effects.

First, the *Guidelines* have made possible for the first time a systematic overview of planned and adopted legislation. This created one prerequisite for a meaningful coordination in the collegial government. It may be argued that in preparation of the *Guidelines* report the Federal Council did not reserve enough time for substantially harmonizing the various planned measures and legislative efforts. Yet one cannot overlook that the planning of government at least forces the recognition of all projects of the federal administration. The host of subjects which had to be treated frequently forced the prioritization of the specific departmental concerns.

Second, the *Guidelines* have thus led to a better understanding of the limits of feasibility. The strict coupling of the *Guidelines* and finance planning has contributed much to this. Also certainly essential was the deteriorating economic situation of the latter half of the seventies that sharply cut into the pre-1972 distribution of growth. Yet, the finding that it was not possible to successfully implement more than 100 projects during a four-year term has reduced planning ambitions. Instead of 127 projects in 1975, there remained 113 in 1979 and only 67 in 1983. Further, the Federal Council still had to transfer 17 to the following term, on demand of Parliament.[22] If the *Guidelines* were not, as already stressed, a visionary program for the future, they seem on the other hand to have enabled the Federal Council to set bounds for the administration, which was already highly active in legislation.

Third, this could have contributed to limit the flood of legislation. During the term analyzed, important bills for new legislation beyond the government program were addressed to Parliament as exceptions only. Even harsh critics of an "exaggerated" amount of legislation had to concede that the extent of yearly legislation had been stabilized since 1976, perhaps even gradually reduced.[23]

Fourth, it must be noted that the priorities were not necessarily set at the level of the Federal Council as a collegial board and imposed on the departments. The transfer tendency repeatedly noted above suggests that those projects were included which had been designed by the administration in collaboration with experts. All these efforts notwithstanding, a certain departmental perspective cannot be ignored in the *Guidelines*. Finally, as long as a systematic analysis of the selection procedure for *Guidelines* projects is not possible, the presumption remains that the reduction of the legislation program was based on across-the-board cutting, similar to financial saving efforts. The way priorities were set at least supports this presumption.

Conclusion

Altogether, the impression remains that the "small reform" of government has not reached its goals. The *Guidelines* have not become a visionary plan of the Federal Council for designing the future, developed with significant parliamentary participation. It was rather the compelling need for a systematic overview of legislative work, together with the perception of economic limits and financial bottlenecks, that led to the reduction of legislative activity.

To be sure, the Federal Council has been able to maintain, if not slightly to extend, its leading role toward Parliament. Yet, this did not silence the criticisms regarding its lack of leadership. This appears contradictory only on the surface. We presume that the Federal Council could maintain its strong position toward Parliament only because it had an even stronger administration in the background. Public administration itself is in the center of a system of interest mediation outside of Parliament and government. It is influenced by the important interest groups. Pressure groups, lobbies, and public administration evade the influence of both the Federal Council and Parliament; hence, harsh criticism of the lack of leadership should correctly be aimed at both institutions.

The conclusion for the future of government is that smaller reforms within executives do not suffice to strengthen the managerial and leadership functions of governments. For Switzerland, this means that the fundamental structure features outlined in our first section would have to be included in future recommendations for reform. Yet, in view of the long tradition and the limited flexibility of the Swiss political system, it should not be expected that in this century the structures and practice of government in Switzerland will substantially change.

Notes

1. François Da Pozzo, *Die Schweiz in der Sicht des Auslandes* (Bern: Francke, 1975).

2. Max Imboden, *Helvetisches Malaise* (Zürich: EVZ, Polis, 1964); Raimund Germann, *Politische Innovation und Verfassungsreform* (Bern: Haupt, 1975).

3. Paolo Urio, *L'affaire des mirages* (Geneva: Médécine et hygiène, 1972).

4. Kurt Eichenberger, "Die politische Verantwortlichkeit der Regiergung im schweizerischen Staatsrecht," in *Verfassungsrecht und Verfassungswirklichkeit* (Bern: Stämpfli et Cie., 1961).

5. Geschäftsverkehrsgesetz, art. 45 bis, al. 1 (law regulating parliamentary procedures).

6. Ibid., art. 45 quater.

7. Summary in Francesco Kneschaurek, "Entwicklungstendenzen und Probleme der schweizerischen Volkswirtschaft," *Schweiz. Bankverien* 9 (1975).

8. Federal Law of October 4, 1974, on measures to improve the federal budget; art. 2, al. 2, letter 3.

9. Ulrich Klöti, "Zum Werdegang der Richtlinien der Regierungspolitik

1975–79," in *Schweizerisches Jahrbuch für politische Wissenschaft* 17 (1977), 77–92.

10. Ulrich Klöti, *Regierungsprogramm und Entscheidungsprozess: Eine Erfolgskontrolle der Regierungsrichtlinien des Bundsrates für die Legislaturperiode 1975–1979* (Bern: Haupt, 1985).

11. *Guidelines, 1968,* p. 3.

12. Ulrich Klöti, *Konzeptionelle Politik—Erfolgsrezept oder Alibi?* (Zürich: Kleine Studien zur Politischen Wissenschaft, no. 200, 1981).

13. National Council, *Official Bulletin* 3:157.

14. Motion 84,360 of March 14, 1984, in *Uebersicht über die Verhandlungen der Bundesversammlung.*

15. Yehezkel Dror, *Public Policymaking Reexamined* (San Francisco: Chandler, 1968); Carl Böhret, *Entscheidungshilfen für die Regierung* (Opladen: Westdeutscher Verlag, 1970).

16. *Guidelines, 1968,* p. 3.

17. Ibid., p. 2.

18. Ibid., p. 5.

19. Christoph Lanz, *Politische Planung und Parlament* (Bern: Haupt, 1977).

20. A postulate is an instrument that can be used by members of Parliament to ask the government for a report on a certain matter. The instrument is weaker than a parliamentary motion with which members of Parliament ask for new legislation.

21. Hans Zwicky, "Kollegialregierung—Idealbild und Wirklichkeit," in *Schweizer Monatshefte* 65 (1985), 213–22.

22. National Council, *Official Bulletin, 1984* 3:817.

23. Wolf Linder, Schwager Stefan, and Comandini Fabrizio, *Inflation législative? Une recherche sur l'évolution quantitative du droit suisse 1948–82.* (Lausanne: IDHEAP, 1985).

CHAPTER 13

Reforming Central Government Administration

in Australia

John Warhurst

THE CAREER public service in Australia has traditionally been respected and influential. "Among the institutional elites of Australian society, public servants occupy an important place."[1] This judgment by the senior scholar of Australian public administration, the late R. N. Spann, still holds, but for the past ten to fifteen years the Australian public service has been suffering something of a crisis: a crisis in relations between governments and senior public servants, a crisis in public confidence, or at least in public image, and a crisis of service morale. Each aspect of the crisis has fed the others.

At the heart of the crisis are relations between governments and these senior public servants who advise them on policy. Dissatisfaction has been expressed by governments with the senior public service for some time. There are a number of elements to the criticism, yet there is enough common ground for generalizations to be made. Each of the parties, the Australian Labor party on the one hand, and the coalition partners, the Liberal and National parties on the other, have given some support to each of these criticisms.[2] They can be summed up as follows: (1) governments have too little control over their administrators; (2) government policies are being implemented by insufficiently skilled managers; (3) senior administrators are insufficiently sensitive to the wider community and its problems.

The Australian Labor party is identified with distrust of the public service, because of the latter's alleged unwillingness to enthusiastically embark on the implementation of Labor's policies when it is government. Many Labor supporters believe that the public service deliberately flouted the wishes of the Labor government of Gough Whitlam (1972–1975).[3] Yet Whitlam's distrust came to be shared by his Liberal successor as prime minister, Malcolm Fraser (1975–1983).[4] The conventional wisdom in the Liberal party seems now to be summed up in the anti–public service flavor of the BBC television series "Yes, Minister."[5] Party spokesmen now quote from and bastardize sentences from the series. The public service is seen as opponents rather than assistants to ministers. In Jim Carlton's words, "There is absolutely no use in spending twenty years in opposition developing policies . . . only to surrender the real control to a civil service machine."[6]

The Liberal party is more closely identified with the second strand of criticism, that public servants are poor managers. Liberal party opinion contrasts public service management adversely to that in the private sector. Several prominent back-benchers directed their energies to this issue during the Fraser years. After its defeat in 1983, the party's post-mortem concluded, "It is clear from the experiences of Ministers in the previous government that public service managerial techniques fall short . . . and indeed fall well behind the best managerial practice in the private sector."[7]

The third strand of government criticism points accusingly at the privileges of the career public servant. The security of public service employment is mocked. In a time of economic instability and relatively high unemployment, public-sector employees with tenured employment are portrayed as smug, self-satisfied and out of touch with reality. A Labor minister in the Whitlam government scorned senior public servants as "fat cats," while later a Liberal minister spoke derogatorily of public servants "having their snouts in the public trough." The images have been reinforced by the adverse treatment of public servants in the media. They have been applied with particular venom to public servants located in Canberra, the small (population 250,000) and somewhat isolated national capital.

These public servants are the focus of this chapter. As a federal system, Australia has separate public services serving the governments of the Commonwealth, six states, and one territory. The state public services are older than the commonwealth (Australian) service which dates from federation in 1901, and in the two largest states, New South Wales and Victoria, government employment is of comparable size.

The existence of a number of public services is significant. Ideas circulate among them, as do some personnel. Lately, there has been increased mobility of senior officers between the services so that it probably now equals the mobility between the public and private sectors.

Canberra is the home, then, of senior advisors in the central offices of the national government.

The problems in relations between governments and their public servants has generated a great deal of interest in public service reform in the 1970s and 1980s. There had been no major outside inquiry into any Australian public service between 1928 and 1973. Since then the flood of inquiries has scarcely slowed.[8] There have been a number into the Commonwealth Public Service, beginning with a major Royal Commission on Australian Government Administration, commissioned in 1973. Changes of government have not interrupted the flow of inquiries, though they have interrupted the implementation of reports. When the present Hawke Labor government won office in March 1983, there was an expectation in the air of administrative reform, and several reports upon which the new government could draw if it wished. But the history of administrative reform efforts between 1973 and 1983 must follow a short introduction to the Commonwealth Public Service.

The Commonwealth Public Service

The Commonwealth Public Service has grown dramatically since the outbreak of World War II. By June 1984, it numbered about 170,000 permanent staff (165,999 full-time, 3518 part-time), and was growing at a rate of more than 5 percent per annum. The comparable figures (excluding agencies no longer part of the public service proper) in 1939 was less than 8,000.[9] Total federal government employment is more than 400,000 (see table 13.1).

Officers serve in about twenty-seven departments with their head offices in Canberra and the bulk of the staff elsewhere in the country, mainly in the capital cities. In 1984 less than a third of the officers were located in the national capital (42,252 out of 165,999 permanent full-time staff). Careers tend to be made within departments, as mobility between departments is limited.

The service is divided into four divisions according to seniority. Departments are headed by First Division officers. They are assisted in senior administrative and advisory tasks by officers of Second Division rank, who number about 1,600. The second largest division is the Third, the clerical division, from whom the senior ranks are drawn, and whose own senior members have significant policy roles. It numbers about 80,000 and its members are now recruited mainly from among university and college graduates. The Fourth Division comprises blue-collar and

TABLE 13.1
Civilian Government Employees in Australia, June 1983
(in thousands)

	Men		Women		Total	
	N	%	N	%	N	%
Australian public service*	97.8	10.0	59.8	9.9	157.6	10.0
Other Australian government*	178.9	18.3	72.7	12.0	251.6	15.9
State government						
New South Wales	192.7	19.7	147.3	24.4	340.0	21.5
Victoria	158.3	16.2	118.7	19.6	276.9	17.5
Queensland	99.8	10.2	57.8	9.6	157.6	10.0
Southern Australia	53.1	5.4	47.4	7.8	100.5	6.4
Western Australia	62.7	6.4	47.0	7.8	109.7	6.9
Tasmania	20.1	2.1	15.8	2.6	35.9	2.3
Northern Territory Government	7.7	0.8	6.5	0.1	14.3	0.9
Local Government	107.1	10.9	31.1	5.1	138.2	8.7
Total	978.1	100.0	604.1	100.0	1,582.2	100.0

Sources: Australian Public Service, Public Service Board *Statistical Yearbook 1982–83*
(Canberra; Australian Bureau of Statistics, Canberra).
Note: Excludes defense forces and workers in agriculture and overseas. Any discrepancies
between totals and sums of components are due to rounding.
    *Staff of the Departments of the Parliament are included with "Other Australian govern-
ment."

secretarial support staff and has a permanent force of about 85,000 supple-
mented by a large number of temporary employees.

The permanent service is about 37 percent female (62,750 out of
165,999). However, the first female department head was appointed only
in 1985 and the Second Division is less than 2 percent female.[10]

The service has traditionally been a career service with a typical
career beginning at the most junior point of entry. Recruitment of outsiders above the base grade has traditionally been seen as exceptional. A
number were appointed while the service was growing quickly in the
1940s, but there were few such appointments over the next twenty years.
It was not until the Whitlam government years that a sizable number of
outsiders was recruited. In one year about 250 lateral appointments were
made at a relatively senior level.[11]

Central Departments and Agencies

At the center of policymaking within the Commonwealth Public Service are the departments and agencies working to the prime minister and
treasurer. Here, there have been developments in recent years.

The career public service advisors to the prime minister are located in the Department of Prime Minister and Cabinet (PMC), which currently numbers about 550 officers.[12] It includes the Cabinet Office and as many other divisions (in 1984 there were ten) as the prime minister deems appropriate. The divisions are organized around functional lines to cover most fields of government activity. It serves the cabinet and both initiates and coordinates policy. The department's role in policy formulation has grown greatly over the last twenty years as prime ministers have sought an independent source of support and advice.[13] This growth has been controversial, and has been opposed by line departments and their ministers.

An even more recent development in the provision of support for the prime minister has been the growth of a private office, which has occurred during the last ten to twenty years, beginning during the Whitlam government. It is a small office, of about thirty to forty staff, nearly all of whom are not public servants. The office includes policy advisers (partisan "political" aides and economic specialists), managerial administrative staff, and a press office.[14]

The prime minister is responsible also for a statutory agency, the Public Service Board (PSB), whose head has first division status. The PSB is the personnel agency for the service. It is responsible for pay and conditions, industrial relations, recruitment and training, and performance monitoring. Traditionally, it has been responsible for the control of staff numbers, but under the Hawke government, that function has been transferred to the Department of Finance. However, it has gained functions too, under Hawke, which gives it still higher standing.[15]

The Treasury has long been the power in the land. It is "incomparably the most influential" department in matters of economic policy, and has had "great staying power."[16] Currently it is about the same size as PMC. Traditionally, it has been responsible not only for general economic policy advice, but also for coordinating and regulating departmental spending. In 1977, the latter functions were transferred to a separate Department of Finance (about 1,000 staff) which was excised from the Treasury. This was done partly in an attempt by the Fraser government to reduce the Treasury's influence. Fraser, like his predecessor Whitlam, had clashed with the department. The Labor party in particular found the Treasury's commitment to laissez-faire economic principes unpalatable. The department has been led by strong permanent heads, until recently John Stone, and previously Sir Frederick Wheeler.

The Treasury had long been opposed to central economic planning and had undermined such suggestions in the past. It had opposed, in particular, the recommendations of the Vernon Committee of Economic Inquiry in 1965.[17] It is thus uncomfortable with a new element in the economic advisory process, the Economic Planning Advisory Council (EPAC). EPAC, a tripartite non–public service advisory body, grew out of the Hawke government's pre-1983 election Prices and Incomes Accord with the representative organ of the labor movement, the Australian Council of Trade Unions, and the April 1983 National Economic Summit of government, business and labor representatives.[18]

The Inheritance of the Hawke Government

The modern history of public service reform in Australia begins with the election of the Whitlam Labor government. The Hawke Labor government, elected a decade later, inherited the situation outlined in the introduction to this chapter, a situation of unresolved problems which demanded to be met. As one commentator concluded a survey of the Whitlam and Fraser years: "The deep-seated problem of the relationship between the government and the bureaucracy remains unresolved."[19]

This decade was distinguished by the sort of government dissatisfaction with the public service discussed earlier, and by a series of government inquiries into the service in an attempt to come to grips with the problems. These inquiries were frustrated by the alternation of government which prevented successive governments implementing the measures advocated in the reports. There was, therefore, a reservoir of ideas in the public domain upon which the Hawke government could draw. There was in addition another reservoir of specifically Labor ideas, which had been handed down and elaborated upon since the fall of Whitlam in 1975. The place of the Whitlam government in Labor thinking is crucial. An outsider needs to understand the hopes which were invested in the Whitlam government by a generation of Labor supporters: the first Labor government for twenty-three years. Yet it was cut down in controversial circumstances only three years later, with the hopes not met. Subsequently, the public service gained a place in Labor's demonology. "Treason of the Clerks?" asked one commentator sympathetic to the government.[20] The Labor party has spent a lot of time chewing over questions such as this. Often the participants were supporters who had either been brought into the administration as lateral recruits in those years, or had been closely associated with the public service.

Government Inquiries

The first inquiry was the Royal Commission on Australian Government Administration (RCAGA), set up by the Whitlam government in 1973 and chaired by a distinguished public figure, Dr. H. C. Coombs.[21] By Australian standards this was a very large inquiry, which in addition to its secretariat, involved as consultants most of the relevant political scientists and students of public administration working in Australian universities.

RCAGA believed that the traditional Westminister system, based upon public service neutrality and anonymity, no longer provided an appropriate model for an Australian public service in the 1970s. It wanted responsive, creative management.

RCAGA reported early in 1976 after the fall of the Whitlam government. In its report and four volumes of appendices it collected a body of research of inestimable value.[22] But it reported after the passing of its sponsor and "under the worst possible conditions for experimentation."[23]

Malcolm Fraser quickly set up a private Administrative Review Committee (ARC) chaired by a senior former public servant, Sir Henry Bland. The ARC's report was never made public. Its brief was to examine departmental expenditure with a view to reducing it, and to "eliminate waste and duplication within and between government departments."[24]

Subsequently, Fraser's main concern was to restrain the growth of public service employment (in which he was successful), and to strictly ensure that the service adhered scrupulously to its position of servant of the government. It was not to concern itself with public service reform until very late—too late—in its period of office.

However, it was during these years that serious interest in public service management and training grew on the government back benches. This interest bore fruit in the bipartisan parliamentary Joint Public Accounts Committee, chaired by an aspiring Liberal member, David Connolly. After investigating a number of individual departments, the committee issued a report on the selection and the development of senior departmental managers.[25] This, again, was too late to be acted upon by the Fraser government. Connolly's personal conclusion was that, within the public service "there is a fundamental lack of managerial philosophy."[26]

Very late in his years as prime minister, Malcolm Fraser did call for an inquiry into the public service in 1982. This inquiry was headed by a prominent businessman, John Reid, and his review of commonwealth administration was made public late in that year.[27]

Labor Party Thinking

Side by side with government inquiries came the work of Labor party supporters. This ruminating was not "ivory tower" reflection, but serious thinking drawing on either years in government service working for

Whitlam and his ministers or years with the RCAGA, which was indirectly working for Whitlam. There was a lot of cross-fertilization. Initially
the work was not done formally at the behest of the Labor party. That
came later. Three individual cases are instructive: those of Patrick Troy,
Geoffrey Hawker, and Peter Wilenski.

Troy, an urban researcher at the Australian National University in
Canberra, worked with Labor party parliamentarians developing the policies
which played such a large part in the urban and suburban quality of life
emphasis in Whitlam's policies. He then joined the government as deputy
head of the newly created Department of Urban and Regional Development
(DURD).[28] At one stage, nineteen out of the twenty-seven Second Division
officers in DURD, were from outside the service.[29] The department was
convinced that it failed to achieve its goals because of the obstruction of the
other, established parts of the service, in particular the Treasury. This is
portrayed in Troy's account of the life span of the department, *Innovation and
Reaction*.[30]

Hawker, an ANU political scientist joined RCAGA as director of
research, heading the research staff.[31] His thinking about public service
reform culminated in a book which mapped out the path for an ALP
government on issues such as representativeness, participation and management in the public service. His attitude toward party government is
also spelled out in the book's title: *Who's Master, Who's Servant?*[32]

The central figure is undoubtedly the third, Peter Wilenski. As a career
public servant, Wilenski was writing papers for Whitlam on government
administration while the latter was still in opposition. Wilenski then became the prime minister's principal private secretary and, in 1975, permanent head of the Department of Labor and Immigration. He spent the Fraser
period as an academic exile at the Australian Graduate School of Management (foundation professor of public administration) and at the ANU. He
wrote extensively, conducted a formal inquiry into the New South Wales
public service for the Labor premier, Neville Wran, took international
assignments, and assisted other Labor state governments.[33] Wilenski's interest in reform is wide-ranging, but the main theme of his work is the issue of
control: Labor governments need to recognize the political nature of the
senior public service and must work to dominate it. For example:

The concepts of the civil service neutrality and the current justifications for a
career service in terms of professional continuity and frank and fearless advice,
are all ex-post justifications. In my view they are also self-serving and attempt
to hide the essentially political role by the civil servant in policy formulation
and implementation.[34]

Once the Labor party began again to think seriously about problems of government in the late 1970s, when it had recovered from the shell shock suffered in 1975, discussions about the machinery of government questions began in the parliamentary caucus. Some "outsiders" like Wilenski were also involved.[35] A first caucus task force was set up in 1979, prior to the 1980 elections in which Labor made advances but was unsuccessful. The second caucus task force was created in 1981, and worked until the successful 1983 election campaign. Patrick Weller concludes that this task force's report on the organization of the cabinet, cabinet-caucus relations, the internal organization of the public service, public authorities, and the relationship between caucus and other organizations "was as thorough, sensible and sophisticated a document as any Opposition is likely to produce."[36] Its suggestions on the internal organization of the public service included a number, such as changing the method of appointing departmental heads, and creating a special division in the senior service, which later found their way into government policy. The work of the task force enabled Labor's plans to be presented in detail during the election campaign. Hawke and the task force chairman, Senator Gareth Evans, launched *Labor and the Quality of Government* on February 9, 1983. Labor was concerned to reassure the senior public service amid rumours that if elected, as seemed likely, the new government would confront the public service. Hawke spelled out his own attitude:

I would take the attitude towards senior public servants with whom we may have had differences to say to them, "you will be aware that there's been a change of government." Second, "you will be aware that there is not just a change of government, but a change of policies. It will be the government which will be making the policies of this country, not just the public service. I will expect that you have a commitment as a public servant to loyally give effect to these policies." Third, I will be saying that I don't want any sycophants in the public service. If you have views about our policies I want to hear them. If, having put your point of view, you don't feel yourself totally able to give effect to government policies, then you go. If you feel that you can loyally serve this government and its policies, then you stay.[37]

Labor entered government with the party divided between those, probably including Hawke himself, who wanted business as usual with the public service to avoid the adverse publicity of the Whitlam years, and those who felt strongly that reform of the public service was necessary if the government's policies were to be fully implemented. Many party members strongly believed that a new Labor government needed to impress its will on the public service. It was believed, in particular, that some senior public servants should be removed from their positions. Preeminent among them was to be the permanent head of the Treasury, John Stone.

The White Paper on the Australian Public Service

The Hawke government, by December 1983, was able to publish a white paper, "Reforming the Australian Public Service: A Statement of the Government's Intentions." That it was able to do this so relatively quickly reflected the previous official and party investigations. Hawke was right to claim in introducing the paper that his was "the first federal government elected with a detailed policy statement in this area."[38]

The government's intentions were focused on three main themes: the senior public service, central resource allocation and review, and personnel policies and methods for handling grievances and appeals.[39] The paper details the government's intentions in regard to both career and noncareer advisers. This section is in fact the bulk of the report. Permanent heads were now to be called department heads. They had always in fact been appointed by governments rather than the PSB, but this was now to be publicly stressed, and after five years' service it was to become the practice for department heads to be rotated to another position. A senior executive service was to replace the existing Second Division. The aim was to increase the mobility of staff in the senior ranks of the public service. And the pool of talent would be increased by actively seeking applications from outside the service. Recognizing that, contrary to talk about "fat cats," public service salaries had become "noncompetitive with those for people with comparable qualifications and responsibilities in the private sector," the remuneration of senior public servants were to be examined. Special legislative arrangements were to control the appointment of ministerial consultants and the personal staff of ministers and other members of Parliament. Referring to a large number of reports, including the September 1983 Liberal Party Committee of Review, the paper is able to point to "a general agreement among political parties, and among those who have reviewed the service in recent times, that the balance of power and influence has tipped too far in favor of permanent rather than elected office holders." Hence, ministers needed more political assistants. "The common thread to their proposals is that ministerial—that is, democratic—control will be bolstered only if larger numbers of politically committed people can have close involvement in the development and implementation of policy."

The new arrangements, in a concession to the views of the service, were to separate career and noncareer appointments more clearly than in earlier Labor thinking. The Fraser government had controlled the service by the staff ceilings mechanism. The new government stated its intention to abolish the staff ceilings system, and to integrate financial and staffing policy by "transferring from the Public Service Board to the Department of Finance the responsibility (and personnel) for advising on and administering controls on staff numbers and profiles by salary level." While the PSB lost this responsibility, it gained elsewhere. Department heads were to be asked to produce a management improvement plan each year for ministers, and the PSB was to "consult annually with department heads and ministers concerning general managerial performance." PMC was given responsibility for overseeing effectiveness reviews of program implementation. The whole process of resource allocation and priorities was to be reviewed regularly—at least annually—at a ministerial retreat, following Canadian, British, and American examples.

The government stated its intention to adopt a number of the modern personnel policies currently winning acceptance in the wider community, such as equal opportunity management programs, permanent part-time work (pioneered in the Australian public sector by the South Australian public service), and industrial democracy, also pioneered by the South Australian Dunstan Labor government.[40] The government also proposed to establish a new, independent "employees grievance appeals and rights protection authority."

Reaction to the White Paper

The white paper appeared while the Hawke government was still extremely popular.[41] This factor clearly helped in easing the way for its proposals. The general response was cautiously approving. The modesty of the proposals was recognized, as was their debt to the previous reports. The opposition parties sensed this mood, and made sure that they took their share of the plaudits. As David Connolly said, "Having spent so much time during the past three years working on public service reform, it is one of the ironies of politics that my political opponents would ultimately accept the merits of much of the Public Accounts Committee's 202nd Report on the Selection and Development of Senior Managers."[42]

Critics pointed to the paper's concentration on central government and management rather than relations with the general public. Career servants past and present, as well as the Opposition, expressed concern, on the basis of their view of the Whitlam experience, that the Hawke government would politicize the service by making partisan senior appointments. For this reason they were skeptical of arrangements for appointing permanent heads, ministerial consultants, and ministerial staff and about the SES. Nevertheless the Opposition concluded, "The time has come for some fundamental changes to the public service."[43] And a former member of RCAGA and senior public servant approved: "I believe the package as presented by the government presents us all with an accomplishable set of improvements. If they are taken up, as I am sure they will be, positively and constructively, they will lead to a more efficient and effective public service."[44]

Implementation: A Midterm Assessment

The government, in line with its consensus philosophy, proceeded to discuss its intentions with departmental management, staff associations, the wider trade union movement and other parties. Not all agreed, but with minor concessions the ideas of the white paper were enshrined into legislation which was introduced into Parliament on May 9, 1984 and subsequently was adopted.[45]

Most attention has been focused on government policy on the staffing of the senior service. The national magazine, the *Bulletin*, in February 1985 carried an article by the former head of Malcolm Fraser's press office which dramatically accused the government of revolutionary changes:

The Federal Government has completed the groundwork for what may prove to be the destruction of the Australian Public Service, to general applause and with bipartisan support; . . . the government has got away with a revolution, turning an institution modelled on British traditions of independent advice and impartial service to elected regimes into something resembling the United States political bureaucracy with all its scope for patronage.[46]

This is a startling exaggeration. The government has made some striking appointments, but on the whole has moved cautiously. The immediate actions of the new government were far from radical. Only three new departments were created, fewer than in a midterm shuffle by the Fraser government less than a year before. The central departments were left untouched. Few changes of senior personnel were made. Only one permanent head, thought to have been too close to the previous prime minister, was clearly pushed sideways (and he later returned to favor). To the dismay of many in the Labor party, Stone was retained as head of the Treasury. Of those career servants identified with the Whitlam government, John Menadue, by this time head of the Department of Immigration and Ethnic Affairs, was moved closer to the heart of the government as the head of the Department of the Special Minister of State. Wilenski was brought back from exile to head the relatively junior Department of Education and Youth Affairs. There was little for the opposition to criticize.

The Hawke government also set out to avoid a repeat of the controversy over the employment and deployment of ministerial political advisors by the Whitlam government.[47] A new procedure was followed in an attempt to show that nepotism and cronyism were out and that the talented were being sought. Public advertisements were placed and a panel was set up, including Wilenski, to screen applicants and to advise ministers upon likely recruits. The Prime Minister was to hold a veto over all appointments. The outcome appears to have been disappointing, however. Only about a dozen of the eighty most senior non–public service staff were recruited in this formal manner. The remainder, as before, appear to have been mostly committed supporters who had worked for the Labor party in opposition, or had been personally known to the ministers.

More dramatic appointments were made later. Most significant, in November 1983, Wilenski, the Opposition's bête noire, condemned by the leader of the opposition as a "crony" and "servant" of the Labor party, was appointed PSB chairman.[48] Another former Labor advisor, Darcy McGaurr, replaced Menadue as head of the Department of the Special Minister of State, when the former moved to be head of the Department of Trade. Three other outsiders were brought to head departments (one from a state public service, two from academia). One of these appointments was to the Department of Foreign Affairs. Stone, the head of Treasury, resigned in a blaze of publicity in September 1984, and immediately became an articulate public critic of all governments, including the present one.[49] He was replaced by his deputy.

The government also moved cautiously at the next level, the Senior Executive Service. Despite public criticisms of particular appointments of outsiders, only ten such appointments had been made to that level between April 1, 1983, and April 30, 1984, which is less than 1 percent of officers in that group.[50] Nevertheless, the government was implementing its policy of advertising widely for vacant SES positions.[51]

Much of the remaining implementation occurred within the PSB itself which was reorganized in July 1984. The government's promises on matters such as management improvement, permanent part-time employment, promotion of equal employment opportunity, and industrial democracy have been recognized initially by upward reclassification of the relevant officers.[52] Departments have also been encouraged to upgrade appropriate units. In fields such as industrial democracy there is certainly a great deal of activity, and modest yet positive beginnings appear to have been made to implement government policy.[53]

Conclusion

The Australian Public Service is being changed. There is no going back. Nor do any of the major political parties wish to. A ratchet effect has been at work over the past fifteen years. The thinking that has been going on within both sides of party politics, officially and informally, now has a chance to take root. The reelection of the Hawke Labor government in December 1984 for a further three-year term ensures this. More mobility, flexibility, and responsiveness are being engendered. The model of the self-effacing, neutral senior public servant appears to be passing. Definite political beliefs, whether partisan or not, are now much more freely shown. This is not to say that the final product will be what the parties want. Other parts of the system also need to improve their performance. The capacity of ministers to adequately carry out their functions, for example, is very much under the microscope.[54] Both the Parliament and the political parties are building greater professional expertise. The organizational changes have now been made. Yet it is not clear whether behavioral change will follow. It may be the end of the decade before we will be able to judge the lasting effectiveness of this package of reforms.[55]

Notes

1. R. N. Spann, *Government Administration in Australia* (Sydney: George Allen & Unwin, 1979), p. 36.

2. For general political background, see H. R. Penniman, ed., *Australia at the Polls: The National Elections of 1980 and 1983* (Sydney: George Allen & Unwin for the American Enterprise Institute, 1983).

3. M. Sexton, *Illusions of Power: The Fate of a Reform Government* (Sydney: George Allen & Unwin, 1979), p. 283.

4. E. Thompson, "The Public Service," in *From Whitlam to Fraser*, ed. A. Patience and B. Head (Melbourne: Oxford University Press, 1979), p. 71; Thompson, "Ministers, Bureaucrats and Policy-Making," in *Government, Politics and Power in Australia*, 3d ed., ed. D. Woodward et al. (Melbourne: Longman Cheshire, 1985), p. 44.

5. See J. Lynn and A. Jay, eds., *Yes, Minister: The Diaries of a Cabinet Minister by the Rt. Hon. James Hacker MP*, vol. 3, BBC, London, 1983.

6. J. Carlton, "Putting Philosophy and Objectives into Practice in Government: The Least Understood Component of Effective Politics," *Canberra Bulletin of Public Administration* 11, no. 1 (Autumn 1984), 23. This paraphrases a saying of the ministerial star of the television series, who says: "What on earth is the use of spending thirty years developing a political philosophy, three years in opposi-

tion developing policies, and then coming into office and handing the whole thing over to Sir Humphrey?" Quoted in *Facing the Facts: Report of the Liberal Party Committee of Review* (Canberra: Liberal Party of Australia, 1983), p. 105.

7. Carlton, "Putting Philosophy and Objectives into Practice," p. 111.

8. R.F.I. Smith and P. Weller, eds., *Public Service Inquiries in Australia* (St. Lucia: University of Queensland Press, 1979).

9. For a history of the service, see G. C. Caiden, *Career Service* (Melbourne: Melbourne University Press, 1965). For 1984 employment figures, see Public Service Board, *Annual Report 1983–1984* (Canberra: Australian Government Publishing Service, 1984); for statistical detail, see Public Service Board, *Statistical Yearbook 1982–1983* (Canberra: Australian Government Printing Service, 1983). When temporary staff are included the total is about 192,000. For 1939 employment figures see Public Service Board, *Annual Report 1939*, p. 10, Appendix B.

10. J. Clarke and K. White, *Women in Australian Politics* (Sydney: Fontana, 1983), pp. 135–52.

11. Spann, *Government Administration in Australia*, p. 318. In 1975, 36 Second Division officers and 214 senior Third Division officers were recruited from outside the service. Subsequently, under Fraser, the numbers fell again.

12. For recent survey of central agencies, see P. Weller, "Australia," prepared for the Conference on Policy Advice and Decision-Making at the Top Level of Government, Royal Institute of Public Administration and Policy Studies Institute, Wilton Park, Sussex, Great Britain, Nov. 25–27, 1984.

13. For background, see G. Hawker, R.F.I. Smith, and P. Weller, *Politics and Policy in Australia* (St. Lucia: University of Queensland Press, 1979), pp. 111–24; F. A. Mediansky and J. A. Nockles, "The Prime Ministers's Bureaucracy," *Public Administration* 34, no. 3 (1975); Sir G. Yeend, "The Department of Prime Minister and Cabinet in Perspective," *Australian Journal of Public Administration* 38, no. 3 (1979).

14. Weller, "Australia," pp. 7–10; F. A. Mediansky and J. A. Nockles, "Malcolm Fraser's Bureaucracy," *Australian Quarterly* 53, no. 4 (1981).

15. Weller, "Australia," pp. 2–3; Spann, *Government Administration in Australia*, pp. 297–99; see also PSB annual reports.

16. Spann, *Government Administration in Australia*, p. 459; P. Weller and J. Cutt, *Treasury Control in Australia* (Sydney: Novak, 1976).

17. Committee of Economic Enquiry, *Report*, 2 vols. (Canberra: Government Printer, 1965).

18. National Economic Summit, *Documents and Proceedings*, 3 vols. (Canberra: A.G.P.S., 1983); J. Warhurst, "The Integration of Australian Interest Groups into Party and Bureaucratic Politics," Strathclyde Papers on Government and Politics, no. 32, Dept. of Politics, University of Strathclyde, 1984, pp. 12–16; G. Singleton, "The Economic Planning Advisory Council," *Politics* 20, no. 1 (1985), 12–25.

19. Thompson, "The Public Service," p. 87.

20. Sexton, *Illusions of Power*, pp. 177–200.

21. Hawker, Smith, and Weller, *Politics and Policy in Australia*, pp. 232–50.

22. Royal Commission on Australian Government Administration, *Report* and *Appendices*, 4 vols. (Canberra: A.G.P.S., 1976).

23. Thompson, "The Public Service," pp. 79.

24. Ibid., p. 80; quote from governor-general's speech, opening of Parliament, Feb. 1, 1976.

25. Joint Committee of Public Accounts, 202nd Report, *The Selection and Development of Senior Managers in the Commonwealth Public Service* (Canberra, 1982).

26. D. Connolly, "Reforming the Australian Public Service—III," *Canberra Bulletin of Public Administration* 11, no. 1 (Autumn 1984), 14.

27. Review in Commonwealth Administration, *Report* (Canberra: A.G.P.S., 1982).

28. See, in general, L. Sandercock, "Urban Policy," in *From Whitlam to Fraser*, ed. Patience and Head, pp. 140–56, esp. p. 145.

29. Spann, *Government Administration in Australia*, p. 277.

30. C. Lloyd and P. Troy, *Innovation and Reaction* (Sydney: Allen & Unwin, 1981).

31. G. Hawker, "The Bureaucracy Under the Whitlam Government and Vice Versa," *Politics* 10, no. 1 (1975), 15–23.

32. G. Hawker, *Who's Master, Who's Servant?* (Sydney: Allen & Unwin, 1983).

33. For Wilenski's biographical details, see A. Ramsay, "The Egghead Turns Mandarin," *National Times*, December 9–15, 1983; P. Wilenski, "Labor and the Bureaucracy," in *Critical Essays on Australian Politics*, ed. G. Duncan (Melbourne: Edward Arnold, 1978), and "Reform and Its Implementation: The Whitlam Years in Retrospect," in *Labor Essays 1983*, ed. G. Evans and J. Reeves (Melbourne: Drummond, 1980); P. Wilenski and D. Yerbury, "Reconstructing Bureaucracy: Towards a Vehicle for Social Change," *Labor Essays 1983* (Melbourne: Drummond, 1983), pp. 154–81. Wilenski's thinking is brought together in P. Wilenski, *Public Power and Public Administration* (Sydney: Hale & Iremonger, 1986).

34. P. Wilenski, "Ministers, Public Servants and Public Policy," *Australian Quarterly* 51, no. 2 (June 1979), quoted in Ramsay, "Bureaucracy: The Wilenski View."

35. Labor party developments are traced in P. Weller, "Transition: Taking Over Power in 1983," *Australian Journal of Public Administration* 42, no. 3 (September 1983).

36. Ibid.

37. P. Weller, *Canberra Times*, February 10, 1983.

38. "Reforming the Australian Public Service: A Statement of the Government's Intentions" (Canberra: A.G.P.S., 1983), p. iii.

39. Ibid., pp. 3–6, 9–26; pp. 6–7, 27–31; pp. 7–8, 32–37.

40. J. Warhurst, "The Public Service," in *The Dunstan Decade: Social De-*

mocracy at the State Level, ed. A. Parkin and A. Patience (Melbourne: Longmans, 1979).

41. See, in general, "Public Service Reform 1984," Symposium, *Canberra Bulletin of Public Administration* 11, no. 1 (Autumn 1984), 4–18.

42. Connolly, "Reforming the Australian Public Service—III," and "Public Service Changes," Letter to the editor, *the Bulletin,* January 10, 1984.

43. Connolly, "Reforming the Australian Public Service—III," p. 15.

44. P. H. Bailey, "Reforming the Australian Public Service—IV," Symposium, *Canberra Bulletin of Public Administration* 11, no. 1 (Autumn 1984), 18.

45. There are three pieces of legislation: Public Service Reform Bill 1984; Merit Protection (Australian Government Employees) Bill 1984; and Members of Parliament (Staff) Bill 1984. For accounts of this legislation, see Public Service Board, *Annual Report 1983–84,* pp. 3–8.

46. D. Barnett, "Mandarins Feel the Squeeze," *Bulletin,* February 5, 1985, p. 32.

47. R. F. I. Smith, "Ministerial Advisers: The Experience of the Whitlam Government," *Australian Journal of Public Administration* 36, no. 2 (1977), 133–58. See also J. Walter, *The Ministers' Minders: Personal Advisers in National Government* (Melbourne: Oxford University Press, 1986).

48. Procedure adopted by Hawke described in Weller, "Transition" and J. Walter, "Ministerial Staff Under Hawke," *Australian Journal of Public Administration* 43, no. 3, September 1984, 203–19.

49. Stone's speeches, "1929 and All That," *Quadrant* 205, XXVI, no. 10 (October 1984); and "What Kind of Country?" *Quadrant* 207, XXVIII, no. 12 (December 1984).

50. House of Representatives *Debates,* August 21, 1984, table of "Appointments of Permanent Staff to the First, Second and Third Divisions from April 1, 1983 to date" presented to John Dawkins, minister assisting the prime minister in public service matters.

51. For example, see the *Canberra Times,* February 16, 1985.

52. See, in general, Public Service Board, "The Public Service Reforms—An Overview," *Annual Report 1983–84,* pp. 95–103.

53. "Industrial Democracy in the Public Service," papers from the 1984 RAIPA workshop, in *Canberra Bulletin of Public Administration* 11, no. 3 (Spring 1984), 166–82.

54. P. Weller and M. Grattan, *Can Ministers Cope?* (Melbourne: Hutchinson, 1981).

55. See also the assessment by J. R. Nethercote in "Government Changes and Public Service Reform," in *Australian Commonwealth Administration 1984: Essays in Review,* ed. J. R. Nethercote, A. Kouzmin, and R. Wettenhall (Canberra College of Advanced Education, 1986), pp. 1–25.

CHAPTER 14

Major Administrative Reform
and Reorganization Efforts in Bangladesh,
1971–1985

૨૦

Mohammad Mohabbat Khan

In developing countries, higher civil servants in particular and civil servants in general have considerable influence on almost every aspect of a citizen's life. This is because of their intimate and active involvement in the formulation, implementation, and evaluation of public policies. Moreover, they oversee and monitor compliance with the government's allocative, redistributive, and regulatory policies on the part of nongovernmental organizations.[1] The influence of civil servants on national life is so pervasive in developing nations that they have been characterized as "political actors, essential ingredients of the political system," "power centers, pressure groups, systems stabilizers," "political stabilizers, social elites, interest articulators," and "decision brokers and environment determinants."[2] The above characterizations of civil servants not only testify to their multifarious roles but at the same time point to their impact on the surrounding social, political, economic, and cultural environment. The influence of the social environment on the actions and activities of the civil servants has now been generally accepted.

The interest of Western scholars in systematically studying the civil services in the developing countries is relatively new. This interest can be traced to a number of developments in the last forty years. First, World War II allowed many younger scholars in Western countries to observe administrative systems of developing countries at close range. They not only found dissimilarities with administrative systems at home but also were not able to explain the peculiarities thus observed by utilizing the traditional Weberian, ideal-type model.

The forties and fifties saw the emergence, mostly in Asia and Africa, of a host of independent countries. The civil servants of these newly independent countries were at a loss to change at a rather short notice their orientation from law and order to developmental administration. External assistance was required to reach their countries' developmental goals. Aid came from Western countries, especially the United States, in the form of technical assistance. Such assistance also brought with it experts who carefully observed the operation of the civil services in recipient countries. Like their predecessors, they discovered that prevailing theories and models available were culture-bound and of little help in analyzing the situation in developing countries.

Third, the formation of the Comparative Administration Group (CAG) under the American Society for Public Administration (ASPA) signaled the determination of a number of American scholars to study civil services in different cultures.[3] This move was also seen as an attempt to broaden the base of public administration as an academic discipline which until then was solely based on American experiences. The CAG-based scholars were sustained by the generous financial assistance of the Ford Foundation for field trips and research in developing countries.

As a result of the foregoing developments, theory building vis-à-vis developing countries became a preoccupation of many Western scholars.[4] They concentrated especially on two types of theories—general and middle-range. The most prominent among the general theories are Fred W. Riggs's "agraria and industria" typology and his theory of the prismatic society.[5] The best example of middle-range theory is Max Weber's ideal-type bureaucracy.[6]

Riggs has played a pioneering role in introducing the ecological approach to the study of administrative systems in the context of developing countries.[7] Using an inductive approach, Riggs constructed two polar types—agraria and industria—to distinguish between societies in which "agrarian institutions predominate" and those that are "predominantly or characteristically industrial."[8] In the face of mounting criticism, Riggs abandoned the agraria-industria typology in favor of what became known as his theory of prismatic society.[9]

In Ferrel Heady's opinion, "For developing countries, the most elaborate model has been formulated by Riggs in his 'Sala' administrative subsystem in the prismatic model for transitional societies."[10] The focus of Riggs's attention is the analysis of a few critical elements of the social structure in a prismatic society and their interaction with the "Sala."[11] He identifies these as heterogeneity, formalism, and overlapping. The power structure in a prismatic society is crucial for understanding the role of public bureaucracy in it. Here the bureaucrat's range of participation in decision making is very wide. This fact results in a serious imbalance between political and bureaucratic growth which allows bureaucrats— especially higher civil servants—to compete with politicians and political institutions for a share of the state power. At the same time, the imbalance encourages senior officials to interfere directly in the political process. The sala, thus, is "associated with unequal distribution of services, institutionalized corruption, inefficiency in rule application, nepotism in recruitment, bureaucratic enclaves dominated by motives of self-protection, and, in general, a pronounced gap between formal expectations and actual behaviour."[12]

Riggs's emphasis on the negative aspects of administrative behavior in developing countries, though criticized by many scholars, has paved the way for a more realistic analysis and evaluation of public bureaucracies in developing countries.[13] It also can be deduced from the Riggsian analysis that reforming such institutions is no easy task.

Heady suggests that it is useful to concentrate on basic structural aspects, such as hierarchy, differentiation of specialization, and the qualifications or competence of the bureaucracy, in any comparative study of civil service systems. He claims that "selecting a structural focus in defining bureaucracy . . . allows us to consider all patterns of behaviour that are actually found in bureaucracies as equally deserving to be called bureaucratic behaviour."[14]

For comparing administrative systems in developing countries, Riggs's "Sala" model as well as the bureaucratic approach associated with Heady can be utilized. One complements the other and allows the simultaneous adoption of micro and macro perspectives.

Likewise, major administrative reforms undertaken by the developing countries may be understood in terms of the interaction between administrative and political subsystems within the social system.[15] The resulting interactions are influenced and shaped by the society, and the society in turn is also molded by the outcome of such interactions. The objectives, goals, strategies, and probabilities of success in implementing major administrative reforms is very much dependent on the surrounding environment. Context is very crucial. Developing countries differ among themselves with regard to their administrative and political systems, economic stage of development, and cultural heritage. These differences, among other things, have made it extremely difficult to develop a universal and operational model with which to observe and evaluate the experiences of developing countries who undertake major administrative reforms.

The experiences of many developing countries indicates that reforming a traditional civil bureaucracy can prove to be difficult indeed, as resistance develops, matures, and is sustained by vested interests. On the other hand, these countries are under increasing pressure to undertake major reforms to keep pace with complex social, political, and economic realities. Sometimes, major reforms must be initiated and implemented within a short time and against powerful opposition.

This chapter will discuss Bangladesh's efforts to reform and reorganize its civil service. To place the analysis in a broader perspective, this chapter will relate its findings to the general issue of bureaucratic reform and reorganization in developing countries. Two central questions and a number of other issues will be raised and analyzed.

First, why have the far-reaching proposals of reform bodies been resisted and not implemented in Bangladesh? In this regard, special attention will be given to the Administrative and Services Reorganization Committee (ASRC) which called for the radical overhaul of the administrative system and advocated drastic changes in the powers, positions, and status of the encadred generalist civil service elite. Why, on the other hand, were major recommendations of another reform body—the Pay and Services Commission (PSC)—enthusiastically supported by the same civil servants?

The other questions also raised include the following: Why have such meager results issued from so many successive inquiries? Why is the military so comfortable with the bureaucracy? Why has decolonization never really penetrated the bureaucracy? How did a bureaucracy with substantial Weberian trappings evolve, notwithstanding the apparent absence of a congruent social base? To what degree is the civil service reform seen as the real problem in Bangladesh?

Background

The British colonial domination of the Indian subcontinent for almost two centuries has clearly had a significant impact on the two key institutions of Bangladesh, the civil bureaucracy and the military. The British rulers established a highly centralized and elitist administrative system intended to strengthen and perpetuate their control over the native population.[16] In independent India and Pakistan, the same administrative system was continued with minor changes in the nomenclature. In fact, the Indian Administrative

Service (IAS) and the Civil Service of Pakistan (CSP) were modeled after the Indian Civil Service (ICS) of British days. The politicians of these two newly independent countries were preoccupied with the task of consolidating their hold over newly acquired power, and hence were forced to rely on an administrative system that had very little relevance for an independent country. In Pakistan, until 1971, the members of the CSP, like their ICS counterparts during British rule, continued to occupy the key policymaking and policy implementing positions at the central and provincial governments in the field, that is, at the subdivision, district, and division level as well as in the head office, or the secretariat. This has been at the expense of other officials—generalists and specialists—employed by the central and provincial governments.

It is no surprise then that between 1947 and 1971 Pakistan rejected the far-reaching recommendations of Rowland Egger, Bernard Gladieux, and the Pay and Services Commission.[17] These included unifying all the services into one, restructuring district administration and overhauling the secretariat setup, basing recruitment and promotion on merit, enhancing the role of specialists in the administration, common training arrangements for all civil servants, and abolishing the system of reserving key posts for the CSP officers.[18]

The institutionalized nature of the CSP and its members' superiority complex, an elitist British heritage, prolonged military rule, and chronic political instability all contributed to the failure of major administrative reform efforts in Pakistan.[19] The members of the CSP successfully resisted the implementation of major administrative reforms, as they had become a "ruling elite" who faithfully adhered to the colonial administrative heritage.[20] Their position was immensely strengthened by the fact that the majority came from upper-class families and from one region (formerly West Pakistan, now Pakistan) and were closely linked by birth and marriage with large and influential landowning, industrial, and commercial families. Coincidentally, the officers of Pakistan's armed forces mostly came from the same region and similar backgrounds.[21]

Major Administrative Reform and Reorganization Efforts in Bangladesh

On December 16, 1971, Bangladesh emerged as an independent state after a nine-month war of national liberation. At independence, the new state had inherited not only a colonial administrative system but also one ravaged by war and factionalism. Initially, the scope of reform was limited to revitalizing the administrative system by reorganizing the secretariat and restoring civil administration in the field.

A six-member Civil Administration Restoration Committee (CARC) was constituted under the chairmanship of a generalist civil servant.[22] A week later, CARC submitted a report that was promptly accepted by the government. The report provided for a trimmed secretariat with twenty ministries and a mechanism for rehabilitation of civil administration at various levels—that is, divisional, district, subdivisional, and *thana* (or subdistrict, now called *upazila*). But, more important, this interim committee provided the setting for the appointment of major reform committees and commissions in later years.

So far, Bangladesh has appointed six major administrative reform commissions or committees. The Awami League government of Sheikh Mujibur Rahman came to power immediately after independence. Consistently with its advocacy of greater political control of civil bureaucracy, the government appointed two high-powered bodies, the Administrative and Services Reorganization Committee (ASRC) and the National Pay Commission (NPC). Lieutenant-General Ziaur Rahman—who came to power amid political chaos through a military coup in September 1975 and who remained at the helm until his assassination in May 1981—appointed the Pay and Services Commission (PSC). Finally, the present ruler of Bangladesh, President and Chief Martial Law Administrator (CMLA) Lieutenant-General Hossain Mohammad Ershad—who seized power in a bloodless coup in March 1982—has already appointed three major reform bodies. These are the Martial Law Committee for Examining Organizational Setup of Ministries/Divisions, Departments, Directorates, and other Organizations under them (MLC), the Committee for Administrative Reorganization/Reform (CARR), and the National Pay Commission (NPC II).

Objectives and Membership of Reform Commissions in Bangladesh

The terms of reference of a reform body indicate, among other things, the political philosophy and political objectives of the government in power. Also, they give an idea as to how the government wishes to solve some of the more pressing problems facing the public sector.

The choice of members for a reform commission or committee to a large extent determines it fate. The members may be drawn from within and/or outside the civil service. In choosing its members, a government should give careful consideration to a number of factors. High expertise, experience, and status among members not only enable them to carry on their investigation in a forthright manner but also considerably facilitate the chances that the resultant recommendations will be accepted both by the government and by conscious and vocal sections of the population.

The Administrative and Services Reorganization Committee (ASRC) was appointed on March 15, 1972. The responsibilities of ASRC included considering the structure of various services and their amalgamation into one unified service, determining of the future recruitment policy for the unified service and preparing a comprehensive scheme for administrative reorganization.[23] A noted academician was made the chairman of this four-member committee. The other three members included an eminent economist, a member of Parliament belonging to the ruling political party, and a senior generalist civil servant. The last member was designated as the member-secretary to the committee.

On July 21, 1972, the first National Pay Commission (NPC) was appointed to review the existing pay structure in order to nationalize and standardize pay scales in the public sector.[24] The NPC was instructed to work in close cooperation with the ASRC. The ten-member commission consisted of five full-time and five part-time members. Of the full-time members, one was a retired senior civil servant who chaired the committee; three were civil servants; and the fifth was an academician. One of the civil servants was given the additional responsibility of serving as a member-secretary to the commission. The part-time members included the deputy chief of staff of the army, two civil servants, and two professionals.

A seventeen-member Pay and Services Commission (PSC) was appointed on February 20, 1976. The policy guidelines and objectives of the PSC were to examine the pay and service structure of public-sector employees and to recommend suitable reforms in recruitment, training, and development.[25] One of the major responsibilities of the commission was to devise rational and simple principles for amalgamating all civil service groups performing similar functions. The PSC was specifically directed to keep in view the recommendations of the ASRC and the NPC and the implementation of some of the recommendations of the latter body. The PSC, like NPC, was chaired by a retired senior civil servant and had full-time and part-time members. The six full-time members included four retired senior civil servants and a current civil servant who was also made member-secretary to the commission. Among the eleven part-time members, six were senior civil servants belonging to key ministries and the rest represented professional groups including accounting, medicine, engineering, business, and journalism.

The Martial Law Committee for Examining Organizational Setup of Ministries/Divisions, Departments, Directorates and other Organizations under them (MLC) was appointed on April 18, 1982. The Committee was asked to rationalize the organization and functions of the government, review the duties of officers, scrutinize the existing or sanctioned personnel and recommend measures to improve efficiency in the civil service.[26] The five-member MLC was headed by a brigadier. The other members included two lieutenant colonels, one major, and one middle-ranking civil servant. The last member was tapped as the secretary to the committee.

A seven-member Committee for Administrative Reorganization/Reform (CARR) was appointed on April 28, 1982. The committee was charged with reviewing the structure and organization of the existing civilian administration and to recommend an appropriate, sound, and effective administrative system based on delegation of authority and responsibility with the objective of bringing the administration nearer to the people.[27] The then deputy chief martial law administrator (DCMLA) and chief of the naval staff was made the chairman of the committee. The other members of CARR included three senior civil servants, a minister, a senior army officer, and a university professor. The civil servant with least seniority was designated to be the secretary of the committee. The committee in its first meeting, held on May 2, 1982, co-opted three more members. Of the three, one was a veteran journalist. The other two were senior civil servants, one in active service and the other retired.

On May 31, 1984 a second National Pay Commission (NPC II) was appointed. The commission was asked to make its recommendations for suitable pay structure, allowances, and other benefits for all civil employees in the public sector, taken into consideration prevailing wages and benefits in other sectors of the country.[28] The fifteen-member commission was headed by a justice of the Supreme Court. The five full-time members included a distinguished academician, a retired senior civil servant, a former member of the planning commission, and a senior civil servant, who acted as secretary to the commission. The part-timers consisted of a senior civil servant, a retired senior civil servant, the president of the Federation of Chamber and Commerce, a chartered accountant, a professor of medicine, a managing director of a private commercial bank, a retired educator, a senior officer from the Ministry of Finance, and a representative from the University Grants Commission.

Methodology

An investigative body needs to follow certain methods to collect, collate, and interpret data. The findings and recommendations of such a group are also influenced and shaped by the kind of methodology used in conducting a formal inquiry. The five committees or commissions used a number of methods including interviews, questionnaires, briefings, memoranda, analyses of the representations of interest groups, and tours both within and outside the country.

The NPC II submitted its report in December 1984, but a year later its deliberations had not been made public by the government. The ASRC interviewed thirteen ministers, fifty-five senior officials, and a large number of people representing different interests. The committee also heard representations from 183 service associations, and visited the Soviet Union and two major districts in Bangladesh.

The NPC, through circulation of a questionnaire, collected information pertaining to pay, allowances, and fringe benefits from ministries, autonomous and semiautonomous bodies, and nationalized enterprises. Also, various service associations and members of the public were invited to submit their suggestions on matters relating to pay. The committee received submissions resulting in some five hundred sets of recommendations. The Ministry of Finance and the Planning Commission helped the NPC with projections of available governmental resources and trends in the cost-of-living index. The NPC held over a hundred sessions to complete its deliberations including several joint sessions with the ASRC. The commission reviewed the pay structure of various developed and developing countries.

The PSC interviewed a number of eminent personalities including government secretaries, vice-chancellors of universities, chairmen of public corporations, and representatives of service associations. A questionnaire was circulated among top officials of the government as well as prominent professionals. The commission also visited a number of countries to study the pay and service structures and other relevant facets of their civil services. Members also toured Bangladesh to obtain first-hand information pertaining to various tiers of administration. The commission held seventy sessions. The commission was ably supported in its work by a staff of fifty-five persons, under the leadership of the member-secretary, which produced twenty-four working papers and several more studies prepared by individual staff members. The PSC report was finalized by three drafting committees: the first group drafted the report on the services, the second on pay, and the third moderated the reports of the first two.

The MLC briefed and submitted memoranda to approximately 300 senior civil servants in the process of obtaining its information. They also met some of the advisers to the CMLA, government officials of all categories, interviewed a few educators and visited most of the ministries/

divisions. Circulation of a questionnaire to relevant authorities, visits to a number of *thana*s in six districts in Bangladesh, and interviews of a few selected social scientists were the methods used by the members of CARR to gather data for their report.

Major Findings

Findings of administrative reform committees or commissions generally focus on the dysfunctions afflicting various segments of the civil service system and attempt to discern their inherent causes. The five reform groups under review here unequivocally condemned a number of deficiencies in the administrative system of Bangladesh. The ASRC found that "the existing services divided into too many distinct entities with artificial walls built around them, with varying career prospects, lacking in professionalism and too much class and rank-oriented, with very little opportunities to rise to the top for those who started their career in the lower ranks."[29] It observed that the service structure designed to suit a colonial, capitalist, and federal system of government was inappropriate for a newly independent country with a socialist bent and unitary system of government. The structure was outmoded, sluggish, and unresponsive to the needs of the people. Also, its procedures were complicated, confusing, and ponderous.

The NPC identified a number of anomalies and inadequacies in the pay structure which it termed "anachronistic." A multiplicity and diversity of scales characterized the pay structure. Indeed, the commission found 2,200 different pay scales in the public sector. The situation was further complicated by diversity in rates of increment and efficiency bars for similarly classified jobs.

The PSC found that administrative inefficiency was one of the principal factors adversely affecting the planned development of the civil services. It, like the ASRC, found the status of the civil service to be ambiguous.[30] It noted that the government was unwilling even after six years of independence to clarify the position of the former elite service—that is, the Civil Service of Pakistan (CSP)—vis-à-vis other services. The MLC found that many senior civil servants flouted rules and disregarded norms by directly contacting the chief executive over the head of the Establishment Division when creating new ministries or divisions or when expanding existing ones. This contributed materially to unnecessary personnel increases. The committee had little option but to comment, "Parkinson's Law about proliferation of organization found its full play in Bangladesh."[31] It observed that, in many instances, recruitment was conducted directly by departments, without the scrutiny of the Public Service Commission.

The CARR findings pointed up a litany of difficulties. These included: a lack of appropriate and uniform personnel policy to recruit, train, and promote public servants; an absence of a durable political process; weak local governments; a need to create parallel political and administrative institutions; an overly complex and recommendation-based decision-making system; an excessive compartmentalization of functions; a continuation of vertical-functional departmentalism which impairs area-based coordination; and a reluctance on the part of the political authority to devolve power to the local level.

Major Recommendations

All the reform bodies made painstaking and detailed recommendations to revamp the country's civil service system. Two of them (ASRC and CARR) went beyond the domain of the traditional civil service system and firmly recommended democratization of administration and devolution of power to elected local governments. The recommendations of the ASRC, which submitted its report in April and October 1973, were influenced by the deliberations of the Fulton Committee in Britain. As well, they invoked four guiding principles of the newly founded state—namely, nationalism, secularism, socialism, and democracy. The committee called for the abolition of divisions among different civil services and recommended in its place a Unified Grading Structure (UGS) containing ten grades.[32] To inculcate professionalism among civil servants all posts would be broadly divided into "functional and area group posts."[33] The committee also advocated the creation of "senior policy and management posts" (SPMP) to be filled by the most competent civil servants on the basis of examinations and career records. The committee also made a number of recommendations to streamline the public personnel management system. It called for the adoption of merit as a cardinal principle for personnel selection. It argued, thus, for establishment of a Personnel Division, an Administrative Management and Reforms Division, a Training Wing in the proposed Personnel Division, and creation of training cells in large ministries along with three servicewide training institutes for postentry, midlevel, and senior-level officials. All of these reforms were intended to develop a system of career management that put a premium on merit and quality. The committee further suggested that the proposed Administrative Management and Reforms Division be placed under the overall supervision of the prime minister and be given the responsibility to work out the details for the implementation of UGS.

With respect to administration, the ASRC made a number of recommendations for democratization at all levels. It strongly argued for substantial devolution of power and authority to the elected local governments at successive levels. Local representatives would be responsible for developmental activities within their jurisdictions, with grants from the central government. They would be empowered to levy taxes within their areas. A "Local Government Service" (LGS) would be created and controlled by the central government. Its members were to be recruited and trained by the central government for placement at different local levels. Other significant recommendations included the abolition of the division as a tier of administration, conversion of subdivisions into districts, substantial reduction of the functions of deputy commissioners (the chief functionary of the central government in the field), separation of executive from judicial functions, and restriction of the role of the central secretariat to the formulation, planning, and evaluation of policies.

The NPC recommended a nine-tier administrative structure with corresponding pay scales. Of the nine tiers, four would be normal direct-entry tiers, three would be promotion tiers, and two, conversion tiers. Subsequently, it recommended ten scales of pay to match the ten service grades recommended by the ASRC.

The PSC's major recommendations included the amalgamation of all former services within an all-purpose civil service. This would include all those employed in the traditional public sector. The new system would emphasize merit as the determining factor for recruitment and promotion. It would remove barriers between the former CSP and other services through the introduction of initial pay scales and provisions for equitable advancement toward the top of the hierarchy. This would entail constituting a new apex cadre with "talented, efficient and experienced" officers drawn from all functional cadres through appropriately designed tests for providing administrative leadership and high-level coordination, adopting the cadre concept of the civil service structure for major functional areas in the government as opposed to the position concept, and organizing cadre services at the top tier to comprise the nucleus of the civil service structure.[34] The other recommendations of the commission included a four-tiered, broad-based civil service in hierarchical order, and the establishment of twenty-nine organized services within the nation's administrative structure.[35]

The PSC recommended fifty-two scales of pay to reduce the multiplicity of pay scales as well as to allow alternate sets of scales for particular categories without disturbing the overall pay structure. Highly qualified professionals were to be adequately remunerated. Proper valuation and upgrading of jobs requiring exceptional creativity and imagination were to be undertaken on a priority basis.

The MLC completed its task in two phases. The reports on ministries and divisions was presented to the government in May 1982, and the assessment of departments, directorates, and subordinate offices followed in December 1983. The committee's most significant recommendations included the reduction of ministries from forty-four to ten, divisions from sixty to forty-two, and secretarial staff from 9,440 to 6,118.

The MLC estimated that the above measures would drastically reduce governmental expenditure. Its other recommendations included cutting the decision layers in the secretariat, restricting the role of the secretariat to policy formulation and planning while giving the department and other executive organizations responsibility to implement policies and programs, formalizing and regularizing the recruitment process, fixing the supervisory ratio at 1:3, delegating financial and administrative powers, finalizing the seniority of cadre offices, setting up a Public Accounts Committee, emphasizing the use of the merit principle for internal promotions, and providing training to civil servants.

The CARR submitted its report in June 1982. Its principal proposal called for direct election of chairmen of *zilla*s (districts), *parishad*s (councils), *thana* assemblies, and union assemblies. These chief coordinators would be provided with full staff support. As well, elected councils at all levels were to enjoy full functional control over officials working under them. Finally, elected chairmen of lower councils were to be ex-officio members of the immediate superior councils.

Implementation of Reform Measures

The experiences of many countries—developed and developing—indicate that major administrative reorganization efforts often fail at the most crucial stage of the reform cycle, namely, implementation. This has certainly been the case with civil service reform efforts in Bangladesh. To begin, the far-reaching recommendations of the ASRC were not implemented by the government of the day. The committee's voluminous report met the unhappy fate of being marked secret and was debarred from public circulation. The NPC fared little better. Only a few inconsequential segments of its recommendations, none of which threatened any powerful interest group within the civil service, were implemented.

Initially, the Zia government responded to the PSC report with calculated silence. Only after a lapse of two years did the government take concrete actions to implement, albeit in modified form, some of the PSC's major recommendations. Five cabinet committees were constituted to work out the details of implementation. The government's action included the creation of twenty-eight services under fourteen main cadres, the constitution of the Senior Services Pool (SSP), and the introduction of New National Grades and Scales of Pay (NNGSP).[36]

The present military government of Lieutenant-General Ershad moved quickly to implement some of the major recommendations of the MLC and CARR. In July 1982, the CMLA appointed a four-member Committee for Finalization of the Reorganization of Ministries/Divisions and Public Statutory Corporations (FRMDPSC) under the chairmanship of the principal staff officer to the commander-in-chief. Other members of the committee were the secretary to the concerned ministry or division, an additional secretary from the Establishment Division (O & M Wing), and a brigadier from the CMLA's secretariat. The O & M Wing of the Establishment Division was designated to act as the secretariat of the committee. The committee was asked to examine the recommendations of MLC as well as the comments of the concerned ministry or division, and finalize the revised organizational setup of ministries, divisions, or departments. The committee submitted its proposals to the CMLA in August 1982. The government then approved the recommendations of the MLC pertaining to reduction of personnel as well as the charter of duties for the officers and staff of the secretariat. In December 1983, the cabinet secretary of the government informed all concerned that the tables of organization of all departments or directorates and subordinate offices as recommended by MLC had been formally approved.

The idea of a national implementation committee (NIC) as well as other major recommendations of CARR were accepted by the military government of Ershad. That is, a short period after the submission of the CARR report, the government constituted the National Implementation Committee for Administrative Reorganization/Reform (NICARR).[37] This body was headed by the chairman of CARR. Its members included quite a few ministers, high-ranking civil military officers, as well as two of the members of CARR. The committee was given wide-ranging responsibilities by the government to facilitate and monitor the implementation of CARR's recommendations.[38] It continues to meet on a regular basis. Among other things, it has identified subdivisions (*thanas*) for upgrading into *upazilas*, fixed the number of officers and staff at *upazilas*, called for allocation of *taka* fifty *lac* for developmental activities to each *upazila* for one financial year, approved Thana Parishad Business Rules (1983), and

Upazila Parishad (Taxation) Rules (1983), and decided to convert sixty-four urban *thana*s into *upazila*s.[39]

The government implemented, within a year (from November 1982 to November 1983), most of the major recommendations of CARR. Four hundred sixty *upazila*s have been created by upgrading *thana*s. The promulgation of a number of ordinances, delegation of substantial administrative authority, and allocation of considerable financial resources at the *upazila* level indicate the direction in which the government is moving.[40]

Analysis and Evaluation of Major Administrative Reform and Reorganization Efforts in Bangladesh

Earlier sections of this chapter have discussed various facets of reform and reorganization efforts in Bangladesh from terms of reference to implementation. This section contains analysis and evaluation of Bangladesh's experience in major administrative reforms and reorganizations in light of the questions raised in the introductory section. Three key variables are utilized here. These derive from a conceptual framework designed to facilitate the analysis which follows. The variables are bureaucratic dominance, military-bureaucratic alliance, and political instability.

Bureaucratic Dominance

Bureaucratic dominance in this context means the overwhelming influence of the senior generalist elite civil servants of the former CSP—now encadred in BCS (Administration)—in the formulation and implementation of major administrative reforms and reorganization policies. These civil servants, though few in number, wield disproportionately great power and influence. Maintenance of most strategic posts has allowed them to control the apex of power and to remain in constant interaction with those with ultimate authority over the apparatus of state. They also receive support from some of the senior members of the former EPCS now also encadred in BCS (Administration) when the interests of generalist civil servants appear to be threatened.

The overwhelming influence of these elite civil servants can be demonstrated by the extent of their involvement in any major reform effort. First, the majority of the members of the commissions or committees were generalist civil servants. The key position of member-secretary in all the reform bodies, except one, went to a former CSP member. NPC and PSC were both headed by retired senior civil servants. The civil servants have tended to fight the corner of their group. For instance, it is claimed that the first member-secretary of PSC went to the extreme of manipulating the opinion of fellow members in favor of his cadre while they drafted their report.[41] Second, the role of the generalist elite civil servants is very critical in the implementation or nonimplementation of major reforms or reorganization. Besides being members of specifically designed implementation bodies like NICARR, they occupy top positions of secretaries and additional secretaries in strategic ministries or divisions like Establishment, Cabinet, Finance, Home, and Local Government. These bodies remain intimately involved in almost every aspect of implementation of any major reform effort.

In Bangladesh there seems to be an inverse relation between the severity of a reform proposal and its prospects for implementation. Major and substantial reforms have been difficult to implement because of resistance from vested interests who benefit from the status quo. The nonimplementation of the far-reaching recommendations of the ASRC and the NPC are examples. By the time reports of the committees were submitted to the political leadership, the situation in the country had changed. A combination of a number of factors—specifically, the deteriorating economy, abandonment of democratic forms of governance by the ruling political party in favor of a totalitarian monolith, and the gradual alienation of the general masses from the government—compelled the political leadership to depend increasingly on the senior generalist civil servants to stay in power. In turn, these civil servants exploited this opportunity to consolidate and strengthen their positions. They convinced the political leadership to maintain the administrative status quo by keeping their positions intact.

The opposition to implementing the ASRC recommendations was successfully led and orchestrated by the senior members of the elite generalist civil servants of the former CSP cadre. Thus, the first major effort in administrative reform failed due to bureaucratic resistance, intrigues, and maneuvers reminiscent of the days of United Pakistan.[42] Failure to revise pay scales for higher-level civil servants, as recommended by NPC, also resulted from the opposition of the senior members of the two generalist civil services formerly belonging to the CSP and the East Pakistan Civil Service (EPCS). Both groups demanded enhancement of their salaries and other associated fringe benefits and were unhappy with the fact that NPC recommended pay cuts for them. A number of cabinet committees were appointed by the government to allow civil servants to appeal against "discrepancies" in pay adjustments. Predictably, these committees were supported by staffs consisting mostly of senior generalist civil servants.

The picture is completely different when the elite generalist civil servants favor certain reform/reorganization measures. A case in point was the creation of the Senior Service Pool (SSP) as recommended by the PSC.

Professionals and members of various nongeneralist services felt betrayed when it became clear that the SSP, an apex policy cadre, would provide an almost insignificant number of spaces for members of their groups, contrary to the recommendations of the PSC. It has been repeatedly alleged that selection to the SSP was made not on the basis of merit but on personal preference and favoritism. In fact, the establishment of the SSP immensely increased the mobility and promotion prospects of elite generalist civil servants. There is little doubt that the then Zia government favored particular segments of civil servants, that is, former CSP and EPCS members. It pitted these in an uneven and unjust contest against the professionals and members of other civil services who gained very little, if anything, from creation of the SSP.

Military-Bureaucratic Alliance

The alliance between the military and the bureaucracy results from a realization that interests of both are similar and need to be protected and, if possible, enhanced. These alliances are forged because the senior members of both the military and the bureaucracy enjoy privileges and benefits far disproportionate to their numbers and contribution to the country's progress and prosperity. In Bangladesh, military intervention in politics is a recurrent phenomenon. The military seizes state power at regular intervals by toppling elected governments with ease and impunity. The first action of a military government is to form an advisory council, the membership of which is dominated by senior military and civil servants. Many senior civil servants who join the military government as advisers subsequently become ministers once a council of ministers is struck. But throughout their active association with the military they maintain close and regular contact with their colleagues in the civil service. Another tendency of military regimes in Bangladesh is to increase their influence within the civil service system by placing a large number of persons from various defense services (both in active service and retired) in strategic positions. This practice has been mostly condoned by senior generalist civil servants who wish to maintain the good will of the higher-ups in the military hierarchy. In effect, the unrepresentative character of both groups promotes imperious approaches to governance.

Under the circumstances, it is only to be expected that any reform proposals that call for increasing public access to and involvement in administration will be resisted. Both the ASRC and the CARR made far-reaching recommendations to ensure popular participation in administration by allowing increasing devolution of power and authority at various subnational levels. What happened to their recommendations? The ASRC report was summarily rejected. As we have seen, the civil bureaucracy alliance in power in Bangladesh today accepted in principle all the recommendations of CARR, including devolution of power to various subnational levels. Accordingly, the *upazila*s were created, financial resources were put at their disposal, and the requisite infrastructures built. Yet, free elections have not been held. The people continue to be ruled by centrally recruited, deputied, and controlled civil servants. The most powerful officer at the *upazila*s is the *upazila nirbani* officer, a generalist civil servant who is both the chairman of the upazila *parishad* (or council) as well as its chief executive officer. Devolution of power to the elected representatives of the people, as recommended by CARR, has not taken place. In fact, generalist civil servants continue to head local administrations as in the past. Divisions, as an administration tier, have not been abolished as recommended by CARR.

It is apparent that actual elections for the post of chairman at the *upazila* level, introduction of a democratic governance system at the district level, and the abolition of divisions as an administrative tier would not only have put the civil servants under the control of the people's representatives but at the same time would have resulted in considerable reduction in their power and responsibilities. Reduction of power, in the eyes of the generalist civil servants, is synonymous with degradation of their status and importance. As a result, their tendency is to constantly increase their power and responsibilities. This tendency to expand even when there is no need was pointed out by the MLC. Although the committee's recommendations were accepted and the number of divisions and ministries were reduced, these soon returned to or exceeded their old complements. One need not have to go too far to understand why that happened. The "empire-building tendency" is not dead with civil servants in Bangladesh, but has been given a new lease on life by their partner, the military.

Political Instability

In Bangladesh, political instability allows elite civil servants to form a working alliance with the military in order to protect their interests and privileges. In the transaction, the military obtains the opportunity to be the senior partner and assumes the direct charge of the country. The military is ably supported by the elite civil servants.

In Bangladesh, the unrepresentative character of the political leadership, their shortsightedness and their unwillingness to initiate or implement fundamental changes in the social, political, and economic system creates a situation in which a representative governance system cannot function. This state of affairs inevitably results in the leadership's increasing dependence on senior civil servants. It becomes isolated from the people and fails to tackle the multifarious problems facing the country. Discontent and disaffection among the people continue to grow. Political leaders—weak and indecisive—become the prisoners of their own shortsighted policies and actions.

The Mujib government thus provided a textbook case for frittering away a massive mandate of popular support. The head of the government at independence turned into a charismatic leader with a massive following. The same government which promised so much in the beginning delivered so little in the end. The far-reaching proposals of the ASRC to overhaul the civil service system and to convert subnational administrative units into representational systems were not implemented. This was despite the fact that two members of the committee (including the chairman) were well-known academics who enjoyed close ties with Sheikh Mujibur Rahman, the head of the government. Even the third member belonged to Parliament and sat with the Awami League, the ruling party. Only the last member of the committee belonged to the elite civil service. The recommendations of the NPC pertaining to pay of senior civils were also not implemented. The recommendations of both the ASRC and the NPC were in line with the then four guiding principles of the state, that is, nationalism, socialism, secularism, and democracy. In every case, the weak political leadership was no match for the trained and experienced civil servants who refused to carry out their directives.

Conclusion

Since independence in 1971, a number of high-powered committees and commissions have been appointed in Bangladesh, with a broad mandate to diagnose the ills afflicting the civil service system and to recommend appropriate corrective measures to transform it into an effective vehicle for the nation's development. After painstaking investigations, these reform bodies, especially the ASRC and CARR, made a number of significant recommendations. Yet they were not carried out.

Notwithstanding the volumes of reports, major reform proposals that called for wide-ranging changes in the civil service system were not implemented because of the internal dynamics of the administrative system and its linkages with the society at large. As I have explained, this nonimplementation is the result of three variables: bureaucratic dominance, the military-bureaucratic alliance, and political instability.

It should be emphasized here that reforming an institutionalized elite bureaucracy that maintains a close and cordial relationship with the military, dismisses politicians, and patronizes the people at large, is a herculean task. It can only succeed if such fundamental changes are initiated simultaneously with others designed to treat the sociopolitical and economic ills of the country. Major administrative reforms and reorganizations, if undertaken in isolation, will be resisted by vested interests and will not be implemented. The experience of Bangladesh has demonstrated this clearly.

Notes

1. Selcuk Ozgediz, *Managing the Public Service in Developing Countries: Issues and Prospects* (Washington, D.C.: World Bank Staff Working Paper No. 583, 1983), p. 1.

2. Gerald E. Caiden, *Public Administration* (Pacific Palisades, Calif.: Palisades Publishers, 1982), pp. 238–39.

3. For an overview of developments on comparative public administration in general and the CAG in particular, see: Ramesh K. Arora, *Comparative Public Administration* (New Delhi: Associated Publishing, 1972); Ferrel Heady, *Public Administration: A Comparative Perspective* (New York: Marcel Dekker, 1984); Dwight Waldo, *Comparative Public Administration: Prologue, Problems and Promise* (Chicago: CAG, Society for Public Administration, 1964); Keith M. Henderson, "Comparative Public Administration: The Identity Crisis," *Journal of Comparative Administration* 1, no. 1 (May 1969), 65–84; the entire issue of *Public Administration Review* 26, no. 4 (1976); Jon S. T. Quah, "Comparative Public Administration: What and Why?" *Administrative Change* 4, no. 2 (January–June 1977), 175–90.

4. See Nimrod Raphaeli, "Comparative Public Administration: An Overview," in *Readings in Comparative Administration*, ed. Raphaeli (Boston: Allyn and Bacon, 1967), pp. 1–25; Ferrel Heady, "Comparative Public Administration: Concerns and Priorities," in *Papers in Comparative Public Administration*, ed. Ferrel Heady and Sybil L. Stokes (Ann Arbor: Institute of Public Administration, University of Michigan, 1962); and James Heaphey, "Comparative Public Administration: Comments on Current Characteristics," *Public Administration Review* 28, no. 4 (1968), 242–49.

5. Another general theory which received prominence was Dorsey's information-energy model based on equilibrium theory. See John T. Dorsey, "An Information-Energy Model," in *Papers*, ed. Heady and Stokes, pp. 37–57, and "The Bureaucracy and Political Development in Vietnam," in *Bureaucracy and Political Development*, ed. Joseph La Palombara (Princeton, N.J.: Princeton University Press, 1963), pp. 318–59; William M. Berenson, "Testing the Information-Energy Model," *Administration and Society* 9, no. 2 (August 1977), 139–58;

Charles T. Goodsell, "The Information-Energy Model and Comparative Administration," ibid., pp. 159–68.

6. Scholars like Berger, Presthus, and Heady, among others, have contributed to what may be called comparative studies of bureaucracies in developing countries. Berger and Presthus tested applicability of Weberian ideal-type bureaucracy in Egypt and Turkey, respectively. See Monroe Berger, *Bureaucracy and Society in Modern Egypt* (Princeton, N.J.: Princeton University Press, 1957); Robert V. Presthus, "Weberian v. Welfare Bureaucracy in Traditional Society," *Administrative Science Quarterly* 6 (1961), 1–24, and "Behavior and Bureaucracy in Many Cultures," *Public Administration Review* 19, no. 1 (1959), 25–35; Heady, *Public Administration*, esp. ch. 2.

7. See Fred W. Riggs, *The Ecology of Public Administration* (Bombay: Asia Publishing, 1961), and "Trends in the Comparative Study of Public Administration," *International Review of Administrative Sciences* 28, no. 1 (1962), 9–15.

8. See Fred W. Riggs, "Agraria-Industria: Toward a Typology of Comparative Administration," in *Toward the Comparative Study of Public Administration*, ed. William J. Siffin (Bloomington: Indiana University Department of Government, 1957), pp. 23–110.

9. For a critique of agraria-industria typology, F. J. Tickner, "Comparative Administrative Systems," *Public Administration Review* 19, no. 1 (1959), 19–25; Presthus, "Behavior and Bureaucracy in Many Cultures;" R. S. Milne, "Comparisons and Models in Public Administration," *Political Studies* 10 (1962), 1–14. It is almost impossible to summarize Rigg's theory of prismatic society. See Fred W. Riggs, *Administration in Developing Countries: The Theory of Prismatic Society* (Boston: Houghton-Mifflin, 1964).

10. Heady, *Public Administration*, p. 76.

11. See Fred W. Riggs, "The 'Sala' Model: An Ecological Approach to the Study of Comparative Administration," *Philippine Journal of Public Administration* 6 (1962), 3–16.

12. Heady, *Public Administration*, p. 82.

13. Riggs's prismatic-sala model has been criticized as Western-biased, value-laden, etc. See Arora, *Comparative Public Administration*, pp. 121–24; E. H. Valsan, "Positive Formalism: A Desideratum for Development," *Philippine Journal of Public Administration* 12, no. 1 (1968), 3–6; R. S. Milne, "Formalism Reconsidered," *Philippine Journal of Public Administration* 14, no. 1 (1970), 21–30; and Michael L. Manroe, "Prismatic Behavior in the United States?" *Journal of Comparative Administration* 2, no. 2 (1970), 229–42. Partly in response to criticism made and partly to clarify and update his thinking further, Riggs published another book; see Fred W. Riggs, *Prismatic Society Revisited* (Morristown, N.J.: General Learning Press, 1973).

14. Heady, *Public Administration*, pp. 61–70, at p. 65.

15. See V. V. Moharir, "Administrative Reforms in India," pp. 238–51; D. Hadisumarto and G. B. Siegel, "The Optimum Strategy Matrix and Indonesian Administrative Reforms," pp. 251–71; A. Carillo Castro, "Administrative Reform

in Mexico," pp. 185–212; A. B. Brewar-Carias, "Administrative Reform Experiences in Venezuela, 1969–1975," pp. 213–37, all in *The Management of Change in Government*, ed. Arne F. Leemans (The Hague: Martinus Nijhoff, 1976). For the experiences of Bangladesh, India, Indonesia, Malaysia, Philippines, Sri Lanka, and Thailand, see A. P. Saxena, ed., *Administrative Reforms for Decentralized Development* (Kuala Lumpur: Asian and Pacific Development Administration Centre, 1980). See also Mohammad Mohabbat Khan, *Bureaucratic Self-Preservation: Failure of Major Administrative Reform Efforts in the Civil Service of Pakistan* (Dhaka: University of Dhaka, 1980); Robert La Porte, Jr., "Administrative Reform and the Evolution of the the Administrative System of Pakistan," in *Administrative Systems Abroad*, ed. Krishna K. Tummala (Washington, D.C.: University Press of America, 1982), pp. 127–57; S. R. Maheswari, *Administrative Reforms in India* (Delhi: Macmillan of India, 1981); Krishna K. Tummala, "Higher Civil Service in India," in *Administrative Systems Abroad*, ed. Tummala, pp. 96–126; Mohammad Mohabbat Khan and Habib Mohammad Zafarullah, "Public Bureaucracy in Bangladesh," in ibid., pp. 158–87; and Mohammad Mohabbat Khan and Habib Mohammad Zafarullah, "Administrative Reform and Bureaucratic Intransigence in Bangladesh," in *Strategies for Administrative Reform*, ed. Gerald E. Caiden and Heinrich Siedentopf (Lexington, Mass.: Lexington Books, 1982), pp. 139–51.

16. Mohammad Mohabbat Khan, "Administrative Reforms in the Indian Civil Service" in Khan, *Bureaucratic Self-Preservation*, ch. 3.

17. See Mohammad Mohabbat Khan, "Failure of Major Administrative Reforms in the Civil Service of Pakistan," and "The Civil Service of Pakistan as an Institution: Reasons for Resistance to Change," in Khan, *Bureaucratic Self-Preservation*, chs. 4 and 5.

18. See Khan, *Bureaucratic Self-Preservation*, pp. 112–33; Mohammad Mohabbat Khan, "Ruling Elites and Major Administrative Reforms: The Case of the Civil Service of Pakistan," *Asian Affairs* 5, no. 2 (April–June 1983), 172–200; and Mohammad Mohabbat Khan, "Role of Ruling Elites in the Non-Implementation of Major Administrative Reforms in the Civil Service of Pakistan," *Journal of the Asiatic Society of Bangladesh* 27, no. 2 (December 1983): 1–16.

19. See Khan, *Bureaucratic Self-Preservation*, pp. 112–33.

20. See Khan, "Role of Ruling Elites."

21. Morris Janowitz states that "sons of leading families from the northern hill country were recruited in regiments of the Indian Army, which later became core of the Pakistan Army at the time of partition" (*Military Conflict: Essays in Institutional Analysis of War and Peace* [London: Sage Publications, 1975], p. 154).

22. For details, see "Government of the People's Republic of Bangladesh," *Report of the Civil Administration Restoration Committee*, pt. 1, vol. 1, January 1972.

23. Government of the People's Republic of Bangladesh, *Report of the Administrative and Services Reorganization Committee*, pt. 1: *The Services*, April 1973, pp. iii–iv.

24. Government of the People's Republic of Bangladesh, *Report of the National Pay Commission*, vol. 1: *Main Text*, May 1973, pp. 1–2.

25. Government of the People's Republic of Bangladesh, *Report of the Pay and Services Commission*, pt. 1: *The Services*, vol. 1, May 1977, pp. 7–8.

26. Government of the People's Republic of Bangladesh, *Report of the Martial Law Committee for Examining Organizational Set Up of Ministries/Divisions, Departments, Directorates and Other Organizations under Them*, phase 1: *Ministries/ Divisions*, May 1982, p. 2.

27. Government of the People's Republic of Bangladesh, *Report of the Committee for Administrative Reorganization/Reform*, June 1982, p. i.

28. Reported in a national English daily newspaper, *The Bangladesh Observer*, June 1, 1984.

29. *Report of ASRC*, pt. 1, p. iv.

30. At independence in 1971, Bangladesh inherited three main categories of regularly constituted services, i.e., (1) the former all-Pakistan services such as the Civil Service of Pakistan (CSP), and Police Service of Pakistan (PSP); (2) the former central superior services; and (3) the former provincial services.

31. *Report of MLC*, phase 1, p. 9.

32. The ten grades were: (1) Senior Administrative/Top Specialist Grade; (2) Administrative/Chief Executive Grade; (3) Junior Administrative/Higher Executive/Higher Professional Grade; (4) Senior Executive/Senior Professional Grade; (5) Junior Executive/Junior Professional Grade; (6) Lower Executive/Lower Professional Grade; (7) Lower Supervisory/Higher Ministerial/Higher Technical Grade; (8) Lower Ministerial/Lower Technical Grade; (9) Subministerial/Subtechnical (semiskilled) Grade; (10) Subministerial/Subtechnical (unskilled) Grade (*Report of ASRC*, pp. 30–31).

33. The functional posts would be those that require either pre-entry technical or vocational education or postentry training in specialized administrative skill (*Report of the ASRC*, pp. 34–37).

34. Khan and Zafarullah, "Public Bureaucracy in Bangladesh," p. 169.

35. The four recommended tiers would be (1) the Administrative/Top Management/Specialized Group; (2) the Executive/Middle Management Group; (3) the Inspectional/Ministerial/Technical/Support Group; and (4) the Messengerial/ Custodial Group (*Report of PSC*, p. 52).

36. The fourteen cadre services are: (1) Bangladesh Civil Service (BCS) (Administrative) having two subcadres: administrative and food; (2) BCS (Agriculture) having four subcadres: agriculture, forest, fisheries and livestock; (3) BCS (Education) with two subcadres: general education and technical education; (4) BCS (Economic and Trade) with three subcadres: economic, trade and statistical; (5) BCS (Engineering) with four subcadres: public works, public health, roads and highways, and telecommunications; (6) BCS (Finance) with three subcadres: audit and accounts, customs and excise, and taxation; (7) BCS (Foreign Affairs); (8) BCS (Health and Family Planning); (9) BCS (Information); (10) BCS (Judicial); (11) BCS (Postal); (12) BCS (Enforcement) with two subcadres: police and *ansar* (adjunct); (13) BCS (Railways) with two subcadres: transportation and commercial engineering; and (14) BCS (Secretariat).

37. The CARR wanted the NIC to be assigned the following major responsi-

bilities: (1) Identify functions of the various departments which can be transferred to the elected local government at various levels within a time-bound frame; (2) Work out the principles of the control mechanism of the elected *parishads* (councils) over the government functionaries; (3) Work out immediately a decentralized budget and planning mechanism for the elected local government so that the release of ADP funds under the present centralized planning process can further be decentralized to suit local needs and requirements; and (4) Identify and work out the training needs and training contents for both appointed and elected officials so that the new framework of local government administration may work to the best advantage of the people (*Report of CARR*, pp. 173–74).

38. The responsibilities of NICARR include the following: (a) identification of the stages within which reorganization measures be made functional; (b) determination of the minimum number of officials and staff required in each *thana* under the reorganization scheme; (c) identification of those *thanas* from among existing ones which would be chosen for upgrading in the first phase, taking into consideration their structural facilities; (d) fixation of a time table to gradually upgrade *thanas*, create new districts and abolish subdivisions with necessary staff support and other facilities; (e) directing Establishment Division, Law and Parliamentary Division to make necessary plans to select and appoint government officials on the basis of a time table; and (f) directing Works Ministry, Local Government Ministry and Land Administration and Land Reform Ministry to provide facilities regarding land, building, roads, etc., in thanas and districts. As reported in *The Daily Bangla* (a vernacular daily newspaper), September 9, 1982.

39. Mohammad Mohabbat Khan, "Reform for Decentralized Development: Bangladesh's Experience with Major Administrative Reforms/Reorganizations in the '80s," in *Bangladesh: Society, Politics and Bureaucracy*, ed. Mohammad Mohabbat Khan and John P. Thorp (Dhaka: Center for Administrative Studies, University of Dhaka, 1984), p. 160. *Taka* 50 *lac* equals *taka* half a million; 44 *taka* is approximately equal to a pound.

40. The ordinances provided the legal framework wherein the election, composition, terms of office of chairmen and members; powers and functions of chairmen and members of the *upazila parishads* (councils); charter of duties of *upazila nirbahi* officers and all other officers (who are recruited and controlled by the central government); regulatory functions to be retained by the central government; lists of developmental functions transferred to the upazillas and delegation of financial powers to people's representatives and officials at the upazila level. See: (a) Government of the People's Republic of Bangladesh, *Manual on Thana Administration*, vol. 1, February 7, 1983; (b) Government of the People's Republic of Bangladesh, *Manual on Upazila Administration*, vol. 2, September 1983; and (c) Government of the People's Republic of Bangladesh, *Manual of Upazila Administration*, vol. 3, April 1984.

41. Interview with a number of the Pay and Service Commission (PSC), Dhaka, July 30, 1980.

42. See Khan, *Bureaucratic Self-Preservation*, pp. 90–133.

Conclusion

Colin Campbell, S.J.

CERTAINLY NO one who has read this book would deny one unmistakable fact. The past two decades have been an exceedingly experimental era both in the organization of governance and efforts to coordinate and control departments and agencies. However, the conclusions that we might derive about the actual fruits of this sometimes frenetic period might prove as varied as the perspectives from which they are viewed. For instance, our three expressly comparative contributions come out with substantially different lessons. Joel Aberbach and Bert Rockman make much of the enshrinement of policy analysis units as one clear result of all the flux; Richard Rose wants to dampen fears that their increased scale and scope has made governmental organizations less responsive; Norman C. Thomas argues strenuously that the prevailing norms of pluralism have outweighed structural alterations in addressing the problems of economic decline. In the section on Britain, one takes from all of the authors a strong disillusionment with the entire project of government reorganization. They also convey a sense that the competence of the British public service is largely putative. Yet, authors from no fewer than six other countries reveal in their chapters the degree to which their systems struggle with many of the same problems encounterd by Whitehall. Ironically, Commonwealth and Anglo systems often continue to look to the British model as the ideal for a merit-based bureaucracy.

An Effort to Hack Away Some of the Underbrush

Before looking in detail at the contributions of each chapter in this book, this conclusion will propose a theoretical framework that might facilitate the comparative study of bureaucratic reforms. I have argued elsewhere that modern executive-bureaucratic complexes grapple with two conflicting goals.[1] On the one hand, political leaders attempt to leave their mark through responsiveness to the central elements of their perceived mandate for change and adaptability to unforeseen circumstances. Yet they operate under varying circumstances depending upon the nature of their political system. For instance, executive authority in the United States concentrates formally in the office of "president" while in those nations following the Westminster model it resides by convention in the "cabinet." As well, systems differ quite substantially in the degree to which political appointees occupy key posts in departments and agencies.

It is also useful to keep one distinction in mind regarding appointees. Increases in the proportion of such officials who occupy various strata of bureaucratic organizations comprise a different set of issues from those surrounding debates over politicization of the public service.[2] Virtually every system has encountered over the last two decades an intensification of top officials'—appointive or career—conscious involvement in executive-bureaucratic gamesmanship.[3] However, even systems following the Westminster model have followed substantially different practices regarding the appointment of *party*-political advisers and operatives to positions within departments and agencies.[4]

Engagement of the state apparatus constitutes the other goal of any political leadership. Chief executives and/or cabinets all attempt in some degree to seize control of and direct toward their own purposes the ongoing bureaucratic establishment. And this enterprise requires the institutionalization of control and guidance mechanisms in the cores of departments and agencies, and the center of the entire executive branch. In systems where partisan appointees assume key positions in coordinative units, the political leadership will increasingly seek established policy professionals for such roles.[5] In systems that continue to place a high value on the neutrality of officials, prime ministers and cabinet secretaries will nonetheless strive to fill the most sensitive positions with career public servants who possess proven skills of executive-bureaucratic gamesmanship necessary for the integration and implementation of their policy objectives.[6]

Institutionalization also takes in formal machinery for processing executive-branch business. Here much depends on the presence or absence of a constitutional norm whereby executive authority is to be exerted collectively. The former situation has usually resulted—in response to the increasing complexity of government—in the proliferation of standing and ad hoc cabinet committees.[7] In noncabinet systems, such developments rely on proven instrumental utility rather than constitutional conventions. In part, this explains why the evolution in the United States of the shared exercise of executive authority associated with "cabinet government" has lagged behind Westminster systems.

If we were to visualize the interplay between the responsiveness of political leaders and their ability to engage the apparatus of state, we might conceive of four quadrants.[8] (See figure A.) Political leaders who

FIGURE A
Responsiveness, Institutionalization, and Political Styles

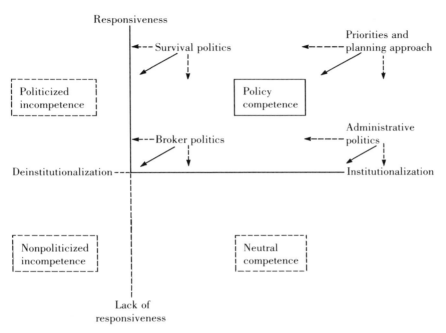

	Emphasis	*Tendency*
Priorities and planning approach	On central agency dominance, countervailing influence	Toward loss of responsiveness, loss of competence
Broker politics	On delegation to line departments, countervailing influence	Toward neutral competence, politicized incompetence
Administrative politics	On delegation to line departments, discrete responsibilities	Toward neutral competence, loss of competence
Survival politics	On central agency domination, discrete responsibilities	Toward politicized incompetence, loss of responsiveness

achieve some level of *policy competence* occupy the area bordered by relatively high responsiveness and engagement of the institutionalized state apparatus. The rare chief executive, indeed, would not strive in some way for policy competence. However, he or she could drift toward another quadrant by failing to achieve an appropriate mix between responsiveness and utilization of the standing machinery of government. Those who stress the former at the cost of the latter run the risk of winding up with *politicized incompetence*. Those who favor institutionalization over responsiveness flirt with a variant of *neutral competence*. This situation leaves observers wondering whether the stylistic and partisan nature of a given political leader makes any real difference. Finally, some governments or administrations might become so mesmerized by imponderables of blending responsiveness and institutionalization that they slip into a weak mixture of both emphases which actually lands them in *nonpoliticized incompetence*.

In chapter 2, I discuss four approaches that might be adopted by political leaders. In delineating these styles, I distinguish between governments or administrations fostering countervailing views in the advisory systems and those which seek to limit conflict. I also differentiate between those that rely heavily upon central agencies and those that prefer as much as possible to have line departments settle quotidian affairs on their own.

Under this framework, a *priorities and planning* style emerges when the political leadership encourages competing advise. It simultaneously entrusts central agencies with the task of developing overarching strategies and assuring that substantive decisions adhere to them. *Broker politics* results when countervailing views abound, but central agencies play only restrained roles in the integration of policies. *Administrative politics* develops when political leaders tend neither to encourage a diversity of views nor rely heavily upon central agencies for guiding and controlling the rest of the executive branch. Finally, *survival politics* prevails when central agencies increasingly draw issues into their orbit and expressly seek to dampen competition between advisers.

With respect to whether governments or administrations ultimately arrive at policy competence, politicized incompetence, neutral competence, or nonpoliticized incompetence, a political leadership's mix of the two determinants of style—degree of responsiveness and degree of institutionalization—can present clear dangers. Figure A summarizes these dangers. A priorities and planning style that emphasizes central agency intervention to the detriment of countervailing views will run the risk of a loss of responsiveness while the opposite condition might lead to diminished competence. With broker politics, tipping the scales toward delegation to line departments lends itself to neutral competence while an overabundance of countervailing positions might bring about politicized incompetence. Under survival politics, overcentralization might result in politicized incompetence while severe reliance upon compartmentalization might hamper responsiveness. And, an administrative politics that rests too heavily upon delegation to departments might slide into neutral competence while one that tries too hard to limit open contestation might suffer a loss of competence.

Priorities and planning, thus, comes out as the safest style from the standpoint of maintaining policy competence. Survival politics and administrative politics tie for second place. For the former, an imbalance toward central agency dominance might end in politicized incompetence; for the latter a skew toward delegation might lead to neutral competence. Broker politics poses two difficulties. First, an overemphasis on delegation could swing the government or administration into neutral competence while moving in the direction of excessive countervaillance could land it in politicized incompetence. Second, a simultaneous decline in delegation and countervaillance could take the political leadership into nonpoliticized incompetence.

Notwithstanding its desirability, the priorities and planning style usually encounters systemic constraints that make it somewhat elusive. We can divide these into institutional and personnel-related factors. With regard to the former, we should keep the following caveats in mind: (1) The absence of reasonably strong policy-oriented shops working directly and exclusively to the chief executive will limit the extent to which he or she will receive countervailing advice. (2) The absence of reasonably strong secretariats dedicated to brokerage of conflicts between departments will hamper a cabinet's capacity for open contestation. (3) The absence of a reasonably structured system of standing cabinet committees will restrict the political leadership's ability to plan rather than simply muddle through. (4) The presence of strong representational imperatives that inflate the size of a cabinet might turn it into a surrogate legislature rather than an executive council. In turn, this situation will cancel out many of the potential benefits to collective responsibility derived from structured committees and secretariats. (5) The absence of reasonably effective analytic and coordinative units within operational departments will impair the ability of these organizations to relate to central agencies and vice versa. Concerning personnel-related constraints, the following points arise: (1) If the legitimacy of party-political advice either in the chief executive's office or in departments is questioned to the point where appointive policy units are too small or restricted to be effective, political leaders will lack the support and imaginative approaches necessary for open contestation of views. (2) A weak tradition of policy-oriented professionalism among party-political appointees can negate the advantages of countervailing views. (3) A very strong ethos of compromise among career civil servants can shield political leaders from sufficiently inclusive consideration of options. (4) Career civil servants with weak analytic orientations and skills will tend to focus their attention on matters of process rather than substantive issues.

Many of the contributions to this book stress the influence of the economic decline on bureaucratic reforms in their countries. During the past fifteen years, this has constricted the art of the possible for the leaders of most industrial nations. This fact prompts one final series of observations about the task of matching style with external conditions. Table A summarizes these points. If we consider four locations in economic cycles, we find that the suitability of one or other style changes within each stage. If growth is accelerating and all other indicators suggest prosperity, immense pressures will bear down upon the political leadership to increase spending in myriad fields. To derive the optimal benefit from the times, priorities and planning should prevail. However, the "candy stores" of possibilities will make it extremely difficult to engage political leaders in such a process. By default, they will lapse into broker politics—which will err administratively—or administrative politics—which will pass up opportunities by being too cautious politically. Survival politics likely will not come to participants' minds as an appropriate style.

As economic conditions begin to tighten, pressures will build to cut expenditures. However, political leaders will focus more on efficiency issues than whether programs merit continuation. Here priorities and planning would be appropriate. Yet, it remains difficult to achieve. Both broker politics and administrative politics become more acceptable, although they remain error-prone. Survival politics would tempt only fiscal conservatives. When, on the other hand, a recession seems imminent, many minds will concentrate on the need to make deep cuts to the point of eliminating ineffective programs. Under these circumstances, priorities and planning might find it less difficult to win over the political leadership. The intensity of pressures means that broker politics and administrative politics will fall still further short of policy competence. Meanwhile, survival politics—while still inappropriate—will increasingly attract support beyond that already secured among fiscal conservatives.

Finally, a severe recession or protracted stagnation would lend credence to those urging radical macroeconomic strokes. These could be Keynesian. However, political leaders currently are more likely to turn to monetarist and supply-side remedies. Thus, survival politics probably will come into its own during periods of acute economic stress. And, it might prove appropriate in such circumstances. Priorities and planning is simply too cumbersome in crisis situations. If selected, both broker politics and administrative politics likely would fail badly administratively *and* politically.

TABLE A
Appropriateness of Leadership Styles to Economic Conditions

	Accelerating Growth	Consolidation	Decline	Recession or Prolonged Stagnation
Priorities and planning approach	Appropriate, but very difficult	Appropriate, but moderately difficult	Appropriate, but somewhat difficult	Inappropriate and too cumbersome
Broker politics	Inadequate administratively	Acceptable, but tending to administrative error	Acceptable, but tending to administrative error	Inadequate politically and administratively
Administrative politics	Inadequate politically	Acceptable, but tending to political error	Acceptable, but tending to administrative error	Inadequate politically and administratively
Survival politics	Unlikely and inappropriate	Inappropriate	Inappropriate, but tempting	Appropriate, but prone to error

The Comparative Perspective

Counting the two chapters which concern major issues associated with organizing governance, five contributions in this book take a crossnational compass. The first of these—Chapter 1 by Guy Peters—reminds those of us educated during the 1960s and the early 1970s that many studies of the structure and organization of government came across as irrelevant and boring. In part, this attitude stemmed from the hidebound traditionalism of much of public administration. However, it also owed to the missionary zeal of the behavioral movement. Researchers wanted to shift attention from how things were supposed to run to how they actually worked. In the process, students of public administration began to lose sight of the overarching importance of government organization—especially dramatic shifts in structural arrangements.

The focus on behavior as against structure was not evenly distributed. Enjoying a relative ease of access to politicians and officials, U.S. scholars leaned furthest toward the behavioral side. America's straightlaced sister—Canada—did not welcome a more bothersome and probing breed of public administration scholar. Still, several very good in-depth inquiries into the actual operation of specific policy sectors emerged during the late 1960s and early 1970s.[9] Whitehall remained a tough nut to crack. This explains the degree to which Hugh Heclo's and Aaron Wildavsky's *The Private Government of Public Money* became viewed as a truly path-breaking work.[10]

Thus, Peters's observations about structure being construed as boring will strike a chord with those who started their studies of public administration two decades ago. Nonetheless, his most salient remarks about rehabilitating the study of structure cut at the heart of what we have tried to embark upon with the inauguration of the International Political Science Association Research Committee on the Structure and Organization of Government. That is, we are not a society banded together for the advancement of scholarly hypnosis. Rather, we are—albeit in the restrained way proper to researchers—saying "fire" in Plato's cave.

In studying bureaucracy, modern political science has spent too much effort tracking the shadows on the wall and not enough on the degree to which structural features might be shaping and altering these images. We are responding to a profound irony. In precisely the period when bureaucratic systems worldwide went thorugh unprecedented structural change, political scientists almost stalwartly refused to pay much attention. Thus, they failed to track adequately the relationship between bureaucratic reorganization and actual performance. That is, they did not assess to the degree necessary the costs and benefits associated with an extremely active period of institutional reform. A deeply encrusted but very wise Whitehall mandarin put this view to me in 1978:

You've got to decide what it is you're going to do and stick with it for a reasonable period of time. The one thing that does reduce efficiency is changing the machinery. Even if you make quite a definite improvement, it's a few years before you collect the payoff. You've got to develop some sort of new esprit de corps so that the staff know who they are and what they are. And, I think we've not had that sufficiently in the front of our minds in the last twenty years. We've chopped and changed around with pretty gay abandon and not considered sufficiently the losses that you do incur. Human beings aren't that adaptable. They do need time to decide where their loyalties are and the rest of it.[11]

My own contribution to this collection—chapter 2—takes up Peters's challenge insofar as it applies to the study of central agencies. The tendency for political leaders to respond to stressful times with organizational reforms has become a principal concern of much of my own research. Even if the view that structures affect outcomes only marginally were entirely validated, political leaders would probably continue to believe fervently in their salience.

One of the greatest dangers emerging from this proclivity is recourse to central agencies to address problems best handled by operational departments. Chief executives and their closest advisers respond all too often to dysfunctions originating in stress between their coordinative machinery and line departments by adding a new degree of intricacy to the former. Frequently, the additional loops that such reforms place in the interrelationships between the center and operational units simply deepen the tensions that they attempted to reduce. All things being equal—and I have discussed the key parameters in the previous section—political leaders should seek tailor-made solutions for particular problems. Only when crises bunch up in ways that clearly suggest that the links between the center and the operational level require substantial alteration should restructuring of these become the order of the day.

Chapter 3 by Joel Aberbach and Bert Rockman makes an important connection between the rapid expansion of central agencies in advanced democracies and diffusion of analytic techniques within bureaucracy more generally. Increasingly, the entire enterprise of coordinating the state apparatus has become a type of warfare between government and subgovernments. Obviously, the fragmentation of political leadership and the bureaucratic establishment in the United States makes American scholars acutely aware of such struggles. However, similar conflicts operate behind the emergence of new central agencies and analytic techniques even in externally tranquil systems.

Aberbach and Rockman are strongly concerned with the conditions under which analytic approaches to the integration of policies can be most beneficial. They clearly view analysis as a means to enhancing policy competence. Looking at the U.S. system, however, they identify a trend running counter to this goal. That is, they point up the dangers of the tendency since the early 1970s for presidents to add to the layers of party-political advisers in departments and agencies.

Although many such appointees qualify as policy professionals, their increased weight in the executive-bureaucratic complex heralds a deinstitutionalization of the state apparatus—both at the center and in departments and agencies. Such officials bring to their work a high degree of political sensitivity and responsiveness. However, their lack of exposure to governance preordains that they will play down the value of continuity and coordination. In addition, they will become hostile toward the custodians of these values in the permanent civil service. The authors certainly put their finger on an important element to the current malaise in U.S. governance. The lessons have applications to Westminster systems that hope to achieve greater political responsiveness while maintaining the tradition of neutrality in the permanent civil service.

Chapter 4 by Richard Rose draws upon a wealth of data available through the author's cross-national study of the growth of government. Rose questions some conventional wisdom about the consequences of growth in governments' scope and the scale of the resources they call upon. His evidence suggests that these developments need not result in the establishment of new departments and agencies at the operational level. Existing organizations have shown immense capacities to cope with additional scale and to incorporate new programs that relate to their central missions. And, the political leadership of most Western European nations has exercised restraint in creation of new ministries. That is, a consensus normally develops regarding the point beyond which a cabinet cannot grow without diminishing returns.

Rose also casts doubt on the common view that political entrepreneurs measure power by the institutional resources at their disposal. He reminds us that frequently the most influential members of cabinets operate from the leanest bureaucratic organizations. Clearly, some systems offer exceptions to the patterns discerned by Rose. Even though some ministers base their power on positioning rather than the size of their departments, those heading operational units will, develop pecking orders linked to resources. This more likely will be the case in large cabinets rather than small ones. As well, some systems face conditions that make it exceedingly difficult to control the size of cabinet. For instance, immense representational pressure might lead to distortions and built-in diseconomies in the number and characteristics of portfolios. The case of Canada comes to mind in this regard.

Rose's analysis takes us far in placing the growth in the size and number of departments and agencies in its proper context. Political leaders, not organizations, have spurred most of the increase in sheer magnitude of government. Rose, thus, makes a strong plea for those seeking fiscal stringency to redistribute some of the blame to the politicians who will not make the tough choices necessary to cut and eliminate programs.

Norman Thomas offers us in chapter 5 a comparative assessment of the U.S., British, and Canadian responses to the economics of decline that prevailed through much of the 1970s and into the 1980s. In each of these countries, political leaders engaged in considerable experimentation with institutional arrangements at the center of government in the search for more coherent responses to the crises associated with stagnation. Thomas argues, however, that these organizational innovations played relatively insignificant roles in shaping the actual contours of the policies that ultimately emerged in the three nations.

Thomas notes as well that—until ideology worked its effects on U.S. and U.K. policies under Ronald Reagan and Margaret Thatcher—the approaches of the three countries to economic crises were remarkably similar. He concludes, thus, that the usual patterns of pluralistic politics in Anglo-American systems—rather than institutional factors—dominated the landscape at least until matters reached the stage where radical solutions took on newfound respectability in the United States and the United Kingdom. By their nature, bold macroeconomic strokes leave little room for fine-tuning either through institutional adjustments or the introduction and honing of new analytic approaches.

Britain as a Model (?) Patient (?)

Whitehall seems to twig the interest of non-British connoisseurs of bureaucracy as readily as bear hats and red coats captivate school-children. This explains why public service broadcasting networks in several English-speaking countries have seized upon the satiric series "Yes, Minister" for their programming. And, any scholar not from the UK who has sought interviews with Whitehall officials for a comparative project will soon find that he or she is part of what has become to weary respondents an endless succession of foreigners probing "how exactly it is done under the Westminster model." Finally—as if its folkways and legacy were not enough—developments over the past twenty years have made a special look at Whitehall still more compelling

Britain has suffered from the agony of industrial failure perhaps more than any other advanced liberal democracy. In time, this fact has provoked the inevitable question: If Whitehall is such a splendid apparatus, why has it proved so helpless as Britain continues its slide into the economics of decline? Richard Chapman's offering—chapter 6—starts us off on this topic. It seems as if certain myths surround conventional views of the Whitehall culture. As Chapman notes, these were badly punctured in 1984 when Clive Ponting—a senior official in the Ministry of Defense who previously had won a commendation from Margaret Thatcher—blew the whistle on the government's efforts to cover up embarrassing circumstances surrounding the sinking of the Argentinian cruiser *Belgrano* during the Falklands War.

The official tradition of civil service discretion—usually to the point of silence—enshrouds a transaction that often undermines both executive responsibility to Parliament and Whitehall's neutrality. Ministers take from this exchange the knowledge that their rendering of the government's handling of issues will never be publicly challenged by the officials best acquainted with the facts. The career civil servants derive the psychological income connected with the anonymous exertion of immense political power. Increasingly, those who hold the most senior positions also find it extremely lucrative, upon retirement, to trade upon their knowledge of Whitehall in private-sector careers.

As if to prove that the Ponting case was not an aberration, another incident arose early in 1986 in which officials in the Ministry of Trade and Industry leaked information in an effort to undercut the credibility of the Minister of Defense. This event, which contributed to the eventual resignation of both ministers, laid bare a sordid fact. The civil service that genuflects more reverently than perhaps any other before the altar of secrecy also could teach the most partisan officials in any heavily appointive system a great deal about tactical leaking.

We might ask what difference this demythologization makes so long as Whitehall remains one of the best civil service establishments in the world? To this, Chapman would appear to say, "You've missed my point." Indeed, he infers a gap between myth and reality in this incisive passage:

What sort of person, one might ask, is attracted to work where satisfactions arise from situations known only to a very small group of colleagues and where the details may never be recorded? . . . Does this mean that selectors at the recruitment stage should ideally be looking for a rather introverted and secretive person who can hide his personality behind the sort of sociable and friendly facade that may impress a selection board?

Chapman raises, thus, the thorny issue of what type of competence might emerge from a civil service with monastic inclinations. Chapman answers his own question by demonstratinng exactly how the young officials are selected and brought along until they are steeped in the "ethos of generalist administration." The process by which the British mandarin is seasoned cultivates a strain of neutral competence heavily oriented toward executive-bureaucratic processes. That is, top Whitehall officials normally lack significant expert knowledge in management sciences or substantive policy fields.

Peter Hennessy's chapter (7) takes us further in this tale by focusing on developments during the Thatcher years. The period since May 1979 has witnessed a radical swing away from efforts to professionalize the senior civil service. At best, the initiatives—which started during Harold

Wilson's first government—produced mixed results. Yet, their pursuit by the political leadership throughout a ten-year period increasingly exposed Whitehall to external and self-criticism about its level of proficiency in the positive craft of administration.

Mrs. Thatcher, Hennessy maintains, has aborted this process by taking a "handbag" to the civil service. Utterly convinced that responsibility for the decline of Britain rests at the mandarins' feet, she has cut away at their complements to the point where most policy units have become stretched beyond their limits, corseted their pay so that the goal of private-sector comparability has faded completely from view, and interfered in their rituals of succession by seeing that the few lads who actually share her views leapfrog to the most cherished Whitehall posts. All of this has demoralized rather than reformed the senior civil service.

Brian Hogwood provides us in chapter 8 with an illuminating account of attempts by U.K. governments from 1959 to 1984 to realign ministries so as to better address changing emphases in industrial strategies. In terms of lasting consequences, the series of reorganizations has diminished the salience of client-based relationships between departments and sectors of the economy. These, of course, tend to fragment industrial policymaking. On the other hand, rationality and organizational follow-through have not always characterized the specific institutional arrangements through which this end has been achieved.

To begin, labels and mandates might not provide one-to-one fits with the desire to consolidate industrial strategy under one roof. Labor's Ministry of Techonology (1964–1969) prophetically highlighted the need to adapt to a postindustrial society. However, technology falls short as a broad-based governmental policy sector. The ministry eventually found itself absorbed. A viable industry department, thus, must achieve more than metaphysical status. Its requires real functions complete with clear administrative powers. Second, crises can occasion damaging breakups of umbrella departments whose original compasses would match—under normal circumstances—broad policy sectors. This appears to be the case with the dissolution of the Department of Trade and Industry as "energy" policy and its new department reached its period of ascendancy in the mid-1970s. Finally, personalities have played heavily in developments. Prime ministers have tried to roll back the fiefdoms of ministers whom, they believe, have become too powerful. As well, some segments of industrial policy have drifted away from the ministers most generally responsible for industrial policy. This usually occurs when ministers lack entrepreneurial skills or believe that the state should intervene less rather than more in specific sectors.

Other National Experiences

Chapter 9 by Johan Olsen shifts our focus from Britain to other nations' efforts to achieve administrative reform. A dramatic transformation in the model operating behind the relationship between the Norwegian welfare state and conventional views of the administrative apparatus has occasioned this chapter.

Olsen maintains that Norway's Conservative-center government has stemmed the process whereby governance was becoming increasingly corporate-pluralistic. That is, the explosion of the welfare state saw the devolution of substantial political discretion to the administrative apparatus. The proliferation of nondepartmental agencies, the enhancement of civil servants' roles in public policymaking, and the multiplication of consultative mechanisms granting direct access of organized interests to governmental decisions all originated from an underlying tendency toward the corporate-pluralistic model. Especially through efforts at privitization and deregulation, the current Norwegian government has attempted, Olsen believes, to recapture the "institutional state." He characterizes this as governance that tries to increase the distance between the state and the various spheres of social activity.

A number of points of broader comparative interest emerge from Olsen's chapter. First, the concepts of administration that predominate among the political leadership and the bureaucratic elite must correspond to their models for governance. Instrumental approaches fit when the consensus upholds the sovereign, rationality of the bounded state; evolutionary modes work best under the institutional view; formats that are adaptive—according to changes in constellations of social power—best serve the corporate-pluralistic model; and political responsiveness becomes the central operative criterion when the state serves as the "supermarket" for the "great necessities."

Second, we may derive from Olsen's formulation an important observation. Political leaders often misread their situation to the point where a mismatch arises between their administrative approach and the prevailing image of the state. For instance, Canada's Pierre Trudeau ceaselessly pressed the sovereign-rational approach in a decidedly consociational and, therefore, corporate-pluralistic state. On the other hand, Britain's Harold Wilson and James Callaghan wrestled from 1974 to 1979 with a fundamental incongruity. That is, their adaptive administrative approaches ran up against the fact that the generalized view of the state was shifting back from corporate-pluralistic to institutional.

A third point provoked by chapter 9 leads us right into a consideration of Chapter 10 by Charles Levine and Michael Hansen. Olsen provides a theoretical framework whereby we can interpret changes of emphasis in administrative styles depending upon the applicable model of the state. However, we still must account for the movement to antigovernance. That is, some modern leaders seek more than a tighter line of demarcation between the state apparatus and social institutions. They believe that huge blocks of government functions simply should not exist. Levine and Hansen chronicle the current antipathy between a political leadership and the permanent custodians of the ongoing project of governance. That is, they relate the story of the U.S. career civil service's marginalization under Ronald Reagan.

Levine and Hansen indentify in the Reagan administration an unhappy coincidence of two conditions. First, the U.S. career civil service lacks a secure niche in the American constitutional tradition. To compensate, through most of this century it built the legitimation of its role on subject-matter expertise. Even if they did not enjoy a monopoly of information and analysis in every policy sector, permanent officials always maintained a sufficiently persuasive grasp of the issues of the day to occupy the role of middlemen between politicians and interest groups. The 1970s and 1980s have, however, seen a substantial erosion of this knowledge base out from under the career civil service. The proliferation of "think tanks" and congressional policy staffs has driven home the fact that "expertise" often speaks with many tongues. In some areas, such as economic forecasting, the resulting babble has left both politicians and the attentive public with the impression that nobody—including the permanent officials—can generate truly objective assessments of policy issues.

The Reagan administration has exacerbated this state of affairs in the degree to which it assigns blame for the decline of the United States' international economic competitiveness to the growth of government and the alleged incompetence of the civil service. Striking out with a vengeance, it has gone beyond simply wholesale abolition of units, sharp reductions in work force, and severe caps on compensation. That is, it wishes as well to bracket civil service as an underclass within the executive-bureaucratic complex.

As Levine and Hansen point up, the likes of Michael Sanera— formerly a Reagan appointee in the Office of Personnel Management and now of the Heritage Foundation—do not mince words on this strategy which the administration has successfully implemented in virtually every department. Each appointive complement in the various agencies was to keep between themselves the specific goals operating behind policy initiatives. They would farm out pieces of the "jigsaw puzzle" to individual

career units. However, they would deliberately discourage permanent officials working on the various parts to coordinate their activities between
themselves. And, they would establish the broad contours of most policies
with as little reference to the career side as possible.

Levine and Hansen outline convincingly the ways in which Reagan's
task is error-prone. As well, they make due note of a genuine irony in the
approach. In recent years, the business community has increasingly recognized that creativity often comes from the encouragement of individual
initiative fairly far down in an organizational hierarchy. Yet, an administration that upholds private-sector techniques almost without question has
reduced the career civil service to "what-iffers." This requires permanent
officials to fill in bits and pieces of policies without receiving more than a
glimpse of their ultimate intent and design.

Peter Aucoin's chapter 11 takes us from Ronald Reagan's flirtation
with politicized incompetence to Canada. There Pierre Trudeau and Brian
Mulroney have grappled with the tradeoffs implicit in the simultaneous
pursuit of political responsiveness and engagement of the state apparatus.
Aucoin's sketch of Trudeau's "scientific management" approach to executive leadership is, quite simply, the best available. Trudeau's fascination
with increasingly intricate machinery for coordinating government policies
stemmed from his and many of his closest advisers' deep conviction that
the right structures and processes should achieve close to optimal responsiveness and competence. However, his highly rationalistic schemes and
designs outstripped by far the capacity for ministers—especially in a
bloated cabinet—to coordinate their policies. As a result, a truncated
administrative politics emerged in which olympian battles between central
agencies waged over matters of form while hosts of substantive issues
remained unattended.

To be sure, Brian Mulroney inherited a huge mess. Yet he too has
failed at achieving a viable mix of responsiveness and competence. Regarding the former, he strengthened the role of party-political advice in
the Prime Minister's Office and appointed a strong rightist to serve as
second in command in his cabinet. In deference to the persistent myth of
civil service neutrality, he did virtually nothing to reform a permanent
bureaucracy which, especially during the Trudeau years, had clearly
aligned itself with the Liberal party agenda. Most critically, he has backed
off from virtually every initiative issuing from his cabinet which encountered the gauntlet of Canadian skepticism about rolling back the welfare
state. In sum, we find under Mulroney a government with a greater party-
political thrust at the center than Trudeau had. Nonetheless, it has failed
to redirect an unsympathetic bureaucracy. As well, its main proposals

have not stood up well against a populace which simply will not entertain radical conservatism.

Chapter 14 by Ulrich Klöti assesses Swiss institutional alterations since the late 1960s. Interestingly, these shared many of the objectives sought by Trudeau through heavy investment in coordinative machinery. Obviously, the Swiss developments did not bear the stamp of a single chief executive or a coterie of institutional engineers. However, they ran up against similar obstacles encountered by Trudeau's efforts toward rationalization of government policies and programs.

Politicians, who tend to focus on the problem of the day, often balk at elaborate schemes to turn their attention to comprehensive plans plotted far into the future. As well, departments usually like to carry on with the clusters of ongoing programs which fit neatly into their own self-image. By reflex, they will respond to requests for innovations and assigning priorities by saying, "This is how what we already do and hope to take on fits with the government guidelines." Perhaps most fatally, economic conditions in Switzerland intruded by the 1970s upon the salad days of the late 1960s when that country—like virtually every advanced democracy—indulged itself with dreams of bold new programs that would satisfy popular expectations in an expansive era. In the subsequent mood of stringency, the constraints of fiscal conservatism have preempted much of the discussion over government guidelines. In fact, systematic analysis has often yielded to the bluntest of policymaking devices—the across-the-board budget cut.

John Warhurst uncovers in chapter 13 a genuine paradox. As most advanced democracies have swung over to right-leaning governments, Australia embraced in 1983 the left-leaning Labor party headed by Bob Hawke. The incongruity emerges from the fact that Labor listed a bill of particulars against the career civil service which bore a marked resemblance to those handed over by conservative governments in other advanced democracies. That is, Labor believed that there was too little political control over the permanent bureaucracy, that civil service managers were insufficiently skilled, and that administrators were not adequately sensitive to the wider community and its problems.

The similarity of these grievances to those of many right-leaning governments elsewhere suggests that some of the tension between current political leaders in advanced democracies and their bureaucracies takes root in the former's alienation from the experience of governance. This becomes especially intense when opposition parties have been the "outs" most of the time over the past fifty years—as is case with the Progressive-Conservatives in Canada and Labor in Australia. It also develops when a party believes that the permanent bureaucray remains the ideological captive of their opposition—as is the case with the U.S. Republicans' view that the civil service is mostly Democratic.

The Hawke government's strategy in response to alienation between itself and the bureaucracy could not contrast more sharply with that of the Mulroney government in Canada. The feeling among Labor politicians that their 1972–1975 government had not been well served by the bureaucracy steeled the resolve of many to vigorously pursue the issue of reform even while in opposition. Once in government, Labor launched a wide array of measures designed to increase both the responsiveness and managerial competence of permanent officials while maintaining their neutrality. Thus, the greater intensity of Australia Labor's frustration—in comparison with Canadian Conservatives'—prompted a more systematic and, in many respects, more effective remedy to alienation from governance.

While it represents our only coverage of civil service reform in a Third World nation, chapter 14 by Mohommad Khan lends a sobering perspective on the degree of carryover in bureaucratic insularity from colonial to revolutionary regimes. Especially in the case of former British colonies, we might expect a certain level of intractability among civil service leaders who learned transplanted Whitehall folkways. In seems, however, that over twenty years of independence had worked relatively little effect on the higher reaches of the civil service of Paskistan.

With independence, the government of Bangladesh faced in 1971 a list of defects strikingly similar to the diagnosis rendered on Britain's civil service in the 1968 Fulton Committee report. These included the excessive segmentation of the bureaucracy into services, inadequate professional esprit and competence, too much adherence to posting by class and rank, and too little intraservice mobility. And, several major examinations of issues surrounding reform since independence have realized very marginal effects. Even regimes responding to intense national aspirations will think twice before tampering with traditional arrangements undergirding the senior bureaucratic cadres.

Conclusion

As an initial effort for a research committee which started in 1984, this book has uncovered a great many unresolved issues connected with efforts at bureaucratic reform in several nations. Doubtless, not even ten research committees working intensely over the next twenty years would make a dent in the vast task of proposing specific ways in which heretofore intractable organizational defects might be overcome. We hope, however, that this volume has helped clarify the dialogue on the genuinely soluble problems.

None of our authors stakes a claim to *the* theoretical framework that makes sense of all the "mess." To the contrary, they all have committed themselves to keeping their conceptual lines of communication open so that they might adjust their viewpoints where necessary according to the findings of comparative research in other settings. Assuming that we will recognize the failing whereby we mortals keep reinventing the wheel, a research committee dedicated to comparative research of government reorganization begins its contribution by recording and transmitting observations about what has worked and what has failed. Along the way, it will attempt to make researchers and practitioners alike more aware of the conditions under which specific types of reforms are likely to prove effective. The last twenty years of organizational experimentation has left most students of comparative public administrtion somewhat out of breath. It is time to pause and take stock from a cross-national perspective.

Notes

1. Colin Campbell, S.J., *Managing the Presidency: Carter, Reagan, and the Search for Executive Harmony* (Pittsburgh, Pa.: University of Pittsburgh Press, 1986), ch. 1.

2. Colin Campbell, S.J., "The Pitfalls of Revisionism Too Eager by Half: An Open Letter to Richard Van Loon," *Canadian Public Administration*, 28 (Summer 1985), 321–25.

3. Joel D. Aberbach, Robert D. Putnam, and Bert A. Rockman, *Bureaucrats and Politicians in Western Democracies* (Cambridge, Mass.: Harvard University Press, 1981), pp. 16–23.

4. Patrick Weller, *First Among Equals: Prime Ministers in Westminster Systems* (Boston: George Allen and Unwin, 1985), pp. 149–62.

5. Lester M. Salamon, "The Presidency and Domestic Policy Formulation," in *The Illusion of Presidential Government*, ed. Hugh Heclo and Salamon (Boulder, Colo.: Westview, 1981), p. 193.

6. Colin Campbell, *Governments Under Stress: Political Executives and Key Bureaucrats in Washington, London and Ottawa* (Toronto: University of Toronto Press, 1983), p. 343.

7. Thomas T. Mackie and Brian W. Hogwood, "Cabinet Committees in Context," in *Unlocking the Cabinet: Cabinet Structures in Comparative Perspective*, ed. Mackie and Hogwood (Beverly Hills, Calif.: Sage, 1985), p. 32.

8. Campbell, *Managing the Presidency*, ch. 1.

9. For example, Kenneth Bryden, *Old Age Pensions and Policy-Making in Canada* (Montreal: McGill–Queen's University Press, 1974); G. Bruce Doern,

Science and Politics in Canada (Montreal: McGill–Queen's University Press, 1971); Freda Hawkins, *Canada and Immigration: Public Policy and Public Concern* (Montreal: McGill–Queen's University Press, 1972).

10. Hugh Heclo and Aaron Wildavsky, *The Private Government of Public Money: Community and Policy Inside British Politics* (Berkeley and Los Angeles: University of California Press, 1974).

11. Campbell, *Governments Under Stress*, p. 216.

Notes on Contributors

Joel D. Aberbach is Professor of Political Science, University of California, Los Angeles, and Professor of Political Science and Public Policy, University of Michigan.

Peter Aucoin is Professor of Political Science and Public Administration, Dalhousie University, Halifax, Nova Scotia.

Colin Campbell, S. J., is University Professor in the Isabelle A. and Henry D. Martin Chair in Philosophy and Politics, Georgetown University.

Richard A. Chapman is Professor of Politics, University of Durham.

Michael G. Hansen is Director of the Federal Executive Institute, Charlotttesville, Virginia.

Peter Hennessy is a Senior Fellow at the Policy Studies Institute, London.

Brian Hogwood is a Senior Lecturer in the Department of Politics, University of Strathclyde, Glasgow.

Mohammad Mohabbat Khan is Professor of Public Administration, University of Dhaka, Bangladesh.

Ulrich Klöti is Professor of Political Science, University of Zurich.

Charles Levine is Distinguished Professor of Government and Public Administration, American University.

Johan P. Olsen is a Professor at the Institutt for Offentlig Administrasjon, University of Bergen, Norway.

B. Guy Peters is Maurice Falk Professor of American Politics, University of Pittsburgh.

Bert A. Rockman is Professor of Political Science and Research Professor, University Center for International Studies, University of Pittsburgh.

Richard Rose is Professor and Director of the Centre for the Study of Public Policy, University of Strathclyde, Glasgow.

Norman C. Thomas is the Charles Phelps Taft Professor and Head of the Department of Political Science, University of Cincinnati.

John Warhurst is Professor of Politics, University of New England, Armidale, New South Wales.

Pitt Series in Policy and Institutional Studies

Bert A. Rockman, Editor